Voluntary Brotherhood
Confraternities of Laymen in Early Modern Ukraine

The Peter Jacyk Centre
for
Ukrainian Historical Research

Monograph Series
Number two

Voluntary Brotherhood
Confraternities of Laymen in Early Modern Ukraine

Iaroslav Isaievych

Canadian Institute of Ukrainian Studies Press

Edmonton   2006   Toronto

Canadian Institute of Ukrainian Studies Press

University of Alberta
Edmonton, Alberta
Canada T6G 2E8

University of Toronto
Toronto, Ontario
Canada M5T 1N7

Copyright © 2006 Canadian Institute of Ukrainian Studies

ISBN 1–894865–02–2 (bound); ISBN 1–894865–03–0 (pbk.)

Library and Archives Canada Cataloguing in Publication

Isaievych, Iaroslav Dmytrovych
Voluntary brotherhood : confraternities of laymen in early modern
Ukraine / Iaroslav Isaievych.

Translation of: Bratstva ta ikh rol' v rozvytku ukrainskoi kultury
XVI–XVIII st.
Includes bibliographical references and index.
ISBN 1–8948865–02–2 (bound).—ISBN 1-894865–03–0 (pbk.)

1. Confraternities—Ukraine—History. I. Title.

HS2046.U38I8313 2006   267'.1819477   C2005–907756–5

This book was published with financial support from the Teodor and Mahdalyna Butrej Fund at the Petro Jacyk Educational Foundation.

A generous grant toward this publication has also been provided by the Skop Family, in memory of Konstantyn Hordienko.

Printed in Canada

Contents

Abbreviations Used in the Book

AGAD   Archiwum Główne Akt Dawnych (Main Archives of Older Records), Warsaw.

AGZ   *Akta grodzkie i ziemskie z czasów Rzeczypospolitej Polskiej*. 25 vols. Lviv, 1868–1935.

AIuZR   *Arkhiv Iugo-Zapadnoi Rossii*. Pt. 1. Kyiv, 1859–1904.

Akty IuZR   *Akty, otnosiashchiesia k istorii Iuzhnoi i Zapadnoi Rossii*. 15 vols. St. Petersburg, 1863–92. Repr. The Hague, 1970.

Album   Album of the Lviv Stauropegion Confraternity (manuscript in the Lviv Historical Museum).

Analecta OSBM   *Analecta Ordinis Sancti Basilii Magni*. Zhovkva and Rome, 1928– .

AZR   *Akty, otnosiashchiesia k istorii Zapadnoi Rossii*. 5 vols. St. Petersburg, 1846–53. Repr. The Hague, 1971– .

BKP   Biblioteka Peremyshl's'koï hreko-katolyts'koï kapituly, zbirka rukopysiv (Library of the Peremyshl Greek Catholic Chapter, manuscript collection; in the National Library, Warsaw, since 1948).

DS   *Diplomata Statuaria a Patriarchis orientalibus Confraternitati Stauropigianae Leopoliensi a. 1586–1592 data, cum aliis litteris coaevis et appendice*. Vol. 2. Lviv, 1895.

HLEUL   Harvard Library of Early Ukrainian Literature. Cambridge, Mass., 1987– .

HUS   *Harvard Ukrainian Studies*. Cambridge, Mass., 1977– .

IuILS   *Iubileinoie izdanie v pamiat' 300–lětiia osnovaniia L'vovskoho Stavropigiona*. Lviv, 1886.

IuSLS	*Iubileinyi sbornik v pamiat' 350–lĕtiiu L'vovskoho Stavropigiona.* Lviv, 1936.
LNB	L'vivs'ka naukova biblioteka imeni V. Stefanyka Natsional'noï akademiï nauk Ukraïny, viddil rukopysiv (Vasyl Stefanyk Scholarly Library of the National Academy of Sciences of Ukraine, Lviv, Manuscript Division).
MCS	*Monumenta Confraternitatis Stauropigianae Leopoliensis.* Ed. W. Milkowicz. Lviv, 1895.
MUH	*Monumenta Ucrainae Historica.* Comp. Metropolitan Andrei Sheptyts'kyi. Rome, 1964– .
NBUV	Natsional'na biblioteka Ukraïny im. V. I. Vernads'koho Natsional'noï akademiï nauk Ukraïny (Volodymyr Vernadsky National Library of Ukraine, National Academy of Sciences of Ukraine, Kyiv)
NM	Natsional'nyi muzei u L'vovi, zbirka rukopysiv (National Museum in Lviv, manuscript collection).
PBSh	*Pam'iatky brats'kykh shkil na Ukraïni: Kinets' XVI–pochatok XVII st. Teksty i doslidzhennia.* Ed. V. Shynkaruk, V. Nichyk, and A. Sukhov. Kyiv, 1988.
Pershodrukar	Ia. D. Isaievych. *Pershodrukar Ivan Fedorov i vynyknennia drukarstva na Ukraïni.* Kyiv, 1975. 2d ed. Lviv, 1983.
PKK	*Pamiatniki, izdannyia Kievskoiiu komissieiu dlia razbora drevnikh aktov.* 2d ed. Kyiv, 1897–98.
PKM	*Pam'iatky knyzhkovoho mystetstva na Ukraïni: Kataloh starodrukiv, vydanykh na Ukraïni.* Comp. Ia. Zapasko and Ia. Isaievych. Vol. 1, 1574–1700. Lviv, 1981. Vol. 2, pts. 1–2, 1700–1800. Lviv, 1984.
RGADA	Rossiiskii gosudarstvennyi arkhiv drevnikh aktov (Russian State Archive of Ancient Acts), Moscow.

TKDA	*Trudy Kievskoi dukhovnoi akademii.* Kyiv, 1861–1917.
TsDIAL	Tsentral'nyi derzhavnyi istorychnyi arkhiv Ukraïny u misti L'vovi (Central State Historical Archive of Ukraine in Lviv).
UIZh	*Ukraïns'kyi istorychnyi zhurnal.* Kyiv, 1959– .
ZNTSh	*Zapysky Naukovoho tovarystva im. Shevchenka.* Lviv, 1892– .

Illustrations

Note on Transliteration

In the text of this book, the modified Library of Congress system is used to transliterate Ukrainian, Belarusian, and Russian personal names and toponyms. In surnames, the masculine ending –ий is simplified to –y (for example, Zubrytsky, not Zubryts'kyi). This simplified transliteration has the virtue of presenting East Slavic names to the reader in a form well adapted to standard English orthography.

In the bibliography and bibliographic references in the notes, the full Library of Congress system (but with ligatures omitted) is used in order to make possible the precise reconstruction of the original Cyrillic spelling.

For details of the Library of Congress transliteration system, the reader may consult the *ALA-LC Romanization Tables*, which are available on-line at www.loc.gov/catdir/cpso/roman.html.

Foreword

With the publication of Iaroslav Isaievych's *Voluntary Brotherhood* as part of its monograph series, the Peter Jacyk Centre for Ukrainian Historical Research (PJC) continues to fulfil its mandate to issue translations of important works in Ukrainian historical studies. The PJC has done so primarily through its principal project, an annotated English translation of Mykhailo Hrushevsky's ten-volume (twelve books) *History of Ukraine-Rus'*, of which four volumes have appeared to date. It has also done so by establishing a Ukrainian translation series to make the best Western works in Ukrainian history available to Ukraine's reading public. The four volumes published so far in this latter series include a translation of Ihor Ševčenko's *Ukraine between East and West: Essays on Cultural History to the Early Eighteenth Century.* The PJC has also sponsored the publication of a volume of documentary source materials on the Ukrainian Cossacks preserved in Russian archives.

Through its monograph series, the PJC fosters the publication of new research, textbooks, seminal articles, source materials, and translations of classic works in Ukrainian history in order to broaden the scope of research available in English and promote the teaching of Ukrainian history in the West. *Voluntary Brotherhood* is a translation of one of the best works on early modern Ukraine to appear in the USSR after the 1920s. It is also a revised and updated work: the author has not only deleted terminology imposed by the Soviet censors before the book could be published as *Bratstva ta ïkh rol' v rozvytku ukraïns'koï kul'tury XVI–XVIII st.* (Kyiv, 1966), but has also broadened the scope of his discussion of the early modern Ukrainian Orthodox confraternities by utilizing a comparative approach and taking into account the literature on the subject published in the past four decades. The Centre is grateful to Marta D. Olynyk for translating a substantial part of this volume, and to Myroslav Yurkevich for editing the text.

In his introduction, Iaroslav Isaievych gives us an insightful commentary on the conditions under which he originally wrote and published *Bratstva ta ïkh rol'*. He mentions the significance foreign reviews of this book had and, at the same time, the dangers of receiving praise from abroad. Professor Isaievych expresses gratitude for the serious yet critical manner in which his works were discussed in the Harvard Ukrainian Research Institute's review of Soviet Ukrainian scholarly books, *Recenzija*. Because that journal condemned the passages in which he had toed the official Soviet historiographic line, he was not negatively branded in the USSR as having received praise from Western imperialists or Ukrainian bourgeois nationalists. As one of the editors and authors of *Recenzija*, I must admit that at that time we were not so sensitive or aware of Professor Isaievych's situation that we considered ways of shielding him from any possible consequences of a positive appraisal of his works. We did, however, admire his erudition and historical vision. The Soviet Ukrainian thaw in culture and scholarship in the 1960s had led our small group of American graduate students in Ukrainian studies to found *Recenzija* in 1970. Iaroslav Isaievych's monograph convinced us that the thaw had made possible a rebirth of scholarship in Ukraine. Tragically, the window of opportunity turned out to be all too narrow: with the mass arrests of members of the Ukrainian intelligentsia and scholars in 1972, it was shut for nearly two decades. By that time, however, Professor Isaievych had managed to write and publish another excellent book— *Dzherela z istoriï ukraïns'koï kul'tury doby feodalizmu, XVI–XVIII st.* (Sources on the History of Ukrainian Culture of the Feudal Period, Sixteenth–Eighteenth Centuries, Kyiv, 1972)—and numerous articles on early modern Ukrainian culture.

Thankfully, the Soviet Union is no more, and since its demise Professor Isaievych has been able to speak and write with his true voice. The PJC is honoured to make his pioneering work available to the Western reading public. Ukraine has resumed its place in the community of nations, and *Voluntary Brotherhood* is proof that the nation's academics are once again able to participate in international scholarly discourse.

Frank E. Sysyn

Introduction

Medieval religious brotherhoods of laymen, often called confraternities, were in many respects forerunners of those voluntary associations that now constitute the organizational framework of modern civil society. In countries like Ukraine, such associations now attract the attention not only of professional scholars but also of intellectuals urgently searching for democratic traditions so necessary for the political education of society.

In public opinion, religious brotherhoods are almost always viewed positively. Even in everyday usage, words expressing the concept of "brotherhood" elicit positive emotions in all languages. Only in totalitarian states were expressions like "fraternal friendship" or "brotherly unity" first debased and then made tools of propagandistic brainwashing. Fortunately, in the course of social renewal, words are regaining their pristine, uncorrupted meaning. This is also true of the word "brotherhood," which expresses a longing to promote among unrelated people a spirit of unity, sincerity, and mutual assistance that is perceived—ideally, at least—as an attribute of a family. Thus it is quite natural that the word "brotherhood" appears so often in the names of associations whose members are united not by blood ties but by common views and goals. The word has been popular with political parties, as well as with religious, professional, and other unions. The Roman Catholic Church, with its tradition of legal uniformity and clarity, reserved the word "confraternity," often synonymous with "brotherhood," for unions of laymen whose goal was to promote Christian piety.

In Ukrainian and Belarusian history, the words "confraternity" or "brotherhood" refer in most cases to lay parish associations that served, in addition to their religious activities, as centers of national life. Their role was especially important in the late sixteenth and early seventeenth centuries, when Orthodox confraternities catalyzed many initiatives undertaken to preserve religious and national identity. At a time when Ukraine and Belarus were under foreign rule, confraternities became, to a degree, surrogates for indigenous state structures, attempting to organize a kind of ethnic-oriented self-government. The leading confraternities, especially in their first stage of development, realized several Reformation postulates. Later, in both the Orthodox and Greek Catholic (Uniate) churches, there appeared confraternities of another type, subordinate to the clergy and performing auxiliary functions in church life.

In no other country did religious lay associations, confraternities, and brotherhoods play as important a national role as in Ukraine and Belarus. Virtually all scholars agree that these associations contributed in great measure to the religious and national revival of the late sixteenth and early seventeenth centuries. This aspect is duly stressed in specialized studies,[1] as well as in most textbooks and general surveys of Ukrainian and Belarusian history.[2] However, until recently the Ukrainian and Belarusian confraternity movement had not been studied against the background of general religious history. Conversely, studies on the confraternities in Western Europe continue to ignore the existence of analogous institutions among Christians of the Eastern rite, namely in the Orthodox Church of Ukraine and Belarus and, later, in the Greek Catholic Church of these countries as well.[3] Comparative study of the confraternity movement in various regions of Europe can enhance our understanding of this phenomenon. The present study is the first such attempt.

---

1.   G. Gajecky, "Church Brotherhoods and Ukrainian Cultural Renewal in the 16th and 17th Centuries," in *Millennium of Christianity in Ukraine: A Symposium* (Ottawa, 1987), 67–78; idem, "The Stauropegian Assumption Brotherhood of Lviv," ibid., 127–37.

2.   See e.g., D. Doroshenko, *A Survey of Ukrainian History*, edited and updated by O. W. Gerus (Winnipeg, 1975), 148–51; M. Hrushevs'kyi, *Istoriia Ukraïny-Rusy*, vol. 6 (Kyiv, 1907; repr. New York, 1955, and Kyiv, 1995), 499–538.

3.   One of the rare exceptions is Robert Stupperrich's article "Bruderschaften/ Schwesterschaften/Kommunitäten" in *Theologische Realenzyklopädie*, vol. 7 (Berlin and New York, 1981), 200. With regard to the Orthodox confraternity in Lviv, the author draws on outdated works, although he also cites some newer studies.

Two interpretations of the history of confraternities are possible. Some scholars, who define them as "artificial families in which all members are united by voluntary brotherhood,"[4] study religious confraternities in the context of the history of all voluntary associations, which "can be found in all civilizations, past and present."[5] Such an approach can be fruitful for the purpose of anthropological and sociological studies. However, while comparative sociological research may certainly be invaluable, historians of institutions should nevertheless concentrate on those types of institutions that are genetically connected and/or function in a comparable way. Inconsistencies of terminology in the sources[6] compel historians to choose their terms in such a way as to assign a separate term to each particular phenomenon. Thus, the choice of terms reflects a historian's concept of what he considers essential in the phenomenon under discussion. In English-language scholarly literature the word *confraternity* (which derives from the Latin *confraternitas* and is related to the Italian *confraternita*, the Spanish *cofradía*, and the French *confrérie*) is generally used for Roman Catholic religious associations, but the term *brotherhood* is more frequent when referring to similar Orthodox institutions (*bratstva*). Nevertheless, given the common features of Catholic and Orthodox associations, it is preferable to use a single term, *confraternity*, for both phenomena.[7] On the other hand, the word *brotherhood* (which is close to the German *Bruderschaft*) may be used as a general term for all associations that aspire to replace kinship ties with a commitment to shared goals, principles, or ideologies. Later in this study the word *brotherhood* will be used with reference to pre-Christian and early Christian associations, whose structures are little known; it is certain, however, that they

---

4.   G. Le Bras, *Études de sociologie religieuse*, vol. 2 (Paris, 1956), 423.

5.   Ibid., 462.

6.   See L. Remling, *Bruderschaften in Franken: Kirchen- und sozialgeschichtliche Untersuchungen zum spätmittelalterlichen und frühneuzeitlichen Bruderschaftwesen* (Würzburg, 1986), 12–16, 25–26, 51–52; V. Bainbridge, *Gilds in the Medieval Countryside: Social and Religious Change in Cambridgeshire, c. 1350–1558* (Woodbridge, 1996), 6, 11.

7.   In Latin-language documents in Ukraine, the word *bratstvo* was invariably rendered as *confraternitas*.

differed from the structures of medieval and early modern Christian confraternities.

Definitions of religious confraternities of laymen may be found in theological works printed in Italy as early as the late fifteenth century.[8] Later, special studies were devoted to the history and juridical character of confraternities.[9] Statutes and other documents of numerous confraternities were published, as were studies of individual confraternities and, to a lesser extent, of the confraternity movement in particular regions. Despite the abundance of case studies, modern historiography offers no comprehensive examination of this phenomenon in a general European context. The only general surveys are to be found in encyclopedia entries[10] and in several informative articles.[11] No general bibliography of the confraternity movement is available,[12] and historiographic studies are extremely scarce.[13] Among the rare exceptions are an article by André Vauchez and the historiographic introduction to Virginia Bainbridge's monograph on the confraternities (which she calls "gilds") of Cambridgeshire.[14] Vauchez correctly notes

8.   See Remling, *Bruderschaften in Franken*, 26–29.

9.   I. B. Bassi, *Tractatus de sodalitiis seu de confraternitatibus ecclesiasticis et laicalibus* (Rome, 1725); A. Guzman, *Tratado del origen de la Confraternidad* (Madrid, 1730); L. A. Muratori, "De piis laicorum confraternitatibus, earumque origine, flagellantibus et sacris missionibus: Dissertatio septuagesimaquinta" in his *Antiquitates Italiae Medii Aevi*, vol. 6 (Milan, 1747), cols. 449–82.

10.   H. Durand, "Confrérie" in *Dictionnaire de droit canonique*, vol. 4 (Paris, 1949), 128–76.

11.   Perhaps the best known is the study by G. Le Bras, "Les confréries chrétiennes: problèmes et propositions," *Revue historique de droit français et étranger* (1940–41): 310–63, repr. in *Études de sociologie religieuse*, 2: 423–62. See also J. Duhr, "La confrérie dans la vie de l'Église," *Revue d'histoire ecclésiastique* 35 (1939): 437–78.

12.   The richness of the printed sources may be gauged from the fact that a bibliography devoted to the confraternities of one Italian city includes 5,652 entries. See O. Marinelli, "Le confraternite di Perugia dalle origini al sec. XIX: bibliografia delle opere a stampa" (Perugia, 1965) (offprint from *Annali della Facoltà di lettere e filosofia*, vols. 2–4).

13.   There is no monograph on the historiography of the subject, although some studies have historiographic introductions: see, e.g., Remling, *Bruderschaften in Franken*, 36–42.

14.   A. Vauchez, "Les confréries au Moyen Age: esquisse d'un bilan historiographique," *Revue historique* 275 (1986): 267–77, repr. in his *Les laics au Moyen Age* (Paris, 1987), 113–22; and Bainbridge, *Gilds in the Medieval Countryside*. See also A. Czacharowski, "Die Bruderschaften der mittelalterlichen Städte in der gegenwärtigen polnischen Forschung," in *Bürgerschaft und Kirche*, ed. J. Sydow (Sigmaringen, 1980), 26–37.

that scholarly interest in the history of European confraternities arose in the post-Romantic period and was associated with the idealization of primitive forms of socialization and of traditional pre-industrial cultural patterns. In the context of the present study, it should be added that the idealization of confraternities was also typical of post-Romantic populist historiography in Ukraine and Russia.

More recently, particularly since the 1970s, after the Roman Catholic Church proclaimed the importance of lay involvement in ecclesiastical administration and activity, some Roman Catholic historians have begun to detect a trend toward Catholic reform in the historical record of the confraternities. As a result of the higher status now accorded to lay religious associations, church historians have been inspired to seek the historical roots of the modern lay movement in medieval and post-Tridentine confraternities. Among the monographs written from such a viewpoint, perhaps the most significant is the three-volume Italian-language study of Gilles Gérard Meersseman.[15] One reviewer even wrote that, along with the studies of Etienne Delaruelle, Meersseman's book produced "a Copernican revolution in the field of church history," since these works posited the spontaneous religious activity of the common people, not official ecclesiastical structures, as the true center of Christian life.[16] In contrast to the Roman Catholic view, C. M. Barron wrote: "Lay involvement in the running of the parish church is not something that emerges with Protestantism, indeed it may be argued that the Reformation was but an extreme expression of that lay interest."[17]

The Italian confraternity movement constitutes a classic example, and it has been examined quite intensively.[18] Since

---

15. G. G. Meersseman, *Ordo fraternitatis: Confraternite e pietà dei laici nel Medioevo,* 3 vols. (Rome, 1977).

16. Vauchez, *Les laics au Moyen Age,* 95.

17. C. M. Barron, "The Parish Fraternities of Medieval London," in *The Church in Pre-Reformation Society: Essays in Honour of F. R. H. Du Boulay* (Woodbridge, 1985).

18. G. De Sandre Gasparini, "Appunti per uno studio sulle confraternite medievali: problemi e prospettive," *Studia patavina* 15, no. 1 (1968): 116–22; K. Eisenbichler, "Italian Scholarship on Pre-Modern Confraternities in Italy," *Renaissance Quarterly* 50, no. 2 (1997): 567–80.

1960, the 700th anniversary of the emergence of the flagellant movement, Italian scholars have organized several conferences devoted to confraternities.[19] These were followed by conferences in other countries that resulted in the publication of important collections of papers. Materials of a round table organized by the University of Lausanne were published under the title *Le mouvement confraternel au Moyen Age: France, Italie, Suisse.*[20] Two conferences were organized in Britain by the Ecclesiastical History Society, and their proceedings appeared in a volume entitled *Voluntary Religion.* The title is explained in the preface as follows: "Informal and voluntary associations constituted a voluntary religion opposed to that institutionalized in churches which constrain and discipline their members."[21] It is also stressed that ideals of fraternity contributed to the formation of corporate identities and horizontal links between members of associations, limiting to some degree the absolutization of hierarchical structures.[22] Recent studies have also focused on the significance of ritual kinship in medieval society, as well as on the shift of confraternities toward more hierarchical models, which reflected the general process of aristocratization in early modern society.[23] There are now more studies on confraternal rituals and the involvement of confraternities in the theatre, music, and works of charity; related to this was their role in offering their members higher status and religious legitimation of their interests.[24]

---

19. A. Monticone, G. De Rosa, G. Alberigo, G. De Sandre Gasparini, C. de la Roncière, and G. Vitolo, "La storiografia confraternale e le confraternite romane," in *Le Confraternite romane: esperienza religiosa, società, commitenza artistica,* ed. L. Fiorani (Rome, 1984), 19ff.; L. Fiorani, "Discussioni e ricerche sulle confraternite romane negli ultimi cento anni" in *Storiografia e archivi delle confraternite romane,* ed. L. Fiorani (Rome, 1985), 11–105.

20. *Le mouvement confraternel au Moyen Age: France, Italie, Suisse. Actes de la table ronde organisée par l'Université de Lausanne avec le concours de l'École française de Rome et de l'Unité associée 11011 du CNRS, Lausanne 9–11 mai 1985* (Geneva, 1987).

21. *Voluntary Religion: Papers Read at the 1985 and 1986 Meetings of the Ecclesiastical History Society. Studies in Church History* 23 (Worcester, 1986).

22. *Corpi, "fraternità," mestieri nella storia della società europea,* ed. D. Zardin (Rome, 1998), 9–49.

23. See Nicholas Terpstra's introduction to *The Politics of Ritual Kinship: Confraternities and Social Order in Early Modern Italy,* ed. N. Terpstra (Cambridge, 2000), 7.

24. Ibid., 4–5.

With few exceptions, authors of books and articles on confraternities in Mediterranean countries have not engaged in the comparative analysis of similar institutions in other regions, especially Northern Europe before the Reformation. On the other hand, because of the suppression of confraternities in Great Britain during the Reformation, the religious side of their activities was insufficiently appreciated. Among recent studies of this problem, mention should be made of the excellent historiographic introduction to Virginia Bainbridge's book on confraternities in Cambridgeshire. From the variety of established terms denoting the religious lay confraternities, the author has chosen the appellation "religious or social gilds," while stressing their differences from craftsmen's and merchants' gilds (usually spelled "guilds").[25]

A new approach to the problem of ecclesiastical confraternities has been proposed by Wolfgang Hardtwig. He sees these institutions as forerunners of modern voluntary associations (*Vereine*), so important for the functioning of civil society since the nineteenth century.[26] In 1990 confraternal scholars founded their own "confraternity," the Society for Confraternity Studies, with its seat at the University of Toronto. The society and its bulletin, *Confraternitas*,[27] are useful instruments for developing the informational infrastructure for this particular area of historical and religious research. Tables of contents of all issues are available on the Internet. It may be added that on 27 May 2001 the Google search engine found 2,930 occurrences of "confraternities" on the Internet and 2,520 occurrences of "cofradías" (including sites of present-day Roman Catholic confraternities and information on books in print devoted to confraternity studies). The first search took 0.14 seconds and the second 0.42 seconds. Several monographs devoted to medieval and early modern confraternities in a

---

25. Bainbridge, *Gilds in the Medieval Countryside*, 6, 17.

26. W. Hardtwig, *Genossenschaft, Sekte, Verein in Deutschland*, vol. 1, *Vom Spätmittelalter bis zur Französischen Revolution* (Munich, 1997), 70–97. Cf. D. Reid, "Measuring the Impact of Brotherhood: Robert Putnam's *Making Democracy Work* and Confraternal Studies," *Confraternitas* 14, no. 1 (2003): 3–12.

27. *Confraternitas: Bulletin of the Society for Confraternity Studies*, ed. K. Eisenbichler, vols. 1–14 (1990–2003) ff.

number of European countries have been published in the past two decades.[28] The sociological and anthropological study of present-day confraternities in Roman Catholic countries, especially France,[29] Spain, and Latin America, is still at an initial stage.[30]

As far as Orthodox confraternities are concerned, surveys of the scholarly literature are available in Mykhailo Hrushevsky's *History of Ukraine-Rus'* and in a much more recent article by Myron Kapral on the Lviv Dormition Confraternity, while brief bibliographic references are appended to the essay by Ivan Ohiienko (Metropolitan Ilarion of Winnipeg), "Ukrainian Church Brotherhoods: Their Activity and Significance," as well as to articles in many encyclopedias and textbooks.[31] There is a bibliographic survey of studies on Ukrainian church history by Isydor Patrylo.[32] Consequently, we may limit ourselves here to general historiographic remarks, citing mainly the most important works. As in Western Europe, so too in Ukraine the history of confraternities was initially studied by their members themselves. The principal reason for this was undoubtedly that historical arguments were important for defending the legal rights of these associations. Only later did historical studies per se begin to appear. In 1825, an elder of the Lviv Stauropegion Institute, Oleksander Illiashevych, produced

---

28.   C. F. Black, *Italian Confraternities in the Sixteenth Century* (Cambridge, 1989); M. Flynn, *Sacred Charity: Confraternities and Social Welfare in Spain, 1400–1700* (Ithaca, N.Y., 1989); H. Pátková, *Bratrstvie ke cti Božie: poznámky ke kultovní činnosti bratrstev a cechů ve středověkých Čechách* (Prague, 2000); J. Mikulec, *Barokní náboženská bratrstva v Čechách* (Prague, 2000).

29.   M. Segalen, *Les confréries dans la France contemporaine; les charités* (Paris, 1975); G. Michelin and M. Segalen, *La Confrérie des Pénitents blancs du Puy* (Paris, 1978).

30.   Especially important are studies on particular features of the late Spanish and Latin American confraternities. See O. Celestino and A. Meyers, *Las cofradías en el Perú, región central* (Frankfurt am Main, 1981); A. Meyers and D. E. Hopkins, ed., *Manipulating the Saints: Religious Brotherhoods and Social Integration in Postconquest Latin America* (Hamburg, 1988); I. Moreno Navarro, *Cofradías y hermandades Andaluzas: estructura, simbolismo e identidad* (Seville, 1985).

31.   Hrushevs'kyi, *Istoriia Ukraïny-Rusy*, 6: 631–33; I. Ohienko [Ohiienko], *The Ukrainian Church*, vol. 1 (Winnipeg, 1986).

32.   I. Patrylo, *Dzherela i bibliohrafiia istoriï Ukraïns'koï tserkvy* (Rome, 1975–95), offprint from *Analecta OSBM*, ser. 2, sec. 1, vols. 33, 46, 49.

a brief manuscript on the history of the Lviv Dormition Confraternity, and in 1836 Denys Zubrytsky completed his "Chronicle of the Lviv Confraternity," which greatly influenced subsequent historiography.[33] Zubrytsky's "Chronicle" was written in such a way that scholars perceived it as a compilation of documentary citations, although the author often expressed his own hypotheses in the form of chronicle entries. One of his errors, repeated even today, is that the Lviv Confraternity was founded as early as 1439, 1463, or 1469. For example, Wolfgang Heller accepted the first of these dates, while Karl Christian Felmy considers that Orthodox confraternities became clearly defined in the fifteenth century.[34] Contrary to this, as early as 1842 Mykola Kostomarov expressed his conviction that the very concept of the confraternity came to Ukraine "from the Western Church" in the late sixteenth century and that "the earlier existence of confraternities is not confirmed by indubitable evidence."[35] In the second half of the nineteenth century, the history of the Lviv Confraternity was studied by Iakiv Holovatsky, Anton Petrushevych, and Isydor Sharanevych. The rather superficial monograph by Amvrosii Krylovsky, *The Lviv Stavropegion Confraternity*, added some new information, but also introduced new misconceptions and errors.[36] Mykhailo Ziber and Oleksandra Iefymenko interpreted confraternities as direct descendants of the primordial family, clans, and tribal associations. This reflected both Romantic idealization of the preindustrial way of life (very similar to that noted by André Vauchez with regard to Western historiography) and a populist view of the "democratic heritage" of Slavic paganism and

---

33. His study, written originally in Polish, was published only in Russian translation in *Zhurnal Ministerstva narodnago prosveshcheniia* (1849–50); 2d ed. (Lviv, 1926). Cf. N. Tsar'ova, "Oleksander Iliashevych ta persha rozvidka z istoriï L'vivs'koho Uspens'koho Stavropihiis'koho bratstva," *Visnyk L'vivs'koho universytetu*, Seriia istorychna, issue 37, pt. 2 (Lviv, 2002): 73–87.

34. W. Heller, "Orthodoxe Bruderschaften und ihre Schulen in Polen-Litauen im 16. und 17. Jahrhundert" in *Der Ökumenische Patriarch Jeremias II. von Konstantinopel und die Anfänge des Moskauer Patriarchates* (Erlangen, 1991), 115; K. C. Felmy, "Der Aufbruch der orthodoxen Laien in Polen-Litauen im 16. und 17. Jahrhundert," *Zeitschrift für Kirchengeschichte* 98 (1987): 379.

35. N. Kostomarov, *Istoricheskie proizvedeniia. Avtobiografiia* (Kyiv, 1990), 116–17.

36. See the excellent critical review by Fedir Sribnyi in *ZNTSh* 75 (1907): 171–95.

"popular" customs.[37] The impact of confraternities on cultural development was studied by Kyrylo Studynsky, Mykhailo Vozniak, Ivan Krypiakevych, and others. Generally speaking, a characteristic feature of Ukrainian historiography was the predominantly secular approach that influenced even church historians.

Beginning in the mid-nineteenth century, Russian historiography hailed confraternities as defenders of Orthodox interests, which were identified with the interests of the Russian Empire. The term "West Russia" was coined in order to incorporate the Ukrainian and Belarusian heritage into the mainstream of imperial Russian history. At the same time, Russian historians contributed to the popularization of the confraternity movement and initiated a discussion on the origins of these associations. The prominent Russian historian Sergei Soloviev saw those origins in the Old Rus' *bratchiny*, loose associations known mostly for their role in organizing feasts of patron saints feasts in some parishes.[38] Ivan Flerov, Mikhail Koialovich and, most particularly, Nikolai Skabalanovich noted similarities of organizational structure between confraternities and Western trade guilds.[39] To some extent, their conceptions resemble those of Wilhelm Eduard Wilda, who stressed the transformation of pagan fraternal institutions under the influence of Christian associations. Later, the Russian author Aleksandr Papkov produced a rather superficial book on confraternities, associating them with the Old Rus' parish structure.[40] Many facts about the history of confraternities were gathered by Stepan Golubev, who saw confraternities primarily as a form of collective patronage of churches.

---

37.   A. Efimenko, *Iuzhnaia Rus'*, vol. 1 (St. Petersburg, 1905), 108, 200–309. Cf. Doroshenko, *Survey of Ukrainian History*, 149.

38.   S. Solov'ev, "Bratchiny," *Russkaia beseda*, 1856, no. 4: 108–17.

39.   I. Flerov, *O pravoslavnykh tsekovnykh bratstvakh, protivoborstvovavshikh unii v Iugo-Zapadnoi Rossii v XVI, XVII, XVIII stoletiiakh* (St. Petersburg, 1857); M. O. Koialovich, "Chteniia o tserkovnykh zapadnorusskikh bratstvakh," *Den'*, no. 36 (1862); N. A. Skabalanovich, "Zapadnoevropeiskiia gil'dii i zapadnorusskiia bratstva," *Khristianskoe chtenie*, 1875, nos. 9–10.

40.   A. Papkov, *Bratstva: Ocherk istorii zapadno-russkikh pravoslavnykh bratstv* (Sergiev Posad, 1900).

The only important general study on Ukrainian confraternities produced in the 1920s was a monograph by Pylyp Klymenko, *Guilds in Ukraine*.[41] Adopting a very broad concept of guilds, he gathered important material on various types of parish confraternities and craftsmen's guilds, focusing on the popular customs adopted by these associations or created by them. Unfortunately, only the first, mainly historiographic, part of the work was published before imprisonment interrupted Klymenko's scholarly activities. After World War II, historiography in Ukraine largely reflected alternating periods of active suppression of Ukrainian culture and those of relative "thaw." In more liberal times, a limited Ukrainian patriotism was tolerated by some officials and even encouraged by others on condition that historians use Marxist formulas and, still more important, glorify the "eternal friendship" of Ukrainians with Russians and their "strivings for reunion" with the Russian people. Consequently, some historians were predisposed only to serve the official ideology, while others used the official phraseology, consciously or even subconsciously, only as a smoke screen that enabled them to publish studies based on documentary sources.[42] It was in such an atmosphere that my monograph *Confraternities and Their Role in the Development of Ukrainian Culture from the Sixteenth to the Eighteenth Century*[43] was written and, notwithstanding many obstacles, finally published. In mentioning this, I take the liberty of offering some reflections *pro domo sua*—not only because that book was the first version of the present study, but also because the story of its publication can help promote understanding of the factors that shaped Soviet Ukrainian historical writing.

On the advice of the dean of Ukrainian historiography, Professor Ivan Krypiakevych, then director of the Lviv

---

41. P. Klymenko, *Tsekhy na Ukraïni* (Kyiv, 1929).

42. This situation is aptly characterized in Ivan Myhul's unpublished dissertation, "Politics and History in the Soviet Ukraine: A Study of Soviet Ukrainian Historiography," Ph.D. diss., Columbia University, 1971, 114–17. See also my introduction to the reprint of Ivan Krypiakevych's monograph *Bohdan Khmel'nyts'kyi* (Lviv, 1990).

43. Ia. Isaievych, *Bratstva ta ïkh rol' v rozvytku ukraïns'koï kul'tury XVI–XVIII st.* (Kyiv, 1966).

Institute of Social Sciences of the Ukrainian Academy of Sciences, I devoted my first monograph to the Lviv Dormition (Stauropegion) Confraternity, the only one that left an extensive archival legacy. Initially, the manuscript was rejected outright by the Naukova Dumka publishing house in Kyiv with the explanation that "wasting money on a book devoted to one city would be a luxury." Eventually, Professor Ivan Hurzhii, then chairman of the History and Philosophy Division of the Ukrainian Academy of Sciences (a kind of superstructure of the historical and philosophical institutes of the Academy) declared that he would support its publication if the author changed the title and added some material on other towns. It proved possible to prepare an expanded version relatively quickly, as historical data on confraternities other than that of Lviv are scarce.

In order to have book finally accepted for publication, the author had to persuade the officials of Knyhotorh (the state book distribution firm) to order such an allegedly "commercially unattractive" book. This could be achieved only with the help of some modest bribes. When the editor read the manuscript, she urged the author to "eliminate words such as 'archimandrite' or 'diocese,' which are alien to the Soviet people" (a quotation from the *redaktsiinyi vysnovok* [editorial evaluation] in the author's possession). With some cosmetic changes, the book was finally printed, only to face the major hurdle. In order to be published in the Soviet Union, every book had to pass three stages of censorship: first, the typescript had obtain the censors' resolution *do naboru* (approved for typesetting); the typeset text had to be inscribed *do druku* (approved for printing); and, once all copies were ready, yet another stamp was obligatory: *v svit* (literally, "into the world"), which meant permission to release the print run. Finally, the Komvydav (a kind of ministry for publishing and the book trade) held all copies in a warehouse until it procured a "closed [i.e., confidential] review" (*zakryta retsenziia*) of the so-called signal copy. Fortunately, the reviewer engaged in this case was Dr. Olena Kompan, who then still belonged to the academic establishment, although she was later persecuted. She was not at all pleased with my introductory quotations from official sources (Lenin; party documents) on "friendship with fraternal Russia" or on "religious forms being only a guise for class interests." Nevertheless, as she informed me, she reproduced those quotations in her review in order to demonstrate that the book was "ideologically correct" and could be released.

Only one of the Western reviewers, Vasyl Lutsiv, dismissed the book as an example of Soviet materialist distortion of history.[44] Other reviewers were less severe. Most of them accepted my conclusions and made valuable suggestions for further research. Especially important in this regard were the review articles of the distinguished Polish scholar Juliusz Bardach in *Kwartalnik Historyczny* (Warsaw) and of Lubomyr Hajda,[45] whose review opened the inaugural issue of *Recenzija*, an excellent (and still unsurpassed) periodical devoted to information on and criticism of Ukrainian publications in the humanities. I am especially grateful to Lubomyr Hajda and to Frank Sysyn, a reviewer of my *Sources for Study of Ukrainian Culture in the Age of Feudalism* (which included a chapter on sources for the study of confraternities)[46] for criticizing my Marxist declarations; without such criticism, a positive review in a "nationalist organ financed by American imperialists" could have had negative consequences for my scholarly career. From today's perspective, it is clear to me that I exaggerated the importance of confraternities in some spheres of cultural life, not to speak of offering simplistic explanations of some social phenomena. Later I tried to give a more comprehensive treatment of selected problems, among them the history of confraternity publishing activities.[47] I would like to add that a collection of articles including my paper on "Confraternities and the Zaporozhian

44.   V. O. Lutsiv, "Tserkovni bratstva v Ukraïni," *Bohosloviia* 37 (1973): 89–90, 92.

45.   J. Bardach, "Bractwa cerkiewne na ziemiach ruskich Rzeczypospolitej w XV–XVIII w.," *Kwartalnik Historyczny*, 1967, no. 1: 77–82; L. Hajda, "Bratstva ... ," *Recenzija* (Cambridge, Mass.) 1, no. 1 (Fall 1970): 3–12.

46.   F. Sysyn, review of Ja. D. Isajevyč, *Džerela z istoriji ukrajins'koji kul'tury doby feodalizmu, Recenzija* 4, no. 2 (Spring–Summer 1974): 14–32.

47.   Ia. Isaevich, *Preemniki pervopechatnika* (Moscow, 1981), 20–30, 90–110.

Cossacks"[48] was confiscated for alleged nationalist deviations and, as a result, I was officially reprimanded by the Presidium of the Academy of Sciences for "exaggerating the impact of the Cossacks on the confraternities." Ironically, my purpose was quite the opposite: to show the influence of the confraternity movement on the ideology of the Ukrainian Cossacks.

From among the views expressed in my monograph on confraternities and their role, most researchers did not accept, or perhaps did not consider important, the concept of diversity within the confraternity movement. More often than not, activities typical only of a few leading associations are still being attributed to the confraternity movement as a whole. On the other hand, the idea of Protestant inclinations among Ukrainian and Belarusian confraternities has become increasingly popular.[49] Moreover, this aspect of the confraternal movement is often exaggerated or interpreted in a non-nuanced way.[50] In part, this can be explained by the desire of contemporary Ukrainian intellectuals to see Ukraine as sharing in general trends of European intellectual development.

The most significant contributions to the field in the past decade are Myron Kapral's articles on the initial stages of the history of the Lviv Dormition (Stauropegion) Confraternity and on its most prominent leaders, Ivan Krasovsky and Iurii Rohatynets, as well as his above-mentioned essay on the historiography of this confraternity.[51] Kapral has produced the best and fullest collection of so-called "privileges" (documents

48.   Ia. Isaievych, "Zv'iazky bratstv z Zaporoz'kym kozatstvom," *Seredni viky na Ukraïni,* issue 2 (Kyiv, 1973), 149–53. Concerning the background of the ban on this article, see my comments in *Kyïvs'ka starovyna* (1992, no. 1: 7–11) on its second edition, which was free of distortions. The article was denounced as "politically incorrect" by Ivan Bilodid, vice-president of the Academy of Sciences of the Ukrainian SSR, even though it was written according to the then obligatory rules of self-censorship.

49.   M. Kashuba, "Reformatsiini ideï v diial'nosti bratstv na Ukraïni: XVI–XVII st.," in *Sekuliaryzatsiia dukhovnoho zhyttia na Ukraïni v epokhu humanizmu ta Reformatsiï* (Kyiv, 1991), 26–51.

50.   For example, it is difficult to accept the notion of Antitrinitarian influence on the confraternity movement. Cf. O. Matkovs'ka, *L'vivs'ke bratstvo: kul'tura i tradytsiï (kinets' XVI–persha polovyna XVII st.)* (Lviv, 1996), 50–58.

51.   On Kapral's approach to the problem of the founding of the Lviv Confraternity, see below, pp. 17–18.

regulating legal status) obtained by the Lviv Dormition Confraternity from ecclesiastical and state authorities. Volodymyr Aleksandrovych discovered the earliest documents on confraternities in Peremyshl (Przemyśl). He also provided comprehensive documentation of the influence of the confraternities on the development of icon painting and church architecture. At the same time, he has shown that some works of art have been attributed quite arbitrarily to confraternity initiative.

Despite its brevity, a collection of conference papers devoted to the 400th anniversary of the Lviv Dormition Confraternity has adduced some new materials and concepts.[52] The role of the confraternities in the development of schooling has been studied by Evgenii Medynsky and Olena Dziuba. Also active are historians of philosophy, most of whom ascribe considerable importance to the influence of confraternities on the shaping of Ukrainian and Belarusian spiritual identity. A collection of texts entitled *Monuments of Confraternity Schools in Ukraine (Late Sixteenth and Early Seventeenth Centuries)* appeared in 1988 as the first volume in the series "Monuments of the Philosophical Culture of the Ukrainian People."[53] Some texts included in this collection had never been published, while others, previously printed with distortions and omissions, were corrected on the basis of manuscript originals. Alongside documents indisputably connected with the confraternity movement, the volume also includes texts not related either to confraternity schools or to confraternities. Apparently, this was done to establish the background of confraternity activities, but in some cases, the authors of commentaries insist on linking such texts with the confraternities. A similar desire to attribute texts of other provenance to the confraternities is apparent in some late Soviet Belarusian publications.[54]

---

52. The conference was organized by Dmytro Bandrivsky under the auspices of the Institute for Religious Studies at the Lviv Museum of the History of Religion and the Vasyl Stefanyk Library of the National Academy of Sciences. See *Uspens'ke bratstvo i ioho rol' v ukraïns'komu natsional'no-kul'turnomu vidrodzhenni: Dopovidi i povidomlennia naukovoï konferentsiï 4–5 kvitnia 1996 roku* (Lviv, 1996).

53. *Pam'iatky brats'kykh shkil na Ukraïni: Kinets' XVI–pochatok XVII st. Teksty i doslidzhennia*, ed. V. Shynkaruk, V. Nichyk, and A. Sukhov (Kyiv, 1988).

54. E.g., H. Halenchenka, "Bratskae knihadrukavanne" in *Frantsysk Skaryna i iaho chas. Entsyklapedychny davednik* (Minsk, 1988), 269–73.

The history of the confraternities has become a subject for dissertations. Thus, Iulia Shustova provides a good survey of sources related to the history of the Lviv Dormition Confraternity,[55] while Oksana Fefelova and Liudmyla Hurska see confraternities mainly as a factor in the religious life and social activity of burghers.[56]

It is a real pleasure to end this historiographical survey with a book that constitutes a milestone in research on the early modern Ukrainian church and society. I refer to Borys Gudziak's *Crisis and Reform: The Kyivan Metropolitanate, the Patriarchate of Constantinople, and the Genesis of the Union of Brest*.[57] The author, first an associate of the Harvard Ukrainian Research Institute and then professor and rector at the Lviv Theological Academy and the Ukrainian Catholic University, has managed to produce a comprehensive synthesis of a subject previously approached mostly from parochial points of view in the spirit of conflicting historiographic and confessional traditions. The early history of the Ukrainian and Belarusian confraternities is treated within the context of the movement toward church reform initiated by the laity (representatives of the Orthodox nobility and leaders of the urban confraternities) that was joined only later by the ecclesiastical elite. Gudziak shows that "At a time when the hierarchy and clergy were only beginning to recognize the need for the revitalization of the Eastern Christian community, the Orthodox burghers of Lviv sought to establish structures allowing them to address the crisis in the Ruthenian Church." A well-balanced analysis of the confraternities' educational initiatives and their participation in religious conflicts provides a background for

55. Iu. Shustova, "Dokumenty L'vovskogo Stavropigiiskogo bratstva kak istoriko-antropologicheskie istochniki po istorii Ukrainy XVI–XVIII vv.," in *Istoricheskaia antropologiia: mesto v sisteme sotsial'nykh nauk, istochniki i metody interpretatsii. Tezisy dokladov i soobshchenii nauchnoi konferentsii* (Moscow, 1998), 233–35.

56. O. Fefelova, *Pravoslavnye bratstva na vostochnoslavianskikh territoriiakh Rechi Pospolitoi vo vtoroi polovine XVI–pervoi polovine XVII vekov* [dissertation abstract] (Tomsk, 2001); L. Hurs'ka, *Pravoslavni bratstva v Ukraïni iak chynnyk formuvannia natsional'noï samosvidomosti (kinets' XVI–persha polovyna XVII st.)*, dissertation abstract (Kyiv, 2000).

57. Cambridge, Mass., 1998; the Ukrainian version published in 2000 includes updated bibliographic information.

the conclusion that "in Lviv, and subsequently following its example in other towns, Ruthenian confraternities, with their relatively broad base, patriarchally endorsed legitimacy, and comprehensive charitable and cultural program, became centers for the forging of a new, gradually emerging, early-modern Ruthenian religious identity."[58]

With the exception of Father Gudziak's book and some popular essays, virtually all existing Ukrainian and Belarusian studies fail to take account of the purely religious motives for confraternity activity.[59] It should also be noted that most historians have concentrated their attention on the early stages of the history of the confraternities, often ignoring the later period. The Orthodox and Greek Catholic confraternities in small towns and villages have never been the subject of special investigation. This gap can be filled only after the completion of monographic research on the various types of confraternities.

The principal objective of the present study is to survey the main aspects of the activities of Ukrainian confraternities from the sixteenth through the eighteenth century. As mentioned earlier, confraternities of the same type existed in Belarus. This is quite natural, as the social and cultural development of both peoples was for the most part inseparable, and their church life also developed within the same ecclesiastical structure—the Kyiv Metropolitanate, originally united but later split into two separate metropolitanates, the Orthodox and the Catholic of the Greek (or, rather, Ruthenian) rite. Focusing on Ukrainian confraternities, this study also takes account of some Belarusian material in order to show that the confraternities functioned in the framework of a broader cultural entity of both peoples.

The introduction, the first chapter, large portions of the fifth chapter, and the summary have been newly written for the present edition. Other parts of the text are translated from the Ukrainian publication of 1966, with alterations and additions. Originally, I had planned to include information on the primary sources for this study in the new introduction.

---

58. Ibid., 160, 147.

59. See, however, Iu. Shustova, "Ukraïns'ki bratstva iak providnyky diial'noï relihiinosti v kintsi XVI–na pochatku XVII st.," in *Istoriia relihiï v Ukraïni: Materialy VIII mizhnarodnoho kruhloho stolu* (Lviv, 1998), 291–93.

However, considering that the archival activities of the confraternities were part of their contribution to cultural life, I finally decided to devote a separate chapter to the subject.

It would be difficult to enumerate all the individuals and institutions that helped bring this project to fruition. First and foremost, before the widespread availability of xerography, it was my mother, Natalia, daughter of Andrii Chaban and Maria Iablonska from the Stryi suburb of Lany Horishni, who copied innumerable excerpts from published sources for me. At various stages, I was fortunate to benefit from the advice of Academician Ivan Krypiakevych; the prominent and extremely altruistic bibliographer Fedir Pylypovych Maksymenko; the self-taught expert on Lviv manuscripts Iosyp Hronsky; Aleksandra Guseva, the author of many excellent descriptions of old Ukrainian imprints and their engravings; and Lubomyr Hajda, who contributed to the editing of the English version of the text. I have also benefited from the cooperation of Ihor Mytsko, Marta Boianivska, Borys Gudziak, Tom Hubka, and others. I am especially grateful to the Peter Jacyk Centre for Ukrainian Historical Research and to its director, Frank Sysyn, for the proposal to prepare the English version for publication in Canada. Dr. Sysyn and Dr. Roman Procyk, director of the Ukrainian Studies Fund at the Harvard Ukrainian Research Institute, helped overcome various obstacles and solve many problems on the tortuous path from manuscript version to published book. The assistance of the Ukrainian Studies Fund made it possible for me to visit American libraries in order to acquaint myself with modern Western research on my subject.

* * *

Medieval and early modern sources refer to Ukraine under different names, such as Rus', Little Rus' (a term that emerged in the fourteenth century, perhaps under the influence of the Greek concept of *Mikra Hellas*), and, in the seventeenth and eighteenth centuries, "the Land of the Cossacks." "Rus'," which was rendered in Latin as "Ruthenia" or "Russia" and in Greek as "Rosia," had several meanings. In the broadest sense, it designated all East Slavic nations, but in Western Europe during the period under discussion it was most often used for Ukraine and Belarus together, as opposed to Muscovy or Russia per se. In modern scholarly usage, the term "Ruthenian" is employed mostly to define phenomena common to both Ukrainians and Belarusians during the medieval and early modern periods of their history. The palatinate of Ruthenia (Latin: Palatinatus Russiae; Ukrainian: Rus'ke voievodstvo) comprised most of the territory of the former Galician (Ruthenian) Kingdom.

In order to avoid misunderstanding when referring to any distinctive historical phenomenon, it is advisable to use the same term for all periods of its existence. Thus, in the present study, the ethnonyms "Ukrainians" and "Belarusians" are also used retrospectively for the period when those nations were known by other names (understanding "nation," according to East European usage, as an ethnic community rather than a polity). By the same token, the terms "Greek Catholics" and "Greek Catholic Church" are applied to all stages of the history of this church, although initially the Greek Catholics of Ukraine and Belarus were officially designated "Catholics of the Greek rite united with the Roman rite" ("Catholici ritus Graeci Romano uniti"), "Ruthenian Catholics" or, less formally, "Uniates."

I

The Origins of the Confraternities

The origin of Christian confraternities is one these historical problems that defy easy solution, owing both to the paucity of sources and to the lack of terminological consensus. It is especially difficult to determine in which cases early brotherhoods possess attributes that might allow them to be considered forerunners of the medieval Christian confraternities.

As mentioned previously, some church historians trace the history of the confraternity movement to various pre-Christian rites and "fraternal" associations.[1] Strictly Christian brotherhoods, which included both laymen and clerics, are known to have existed in the Christian East as early as the fourth century.[2] The legalization of the Christian religion may have led inevitably to a split between official church structures and those that were initially informal. Many church historians, especially in Italy, assume that medieval lay confraternities were direct descendants of early Christian brotherhoods, which in turn grew out of the *collegia* and other "fraternal" associations of ancient Rome.[3] Other scholars, particularly in Germany and the Scandinavian countries, see the prototype of religious and craft confraternities in the traditional Nordic associations known as guilds.[4] Still others trace their derivation to both sources, writing about the modification of Nordic guilds un-

---

1.   J. Deschamps, *Les confréries au Moyen Age* (Bordeaux, 1958), 9–35.

2.   E. Wipszycka, "Les confréries dans la vie religieuse de l'Egypte chrétienne," *Proceedings of the XII International Congress of Papyrology* (1970), 511–25; cf. idem, "Świeckie bractwa w życiu religijnym chrześcijańskiego Egiptu," *Przegląd Historyczny* 59 (1968): 447–62; P. Horden, "The Confraternities of Byzantium," *Studies in Church History* 23 (1986): 42.

3.   R. Fiamingo, *Le confraternite nel diritto canonico e civile* (Naples, 1917), 7; K. Zoric, *Le confraternite in Dalmazia studiate nei lor manoscritti ed il loro influsso sulla vita religiosa* (Rome, 1949), 9.

4.   See, e.g., M. Pappenheim, *Die altdänischen Schutzgilden* (Breslau, 1885).

der the influence of Christian brotherhoods. Such a view was propounded early on by Wilhelm Eduard Wilda, whose work strongly influenced later German historiography.[5] It is difficult to reach a definitive conclusion, since our information about pre-Christian Germanic brotherhoods is extremely scarce.[6] The same may be said of the East Slavic *bratchiny*, loose associations that organized "fraternal" feasts.

One of the best-known sources describing early medieval brotherhoods is the "Capitula presbyteris data" (852) of Hincmarus, bishop of Reims. In this document, the bishop admonished "guilds or confraternities" (*geldonias vel confratrias*) to confine themselves strictly to religious activities, such as attendance at burial services, provisioning churches with candles, and collecting alms.[7] Some scholars distinguish the early guilds from confraternities, stressing that the former included both laymen and clerics and had as their main aim the organization of mutual assistance and the arrangement of common meals, while the latter were comprised primarily of clerics joining in common rituals to attain salvation.[8] The broad distribution of lay confraternities of the type that later became dominant in Western Christianity can be traced in Italy, France, and Germany only to the twelfth and thirteenth centuries.[9] The activities of the Dominicans initiated a distinctive type of confraternity movement, the flagellants. Important though they were, however, penitential associations of flagellants remained a deviation from the mainstream in the evolution of confraternities. In many countries they never gained a permanent foothold, while non-flagellant confraternities became

---

5.   W. E. Wilda, *Das Gildenwesen im Mittelalter* (Berlin, 1831; repr. Aalen, 1964).

6.   A. Schnyder, *Die Ursulabruderschaften des Spätmittelalters: ein Beitrag zur Erforschung der deutschsprächigen religiösen Literatur des 15. Jahrhunderts* (Stuttgart, 1986), 21–22.

7.   *Patrologia latina*, comp. J.-P. Migne (Paris, 1844–64), vol. 125, col. 777ff.

8.   Schnyder, *Die Ursulabruderschaften*, 28–29.

9.   G. Angelozzi, *Le confraternite laicali* (Brescia, 1978), 16, 23. The oldest known confraternity statute dates from the eleventh century (see Meersseman, *Ordo fraternitatis*, 1: 55–65). As Lester K. Little rightly points out, "the absolute novelty of the new thirteenth-century confraternities consisted in preponderant control by the laity, unfolding from the moment of their founding." See his *Libertà carità fraternità: Confraternite laiche a Bergamo nell'età del comune* (Bergamo, 1988), 12.

extremely popular in all Roman Catholic countries during the fourteenth, fifteenth, and early sixteenth centuries. The further development of lay confraternities was interrupted only by the Counter-Reformation.[10]

The emergence of urban confraternities was influenced by a growing sense of self-confidence among the burghers, who were acquiring greater political and economic power and becoming better educated. In many respects, the lay confraternity movement was also a reaction on the part of the laity to the upsurge of clerical authority.[11] Gradually, confraternities formed a network of religious communities based on voluntary individual membership, as opposed to the obligatory membership in parishes. Initially the clergy did not favor the spread of confraternities and only later began to accommodate them within church structures. Subsequently, confraternities helped strengthen parish administration, introducing limited self-management practices that generally were not opposed to the official church, but rather supportive of it.[12] The social composition of the confraternities has not been properly studied, and only a few scholars have attended to this important question. Still, on the basis of existing studies, it appears certain that the confraternity movement involved all social groups, with the exception of the very highest and lowest ranks of the social hierarchy.[13] Confraternities became a vehicle of social integration, as well as of acquiring status and self-confidence—a factor of special importance to the middle classes. As a general rule, in preindustrial societies voluntary associations were much more prevalent among the urban population, especially merchants, than among the upper classes or plebeians and peasants.[14] Maureen Flynn has aptly noted that in medieval

10. É. Delaruelle, *La piété populaire au Moyen Age* (Turin, 1975), 443–44.

11. Cf. L. Lauwers, review of A. Vauchez, *Les laics au Moyen Age, Revue d'histoire ecclésiastique* (Louvain) 83, nos. 3–4 (1988): 695.

12. D. H. Dietrich, "Confraternities and Lay Leadership in Sixteenth-Century Liège," *Renaissance and Reformation* 13, no. 1 (1989): 29–30.

13. Vauchez, "Les confréries," 470; R. Mackenney, *Tradesmen and Traders: The World of the Guilds in Venice and Europe, c. 1250–c. 1650* (London and Sydney, 1987), 44–73.

14. R. T. Anderson, "Voluntary Associations in History," *American Anthropologist* 73, no. 1 (1971): 213.

communities individuals were not guaranteed specific rights
under the law, and their self-identity reflected corporative or
familial rather than personal status. The mandatory meetings
where questions of common interest were discussed and decided in democratic fashion, as well as the elaborate corporate
ritual prevailing in the confraternities, may be interpreted as
"a concerted effort to realize within the microcosm of membership the spiritual ideals of brotherhood and social equality."[15] Many provisions of confraternity bylaws, especially the
election of officers, show the influence of communal statutes,
while the religious rituals were influenced by the statutes of
monastic congregations.[16] It should be noted that craft guilds
had a very similar organizational structure and conducted the
same pious activities as religious confraternities. Such guilds,
however, were also concerned with a vast range of professional activities, including learning a trade, quality control of
products, regulation of sales, and so on. In many cases a guild
"began as a neighborhood fraternity but then, perhaps because
men following the same craft tended to live in the same area,
these parish associations developed into trade fraternities and
then, later, into trade or craft companies."[17]

Religious lay confraternities in the West were extremely
diverse. The study of local confraternities of various types has
not been coordinated,[18] and even the compilation of catalogs
of confraternities is still in its initial stage.[19] Different as they
were, confraternities had many fields of activity in common.
Confraternities considered common prayer and other religious
rituals, and keeping order in the churches or in their own chapels or oratories, as their primary tasks. Since all confraternities were conceived as unions of living and deceased brethren,

---

15.   M. Flynn, "Rituals of Solidarity in Castilian Confraternities," *Renaissance and Reformation* 13, no. 1 (1989): 53, 66.

16.   J. Henderson, "Confraternities and the Church in Late Medieval Florence" in *Voluntary Religion*, 72.

17.   Barron, "Parish Fraternities," 14.

18.   L. Orioli, "Per una rassegna bibliografica sulle confraternite medievali," *Ricerche di storia sociale e religiosa*, n.s. 17–18 (1980): 79.

19.   J. Krettner, *Erster Katalog von Bruderschaften in Bayern* (Munich, 1980); H. Hochenegg, *Bruderschaften und ähnliche religiöse Vereinigungen in Deutschtirol bis zum Beginn des zwanzigsten Jahrhunderts* (Innsbruck, 1984), 35–225.

prayers and masses for the repose of the souls of the deceased were an important element of their mentality.[20] Indeed, the desire for colleagues who would ensure an "honorable" funeral was a major stimulus to membership in confraternities.[21] Other confraternal activities were also motivated by the desire for salvation. Confraternities promoted or at least proclaimed mutual assistance to their members and for charitable purposes, especially the care of widows and orphans. They often organized hospitals, which were shelters for the disabled rather than medical institutions. Fraternal feasts, probably a legacy from pre-Christian times, were associated with the feast days of patron saints.[22] And since excesses are usually more conspicuous than ordinary activities, as early as the ninth century Bishop Hincmarus of Reims denounced brotherhood members for drinking too much, while Luther later referred to confraternities as associations of drunkards.

A distinctive feature of all confraternities and trade guilds were their organizational practices, which included paying entrance and membership fees, regular mandatory meetings, the election of officers and their accounting to members. All spheres of activity undertaken by Roman Catholic confraternities and their organizational rules were shared by Orthodox confraternities in Ukraine and Belarus. The similarities are so close as to leave little doubt that the Western confraternities and guilds served as models for their East European counterparts. While the models reached Ukraine via Poland,[23] they

---

20. Epidemics, especially the Black Death of the mid-fourteenth century, contributed to the popularity of confraternities, which serving as a kind of surrogate for destroyed or endangered family and social ties. See J. Chiffoleau, "Les confréries, la mort et la religion en comtat venaissin à la fin du Moyen Age," *Melanges de l'École française de Rome: Moyen Age, Temps Modernes* 91 (1979): 818.

21. P. Löffler, *Studien zum Totenbrauchtum in den Gilden, Bruderschaften und Nachbarschaften vom Ende des 15. bis zum Ende des 19. Jahrhunderts* (Münster, 1975), 292.

22. On the sacral significance of feasts and drinking rituals in pagan associations, see Deschamps, *Les confréries au Moyen Age,* 16–21, 62–63.

23. On confraternities in Poland, see B. Kumor, "Kościelne stowarzyszenia świeckie na ziemiach polskich w okresie przedrozbiorowym," *Prawo Kanoniczne* 10 (1967): 289–356; E. Wiśniowski, "Bractwa religijne na ziemiach polskich w średniowieczu," *Roczniki Humanistyczne* 17, no. 2 (1969): 51–81.

were also the result of direct Ukrainian and Belarusian contact with West European countries, especially Germany and Italy.

Orthodox religious confraternities may also have adopted some functions and rituals from the ancient *bratchiny*, which are first mentioned in the twelfth-century Kyiv Chronicle. In an entry devoted to events of 1158 (dated in the chronicle according to the "ultra-March" system as 6667, i.e., 1159), the chronicler states that the people of Polatsk invited Prince Rostyslav Hlebovich "to attend *bratshchina* in the old [church] of the Holy Virgin, on St. Peter's day" (у братьщину к сѣтй Бци к старѣй на Петров днь).[24] As employed here, *bratchina* (*bratshchina*) can mean not only a fraternal banquet, but also the parish association as its organizer. There are various interpretations of this text and later sources related to *bratchiny*, but there is insufficient evidence to consider the *bratchina* a kind of artisan or merchant guild.[25] More likely, the *bratchiny* were forerunners of the "mead brotherhoods," whose main prerogative became to brew beer and mead for sale at parish feasts.[26] The incorporation of pagan traditions of sacrificial meals into the rituals of these brotherhoods is a matter of speculation,[27] although it is theoretically probable.

Artisan guilds (*tsekhy*, from the German *Zeche*) appeared in western Ukraine no later than the fourteenth century, and the first reliable information on the structure of Orthodox religious confraternities is to be found in the bylaws of two confraternities in the suburbs of Lviv, dated 1542 and 1544.[28] In 1538, the mead brotherhood of Orthodox furriers in Vilnius (Ruthenian:

---

24. *Polnoe sobranie russkikh letopisei*, vol. 2 (Moscow, 1962), col. 495; *The Old Rus' Kievan and Galician-Volhynian Chronicles: The Ostroz'kyj (Xlebnikov) and Četvertyns'kyj (Pogodin) Codices* (Cambridge, Mass., 1990), 219; *Litopys rus'kyi za Ipats'kym spyskom*, trans. and ed. L. Makhnovets' (Kyiv, 1989), 272.

25. B. A. Rybakov, *Remeslo drevnei Rusi* (Moscow, 1948), 759–65; *Istoriia kul'tury drevnei Rusi*, ed. B. D. Grekov, vol. 1 (Moscow and Leningrad, 1948–51), 177.

26. Hrushevs'kyi, *Istoriia Ukraïny-Rusy*, 6: 502–504.

27. Rybakov, *Remeslo*, 760, 764.

28. In some historical monographs, the emergence of confraternities in Ukraine is dated as early as the mid-fifteenth century. Although the existence of confraternities at this time cannot be excluded, the documents cited to prove this early date are not reliable. See Ia. Isaievych, "Naidavnishi dokumenty pro diial'nist' bratstv na Ukraïni," *Istorychni dzherela ta ïkh vykorystannia* (Kyiv), 2 (1966): 13–18.

Vilno; Polish: Wilno) became a guild, retaining the name "brotherhood," which was also used by other guilds. The Vilnius
Orthodox guilds (*bratstva*) of tanners and merchants emerged
in a similar way. They differed from regular Orthodox confraternities not only in their openly professional orientation, but
also in their lack of connection with a particular parish; instead,
they provided supplies of wax and rendered financial support
to several churches.[29] Unlike many other scholars, we consider
these developments in Vilnius an exception rather than the rule.
In most cases, particularly in Ukraine, guilds and confraternities
of the Western type emerged independently from ancient mead
brotherhoods, although some guilds and confraternities, especially in the eastern regions of Ukraine, were later influenced
by traditional brotherhood rituals. Similar conclusions were
reached concerning Greek Orthodox confraternities in the lands
under the rule of Venice. N. G. Moschonas has stressed that,
although pious corporations were known during the Byzantine
period, the later lay confraternities and guilds on the Ionian
islands followed the model of the Venetian confraternities and
should be analyzed against the background of the European
corporative movement.[30]

In this study we shall leave aside guilds that should be
studied in the context of social and economic history and
consider only confraternities of a mainly religious character.
It may be assumed that initially confraternities were not widespread and coexisted with more archaic forms of parish activity. Sharing many features with Roman Catholic confraternities
in their organization and functions, Orthodox confraternities
also had important peculiarities from the very beginning. First,
in the Orthodox Church, confraternities of priests such as the
Kalandbruderschaften in Germany were unknown. Most Eastern
Orthodox confraternities had a purely lay membership, and
mixed confraternities that also accepted monks and/or priests
should be considered rare exceptions. The Orthodox confraternities never claimed any formally regulated rights or privileges

---

29.   Cf. Hrushevs'kyi, *Istoriia*, 6: 505.

30.   N. G. Mosxona, "Threskeutikes adelphothetes laikon sta Ionia nesia,"
Ethnikon idryma epeunon Kentron Byzantinon epeunon symmeikta, 7 (1987): 193–204.

related to the absolution of sins such as those offered by papal diplomas or grants of indulgences for many confraternities.[31] In the Roman Catholic Church, moreover, alongside the parish confraternities,[32] there were many specialized confraternities associated either with particular forms of devotion or with a special type of membership, such as confraternities for the veneration of the Corpus Christi, rosary confraternities, "confraternitates litteratum," and national or ethnic confraternities,[33] not to speak of confraternities of flagellants and other sectarian associations. Very often there were several confraternities associated with particular chapels or altars in a single church, and, conversely, other confraternities whose activities involved more than one parish. By contrast, only parish confraternities were known in the Ukrainian and Belarusian Orthodox Church. Such non-parish confraternities as the Marian sodality in the Kyiv Mohyla Academy were rare exceptions.[34] Perhaps even the very concept of a parish confraternity as a form of religious and ethnic organization was influenced both by Greek Orthodox brotherhoods in Italy and by local Catholic lay confraternities in the Polish-Lithuanian Commonwealth.[35]

In the late sixteenth and early seventeenth centuries, the character of confraternities changed drastically both in West-

---

31. Certain analogies, however, may be discerned in the confreres' belief in the importance of confraternal rites and ceremonies for salvation of the soul.

32. They were especially typical for villages, where in many cases a parish and a confraternity could become almost synonymous. See Henderson, "Confraternities," 70; C. M. de La Roncière, "La place des confréries dans l'encadrement religieux du contado florentin: l'exemple de la Val d'Elsa," *Mélanges de l'Ecole française de Rome* 85 (1973): 31–77, 633–71.

33. G. G. Meersseman (*Ordo fraternitatis*, 188) suggests that the confraternities of Lombards at the University of Bologna were forerunners of the later "nationes," which took on a totally secular character.

34. P. Hradiuk, "Do istoriï Mariis'kykh Druzhyn v Ukraïni," *Analecta OSBM*, ser. 2, vol. 1 (7) (1953): 648–61. Another exception was the attempt to establish a confraternity in Zhyrovychi under the patronage of Our Lady of Mercy including both Uniates and Roman Catholics, laymen and clergy. The regulations of this confraternity were sent to Rome for approval in 1668. See *MUH* 2: 204; S. Senyk, "Marian Cult in the Kievan Metropolitanate XVII–XVIII Centuries" in *Intrepido pastori* (Rome, 1984), 271.

35. Interestingly, in contrast to cities of Western Poland, medieval Cracow had only parish confraternities (cf. Czacharowski, "Bruderschaften," 37). The question of possible interaction between regional variants of Polish Catholicism and Orthodoxy has yet to be studied.

ern Europe and in those Orthodox countries where confraternities already existed. These changes, however, went in opposite directions. After the Council of Trent, the Roman Catholic Church began to revitalize and promote confraternities as a form of Counter-Reformation activity.[36] In 1562, a decree of the council instituted strict episcopal control over confraternities and other lay associations. Later, the papal constitution "Quaecumque" of 7 December 1604 postulated the canonical establishment of confraternities, as well as the obligatory confirmation of their statutes by local bishops.[37] The practice of granting indulgences to confraternity members became firmly established and, at the same time, confraternities began to take part in disseminating those forms of devotion that were rejected by Protestants. As the Polish scholar Krystyna Kuźmak suggests, some Roman Catholic confraternities in Ukraine were conceived as an "antidote" to confraternities connected with the Eastern Church.[38] Most Catholic confraternities were involved in organizing such typically baroque forms of religious ritual as stately public ceremonies and processions.[39] They also contributed to the standardization of rituals and encouraged individual forms of affective piety.[40]

As Roman Catholic confraternities were finally being subordinated to the clergy, Ukrainian and Belarusian burghers began to organize Orthodox parish confraternities that were often anticlerical and occasionally even adhered to the semi-Protestant notion of lay control over priests and bishops. In

---

36. Remling, *Bruderschaften in Franken*, 30–32; Wiśniowski, "Bractwa religijne," 81.

37. Schnyder, *Die Ursulabruderschaften*, 33–34; M. Mombelli Castracane, "Ricerche sulla natura giuridica delle confraternite nell'età della controriforma," *Rivista di storia del diritto italiano* 55 (1982): 1–73.

38. K. Kuźmak, *Bractwa Matki Boskiej Wspomożycielki Chrześcijan na ziemiach polskich w XVIII st.* (Rome, 1973), 80, 189–90.

39. W. Katzinger, *Die Bruderschaften in den Städten Oberösterreichs als Hilfsmittel der Gegenreformation und Ausdruck barocker Frömmigkeit in Bürgerschaft und Kirche* (Sigmaringen, 1980), 106–10.

40. G. Schreiber, "Der Barock und das Tridentinum: Geistesgeschichtliche und kultische Zusammenhänge" in *Das Weltkonzil von Trient*, vol. 1 (Freiburg, 1951), 406–16; J. Kopiec, "Bruderschaften als Ausdruck barocker Frömmigkeit," *Archiv für schlesische Kirchengeschichte* (Sigmaringen) 44 (1987): 81–91.

addition, these new Orthodox confraternities were generally much more involved in cultural and political activities than Roman Catholic ones.[41]

There is an almost complete dearth of authentic sources about organizations that can be considered forerunners of the Orthodox parish confraternities. As previously stated, there is some evidence that the so-called *bratchiny* existed as early as the twelfth century, but only from the mid-fifteenth century do we have more precise information about the laity's role in Orthodox parish structures. In the proceedings of the city court collegium (*lava*) of Peremyshl, entries from 1447 and 1452 mention the overseers (*vitrici*) of St. John's Cathedral.[42] The Latin term *vitricus* was sometimes rendered as *vytrykush*, and the Greek word *ktitor* was also used in a similar sense.[43] Documents related to the Nativity Church in Ternopil provide some information about the duties of these overseers. Although the legal status of the lay parishioners was defined only in the sixteenth century, the relevant documents reflect earlier relations. Traditionally, the whole Orthodox community chose four persons, holding life tenure, to nominate and dismiss parish priests and oversee the hospital and school.[44] The organization did not always function in an orderly fashion; for example, by-elections were not always held on time.

Although the oldest documents about the organizational structure of the Orthodox community in the city of Lviv are extremely fragmentary, their terminology provides evidence that parish institutions in Lviv were similar to those of Ternopil. An entry in the Lviv city magistracy records from 1472 indicates that Ukrainians (*Rutheni*) claimed

---

41.   For Roman Catholic confraternities, strictly cultural activities appear to have been the exception. For example, there was a confraternity publishing house, "Academia Amoris," in Wrocław. In Lviv there was a printing press owned by the Roman Catholic Holy Trinity Confraternity, but its publishing activities were under the complete control of the clergy. See *PKM* 2, pt. 1: 111.

42.   *Pomniki dziejowe Przemyśla*, vol. 1 (Przemyśl, 1936), 150.

43.   A. Dobrianskii, *Istoriia episkopov trekh soiedinennykh eparkhii* (Lviv, 1893), period III, 74.

44.   O. Terlets'kyi, *Vasyl' Konstantyn kniaz' Ostroz'kyi: Istoriia fundatsii kniazia Ostroz'koho v Ternopoli* (Ternopil, 1909), 37–40. In his own comments, Omelian Terletsky used the word "confraternity" for elected church wardens, but that term does not appear in his sources.

the right of the Dormition Church to a parcel of land bequeathed by a woman called Dobrusha. It may be assumed that the general term *Rutheni* refers here to an organization of burghers who oversaw the Dormition Church. In 1502, Marko the Merchant (Kramar) and Borys the Furrier (Kushnir) are mentioned as overseers of the city church.[45] In 1504, the overseers were Andrii Lysyi, Borys, and Kost the Furrier. In 1515, the Ukrainian burghers bought a piece of velvet "with money from their common fund," and in 1524 they acquired a building in the city. As early as 1530, Makar (Tuchapsky), Omelian, and Stetsko are mentioned as church overseers and patrons elected by the Ukrainian community. In 1544 the Ukrainian elders (*seniores Ruthenici*), superintendents (*provisores*), and senior overseers of the church named Davydko Maletsky, Omelian, and Matvii, "in their own name and in the name of other brothers and neighbors, patrons of the church,"[46] were involved in a lawsuit concerning a book and twelve paintings on parchment donated to the church by Iatsko the Cantor. In 1558 and 1559, burghers who had undertaken the construction of a new church edifice sent their representatives Volos, Davyd Maletsky, and Bohdan to Prince Alexandru Lăpuşneanu of Moldavia to seek financial assistance. Prince Alexandru's letters in this matter were addressed "to the honorable Lviv burghers Davyd, Demyd Krasovsky, Toma, Volos," and in other instances to "Volos, Davyd, and others," "to the parishioners of the Dormition Church," or "to the priest Herasym and the parishioners Davyd and Volos." The prince not only provided financial support for the construction of the church but also promised to defray the costs of feasts to celebrate the feast of its patron.[47]This custom of commemorating feast days may have been inherited from the ancient *bratchyny*.[48]

---

45.   I. Kryp'iakevych, "L'vivs'ka Rus' v pershii polovyni XVI st.," *ZNTSh* 78 (1907): 23, 30, 47.

46.   TsDIAL 52/2/11: 191, 137. References to archival files consist of three (*fond/opys/*file or volume) or two (*fond/*file) figures. Thus, 52/2/11 means *fond* 52, section 2, file 11. A *fond* is a group of files created by one institution or person; an *opys* is a section of a *fond*.

47.   *IuILS*, vol. 1, nos. 7–22.

48.   I. Franko, *P'ianyts'ke chudo v Korsuni* (Lviv, 1913), 5.

Considering themselves the true masters of church property, the burghers tried to limit the influence of parish priests as much as possible. The same Prince Alexandru reproached the Ukrainian burghers of Lviv for not accepting the authority of their parish priest.[49]

The parishioners' association of the Dormition Church did not confine its activities to ecclesiastical affairs. Occasionally its leaders claimed to be "the elders of the Ukrainian nation in Lviv" and led the movement of Orthodox burghers for greater political liberties. During the 1520s, the merchants Makar (Tuchapsky), Hnat, Makar's father-in-law, Illia, and other church overseers distinguished themselves as representatives of the Ukrainian community in a lawsuit against the city magistracy, which had violated the Orthodox burghers' rights.[50] They and other Ukrainian burghers, along with representatives of the middle and lower nobility, were involved in protracted efforts to end their humiliating dependence on the Roman Catholic archbishops. In a letter of 1536, they described their own efforts and those of "their ancestors, grandfathers, and fathers" to obtain royal permission for the establishment of an Orthodox episcopal see in Lviv. Not only did they have to send bribes (several hundred oxen) to individuals at the court of Queen Bona Sforza and to the king himself, but also to defend their episcopal candidate with arms in hand, "because they were afraid that the archbishop or some Polish lord would overtake him and order him killed" (боячися, аби арцибіскуп або который лядський пан єго догонил, а не казал єго забити).[51] In 1538, Ukrainian burghers were denounced to the city magistracy "for having arranged a secret meeting where they elect Ukrainian burgomasters and councillors from among themselves and conspire against the authority of the city magistracy."[52] Significantly, such charges were voiced just before the Ukrainian burghers and noblemen managed to

---

49.   IuILS, vol. 1, no. 17; Kryp'iakevych, "L'vivs'ka Rus'," 25–26.

50.   AIuZR, 10: 13. See also MCS, 2, 3, 9; Kryp'iakevych, "L'vivs'ka Rus'," 10.

51.   AZR, 2: 359. The original royal charter of 1539 on the recognition of Makar as an Orthodox bishop is preserved in NBUV, fond of the Greek Catholic Metropolitan Consistory (fond 18, no. 6).

52.   Kryp'iakevych, "L'vivs'ka Rus'," 13; TsDIAL 52/2/10: 789–90.

extricate themselves from the spiritual control of the Roman Catholic archbishops.

In the second half of the sixteenth century, the Ukrainian burghers of Lviv organized the solemn burials of two Molda-vian rulers executed by the Polish authorities, Ştefan Tomşa (1564)[53] and Ivan Pidkova (Potcoavă) (1578).[54] These events were generally perceived as acts of political opposition.

The most active leaders of the Lviv Orthodox burgher community were Makar Tuchapsky (in 1538 he became the first bishop of the newly created Orthodox diocese of Lviv), the cobbler Volos (in 1553, he was the "elder of Ukrainian cobblers" and as such was mentioned among the *tsekhmistry* or guild elders),[55] the tailor Demko (Demyd, Diomyd) Kraso-vsky, and the merchants Davydko Maletsky and Ivan Babych. It is not surprising that the first Orthodox bishop of Lviv came from this milieu. On the other hand, the burghers came into conflict with Bishop Arsen Balaban, who belonged to the nobility and tried to limit the prerogatives of the laity in par-ish life (in particular, he sought to bring the St. Onuphrius Monastery under his direct jurisdiction). Urban parishioners were also interested in cultural affairs and took care of hos-pitals. Thus it is difficult to agree with the assertions of some historians that the early parish associations had a merely charitable character. As we have seen, they were already in-volved (albeit to a limited extent) in the cultural and political activities that later became the domain of the confraternities.

In the mid-sixteenth century some parish associations accepted the designation of "confraternity" and adopted written statutes. The earliest known statutes of Orthodox con-fraternities are those of two organizations in the Pidzamche (Subcastle) suburb of Lviv—the confraternity at the Annuncia-

---

53. *AGZ*, 1: 34.

54. Bartłomiej Zimorowicz, a Lviv city chronicler, states that Ivan Pidkova was buried by the Ruthenian confraternity. This was written in 1665–67, apparently under the influence of the later usage of the word (J. B. Zimorowicz, *Opera* [Lviv, 1899], 136).

55. "Starosta sutorum Ruthenicalium" (K. Badecki, *Zaginione księgi średniowiecznego Lwowa* [Lviv, 1928], 48).

tion parish (1542)[56] and the St. Nicholas Confraternity (1544)[57]—
and the confraternity in the town of Sudova Vyshnia (1563).[58] A
diploma presented in 1556 by Bishop Antonii Radylovsky of
Peremyshl to the Confraternity of the Elevation of the Holy
Cross in Drohobych is known only from the Latin summary
discovered by Volodymyr Aleksandrovych in the archive of
the Peremyshl Roman Catholic bishopric: "Privilegium confraternitatis ecclesiae Exaltationis S[anct]ae Crucis drohobycensis
per ill[ust]r[issi]mum olim Antonium Radylowski episcopum.
Privileg[ium] dat[um] post septem mille annorum a condice
mundo alias, ut ad marginem eiusdem privilegii adnotatum est,
anno Christi 1556, in pergameno cum sigillo pensito." A document dated 1571 mentions "provisores seu seniores contubernii
Sancti Ioannis seu Iwanonis ritus Raeci (sic)," i.e., "guardians or
guild elders of St. John's [Church] of the Greek rite."[59] The late
Latin term contubernium usually meant a craft guild, but the
distinction between confraternities and guilds was not clear-
cut, and in this case contubernium referred to the church confraternity (this is apparent from its being named after St. John). At
that time, the Orthodox hierarchy in the Peremyshl and Lviv
eparchies was probably involved in organizing confraternities
of the Western type, but they evinced no activity capable of
influencing society in general. At least, the lack of information
to that effect, as compared with the abundance of data after the
late 1580s, may be interpreted as evidence that the new confraternities remained rather passive on the public scene. All three
known early statutes were concerned with a limited number of
issues, such as the entrance fee (ukup), frequency of meetings,
rules for the election of elders, and the obligation of members
to help sick colleagues take part in common church services

---

56.   NBUV, Manuscript Institute, fond 18, no. 8; Vestnik Iugo-Zapadnoi i Zapadnoi
Rossii, 1862, no. 3, 98–100. The charter issued by the Lviv city magistracy in 1545
confirmed the ownership of the Annunciation Church by its parishioners, but did
not use the word "confraternity" (TsDIAL 201/4b/13–14).

57.   TsDIAL 129/1/10; MCS, 13–14; PBSh, 13–15.

58.   AIuZR, 6: 50–52; PBSh, 15–17.

59.   V. Aleksandrovych, "Pryvilei peremys'koho iepyskopa Antoniia
Radylovs'koho dlia drohobyts'koho Khrestovozdvyzhens'koho bratstva z 1556 r."
in Drohobyts'kyi kraieznavchyi zbirnyk 4 (2000): 332–36. See also Polska-Ukraina. 1000
lat sąsiedztwa (Przemyśl), 3 (1996): 65.

and to arrange the burial of deceased confreres. The statutes of the Lviv suburban Annunciation and St. Nicholas confraternities are very similar, giving grounds to assume that they were modeled on the earlier statute of the confraternity attached to the Dormition Church in central Lviv.[60] Nevertheless, the documents about the internal activities of the city parish association do not use the term "confraternity." Two such acts are known, allowing us to conclude that the structure of this association differed considerably from that of the later Dormition Confraternity.

One of these documents contains the proceedings of a meeting of burghers who conducted an inventory of the Dormition Church property. It runs as follows: "In the year 1579, on the 11th day of May. There was a meeting to inspect the church treasury, utensils, and books. Both elders and juniors took part." A list of those present follows. Fifteen persons are named: Marko the Greek, Hrytsko Duda, Stetsko Morokhovsky, Lesko Maletsky, Khoma Babych, Vasko Tenevych, Sava the Greek, Hrytsko Huba, Ivan Namisnyk, Ivan Mynets, Dmytro Demydovych Krasovsky, Iarosh the tailor, Ivan Bohatyrets, Ivan the merchant, and Ivan the cantor.[61] Following a description of the inspected property, including sixty-three books, there is a note about the election of overseers (*vytrykushi*) of this property: "Finally, all this was entrusted to Master Marko the Greek and to Master Lesko, including the church moneybox, then containing 24 zlotys and half a grosz" (Отож тоє все поручено пану Маркові Гречинові і з паном Леськом, і скриньку церковную, в которой било на тот час піндзей церковних 24 золотих і пулгрош). The next day, the "elders and juniors" met in the suburban St. Onuphrius Monastery for an inventory of the monastery church. Beside those listed above, two other burghers were present, Matsko Ivanovych and Huba's son Khoma, but Hrytsko Huba himself and Ivan Bidlaha could not

---

60. A. Krylovskii, *L'vovskoe Stavropigial'noe bratstvo: Opyt tserkovno-istoricheskago issledovaniia* (Kyiv, 1904), 35–36.

61. TsDIAL 129/1/1114, f. 1, 3, 4. The best text is to be found in V. Kmet', "Inventari Uspens'koï ta Sviatoonufriïvs'koï monastyrs'koï tserkvy u L'vovi 1919 r.," *Visnyk L'vivs'koho universytetu*, Historical Series, 35–36 (2001): 497–506. For a reproduction of the first page of this record, see Isaievych, *Bratstva*, 30.

come because they were away (пана Грицка Губи і пана Івана Бідлаги в тот час дома не било).

The association of "neighbors" divided into "elders" and "juniors" did not yet have elaborated structures and did not meet regularly. This is apparent from the notes, all kept by the same individual, probably Ivan Bohatyrets. These notes are the oldest known documents concerning the internal activity of the organization that was a forerunner of the confraternity. Immediately following an account of the election of Marko the Greek and Lesko Maletsky, we read the following: "In a few days a conflict emerged over the priest Ivan, and Master Marko became angry and resigned from his supervisory office, and Master Lesko also resigned, and once again Master Hrytsko, together with Master Stetsko, stayed in office as before for three years. And then in 1581, on the first of the month of October, when Duda was not able to remain in office, and Master Stetsko did not wish to do so, the latter gave the church keys to Master Marko and to Master Ivan the merchant." After recording new treasury income, the report continued: "In the year 1583, on the Wednesday after Easter, upon due consideration, we elected Master Lesko and Ivan the merchant to be overseers and handed them the church keys and the treasury. And again there was strife. Lesko became angry over the same priest Ivan and did not wish to be in that office, and resigned."[62] The copy of the report ends at this point.

The parishioners' organization of the Dormition Church, headed by the "neighbors and church guardians" who elected church supervisors, sometimes acted as a representation of the "Ukrainian community" of burghers. In some cases, this association is referred to as *confratres et vicini* ("confreres and neighbors," as in a document dated 1544), or even as a "confraternity" (for example, in an entry in the municipal records dated 1573).[63] In all probability, there was no written statute of the kind that was considered the distinguishing feature of a legally recognized entity in the West. Even if a statute existed (some scholars assume that

---

62.   TsDIAL 129/1/1034, f. 3–4.
63.   TsDIAL 52/2/17, f. 963.

statutes of suburban confraternities could not have appeared independently, without the previous model of a burgher institution), it was not strictly adhered to, as may be seen from the inconsistent terminology. In any case, before 1585–86 the organizational structure of the association of overseers of the Dormition Church was neither stable nor clearly defined, and the distinction between parish and municipal functions was blurred. It may be assumed that in that period parishioners of the Dormition Church were organized along traditional lines, as was also the case in most Ukrainian and Belarusian Orthodox church communities.

Although in Lviv the word *bratstvo* (confraternity) was occasionally used much earlier, in the late 1580s both the city magistracy and Ukrainian townsmen called the Dormition Confraternity "new" or "newly established." A ceremony of admission incorporating an oath to fulfill all the duties of a member, regular meetings with reports by officeholders, and disciplinary sanctions were the external features that distinguished confraternities of the new type from their predecessors. Of course, the introduction of a new organizational structure would have been insignificant had members not been active participants in public affairs. It was precisely the upsurge of the social and religious movement that made it urgent to replace outdated forms with more streamlined ones, capable of bringing together the Ukrainian city population more effectively. As Ivan Franko aptly stressed, the strength of the confraternities would lie in their discipline and the cohesiveness of their members.[64] The importance of this factor is underestimated by historians who identify archaic and highly diversified parish institutions (probably related to indigenous traditions, Byzantine practices and, even at this early date, Western influences) with the later confraternities. Such an approach, typical of many older studies, was adopted by Myron Kapral.[65] For example, he takes the fact that in 1583 Ivan Krasovsky acted "on behalf of the overseers" (*curatorum ... iussu*)

---

64.   I. Franko, "Z polia nashoï kul'tury," *Narod* 4 (1893): 228.

65.   M. Kapral', "Chy isnuvalo L'vivs'ke Uspens'ke bratstvo pered 1586 rokom?" in *Uspens'ke bratstvo i ioho rol' v ukraïns'komu natsional'no-kul'turnomu vidrodzhenni* (Lviv, 1996), 9–10

and "in the name of the church" (*ecclesiae ... nomine*) as evidence of Krasovsky's activities in the confraternity.[66] Kapral's main argument is that the Ukrainian community (hromada) was active before 1586 in a variety of fields, including economic life, religious matters, and philanthropy. However, concepts of community and religious confraternity had different origins and functions. Naturally, the old structure prepared a basis for the new, and in that sense the establishment of the confraternity may be called a reform of communal religious life. A very similar way of thinking was evinced earlier by authors who regarded any association of craftsmen as a guild. In order not to blur the distinction between essentially different types of associations, it would be preferable to reserve the term "guilds" (*tsekhy*) for legally regulated craftsmen's corporations of the European type and the term "confraternities" for parish associations known from the 1540s (from the first statutes and foundation charters mentioned above), which began to spread intensively through western Ukraine and Belarus in the 1580s and 1590s. (This would also be in keeping with the terminology of most of the sources.) The confraternities were distinguished from previous associations by their discipline, larger membership, and more active role in cultural and political life. The widespread confraternity movement was initiated by confraternities with written and officially approved statutes or founding documents, first and foremost by the Dormition Confraternity in Lviv, which built with unprecedented zeal on the existing tradition of burgher social activism and became "an important center of education and literary activity."[67] Its example was followed by other confraternities.

* * *

The emergence and evolution of leading Ukrainian and Belarusian confraternities into quasi-political associations was strongly influenced by the social and religious conflicts

---

66.   M. Kapral', "Aktovi materialy do biohrafiï Ivana Krasovs'koho za 1574–1619 rr.," *Ukraïna v mynulomu*, 1993, no. 4: 91–98.

67.   I. Franko, *Narys istoriï ukraïns'ko-rus'koï literatury* (Lviv, 1910), 45.

of the second half of the sixteenth century and later. These conflicts became particularly acute in western Ukraine and in Vilnius, which was not only the capital of the Grand Duchy of Lithuania but also the most important cultural center for the Belarusian Orthodox burghers and nobility. In this period, religious identity was inseparable from national identity. The latter concept is, of course, to be understood in its prevalent East European interpretation: thus, the idea of a "Ruthenian nation" had more of an ethnic than a political meaning. Among its features were historical tradition, language, and a particular church that provided not only ideological underpinnings but also organizational structures for the consolidation of Ruthenians, i.e., Ukrainians and Belarusians.[68] The words "Ruthenians" and "schismatics" (meaning Orthodox) were used interchangeably in Polish documents of the fifteenth and sixteenth centuries.[69] Only the Roman Catholic Church enjoyed absolute freedom, a wide range of privileges, and the protection of the state. The particularistic law of this church, which was enforced in the Polish-Lithuanian state, lumped the "schismatics" (Orthodox, Armenians) and "infidels" (mainly Jews) into the same category—people whose religions were only tolerated.[70]

Authors who wrote about the Commonwealth as characterized by exemplary religious tolerance usually stressed that the official ban on the building of new churches in the Grand Duchy of Lithuania and in some cities of the Kingdom of Poland was never fully implemented. Even if that were so, the very possibility that such a ban could be issued is clear evidence of the degradation of Orthodoxy. It is true that the Orthodox nobility eventually acquired the same political rights as those possessed by Roman Catholic and Protestant

---

68. On religious and ethnic relations in Ukraine, see F. Sysyn, *Between Poland and the Ukraine: The Dilemma of Adam Kysil, 1600–1653* (Cambridge, Mass., 1985), 26–36; T. Chynczewska-Hennel, *Świadomość narodowa szlachty ukraińskiej i kozaczyzny od schyłku XVI do połowy XVII wieku* (Warsaw, 1985).

69. J. Sawicki, "'Rebaptisatio Ruthenorum' in the Light of 15th and 16th Century Polish Synodal Legislation" in *The Christian Community of Medieval Poland*, ed. J. Kłoczowski (Wrocław and Warsaw, 1981), 62.

70. These formulations closely approximate those of Jakub Sawicki, the well-known Polish historian of canon law, ibid., 61–62.

noblemen. Nevertheless, the continuing humiliation of the Orthodox religion was perceived as the humiliation of all its adherents. Although the religious and linguistic assimilation of the Ukrainian nobles to the dominant Poles was not rapid until the upheaval of the mid-seventeenth century,[71] it proceeded steadily nevertheless. While such assimilation appeared spontaneous in most cases, it was generally a result of existing inequalities and even of pressure exerted by the ruling Polish (Roman Catholic) elites.

Religious inequality was especially acute in some towns of western Ukraine, where Orthodox Ukrainians were denied the right to participate in municipal administrative bodies and even in artisan guilds. This situation was further aggravated by the advent of the Counter-Reformation in the Polish-Lithuanian Commonwealth. The Orthodox now faced even more militant adversaries, which provoked an immediate response in the religious sphere.[72] Relations in Lviv, the capital of the palatinate of Ruthenia, became particularly tense. Most of the urban population, including its lower strata, was in conflict with those families that had monopolized membership in the city magistracy. Simultaneously, in 1578–85 the "Ruthenian community" was involved in a lawsuit with the magistracy "over their denial of the liberties and rights enjoyed by the Polish burghers."[73] Ukrainians publicly demanded an end to restrictions on commerce, in trades and crafts, as well as on access to secondary schools for their children. At the end of 1583, the Roman Catholic archbishop of Lviv, Dymitr Solikowski, tried to force the Orthodox to accept the Gregorian calendar, which added to the tension between the Ukrainian Orthodox community and the Roman Catholic clergy. According to Mykhailo Hrushevsky, the vindication by the Orthodox of their right to retain the Julian calendar further emboldened the Lviv Orthodox burghers and helped

71.   H. Litwin, "Catholization among the Ruthenian Nobility and Assimilation Processes in the Ukraine during the Years 1569–1648," Acta Poloniae Historica 55 (1987): 56–83; N. Iakovenko, Ukraïns'ka shliakhta z kintsia XIV do seredyny XVII st. (Volyn' i Tsentral'na Ukraïna) (Kyiv, 1993), 243.

72.   F. Sysyn, "The Cultural, Social and Political Context of Ukrainian History-Writing: 1620–1690," Europa Orientalis 5 (1986): 291–92.

73 .   TsDIAL 9/338: 210; 341: 765.

improve their status not only in Lviv, but also in other cities and towns.[74]

The need for greater consolidation of Orthodox craftsmen and merchants became even more evident when they undertook to organize a school and a printing press. These initiatives were not motivated only by the interests of their social group; on the contrary, the educated burghers began to represent the viewpoint of all nationally conscious elites. After the death of the famous printer Ivan Fedorov,[75] Ukrainian citizens of Lviv decided to redeem his pawned equipment in order to set up a press of their own. By November 1585, fund raising for that purpose was already in progress.[76] Most probably, the action was initiated by the same people who were then busily reforming or, more properly, organizing the Lviv Dormition Confraternity. In order to lend greater authority to the confraternity statute they had drafted, the Ukrainian citizens of Lviv took advantage of the fact that early in 1586 the patriarch of Antioch, Joachim IV Dou, was to pass through their city on his way to Moscow. His official mission there was connected with the establishment of the Moscow patriarchate, but, according to Syrian sources, the main reason for his journey to Romania, Ukraine, and Muscovy was to collect alms to pay the debts of his patriarchate.[77] If subsequent testimony by confraternity members is reliable, Joachim arrived in Lviv on 1 January 1586 and was greeted with a solemn ceremony and a procession.[78] A document dated the same day and written in the patriarch's name contains the text of the confraternity's statute.[79] The preamble, conclusion, and some of the more general articles were written in Old Church Slavonic, but

---

74.   Hrushevs'kyi, *Istoriia Ukraïny-Rusy*, 6: 519; Gudziak, *Crisis and Reform*, 374–75.

75.   On his activities, see chapter 5.

76.   *MCS*, 112; *400 let russkogo knigopechataniia*, vol. 1 (Moscow, 1964), 73; *Pershodrukar*, 80–82.

77.   Episkop Porfirii, *Vostok khristianskii. Siriia: I* (Kyiv, 1846): 83–84. Manuscripts in Arabic concerning the patriarch's journey are in the Manuscript Division of the Institute of Peoples of Asia, St. Petersburg Branch (MSS B. 1228 and B. 1229).

78.   *PKK*, 3: 43.

79.   *MCS*, 113–19; *DS*, 3–15; *Pryvileï natsional'nykh hromad mista L'vova (XIV–XVIII st.)*, comp. M. Kapral' (Lviv, 2000), 500–504. For the original and a contemporary copy, see TsDIAL 129/1/7. For other copies, see TsDIAL 129/1/423, Album, 22–39.

the articles defining the goals, organizational structure, and tasks of the confraternity were in Ukrainian. Presumably, the document was prepared by the citizens of Lviv on the Western principle that an institution without a written statute was legally non-existent. As Professor Gilles Meersseman notes: "Each confraternity in every true society had a statute of its own: ubi societas, ibi lex."[80]

Patriarch Joachim, a speaker of Arabic,[81] corroborated the document with his seal, but not with his signature. The latter appears, however, on a Ukrainian-language letter encouraging clergy and laymen to support the construction of the church, the school, and the printshop in Lviv, as well as on an Arabic-language document condemning digamous (i.e., remarried) priests.[82] The first document was dated 15 January 1586, and the second was written no earlier than 16 January. In both signed documents there is no mention of the confraternity. No doubt the patriarch did not figure as its initiator. Later, the confraternity wrote that on arriving in Lviv the patriarch had found there a confraternity, a hospital, and a school.[83] It appears that the confreres persuaded the patriarch to approve the document, which had been prepared in advance, by convincing him that the confraternity would help eliminate remarriage among priests and other "vile customs" of which he vehemently disapproved. The patriarch may have agreed to issue the founding charter of the confraternity on 1 January, but when it was finally drawn up, he only affixed his seal, without signing the document. Later it was submitted to the metropolitan of Kyiv, Mykhailo Rohoza, and to his protonotary for signing. The seal of Hedeon Balaban was also affixed. While the possibility that Balaban was forced to sign the charter during Joachim's stay in Lviv cannot be excluded, it is more probable that both Balaban and Rohoza approved the document on 22 June 1590 during the Brest (Ukrainian: Berest,

80.   Meersseman, *Ordo fraternitatis*, 1: 18.

81.   "Barkulabovskaia letopis'," ed. M. N. Dovnar-Zapol'skii, *Universitetskiia izvestiia* (Kyiv) 38, no. 12 (1898): 7.

82.   *MCS*, 119–20; I. Krachkovskii, *Izbrannye sochineniia*, vol. 6 (Moscow and Leningrad, 1960), 447.

83.   *Chteniia v Obshchestve istorii i drevnostei rossiiskikh* (Moscow), 1848, no. 6: 57.

Berestia) synod of Ukrainian and Belarusian bishops, which took the side of the confraternity in its conflict with Balaban and approved its statute.[84] During this synod, Balaban agreed to sign a charter exempting the Dormition Confraternity from his authority. Apparently he did so and simultaneously affixed his seal to the confraternity statute as a result of some temporary compromise with the burghers.

It is difficult to imagine that the articles of the statute dealing with the organizational structure of the confraternity, so similar to articles in statutes of Western-type confraternities and guilds, were initiated and formulated by the Arabic-speaking patriarch of Antioch. Although some patriarchs later found it useful to employ confraternities as levers of influence on local hierarchs, it is improbable that the patriarch himself conceived of the unprecedented right to maintain control over other confraternities, clergymen and hierarchs, as well as to act against any bishop whom the confraternity considered an "enemy of truth." The text of the charter, though written in the patriarch's name, helps us appreciate the self-assurance and fervor of the confraternity leaders:

> ... we, Joachim, by the Grace of God, patriarch of Great Antioch, sent by the synod of the patriarchs, command by the power of God that these commissions be firmly observed in perpetuity. And we grant power to this church Confraternity to reprimand by the law of Christ opponents and to banish all disorder from the Church. And if any brother should be excommunicated from his church by his own priest, let not the protopresbyter or the bishop bless such a man until he has reckoned with the Confraternity. And if someone in this city or a church, or some other confraternity is seen or heard to be living not according to the law, be it a layman or religious, a protopresbyter, priest, deacon, or of one of the minor orders, he should be reprimanded in word or in writing. If certain persons are found to oppose the law of truth, they should be reported to the bishop. If the bishop himself acts against the law of truth and does not manage the Church according to the law of the canons of the Holy Apostles and Holy Fathers, corrupting the righteous to injustice, sustaining the hands of

---

84.   Album, 22.

the lawless, such a bishop should be opposed, as an enemy of truth. If the Confraternity makes an accusation to the bishop concerning any brother, the brother cannot be tried until the whole Confraternity stands with him, and together with the bishop let the brothers investigate the cause of the accusation and adjudicate according to the canons of the Holy Fathers. And if in other places disorderly priests or laymen are known or seen, they should be reprimanded in a Christian manner, and an explanation should be sought. If persons are detected who are contrary or insubordinate to the bishop, they should be reported. Moreover, if there were anywhere a Confraternity that did not act according to the rule of this church Confraternity, on which we first in Lviv lawfully bestowed seniority [let it be reported]; and let no one oppose the latter or hinder it through [the use of the rules of] an older confraternity not confirmed by some bishops who have convened. We command that all confraternities everywhere be subordinate to the Confraternity of Lviv. And every city having this lawful confraternity ought to know the life of both priests and laity within it and in surrounding towns and villages, and seeing all lawlessness, shall not conceal it, but shall report it to the bishop.... With all the above written down lawfully, let not the bishop oppose the code granted by us in a spiritual manner to this church for all ages.... Whoever comes to oppose this spiritual code and attempts to abolish it, whether archbishop, bishop, protopresbyter, priest, deacon, or any cleric of the Church, or any from among the rulers, or the laity, our blessing will not be upon him, but rather the anathema of all four ecumenical patriarchs and the anathema of the Holy God-Bearing fathers of the Ecumenical Councils.[85]

The citizens of Lviv also wanted to have the document confirmed by the patriarch of Constantinople, Theoleptos, to whom they wrote: "We are sending you the statute of our confraternity so that you, our pastor, might sign it and corroborate it with your seal."[86] But shortly afterwards Theoleptos was replaced by a new patriarch of Constantinople, Jeremiah II Tranos. On 2 December 1587, he approved the founding of the confraternity, the hospital, the school, and the

---

85.   DS, 13–15; Pryvileï natsional'nykh hromad, 503–4. The translation is by Borys Gudziak (Crisis and Reform, 159–60).
86.   MCS, 139.

press, and in November 1589 he granted the St. Onuphrius Monastery the status of stauropegion, which exempted it from the jurisdiction of the local bishop. On 22 June 1590, the Synod of Brest not only upheld Jeremiah's charters concerning the founding of the Lviv Confraternity but also gave its consent to the formation of similar confraternities in other towns.[87] Jeremiah's diploma for the Nativity of the Theotokos Confraternity in Rohatyn endowed it with rights similar to those of the Vilnius and Lviv confraternities.[88] The parchment original of the Greek-language diploma is now in the Manuscript Institute of the Vernadsky Central Scholarly Library of Ukraine in Kyiv. Subsequently the text was "corrected": passages dealing with the confraternity's dependence on Lviv bishops were deleted and the notion of stauropegial rights was added. The document was later signed by bishops Hedeon Balaban, Kyrylo Terletsky, and Meletii Khrebtovych, as well as by metropolitans Mykhailo Rohoza and Petro Mohyla.[89]

The Orthodox confraternity attached to the Holy Trinity Monastery in Vilnius was allegedly founded by the metropolitan of Kyiv, Onysyfor Divochka, in 1584. It began to participate in church affairs as a result of the city council's placing the Holy Trinity Monastery under the protection of Orthodox municipal councillors.[90] The distinctive feature of this confraternity was close cooperation among burghers, monks, and nobles. It may be assumed that after receiving a copy of the Lviv Confraternity statute, members of the Vilnius Confraternity made some significant changes in their previous version of the text and then published it.[91] Patriarch Jeremiah sanctioned the Vilnius Holy

---

87.   *DS*, 35–38, 93; *MCS*, 203–5, 258.

88.   *DS*, 60–61.

89.   NBUV, Manuscript Institute, fond 18, no. 47. Cf. *Hrets'ki rukopysy u zibranniakh Kyieva. Kataloh*, comp. Ie. Chernukhin (Kyiv, 2000), 209.

90.   B. Floria, "Kommentarii," in Makarii (Bulgakov), *Istoriia russkoi tserkvi*, vol. 5 (Moscow, 1996), 467.

91.   Hrushevs'kyi, *Istoriia Ukraïny-Rusy*, 6: 526–27. The text of the Vilnius statute was published from a manuscript copy acquired by the Museum of the Kyiv Theological Academy from the Pochaiv Monastery. See S. Golubev, *Kievskii mitropolit Petr Mogila i ego spodvizhniki*, 2 vols. (Kyiv, 1883–98), vol. 1, supplement, 235–53.

Trinity Confraternity during his stay in Vilnius in June 1588. In the following year, this confraternity succeeded in obtaining confirmation of its status by Sigismund III, King of Poland and Grand Duke of Lithuania.[92]

As we have seen, the Lviv Dormition Confraternity was already exempted from subordination to the bishop by the statute of 1586 and even empowered to take action against him when it considered his conduct improper. In essence, then, the confraternity claimed its independence from the bishop of Lviv. It did so with the approval of the metropolitan of Kyiv, who hoped to replace the bishop's authority with his own.[93] Eventually, Hedeon Balaban made an attempt to use patriarchal authority against the metropolitan, presenting a copy of a letter (still extant) allegedly signed by Patriarch Jeremiah in July 1592. It contained a demand to abolish the Stauropegion founded by Metropolitan Mykhailo Rohoza of Kyiv "under the bell tower in Lviv," as no one had done anything of the sort "since the times of the great emperor Constantine." This assertion was correct in the sense that in the Byzantine and post-Byzantine church stauropegial rights were accorded to monasteries, not to associations of laymen. The name stauropegial ("bearing the cross") was used because the planting of a patriarchal cross on monastery property was a sign of its direct subordination to the patriarch, bypassing the authority of local bishops or any other ecclesiastical bodies. Nevertheless, in this case the patriarch supported the confraternity and the metropolitan, who established that the patriarchal act abolishing the Lviv Stauropegion was spurious.[94] Allegedly the forged document was prepared with the assistance of Dionysius Rhalis-Paleologos, archbishop of Tŭrnovo and at one time an associate of the Ostrih (Ostroh) circle, who was also suspected of other forgeries and whose attitude to the Ukrainian hierarchy does not appear to have been consistent.[95]

The patriarch's attitude was finally clarified when he issued a charter endowing both the St. Onuphrius Monastery

92.   *AZR*, 4: 22–25; Gudziak, *Crisis and Reform*, 166–167, 190, 402.

93.   Gudziak, *Crisis and Reform*, 409–10.

94.   *MCS*, 361–62, 405.

95.   Gudziak, *Crisis and Reform*, 207.

and the confraternity church with the status of patriarchal stauropegion, released from dependence on the bishop and metropolitan.[96] There is a copy of this document in the confraternity Album (Register of Copies) under the year 1593. Although the patriarchal document refers only to the monastery and the church as possessing stauropegial rights, the Dormition Confraternity itself began using the name Stauropegion Confraternity (in Ukrainian, Stavropihiia) in order to assert its claim to independence from the local ecclesiastical hierarchy. It was only a few years earlier, in 1578, that the same patriarch had granted stauropegial rights to St. George's Greek Orthodox Church in Venice.[97] This probably served the Lviv Orthodox burghers as an example, since western Ukraine maintained close contact, mostly through its Greek residents, with the Venetian Greeks. Perhaps the very concept of a confraternity as a form of organization suitable for a religious and ethnic community arose under the influence of Greek brotherhoods in Italy. The diploma confirming the status of the Lviv and Vilnius confraternities signed in 1592 by King Sigismund may show that at the time the Polish government still had no plans to foster a church union.[98] On the other hand, we do not know whether the king had any opinion of his own in this particular case: very often documents from the royal chancery were obtained through personal contact with court officials, including bribery.

Some Orthodox historians have deplored the granting of stauropegial status to the confraternities as the main cause of the acceptance of the church union by most Orthodox bishops. Even Mykhailo Hrushevsky wrote: "On the part of the patriarch, the granting of such egregious rights to this organization, whose composition was accidental in any case, was not a judicious action. Such rights of the confraternities were decidedly contrary to the whole canonical structure of the Orthodox Church, and their existence could be explained only by the very sad opinion of the patriarchs concerning the

96.   Ibid., 87–90, 107–8.

97.   G. Fedalto, *Ricerche storiche sulla posizione giuridica ed ecclesiastica dei Greci a Venezia nei secoli XV e XVI* (Florence, 1967).

98.   Floria, "Kommentarii," 478.

Ukrainian church and its hierarchy. Such opinions explain
why the patriarch of Constantinople, Jeremiah, ratified
the constitutive charter granted by Joachim to the Lviv
Confraternity and adopted the same position: broad rights
and privileges for the confraternity against the hierarchy. This
had unfortunate consequences: the Ukrainian bishops were
offended by such willfulness on the part of the patriarchs,
and this was one of the more important motives for their
going over to the Union."[99] A similar view was expressed by
Oleksander Lototsky and other scholars.[100] It cannot, of course,
be denied that the patriarchs sometimes agreed to confirm a
confraternity's exceptional status because they hoped that
limitations on episcopal power would reinforce their own
status. Furthermore, they wanted material assistance from
the confraternities. Panteleimon Kulish even considered that
the Stauropegion Confraternity had simply "bought" its
statute.[101] There are even authors who accuse the patriarchs of
intentionally worsening the anarchy in the Ruthenian Orthodox
Church.[102] It seems more likely, however, that the inconsistent
and often contradictory decisions of the patriarchs with regard
to confraternities resulted from insufficient knowledge of the
Ukrainian church, as well as their susceptibility to various
influences. Patriarchal decrees acknowledged the existing
situation instead of creating a new one. As far as the union
of churches is concerned, it had much more profound causes,
and the stauropegial rights of confraternities were a pretext for
the bishops rather than a significant motive. The thesis of the
confraternities' "abuses" as the cause of bishops' "flight" to the
Union was expressed by the bishops themselves, but if it were
true, it would be difficult to explain why the main opponent of
the confraternities, Bishop Hedeon Balaban, remained faithful
to Orthodoxy.[103]

---

99.   M. Hrushevs'kyi, *Kul'turno-natsional'nyi rukh na Ukraïni v XVI–XVII vitsi*
(Kyiv, 1912), 113–14.

100.   O. Lotots'kyi, *Ukraïns'ki dzherela tserkovnoho prava* (Warsaw, 1931), 190.

101.   P. A. Kulish, *Istoriia vossoedineniia Rusi*, vol. 1 (St. Petersburg, 1874), 240.

102.   See for example, M. Stakhiv, *Khrystova tserkva v Ukraïni, 988–1596*
(Stamford, Conn., 1985), 289.

103.   I. Vlasovs'kyi, *Narys istoriï Ukraïns'koï pravoslavnoï tserkvy*, vol. 1 (New
York, 1955), 218.

Essentially, confraternities were founded at the initiative of the burghers themselves, while the patriarchs agreed to confirm their privileges, but remained passive or even hostile to important aspects of confraternal activity. Credit for the establishment of the confraternities is due mainly to such burghers as Iurii Rohatynets, Ivan Krasovsky, Lesko Maletsky, Stetsko Morokhovsky and others. The movement initiated by them quickly spread beyond Lviv to encompass a significant portion of Ukraine.

* * *

The statute of the Lviv Dormition Confraternity contained a clause on the invalidity of "imperfect" confraternity statutes approved earlier by bishops. It declared that all confraternities had to accept the authority of the "elder" Lviv Dormition Confraternity, also known as the "urban" confraternity (because its members were burghers and parishioners of the only church in the central part of the city, the "city proper"). Thus the Dormition Confraternity served as a model for founding new confraternities or reorganizing existing ones in the suburbs of Lviv, as well as in other cities and towns. For example, after 1586, the preamble of the Dormition Confraternity statute, including the endorsement of this confraternity in the name of Patriarch Joachim, was added to the statute of the St. Nicholas Confraternity in the Pidzamche suburb.[104] In 1591, another suburban association, the Theophany Confraternity, was "amalgamated with the urban confraternity," that is, it acknowledged the latter's authority and adopted its statute.[105] As early as 1608, there were confraternities in all the suburban parishes of Lviv. At times, some suburban residents manifested "disobedience and defiance of the authority of the urban confraternity as supreme in all affairs."[106] However, the great majority of the suburban confraternities (there were twelve of

---

104.   *MCS*, 14.
105.   Ibid., 279–81.
106.   *AIuZR*, 11: 128.

them in the eighteenth century)[107] supported the Stauropegion Confraternity in all important questions.

The confraternity attached to the monastery church of St. Onuphrius was considered "junior" to the Stauropegion Confraternity. Similar "junior" (also known as "minor" or "bachelor") confraternities for unmarried men arose in other towns, parallel to the "elder"[108] confraternities. In Kyiv, a "junior" confraternity founded "in the tradition of confraternities of other towns" was confirmed in 1620 by Patriarch Theophanes simultaneously with his confirmation of the "elder" confraternity.[109] The structure of the junior confraternities was similar to that of all others; their task was to prepare young men for activity in regular confraternities.

By the end of the sixteenth century, confraternities had been established in many towns of Galicia, the Kholm (Polish: Chełm) Land, and Podlachia (Pidliashshia). Confraternities were officially founded in Rohatyn and Krasnostav (Krasnystaw) in 1589, in Brest and Horodok in 1591, and in Komarno in 1592.[110] In Lublin, where the Ukrainian population was comparatively small but well organized, a confraternity was established in 1594. Many Belarusian confraternities were founded or reorganized at the same time.

At the Brest synod of 1594, in addition to the confraternities listed above, others based in Halych, Bilsk (Polish: Bielsk Podlaski), "and many other places"[111] were represented. There are early seventeenth-century records concerning the activity of confraternities in Drohobych, Sambir, Sianik (Polish: Sanok), Berezhany, Kamianka Strumylova (now Kamianka-Buzka), Kholm, Zamostia (Zamist; Polish: Zamość)[112] and many other

---

107.   V. Figol', "Tserkovni bratstva Halyts'koï hreko-katolyts'koï provintsiï XVIII st.," *Bohosloviia* 15–16 (1938): 35.

108.   *AIuZR*, 10: 545; *Kievskaia starina*, 1882, no. 2, 156, 158, 159; I. Velyhors'kyi, "Iavorivs'ke molodets'ke bratstvo XVIII st.," *Nasha kul'tura*, 1936, no. 4: 310–13.

109.   *PKK*, 2: 121.

110.   *DS*, 60; *MCS*, 334–48; *AIuZR*, 1: 243; *AZR*, 6: 104; A. Longinov, *Pamiatnik drevnego pravoslaviia v Liubline: Pravoslavnyi khram i sushchestvovavshee pri nem bratstvo* (Warsaw, 1883).

111.   *AZR*, 4: 67.

112.   I. Tsehel's'kyi, *Deshcho pro tserkvy ta chudotvornu ikonu Materi Bozhoï v Kamiantsi Strumylovii* (Lviv, 1932), 19; I. Zastyrets', *Hramota iepyskopa H. Balabana, osnovuiucha bratstvo tserkovne peredmishchan adamkovets'kykh v Berezhanakh* (Lviv, 1905); A. Budilovich, *Russkaia pravoslavnaia starina v Zamost'e* (Warsaw, 1885), 29.

towns, as well a number of villages. For example, it is known that as early as 1607 there was a confraternity in the village of Bila, which belonged to the estates of the Belzecki family.[113] In the same year, confraternities were active in all parishes of Brest. In the course of the seventeenth century, confraternities emerged in virtually all parishes of many other cities and towns.

In Kyiv and Lutsk, confraternities appeared comparatively late. The Kyiv Theophany (Bohoiavlenske) Confraternity was apparently founded at the end of 1615. The material basis for its activity was a gift of the Ukrainian Orthodox noblewoman Halshka Hulevychivna, who donated her property in Kyiv for the establishment of a monastery, a school, and a shelter for pilgrims.[114] The initiative for its foundation came from a group of educated clergymen, mostly from western Ukraine.

The Kyiv Confraternity was active until the mid-seventeenth century and was supported by the Zaporozhian Cossacks. Originally named after the Theophany, it was sometimes called the Confraternity of the Theotokos after it built or, rather, renovated the ancient church named in honor of the Mother of God. Some historians were confused by this and mentioned the Theophany and Theotokos confraternities as separate institutions.[115]

About 1617 a confraternity was founded in Lutsk, the administrative and cultural center of Volhynia. The Lutsk Confraternity was attached to the Church of the Elevation of the Holy Cross (Ukrainian: Vozdvyzhennia); its members included not only burghers but also monks and Orthodox noblemen from the palatinate of Volhynia. In 1620, Patriarch Theophanes of Jerusalem granted stauropegial rights to the confraternity churches of Kyiv and Lutsk,[116] but in 1624 those rights were

---

113.   I. Franko, "Zapysky proty knyhokradiv u starykh knyhakh i rukopysakh," *ZNTSh* 77 (1907): 125.

114.   *PKK*, 2: 385–94; M. Maksymovych, "Zapiski o pervykh vremenakh Kievskogo Bogoiavlenskogo bratstva" in his *"Kiev iavilsia gradom velikim": Vybrani ukraïnoznavchi tvory* (Kyiv, 1994), 112–36; S. Golubev, "Drevniia i novyia skazaniia o nachale Kievskoi Akademii," *Kievskaia starina*, 1885, no. 2: 115–16; M. Hrushevs'kyi, *Istoriia ukraïns'koï literatury*, vol. 6 (Kyiv, 1995), 125–35.

115.   K. Chodynicki, *Kościół prawosławny a Rzeczpospolita Polska. Zarys historyczny 1370–1632* (Warsaw, 1934), 590.

116.   *PKK*, 2: 397–99, 1: 8–9.

revoked. In the years 1620–24, the Kyiv and Lutsk confraternities actually subordinated themselves to the newly reestablished Orthodox hierarchy and never became stauropegial institutions in the full sense of the word. In February 1629, at the request of the Orthodox nobility of the palatinate of Kyiv, the Kyiv Theophany Confraternity was confirmed by the king.[117]

The metropolitan of Kyiv, Iov (Ivan) Boretsky, formerly a teacher and rector at the Lviv Confraternity School, was instrumental in promoting the establishment of confraternities throughout the palatinates of Kyiv and Bratslav. In 1626, he founded a confraternity in the town of Nemyriv, whose founding charter mentions the existence of a confraternity in Vinnytsia.[118] Apparently, at this time confraternities were founded in other towns of Right-Bank Ukraine as well. In 1636, Isaia Kopynsky, acting as a "trans-Dnipro" bishop, issued the founding charter for a confraternity in Lubny in Left-Bank Ukraine.[119]

The growth of confraternities in the late sixteenth and early seventeenth centuries proceeded under the direct influence of the Lviv Dormition Confraternity. Many adopted its bylaws, while others based their statutes on the Lviv model. Members of the Lviv Stauropegion sometimes provided other confraternities with copies of their statute. For example, in 1591, Lviv Confraternity leaders sent the Brest Confraternity a letter on the nature of their activities, as well as the text of their statute.[120] In 1641, Afanasii Filipovich,[121] then a monk of the Brest Monastery, entered a copy of the statute into the Brest castle records, and in 1668 "an extract from the castle books of Brest county" containing the text of the Lviv statute was entered into the Pynsk (Pinsk) castle registers "for various purposes and in case of loss."[122]

The statute of the confraternity in Komarno (1592) is a replica of the statute of the Lviv Dormition Confraternity; in

117.   P. Zhukovich, *Seimovaia bor'ba pravoslavnago zapadnorusskago dvorianstva s tserkovnoi uniei*, vol. 5 (St. Petersburg, 1910), 190.

118.   *Chteniia v Istoricheskom obshchestve Nestora letopistsa*, 1891, vol. 5, otd. 3: 221.

119.   *Kievskaia starina* 52 (1896): 354–57.

120.   *Chteniia v Obshchestve istorii i drevnostei rossiiskikh* (1848), 56–61.

121.   Afanasii Filipovich became known as a polemical writer and an ardent opponent of compromise with Catholicism. In 1648, he was executed by the Polish military for alleged contacts with the Cossacks.

122.   *Chteniia v Obshchestve istorii i drevnostei rossiiskikh* (1848), 55.

1596, the king endorsed the Orthodox confraternity in Lublin "in accordance with the Lviv model," while in 1634 Metropolitan Petro Mohyla granted approval to a confraternity in Bilsk governed "under the same regulations as apply in the Lviv, Vilnius, and other confraternities."[123] As late as the eighteenth century, the statute of the Lviv Dormition Confraternity of 1586 was copied by confraternities in various cities and towns, including some in the central provinces of Ukraine.[124] "Articles of the Kańczuga junior confraternity" in Kańczuga in the Peremyshl Land of the palatinate of Ruthenia drafted in June 1704 contained the text of the Lviv statute of 1586 with the postscript, "Vasylii Charnota copied these articles in the divinely redeemed village of Porokhnyk[125] in the year of Our Lord 1704."[126] In some statutes, the preamble to the Lviv bylaws (which relates how the supervisors of the Lviv Dormition Church came to Patriarch Joachim and asked him to confirm the confraternity's bylaws) was reproduced verbatim, merely replacing references to Lviv with the name of the village or town where the given confraternity was located. Thus, in the bylaws of the St. Paraskeva Confraternity of Drohobych, the words "there came to us ... Lviv burghers" were changed to "there came to us ... sons of the Eastern Church from the St. Paraskeva Church in a suburb of Drohobych."[127] The bylaws of the confraternity of the village of Kamianka Lisna, revived in 1739, began with words attributed to Patriarch Joachim of Antioch: "I arrived in the city of Lviv in the diocese of Lviv and Kamianets (Kamianets-Podilskyi) during the tenure of Bishop Hedeon Balaban in the year ... 1586, on the first day of January. At this time there came before us and in deference to our spiritual rule the community of Kamianka, all them jointly supervisors of the Church of the Theotokos in the village of Kamianka, desiring to organize a confraternity.... "[128]

---

123. Dobrianskii, *Istoriia episkopov*, supplement, 87–89; *AIuZR*, 6: 104; *AZR*, 5: 18–19.

124. National Museum (Lviv), Manuscript Division, nos. 120, 91, 170.

125. In Polish, Próchnik.

126. Taras Shevchenko Institute of Ukrainian Literature, National Academy of Sciences of Ukraine, Manuscript Division, Ivan Franko Archives 3/4833, f. 4–13, 26.

127. LNB, NTSh collection/258, f. 7–25.

128. Ivan Franko Archives 3/4836, f. 5–21.

The peasants of Kamianka did not, of course, meet with Joachim in 1586: the authors of the statute merely substituted Kamianka for Lviv at the appropriate point in the preamble to the Lviv bylaws. Some confraternities sold their statutes to others: for example, in 1686 the statute of the confraternity in the village of Rudiantsi, dated 1650 and identical to the statute of the St. Onuphrius Confraternity in Lviv, was sold to the confraternity in the town of Iarychiv.[129] The statute of the confraternity in the village of Bashnia, which replicates the text of the Lviv statute, was sold in the eighteenth century to the confraternity of Potelych for 11 zlotys.[130] In 1695, the confraternity of Zhovkva decided to translate the Lviv statute into Ukrainian so as to make it more comprehensible.[131]

The Krasnostav Confraternity in the Kholm region distributed the Lviv statute to other confraternities. As early as 1589, when Patriarch Jeremiah visited their town, the Orthodox burghers of Krasnostav showed him a copy of the Lviv statute and asked that "the same regulations" be given to them. The patriarch not only signed this copy but also added, presumably at the request of his hosts, "We permitted them to give copies of this act, authenticated with their confraternity seal, to other towns."[132] The statutes of the confraternity of Oleksandriia (Skole) and of the St. George Confraternity in Drohobych included the text of the Lviv statute, its endorsement by Jeremiah for the Krasnostav Confraternity (1589), and the endorsement issued to the Sambir suburban St. Philippus Confraternity on the basis of the same statute by Exarch Meletios of Ephesus.[133]

The emergence of the Theophany Confraternity in Kyiv (1615) and the Holy Cross Confraternity in Lutsk (1617), as well as their recognition both by the metropolitan of Kyiv and by

129.   Ibid. 3/4835, f. 33.

130.   LNB, NTSh collection, no. 15.

131.   A. S. Petrushevych, *Svodnaia Halytsko-russkaia lětopys' s 1600 po 1700 h.*, vol. 1 (Lviv, 1874), 382.

132.   LNB, NTSh collection/258: 27.

133.   LNB, A. S. Petrushevych collection 449, f. 1–27; Lviv Historical Museum, Manuscript Division, no. 121; Library of the Russian Academy of Sciences, St. Petersburg, Manuscript Division, E. Kaluzhniatskii collection 64, f. 1.

the patriarch of Jerusalem, also contributed to the popularity of the confraternity movement. Endorsements by the supreme Orthodox hierarchs were seen as proof that a given confraternity had achieved high status. Charters acquired by the Kyiv Confraternity were therefore eagerly copied by confraternity members in other cities and towns. Thus, the St. George Confraternity of Drohobych included in its statute the text of a confirmation of the Kyiv Confraternity by Metropolitan Iov Boretsky, while the Dormition Confraternity of Iavoriv copied the charter of ratification issued to the Kyiv Confraternity by Patriarch Theophanes of Jerusalem in May 1620.[134]

As will be shown in later chapters, many confraternities organized in the western Ukrainian lands in the late sixteenth and early seventeenth centuries (those of Rohatyn, Halych, Holohory, Horodok, and others) not only formally accepted the statute of the Lviv Confraternity but also followed its program in their practical activities. While opposing the advance of Catholicism, they also tried to curtail the dominance of the Orthodox clergy in public life. But circumstances were different for the confraternities of Lutsk and, most particularly, Kyiv. There the key offices were taken by representatives of the Ukrainian nobility and clergy, who found it necessary to seek support among the urban population during the period of Catholicism's greatest expansion. In their struggle against a common enemy, the burghers of Lutsk and Kyiv associated themselves with the clergy and nobility but were not strong enough to retain the leadership of the united organizations. As a result, the burghers gave up their efforts to limit the preeminence of the Orthodox clergy in social and cultural life. The negative repercussions of this state of affairs soon became apparent. Once the immediate threat from the Catholic Church had passed and the Ukrainian Orthodox Church consolidated its status, the Orthodox clergy and the Ukrainian nobility that cooperated with it were quick to put an end to burgher influence in the confraternities. This explains why, after an initial period of significant political activity, the Lutsk

---

134.   LNB, NTSh collection 136.

Confraternity declined, while the Kyiv Confraternity was subordinated to Metropolitan Petro Mohyla (to achieve his purpose, he urged the confraternity to accept him as its "elder brother," protector, and "founder," only to do away with it shortly thereafter). Mohyla also managed to take control of other confraternities in his eparchy.[135] In other eparchies, where he did not rule directly but through bishops, he was prepared to support confraternities in their conflicts with local hierarchies.

In the late seventeenth and eighteenth centuries, conditions became less favorable for independent confraternities. Amvrosii Krylovsky even claimed that their numbers began to decline gradually after the 1630s.[136] This was not so: it was precisely in the late seventeenth and eighteenth centuries that confraternities were most numerous. In the western Ukrainian lands, except for Bukovyna and Transcarpathia, they were active in almost all urban parishes, and later also in most villages. There are many statutes and catalogues of confraternities in the towns and villages of the Peremyshl and Kholm eparchies, for example, in the town of Iavoriv, the suburb of Hole in Rava (Rava Ruska), and the villages of Cherneliava, Budynyn, Zapaliv, and Drohomyshl.[137] In the villages of Galicia, Volhynia, and Podillia provinces, there were numerous confraternities.[138] However, the range of activity of most of the confraternities narrowed. Only the Lviv Dormition Confraternity maintained extensive political activity, though on a more limited scale than before. Many confraternities supervised schools and hospitals. The absence of confraternities in Bukovyna, where the Orthodox Church was dominant, may be explained by noting that a confrontational situation was important for the spread of the confraternity movement. Western cultural influences were much weaker here than in the lands discussed above. Perhaps Western

---

135.   A. A. Turilov and B. N. Floria, "K voprosu ob istoricheskoi al'ternative Brestskoi unii" in *Brestskaia uniia 1596 g. i obshchestvenno-politicheskaia bor'ba v Ukraine i Belorussii v kontse XVI–pervoi polovine XVII v.*, pt. 2 (Moscow, 1999), 19.

136.   Krylovskii, *L'vovskoe Stavropigial'noe bratstvo*, xviii.

137.   BKP, MSS 2920, 2921, 2923, 2926, 2933, 2967 (former MSS of the Peremyshl Greek Catholic Chapter Library).

138.   Isaievych, *Bratstva*, 42.

models were more easily accepted in Eastern Europe through the mediation of Poland, Bohemia, and other Slavic lands. At any rate, in Transcarpathia, which was under Hungarian rule, confraternities were rare, and most of those that did exist appear to have been founded by priests from the Ukrainian lands dominated by the Polish-Lithuanian Commonwealth.

In the central and eastern provinces of Ukraine, there were confraternities in many towns and villages in the late seventeenth and eighteenth centuries, and often even later. Some of them are mentioned only in brief notices, such as the marginal inscription on a service book (published, significantly enough, by Hedeon Balaban's printing press in Striatyn) presented to the Novi Sanzhary Church in 1694 in the presence of members of the Holy Trinity Confraternity.[139] Some confraternities are mentioned in municipal records of the late seventeenth century. From one such record we learn that in Poltava the St. Nicholas Confraternity owned its "fraternal home" and that the property of the Dormition Church was managed by "a supervisor (*ktytor*) and the confraternity."[140] There were also confraternities in Starodub and other towns of the Ukrainian Hetmanate.[241]

Only a few of these confraternities had charters regulating their activities. One such charter was issued in 1689 by the metropolitan of Kyiv, Hedeon Sviatopolk-Chetvertynsky, to the confraternity of the town of Sribne (near Pryluky).[242] The decree stipulated that the confraternity should possess a building for meetings, supervise a hospital, carry on charitable activities for the benefit of its members, and ransom prisoners of war. The confraternity did not have a statute enforcing strict discipline on its members.

---

139.   I. Sventsits'kyi, *Opys' Muzeia Stavropihiiskoho instituta, vo L'vově* (Lviv, 1908), 60.

140.   *Aktovyia knigi Poltavskago gorodovago uriada XVII veka*, vol. 3, *Spravy vechistyia 1672–1680 gg.* (Chernihiv, 1914), 6.

241.   "Protokul do zapysovania sprav potochnykh na rok 1690," *Chernigovskiia gubernskiia vedomosti 1852 goda*, nos. 36–45 (Chernihiv, 1852).

242.   V. A., "K istorii iuzhnorusskikh bratstv: Osnovanie tserkvi i bratstva pri nei v m. Sribnom Poltavskoi gubernii, Prilukskago uezda," *Kievskaia starina* 16 (1886): 186–90.

From the Hetmanate, confraternities also spread to Sloboda Ukraine. A confraternity in Kharkiv is mentioned as early as 1700.[243] Aside from regular "church" confraternities in the Dnipro region, mainly in Kyiv province and the northern regions of the Hetmanate, "junior" (bachelor) confraternities appeared in some towns and villages alongside the relatively well-organized "guild brotherhoods" of craftsmen. An example of the latter is the brotherhood of craftsmen in the village of Velyka Zahorivka, belonging to the Borzna company of the Nizhyn regiment.[244] The artisan brotherhoods of eastern Ukraine differed from regular craft guilds in that they had very little to do with such issues as regulating craftsmen's production or professional skill. Like parish confraternities of the Dnipro region, they limited their activity mainly to religious rituals, funeral ceremonies, mead brewing and "fraternal feasts," candle making, the provision of small loans, and so on.[245] Craft brotherhoods and confraternities engaged in a limited scope of activity existed here and there until the second half of the nineteenth century.[246] Only a small number allotted part of their funds to schools.[247]

In Left-Bank Ukraine the maintenance of hospitals and schools, as well as the election of priests, was handled mainly by the urban and rural communities, not by confraternities.[248] Given that confraternities in the western Ukrainian lands (except for a few larger ones) also included the entire community, the difference between these types of social organization should not be exaggerated. The involvement of laymen,

---

243.   N. Sumtsov, "Shpital' v m. Boromle," *Kievskaia starina* 7 (1883): 309.

244.   A. Lazarevskii, *Opisanie staroi Malorossii*, vol. 2 (Kyiv, 1893), 144–45.

245.   Efimenko, *Iuzhnaia Rus'*, 1: 234.

246.   L. Kisilevich, "Vymiraiushchiia tipy ukrainskoi derevni," *Kievskaia starina*, 1884, no. 8: 517–18; K. Vasilenko, "Ostatki bratstv i tsekhov na Poltavshchine," *Kievskaia starina*, 1885, no. 13: 166–68; I. Pavlovskii, "Ostatki bratstv v prikhodakh Pereiaslavskago uezda," *Poltavskiia eparkhialnyia vedomosti*, 1880, no. 5.

247.   I. Srebnitskii, "Sledy tserkovnykh bratstv v Vostochnoi Malorossii," *Trudy IV Arkheologicheskago s"ezda v Kazani*, vol. 2 (Kazan, 1891), 18.

248.   The Ukrainian law code of 1728–44, which was prepared on the basis of the Ukrainian legal tradition but never recognized by the imperial Russian authorities, included a clause on the election of priests by their parishioners. See *Prava, po kotorym suditsia malorossiiskii narod*, ed. A. F. Kistiakovskii (Kyiv, 1878), 78. Cf. *Prava, za iakymy sudyt'sia malorosiis'kyi narod*, ed. Iu. S. Shemshuchenko and K. A. Vyslobokov (Kyiv, 1997), 78–79.

either through confraternities (as was the case in western and, to some extent, Right-Bank Ukraine) or through municipal institutions, in establishing hospitals and elementary schools and exercising a modicum of control over the parochial clergy is evidence of similarity of social and cultural development throughout the land.

Orthodox and Eastern-rite Catholic confraternities continued to survive in some regions of Ukraine, mostly in small towns and villages, until the nineteenth century and even later, primarily as a vehicle for the preservation of traditional rites and customs. The study of such confraternities from the ethnographic viewpoint is potentially a separate area of research, but a historian's attention must focus on those confraternities that played an active role in the political and cultural life of the nation.[249]

---

249.   The present study takes no account of political and religious associations of the late nineteenth and twentieth centuries that took on the name of confraternities and were even inspired by their legacy, but were not genetically linked with the traditional confraternities.

II

The Social Composition and Organizational Structure of the Confraternities

The legal basis for the activities of the confraternities in Ukraine and Belarus was provided by the constitutive documents issued by the Eastern patriarchs and by the synods of Orthodox bishops held in the last decade of the sixteenth century. The confraternities of Lviv, Kyiv, Lutsk, Peremyshl, Stryi, Zolochiv, Brest, Bilsk, and some other towns also obtained charters from the Polish kings guaranteeing their rights.[1] It is well known that in the Polish-Lithuanian Commonwealth royal guarantees were often violated, and kings often granted mutually contradictory "privileges" to the confraternities and their opponents alike. Nevertheless, the documents of the hierarchy and the kings provided a kind of fulcrum for the confraternities in conflicts with those who violated their rights.

By decrees of the Austrian government (21 March 1788) and of the gubernial administration of Galicia (4 April 1788), all confraternities in that province were declared abolished. Responsibility for the needs of churches was transferred to "caretakers of the church and trustees" chosen from among the parishioners. Yet even after these decrees were issued, confraternities continued to exist in many towns and villages of Galicia, and some remained active until the first decades of the twentieth century. However, their activities had no legal basis and developed mainly within the framework of popular common law. The parish confraternities of Right-Bank Ukraine and Belarus operated in similar fashion. In the

---

1. *MCS*, 390; *IuSLS*, 1: 264–74; *PKK*, 1: 5; *Akty IuZR*, 1: 243–44; *Akty izdavaemye Vilenskoiu komissieiu dlia razbora drevnikh aktov*, 33: 137–39; TsDIAL/13/431: 373–76.

course of the nineteenth century, those confraternities that had survived in certain regions lost importance as centers of public life and cultural activity. Gradually, even their role in parish administration declined. Yet even after forfeiting their administrative functions, the confraternities often retained their ancient customs and rites. Generally speaking, parish confraternities were typical for Right-Bank Ukraine, while guild confraternities flourished on the Left Bank. The latter differed from the former in that every tradesman in a given community or neighborhood was obliged to belong the guild confraternity.[2]

In 1862 the Russian historian and publicist Mikhail Koialovich journeyed through Ukraine and Belarus specifically in order to acquaint himself with existing confraternities.[3] He discovered them in numerous villages and towns of Right-Bank Ukraine (Kyiv, Podillia, and Volhynia provinces) and western and central Belarus (Minsk province). But he was unable to locate any functioning confraternities in eastern Belarus (Polatsk and Mahiliou provinces), although here and there he found evidence of surviving customs associated with the confraternities.

Shortly after the publication of Koialovich's report of his journey, the Russian government decided to "revive" the confraternities in Ukraine and Belarus and even to expand them in other regions of the empire for the specific purpose of forcibly introducing official Orthodoxy and "combating Catholic propaganda and the Jews." On 8 May 1864, the tsar, with the blessing of his bishops and the agreement of the provincial governors, signed special regulations governing the establishment of church confraternities. This attempt to exploit the remnants of the ancient confraternities for the establishment of pro-tsarist associations with a Russifying mission proved unsuccessful. Even in those rare cases when concerted efforts led to the founding of such associations, they were unable to gain a foothold in the old Ukrainian confraternities.[4]

---

2.   Efimenko, *Iuzhnaia Rus'*, 247–48, 264.
3.   M. Koialovich, "Chteniia o tserkovnykh zapadno-russkikh bratstvakh," *Den'*, 1862, no. 36.
4.   Efimenko, *Iuzhnaia Rus'*, 268.

As for the most prestigious of them, the Lviv Dormition Confraternity in the Habsburg Monarchy, in the autumn of 1788 the government and provincial administration of Galicia issued additional instructions concerning the supervision of the Dormition Church. According to these instructions, the Greek Catholic burghers of Lviv were to elect "guardians of the church and school," who, from 1790 onward, began to be known as members of the "Stauropegion Institute."[5] As early as 1789, the St. Onuphrius Hospital was transferred to the municipal foundation for the poor, and after a time the school ceased to exist. The Stauropegion Institute, established by an imperial decree of 16 February 1793, was a new institution in terms of its structure and activities, differing completely from the former Stauropegion Confraternity. Its role in civic and cultural life varied at different times, but generally was minor, restricted to administration of the printshop as a commercial establishment and the boarding house for students, as well as trusteeship of the church. To all intents and purposes, the history of Lviv Dormition (Stauropegion) Confraternity ended in the 1780s.

What was the social composition of the confraternities? On this and other questions, the greatest amount of information has been preserved about the Lviv Dormition (Stauropegion) Confraternity from the time it obtained its statute in 1586 until its abolition in 1788. According to the statute, it was to be an organization open to all classes: any Orthodox, regardless of social status, financial circumstances, or ethnic origin, could become a member. The Ukrainian craftsmen and merchants of central Lviv played a leading role. According to some scholars, in the sixteenth and early seventeenth centuries members of the Dormition Confraternity also included representatives of the clergy and the nobility. Amvrosii Krylovsky, for one, believed that Metropolitan Mykhailo Rohoza of Kyiv, Archimandrite Henadii of the Derman Monastery, Presbyter Fylyp Atanasevych of the St. Sophia Cathedral, and Archdeacon Hakovych of Kyiv were members of the confraternity.[6] Indeed, their names appear in its Album, a register of all who joined

---

5.   TsDIAL 129/2/15, f. 7; I. Orlevych, *Stavropihiis'kyi instytut u L'vovi (kinets' XVIII–60 rr. XIX st.)* (Lviv, 2000).

6.   Krylovskii, *L'vovskoe Stavropigial'noe bratstvo*, 45.

the confraternity, but these clergymen signed their names as honored guests, not as regular members. It is apparent from their subsequent correspondence that they did not consider themselves members, nor did the confraternity regard them as such. In the whole history of the Lviv Confraternity, only once (in 1754) was a priest, Antin Levynsky, accepted as a member.[7] This was also the case in other confraternities, with the exception of Kyiv, Lutsk, and a few others.

While remaining lay in composition, the Stauropegion invited priests (monastic clergymen from 1633 to 1758) to conduct divine services in the Dormition (Uspenska) Church.[8] These were predominantly representatives of the poorer clergy. As early as 1561, the prince of Moldavia reproached the burghers for failing to provide for the priest of the Dormition Church, who "lives among you and ekes out a living by retailing: he goes to church, while his wife goes to the market with bread and onions purchased from someone else; they live off whatever she earns from selling this." In 1600 Fedir Drabyk, a member of the confraternity, told the priest that he was "the same as anyone else—a skinflint and a simple fellow."[9] Whenever possible, the Lviv Dormition Confraternity tried to engage church managers who were also competent in printing, engraving, proofreading, teaching, and so on, and could thus be of service to the confraternity. At the same time, it ensured that the clergy did not have a decisive influence on its administration.

On the basis of a letter written on 6 February 1592 to Patriarch Jeremiah by members of the confraternity, Denys Zubrytsky concluded that three Orthodox magnates had joined the confraternity: Fedir Skumyn Tyshkevych, the palatine of Navahrudak; Bohdan Sapieha (Sapeha, Sapiha, Sopiha), the palatine of Minsk; and Adam Potii, the castellan of Brest (later a Greek Catholic bishop and metropolitan).[10]

---

7.   See TsDIAL 129/2/8: 100.

8.   The names of priests and monks serving at the "fraternal" Dormition Church and the St. Onuphrius Monastery supervised by the confraternity are listed in I. Myts'ko, "L'vivs'ki sviashchenyky ta vchyteli XVI–pershoï tretyny XVII st." in Uspens'ke bratstvo (Lviv, 1996), 13–14.

9.   IuILS, no. 17; AIuZR, 11: 60.

10.   D. Zubritskii [Zubryts'kyi], "Lětopis' L'vovskago Stavropigial'nago bratstva," Zhurnal Ministerstva narodnago prosveshcheniia 62 (1849): 65.

In reality, neither this letter nor any other documents provide any grounds to suppose that these magnates were regular members. Indeed, the Album of the confraternity contained the signatures of the princes Adam Vyshnevetsky, Kyryk and Roman Ruzhynsky, as well as Adam Kysil, several Moldavian princes and boyars, and representatives of the Ukrainian Cossack *starshyna* (officers). In the first half of the seventeenth century individual confraternities received a certain amount of material assistance from several nobles of middle rank, such as Lavrentii Drevynsky, the cupbearer of the palatinate of Volhynia (he became a member of the confraternity in 1603), Tetiana Bohovytynivna Malynska, the owner of the village of Verba in the district of Kremianets (she joined the confraternity in 1610 and died in 1618), and Dmytro Karlochii, the starosta of Stare Selo.[11] The names of Orthodox magnates also appear in the roster of the Lublin Confraternity.[12] The nominal membership of magnates and noblemen gave the confraternities legitimacy in the eyes of the secular rulers and clergy.[13] Neither in Lviv nor in Lublin, however, were the magnates regular, active members of the confraternities. When requested by the members, they would occasionally support complaints of the confraternities against the Roman Catholic magnates and make donations for the construction and decoration of churches, but in most cases they did not share the reformational fervor of the confraternities. Indeed, the Moldavian princes, Kostiantyn Ostrozky, and other Ukrainian and Belarusian magnates often sided with a resolute opponent of the confraternities—Bishop Hedeon Balaban of Lviv.

The statute of the Vilnius Confraternity, adopted and printed in 1588, stipulated that individuals "from the three classes—the clergy, nobility, and commoners" could join the confraternity. Among its members were Metropolitan Mykhailo Rohoza; Fedir Skumyn Tyshkevych, the palatine of Navahrudak; Filon Kmita Chornobylsky, the palatine of Smolensk; and a number of

---

11.   *AIuZR*, 10: 125, 11: 371.

12.   Krylovskii, *L'vovskoe Stavropigial'noe bratstvo*, suppl., 3–9; A. Longinov, *Pamiatnik drevnego pravoslaviia v Liubline: Pravoslavnyi khram i sushchestvovavshee pri nem bratstvo* (Warsaw, 1883).

13.   Gajecky, "The Stauropegian Assumption Brotherhood," 132.

other magnates and noblemen from such families as the Sapehas (Sapiehas), Sanhushkos (Sanguszkos), Masalskys (Masalskis), and Ohynskys (Ogiński).[14] But they were only honorary members: the statute exempted nobles and clergymen who lived far away from taking part in monthly meetings and fulfilling other regular duties. They were requested to attend at least the annual general meeting and make themselves available when extraordinary circumstances required. Voluntary membership fees ("at their discretion") were allowed to be transmitted by courier. From this it would appear that only burghers were regular members, while the magnates and noblemen were to provide financial support and act as patrons of the confraternity. More often than not, they were none too willing to perform even this role. Indicative of this is the attitude of Fedir Skumyn Tyshkevych, the palatine of Navahrudak. He was considered a member of the Belarusian Vilnius Confraternity, and it was he who thanked the members of the Lviv Confraternity for having sent a teacher and textbooks to Vilnius. In 1594, along with other magnates, he signed an order to the Brest episcopal synod with a demand for the legalization of confraternities.[15] However, in a letter written in 1595 to the metropolitan of Kyiv, he sharply condemned the Lviv Confraternity and justified Hedeon Balaban's stand on the question of church union. According to Skumin, the bishop, "completely oppressed by the confraternity there, was not only forced into apostasy, but also, I believe, would have been glad to take the devil for his ally."[16]

The magnates' attitude toward the civic and political activities of the confraternities is reflected in the Belarusian Barkalabava Chronicle compiled by the priest Fiodar Filipavich Mstsislavets at the court of the Solomiretski (Salamiretski) princes. Although the Solomiretskis had invited Stefan Zyzanii, a representative of the Lviv Confraternity, to teach their children, they were hostile to the interference of confraternities in church management. "In that year of [15]92," we read in the chronicle, "there was great and irreconcilable discord in the faith owing to the actions of the Romans [i.e., Roman Catholics] against

14.   Makarii, *Istoriia russkoi tserkvi*, 9: 546–47.

15.   TsDIAL 823/1/168.

16.   *MCS*, 615.

the holy Eastern Greek faith. At that time the confraternity in the city of Vilnius enlisted the aid of learned men from the city of Lviv—Iurii Rohatynets and Stefan Zyzanii. They waged a mighty and great war against the Romans, not only in the town halls, markets squares, and roads, but also fierce fighting and conflict inside the church." Having thus described the activities of the representatives of the Lviv Confraternity in Vilnius, the author of the chronicle unexpectedly concludes: "But because of their great stubbornness and the statutes and laws they have thought up, God has never helped them and never will."[17]There are grounds to believe that this attitude toward the statutes and activities of the confraternities was shared not only by the magnates and some of the clergy (especially the higher clergy), but also by a considerable portion of the Orthodox nobility.

Historians have sometimes also exaggerated the role of the wealthiest stratum of burghers in the activities of the Lviv and Vilnius confraternities. Thus, A. Savych wrote that in 1586 the Lviv Confraternity was organized "by the wealthy Lviv bourgeoisie." In order to show how wealthy the bourgeoisie was, he claims that its members "were able to maintain a printing house and school at their own expense."[18] In fact, after its initial period of activity, the printing house not only did not require large expenditures on the part of its members but, on the contrary, brought them great profits. As will be shown subsequently, the maintenance of the school also did not require any great expenditures.

In the first list of the twenty founding members of the Lviv Confraternity, dated 1586, there is no mention of any of the wealthiest patricians. Only the middle strata are represented: the saddlers Iurko and Ivan Rohatynets, the tailor Dmytro Krasovsky, the furrier Luka Huba, and the shopkeepers Ivan Krasovsky, Lesko Maletsky, Khoma Babych, Stetsko Morokhovsky, and Ivan Bohatyrets.[19]

---

17.   "Barkulabovskaia letopis'," 10–11; A. Korshunaŭ, comp., *Pomniki starazhytnai belaruskai pis'mennastsi* (Minsk, 1975), 123.

18.   A. Savych, *Narysy z istoriï kul'turnykh rukhiv na Ukraïni ta Bilorusiï v XVII–XVIII st.* (Kyiv, 1929), 130–40.

19.   F. Sribnyi, "Studiï nad organizatsiïeiu l'vivs'koï Stavropigiï vid kintsia XVI do polovyny XVII st.," *ZNTSh* 106 (1911): 68, 32.

In the second redaction of this list, there is no mention of Ivan Bohatyrets; instead, the names of the shopkeeper Ivashko Zinkovych and the Greek merchants Constantine Korniakt and Manolis Arphanes Marinetos are added. This second redaction appeared no earlier than 1589, as wealthy Greeks began to join the confraternity at a later date, once it had expanded its activities.[20] Korniakt was actually the wealthiest man in Lviv: he traded in Eastern, Western, and local goods, collected customs duty on behalf of the king, and owned a number of villages. Historians of the late nineteenth century (Isydor Sharanevych et al.) exaggerated Korniakt's role in the confraternity, and the issue needs to be clarified. During the seventeenth and eighteenth centuries, the members themselves described the wealthy Greek as one of the founders of the confraternity, but they were guided by practical considerations: in order to protect the confraternity from persecution, it was convenient to emphasize that one of its founders was such an influential person. Korniakt did in fact provide the confraternity with material support, but it was comparatively insignificant, considering his enormous wealth.[21] He never attended meetings, and in 1600 he transmitted 1,100 zlotys to the members through Luka, another member of the confraternity.[22] Moreover, for Korniakt to fulfill his promises to aid the confraternity, it was necessary to enlist the influence of Patriarch Jeremiah. One of the patriarch's letters permits the conclusion that in the conflict with Bishop Hedeon Balaban, Korniakt sympathized with the bishop, not with the confraternity.[23] It is evident that he was not a regular, active member of the confraternity, but, like any ordinary parishioner, a financial contributor to the Dormition Church. Contacts with such an influential person as Korniakt were of course essential to the prestige of the newly organized confraternity.

In the period when confraternity activities reached their peak, its leaders were merchants and craftsmen: the brothers

---

20.   Ibid., *ZNTSh* 108 (1912): 10–11.
21.   Ibid., *ZNTSh* 114 (1913): 56.
22.   *MCS*, 854.
23.   *IuILS*, no. 117 (1589).

Iurii and Ivan Rohatynets, Ivan and Dmytro Krasovsky, and their adherents. Initially, Khoma Babych, one of the wealthiest founders of the confraternity, was a well-off merchant, but by the 1580s he had become so impoverished that his son, Ivan, did not own a house. Dmytro Krasovsky was forced to sell off his property, and Ivan Krasovsky also had to divest himself of some of his holdings.[24] Although Ivan Bohatyrets, Ivashko Zinkovych, and Stetsko Morokhovsky increased their property holdings, the improvement of their status was very relative. Registers of their assets listed mostly inexpensive items in limited quantities; they were considerably less well off than the wealthier merchants.[25] Besides those who owned masonry houses, poorer craftsmen and shopkeepers who did not own homes or workshops and lived as boarders in the city center belonged to the confraternity. In the latter half of the 1580s, a broad range of civic and political activities of the confraternity were initiated by craftsmen and middle (or even impoverished) shopkeepers.

The membership of the confraternity grew quickly. Of the fourteen members who joined in 1591, half were craftsmen, but there were also several wealthier merchants, including the Greek Iannis Affendyk. But by the late sixteenth and early seventeenth centuries, there were only about fifty such members in the confraternity. The scholar and translator Havrylo Dorofeiovych, who had contacts with the higher clergy, expressed scorn for the members of the confraternity: "Who in the confraternity is to judge me—shoemakers, tailors, furriers?"[26] In a letter to Patriarch Theoleptos dated 28 May 1586, the members of the Lviv Confraternity called themselves craftsmen, while in another letter written at the end of the sixteenth century they declared: "We are guildsmen and are being persecuted in the guilds."[27] This makes it apparent that the Lviv Dormition Confraternity remained an organization to which comparatively broad circles of the guild and trading population belonged. It was during this period that the

---

24.   Sribnyi, "Studiï," *ZNTSh* 114 (1913): 25–26, 28, 29.
25.   Ibid., 31; 115: 36–37.
26.   *AIuZR*, 11: 62.
27.   *MCS*, 140, 423.

suburban confraternities were closely grouped around the Dormition Confraternity.

During the second quarter and middle decades of the seventeenth century, many craftsmen joined the confraternity. At this time, conflict deepened between the wealthiest merchants and indigent members.[28] On the one hand, the confraternity included members who had no means of acquiring even petty sums of a few zlotys,[29] while on the other it included wealthy individuals whose names did not appear on earlier membership lists. Of one of the Striletsky brothers, who melted coins into silver for export, it was said that he had melted the sum of several thousand zlotys and, in so doing, had expended more coal than an entire goldsmiths' guild.[30]

At this time, the highest posts in the confraternity were occupied by the wealthy merchants (often of Greek origin) Havrylo Langish, Kostiantyn Mezapeta, and others. During the second quarter of the seventeenth century, the Lviv Dormition Confraternity had, in different years, from five to nine Greeks among its members, making up approximately one-fourth of its total membership.[31] In the 1650s, the most influential members were the rich Greek merchants Theodosios (Teodosii) Tomkevych, Georgios (Iurii) Papara, and Iannis (Ianii) Mazaraki. According to records from 1656, Mazaraki Kryshtofovych, a Greek confraternity member who came from Bar in Podillia, was considered the second richest person in Lviv (his property was estimated by city authorities to be worth 300,000 zlotys). At that time the value of Stefan Nesterovych's property was estimated at 100,000 zlotys, and Vasyl Hryhorovych's at 70,000 zlotys. Even though Lviv had suffered an economic decline in this period, the wealth of the richest confraternity members had obviously increased, reaching the level of the estates of the Catholic patricians. At the same time, the confraternity's activity decreased in every sphere of sociopolitical life. For several years (1616–30) the

---

28.   Sribnyi, "Studiï," *ZNTSh* 115 (1913): 68–69; 114 (1913): 32, 34.

29.   Ibid., 41, 42, 43, 33; *AIuZR*, 11: 130, 160.

30.   Sribnyi, "Studiï," *ZNTSh* 115 (1913): 46–47; W. Łoziński, *Złotnictwo lwowskie* (Lviv, 1889), 21–22.

31.   Sribnyi, "Studiï," *ZNTSh* 108 (1912): 12–14, 22, 7.

printshop stopped publishing; even construction of the church was halted during the years 1617–27.[32] In the 1630s, activity intensified once again, but never reached the level observed in the late sixteenth and early seventeenth centuries.

During the second half of the seventeenth century and the early part of the eighteenth, the situation of the Lviv Dormition Confraternity worsened. The economy was in decline, Polish soldiers imposed systematic requisitions on the urban population, and the political role of the burghers generally fell off. All these factors had a negative effect on social and cultural life. Whereas in the late sixteenth and early seventeenth centuries there were more than 50 active members in the confraternity (not counting noblemen, women, and members from the city of Rohatyn), and in 1633 there were 36, by 1656, after military devastations and severe epidemics, only 16 members remained (four new members joined that year, bringing the final total to 20).[33] Also, in the second half of the seventeenth century several of the richer merchants, as well as impoverished burghers, belonged the confraternity. Some of them even managed to join the nobility. In 1654 the Diet ennobled Roman Striletsky, a member of the confraternity. In 1659 Theodosios Tomkevych, Georgios Papara, and Iannis Mazaraki became nobles, as did Mykola Krasovsky and Iurii Korendovych at a later date.[34] The attainment of noble rank exempted the burghers from the authority of the town council and from paying customs duties and taxes incumbent upon their non-noble counterparts. But in the second half of the seventeenth century, as well as at the beginning of the eighteenth, even nobiliary members were still primarily merchants by occupation, just like ordinary burghers. In the course of the eighteenth century, several other burghers who belonged to the confraternity managed to obtain noble title. Thus, Anton Dziokovsky, an official in the king's chancery and later a leaseholder and administrator of the royal customs duty in Podillia and eastern Ukraine, obtained noble status in 1765.

---

32.   *IuILS*, 5 (article by I. Sharanevych).

33.   Sribnyi, "Studiï," *ZNTSh* 106 (1911): 33, 35, 38.

34.   *Volumina legum*, 4: 296, 297, 304; A. Boniecki, *Herbarz polski*, 16 vols. (Warsaw, 1899–1913), 5: 215, 4: 270; *AGZ*, 10: 422.

In 1768 the Diet granted noble titles to the postmaster Anton Deima and his brother Khrystofor.[35]

From the 1730s, as the position of the Ukrainian burghers grew weaker, hereditary noblemen began to appear in the ranks of the Lviv Confraternity. On 20 October 1730 the members demanded and obtained a privilege from the king granting permission to accept as members of the confraternity individuals, including noblemen, living outside the Lviv municipal boundaries.[36] Indeed, by 1730, the Navahrudak cupbearer and descendant of an erstwhile burgher family, Fedir Papara, was already one of the elders of the confraternity. Gradually, not only petty nobles, but also those of middle rank became more influential. In 1740, Vasyl Kostiantynovych Turkul, subpalatine of the Lviv Land and later colonel of Chernihiv, joined the confraternity.[37] In 1751, Colonel Illia Turkul and the Chernihiv master of the table (stol'nyk) Iakym Hryhorii Turkul were admitted as members. In the years 1741, 1749, 1751, and 1758, Vasyl Kostiantynovych Turkul, who lived in the village of Rozdilovychi and rarely visited Lviv, held the post of elder in the confraternity. The day-to-day administration of its affairs was carried out by his deputies: Anton Dziokovsky in 1741 and 1758, Iakiv Rusianovych in 1749, and Iakiv Gavendovych in 1751.

While most of the confraternity still consisted of burghers, in the second half of the eighteenth century the highest posts were occupied by nobles. Thus, in 1751, the vice-chairman of the confraternity was Iakiv Gavendovych, and Ivan Popel was one of two trustees of confraternity property (both were clerks at the Lviv castle court), while one of the directors of the archives was M. Slonsky, the vicegerent of the Łuków castle registry. In 1758, the nobleman I. Sobolevsky joined the confraternity, as did H. Srokovsky, clerk of the castle office. Thus it was mainly noblemen without large estates, employed as government officials, who joined the confraternity. Other

---

35.　Boniecki, *Herbarz polski*, 5: 215, 4: 270; *AGZ*, 10: 422.

36.　*IuSLS*, 1: 104.

37.　Vasyl Kostiantynovych Turkul was the grandson of Vasyl Turkul, originally from Moldavia, who had attained noble rank in 1676 (K. Niesiecki, *Herbarz polski*, vol. 9 [Leipzig, 1842], 151).

members included burghers in the king's service, clerks in diocesan offices, and nobles employed in local offices. Like the above-mentioned Anton Dziokovsky, Fedir Dobrovliansky was a tax collector in the Zhydachiv district, and Vasyl Iliashevych was a notary in the Lviv consistory.[38] By the second half of the eighteenth century, Ukrainian patricians had obtained posts in the town council; for example, Dobrovliansky was a member of the town court, while Iliashevych was a councillor, and later a magistrate.

Consequently, the social structure of the Lviv Dormition Confraternity changed in the course of the seventeenth and eighteenth centuries. In the late sixteenth and early seventeenth centuries, it had been an association of craftsmen and shopkeepers. From the 1620s to the early eighteenth century, the social stratification of the confraternity became more pronounced: besides impoverished members, it attracted the wealthiest stratum of Ukrainian townsfolk, mainly well-to-do merchants and, to a lesser degree, craftsmen. These wealthy burghers and, from the 1740s, nobles, attained the highest elective posts in the confraternity. During this period, confraternity officers were engaged primarily in the book trade and competed for seats on the town council; only a few members engaged in a broader range of civic activity. In the cultural sphere, the principal contributions of the Lviv Confraternity during this period can be attributed not to its members but to those cultural activists who were grouped around confraternity institutions. This was the "itinerant intelligentsia" of the day: teachers, students, printers, engravers, choir directors and composers, and so on. Almost all of them were poor, for they had no stable income. Unfortunately, archival sources contain only passing references to most of them. By chance, a certificate issued in 1741 to the printer Petro Khanevych has been preserved; it indicates that he was from the village of Hlomcha in the Sianik Land.[39]

The heterogenous composition of the confraternities was a source of contradictory tendencies within them at various

---

38.　　TsDIAL 129/1/1169: 101, 128; *IuSLS*, 1: 243.
39.　　TsDIAL 129/1/1169: 78–79, 39.

times. Nevertheless, in questions concerning religion and education, the activities of the confraternities addressed the needs of the whole Ukrainian (Ruthenian) nation. The members of the Lviv confraternities regarded themselves as "elders of the Ruthenian nation" in the city.[40] At certain decisive moments, notably at the turn of the sixteenth and seventeenth centuries, they were able to attract support from a broad range of the population. Meetings of the Dormition Confraternity were then attended by "all the Ruthenians from the city and its suburbs"; "the entire community, both burghers and residents of the suburbs." The confraternity's most important resolutions were approved in the name of the whole "commonwealth."[41]

Whereas the Lviv clergy was excluded from the confraternity and members of the nobility began to join its ranks when the confraternity movement was in decline, in such cities as Kyiv and Lutsk the social composition of the confraternities was different from the outset. The founders and members of the Lutsk Confraternity of the Elevation of the Holy Cross, in particular, were representatives of the clergy and nobility—the superiors of the Monastery of the Elevation of the Holy Cross, Herasym Mykulych and Isaakii Boryskovych, the noblemen Mykhailo Hulevych, Lavrentii Drevynsky, and others.[42] In 1619, forty-six Orthodox noblemen of the palatinate of Volhynia declared the establishment of the Lutsk Confraternity of the Elevation of the Holy Cross. As they did not live in the city, they entrusted the maintenance of order in the confraternity and the administration of its regular business, most notably the construction of the church, school, and hospital, to their "younger brothers, the Lutsk burghers." For their part, the noblemen were obliged, "as elder brothers, to help and protect" the burghers in all their needs.[43] The monks of the confraternity monastery were also considered its members, one of the reasons being that in the eyes of the lay members, clerics were "people with greater security" who could be relied

40.   Cf. Myron Kapral's introduction to *Pryvileï natsional'nykh hromad*, 12–15.
41.   *AIuZR*, 11, 5, 7, 20, 25, 28, 54.
42.   *PKK*, 1: 3, 4.
43.   Ibid., 7.

upon more than the laity to protect the members' common interests in legal affairs.[44] While the superior of the monastery was elected by the lay members of the confraternity, burghers played a comparatively insignificant role in the administration. In 1655 there were two burghers among the four trustees elected to one-year terms of office, but in 1686, 1695, and 1713, all the trustees were noblemen.[45] As indicated in documents pertaining to the activities of the Lutsk Confraternity, middle-ranking Ukrainian noblemen such as Lavrentii Drevynsky, Khoma Hulianytsky, and Andrii Puzyna were prominent in its affairs.

Of a somewhat different character was the Theophany Confraternity of Kyiv, among whose founders we encounter the names of such learned monks as Zakhariia Kopystensky, Tarasii Zemka, and Iiezekyil Kurtsevych.[46] The aim of its members was to provide "encouragement and support in correct devotion of our Ruthenian stock, the sons of Eastern Orthodoxy, citizens of the Kyiv palatinate, both those of every clerical status and those of secular status—the nobility and the entire municipal republic (*rěch-pospolitaia mestskaia*), and all the Christian people—to practice merciful deeds: both spiritual ones—in multiplying and implanting Christian virtues and a virtuous monastic life, in passing on virtuous teachings, and in training the children of the Christian people, thanks to which the glory of almighty God increases on earth, paternal joy increases at the education of their sons, and the defense and admirable embellishment of the Commonwealth are established and blossom; and corporal works of mercy—in defending widows and orphans and in rescuing all kinds of destitute people."[47] "Numerous" members of the clergy, nobility, and townsfolk joined the confraternity.

The most significant fact in the history of the Kyiv Theophany Confraternity was that its members included Hetman Petro Konashevych Sahaidachny and the whole Zaporozhian Host. Cossack membership was of great importance: by joining,

---

44.   Ibid., 40.

45.   Ibid., 101, 102, 111–13. On the Lutsk Confraternity, see P. Kraliuk, *Luts'ke Khrestovozdvyzhens'ke bratstvo* (Lutsk, 1996).

46.   Ibid., 2: 393–94.

47.   Cited in Hrushevsky, *History of Ukraine-Rus'*, 7: 322.

the Cossacks publicly manifested their solidarity with the confraternity's program and declared that they were taking it under their protection. This increased the popularity of the Kyiv Confraternity and saved it from repression. Thanks to Cossack support, in the first period of its existence the Theophany Confraternity was able to function unhindered.

The clergy and nobility played a leading role in the Theophany Confraternity, but during the initial stages these two groups sought an alliance with the burghers. The need for such an alliance disappeared when the hierarchical church structures grew stronger. By the 1640s the Theophany Confraternity was no longer an active institution, and the leading role in the social and cultural life of Kyiv was played by the metropolitan, the Kyivan Caves Monastery, and the Theophany Monastery. Although in accordance with earlier tradition the Theophany Monastery continued to be known as the "confraternity monastery" (sometimes even "the confraternity"), there was no longer any real cooperation with its lay membership.

The confraternities of the large cities (Lviv, Lutsk, Kyiv) had comparatively small memberships. However, in such matters as the defence of their ancestors' faith and in cultural activities, they enjoyed broad support. Unlike the Lviv Dormition Confraternity, the Kyiv Theophany Confraternity, and the Lutsk Confraternity of the Elevation of the Holy Cross, the many confraternities that arose in small and middle-sized towns counted the entire Orthodox population residing on the territory of a given parish as their members. Thus, at a meeting of the Transfiguration Confraternity in Drohobych, the "whole congress of the Zadvirne suburb" was present. The Confraternity of the Nativity of the Theotokos was simultaneously active as the "community of the Lishnianske suburb," led by a community headman.[48] Among the founders of the confraternity in the town of Stara Sil were poor "tenants, alongside the burghers and residents of the suburbs."[49]

---

48.   TsDIAL 159/8/863, f. 200; 32/3, p. 234; 32/4, p. 59; 32/2, f. 155, 156.
49.   *PKK*, 4, otd. 1: 4.

The statutes occasionally provided that the membership of a confraternity should consist of all persons espousing a given religion (Orthodoxy or, later, Greek Catholicism) in a particular parish. Thus, a diploma issued by Bishop Iurii Hoshovsky of Peremyshl for the confraternity of the village of Valiava (which, incidentally, was the bishops' estate and, frequently, their residence) stated that a "Christ-loving confraternity consisting of three estates—the clergy, nobility, and burghers" was being established at the Church of St. Michael. From the names of the confraternity's founders (Fedir Patchak, Vasko Kuzmych, Ivan Petriv, Kost Meleshkiv), however, it is clear that they were all peasants.[50] In those villages where the whole population or a significant part of it consisted of petty Ukrainian nobles, the confraternities did not differ in any way from those whose members were peasants.

The organizational forms of confraternity activities often remained the same, even when there were changes in their social composition and the scope of their work. These forms were only partially regulated by statutes, which did not reflect many aspects of confraternity life. The Lviv statute of 1586,[51] later adopted by many other confraternities, began by specifying membership dues. "Whoever might wish to become a member of the confraternity, whether a burgher, nobleman, or resident of a suburb, or any common person of any degree, both local and non-resident, must pay an entrance fee of six groszy." Dues of a half-grosz were to be collected at monthly meetings. The election of officers was also regulated. Four "elder brothers" were to be elected annually, and a report of the outgoing elders was to be presented before the election. A quorum was required to decide important matters. In particular, all members could take part in discussions pertaining to the judgement of those who had violated the rules of discipline, and "the elders must resolve a question in accordance with the decision of the junior members," that is, of the whole membership.[52] The members

---

50.   State Archives in Przemyśl, archives of the Greek Catholic bishops, diploma of 18 April 1669.

51.   MCS, 113, 119.

52.   With the exception of elected senior members, all members of the confraternities were "junior."

were required to be intransigent toward amoral actions on the part of confraternity members: "and if a brother shows himself to be a libertine, or an extortionist, or an idol-worshipper, or a drunkard, or a plunderer, one should not even eat with such people." It is interesting to note that elders were to be punished twice or even thrice as severely as regular members for similar infractions. Immoral and disobedient members were punished with expulsion from the confraternity, or even with excommunication from the church. Such a punishment could not be annulled either by an archpriest or by a bishop unless the confraternity itself pardoned the accused. Much emphasis was also placed on the duty of confraternity members to care for ailing members, give interest-free loans from a mutual fund to those "who are in dire straits," and generally help the poor and the infirm.

Every confraternity existed within a parish and took its name from the parish church. Only rarely did a confraternity have its own chapel or altar.[53]

* * *

Alongside regular confraternities, to which only married people could belong, there were "junior confraternities" for unmarried men. Such junior confraternities are known to have existed in Lviv, Zamostia, Kyiv, Mahiliou, and other cities. They gave rise to "bachelor confraternities" that existed in numerous villages of eastern Ukraine until the second half of the nineteenth century. Junior ("minor") confraternities played only a local cultural role, leaving little mark on civic and political life. In the opinion of Volodymyr Peretts, these "junior confraternities" were forerunners of the Marian Sodality of students of the Kyiv Mohyla Academy, established at the end of the seventeenth century.[54] However, the specific forms of pious activity practiced by this sodality, as well as by others in Basilian schools, were modeled on those of sodalities active in Jesuit collegiums.[55]

---

53.   *Akty IuZR*, 1: 243.
54.   V. Peretts, "Novi dani dlia istoriï shkoliars'kykh bratstv na Ukraïni," *Zapysky Istorychno-filolohichnoho viddilu VUAN*, 1923, nos. 2–3: 78.
55.   Hradiuk, "Do istoriï Mariis'kykh Druzhyn v Ukraïni," 652.

The statute of the Vilnius Holy Trinity Confraternity of 1588 made provision for the membership of "sisters," but they did not have the right to take part in meetings, and even had to transmit their membership dues through male representatives. Obviously, the "sisters" in question were noblewomen from whom material assistance could be expected.[56] Indeed, the membership register of this confraternity listed the names of women from noble families. In the catalogues (membership lists) of some confraternities, one can find the names of "sisters" or "female confraternity members" from burgher ranks.[57] They took part in such activities as fund-raising and maintaining churches, even in confraternities whose statutes made no provision for female membership. As noted earlier, the Kyiv Confraternity was established thanks to donations of property from Halshka Hulevychivna. It should be stressed that later, during the nineteenth century and particularly in the twentieth, female participation in confraternities increased significantly.

A specific feature was the existence of confraternities of beggars who lived in hospitals. The small beggar confraternities of eastern Ukraine engaged primarily in the collection of funds for the needs of hospitals and churches.[58]

The Greek Confraternity of Nizhyn, which was organized along the lines of a church confraternity, devoted itself to promoting the international trade in which its members engaged. On the basis of proclamations issued by Hetmans Ivan Vyhovsky, Iurii Khmelnytsky, Ivan Briukhovetsky, Ivan Samoilovych, and Ivan Mazepa, this confraternity enjoyed many privileges, including the right to elect judges from among its members.[59]

Secret initiation rites played a great role in binding together members of various associations. Of particular significance in the confraternities was the "vow," a membership oath similar to a monastic vow. In the Lviv Stauropegion Confraternity,

---

56.   L. Bieńkowski, "Organizacja Kościoła Wschodniego w Polsce" in *Kościół w Polsce*, vol. 2 (Cracow, 1969), 837.

57.   BKP, MSS 2843, 2868, 2933.

58.   Efimenko, *Iuzhnaia Rus'*, 244.

59.   Ia. Padokh, *Sudy i sudovyi protses staroï Ukraïny: Narys istoriï*, vol. 209 of *ZNTSh* (1990): 106.

the entrant was obliged to fulfill all the duties of a member, to "resist his opponents," and to declare that if he should ever "betray or denigrate or disobey this lawful confraternity," he would be subject to ecclesiastical anathema.[60] The vow was pronounced during a solemn ceremony, with candles burning. This ceremony affected some members so deeply that they were afraid to take the oath. In 1620, Patriarch Timotheos of Constantinople called this oath a "cruel and terrible curse," gave absolution to those who had taken it or died in violation of it, and finally abolished the vow as "foolishly conceived." In 1633 the Stauropegion approved an abbreviated text of the vow, with no anathema to be proclaimed against a transgressor. In 1644, discussions were renewed on whether to reinstate the "ancient, terribly severe vow to which our forefathers adhered" or the "later, abridged, and more tolerable vow to which current members adhere." All present affirmed their preference for the lenient version of the vow,[61] which was somewhat indicative of the members' departure from the unconditional devotion to civic and religious matters that characterized the Lviv Dormition Confraternity in its initial period of activity.

Confraternity meetings were convened in the same way as meetings of craft guilds: each member was sent a *tsikha* or emblem of the confraternity (from the German *Zeche*).[62]

The statutes of most confraternities called for annual elections, but quite often they were held once every three or four years, or even less often. At a meeting of the Lviv Dormition Confraternity, after having heard the report of the outgoing officials, the members elected four "senior brothers" (a "collegium of four elders").[63] In the early seventeenth century deputies, or assistants, were elected for each of them, mainly to take their place when they were absent or ill. The first of the elders was the most important: in time, members began calling them seniors and their deputies vice-chairmen.[64] At first, four "table attendants" were elected to

---

60.   *DS*, 1–2; *AIuZR*, 11: 135.
61.   *AIuZR*, 11: 90, 177, 10: 135.
62.   *AIuZR*, 11: 58–59, 86; TsDIAL 129/1/1044, f. 4.
63.   *AIuZR*, 11: 191.
64.   TsDIAL 129/8/2, f. 2, 64, 91, 101; *IuSLS*, 1: 242.

maintain order at the proceedings (at the beginning of the seventeenth century, deputies were elected for them as well); later, only two "assessors of public sessions" were elected. At election meetings, duties were assigned to elders and regular members (confreres): a designated brother was responsible for confraternity property, another for book sales; "trustees of the hospital" were appointed, as well as a superintendent of the printing house, a scribe (secretary) of the confraternity, a treasurer, occasionally a director of the archives, "directors of the library," and "exactors," who raised funds.

At the periodic meetings ("sessions") of most confraternities, new members were admitted and discussions held on all issues in which the confraternities were engaged—the defense of civil rights, religious conflicts, the economic status of the confraternities, and the assistance provided to members and non-members alike. At these meetings, the confraternities chose envoys to the Diet and provincial dietines; they were given instructions and their reports were read; and occasionally teachers were engaged. The meetings tried members for their infractions, particularly for bringing matters over which the confraternity had jurisdiction to the attention of government officials, and so on.[65] In Lviv, even so praiseworthy an activist as Iurii Rohatynets was sentenced to a day's imprisonment and fined one pound of wax for failing to attend a meeting where an important discussion about the "great persecution on the part of the Poles" was to take place. In January 1601, Havrylo Dorofeiovych was permanently struck from the register of the Lviv Dormition Confraternity for betraying its interests during its conflict with Bishop Hedeon Balaban.[66] The confraternity also settled neighborly disputes among its members. Long-term conflicts would sometimes arise within the Lviv membership, for example, between Stefan Liaskovsky and Ivan Chesnykivsky (Rubakh) on the one hand and Semen Hrebenka on the other in the years 1722–23,[67] and between Iakiv

---

65. *AIuZR*, 11: 65, 39–40.

66. Ibid., 58, 62.

67. St. Petersburg Branch, Institute of Russian History, Russian Academy of Sciences, Dobrokhotov collection, no. 315, f. 26–72.

Gavendovych and Anton Dziokovsky from 1752 to 1759.[68] Such disagreements in principle, to which were added disputes of a personal nature, occasionally disrupted the normal activities of the confraternities.

What were the sources of confraternity funds? Besides regular membership dues, funds were raised from time to time for a variety of civic causes. In the fund-raising campaigns conducted by the Lviv Dormition Confraternity to cover the court costs of legal disputes "for rights and freedoms," donations were made not only by members but also by poor servants, tenants, and women.[69] In 1600, tailors' apprentices donated 26 zlotys to the confraternity, while Korniakt, the wealthiest resident of Lviv, contributed only 7 zlotys.[70] Visitors from various Ukrainian towns and merchants from Greece also took part in these fund drives. Donations "for mutual matters" were collected at markets, and members acting as envoys would be sent to neighboring towns "for alms" for the upkeep of schools and printshops, as well as for construction.[71]

Quite often, members and non-members would bequeath funds to the confraternities. Usually the amount of the bequest was registered as a permanent obligation associated with a particular property, whose successive owners were required to make an annual interest payment (generally eight percent of the registered amount) to the confraternity. As a result of bequests and collateral confiscated for unpaid debts, the Lviv Dormition Confraternity acquired real estate, including buildings in Lviv and a meadow with beehives in the village of Bilohorshcha. Rent from houses, stores, warehouses, and meadows was an additional source of income for the confraternity. In order to augment its material resources, members would engage in a variety of financial transactions, trading confraternity funds at profitable rates and occasionally floating loans, with the profits going to the confraternity.[72] In time, the Lviv Confraternity began

---

68. P. Dąbkowski, *Miscellanea archiwalne* (Lviv, 1930), 63–64.
69. *AIuZR*, 11: 27.
70. Ibid., 20–26.
71. TsDIAL 129/1/193.
72. *AIuZR*, 11: 299.

to expand its credit operations, offering secured loans to shopkeepers and craftsmen from the city and suburbs, as well as to Armenian and Jewish traders. But the main source of the confraternity's income in the 1630s was the sale of its printed books.

A significant portion of confraternity expenses was devoted to financing the construction of churches. The Lviv Confraternity expended a great deal of effort on the construction of the new Dormition Church.[73] The initiative shown by the confraternities contributed to the emergence of a new style of construction that combined original features of Ukrainian architecture with Renaissance elements. In 1625 the Kyiv Theophany Confraternity completed a new church that soon began to be known as the confraternity church. Confraternities in other towns engaged in similar activities. The list of expenditures of the St. George Confraternity in Drohobych contains a description of the members' endeavors pertaining to the restoration and reconstruction of their church, which is one of the pre-eminent monuments of Ukrainian wooden architecture. Here we read: "In the year 1657, the 15th of April. After the church was destroyed by fire, we approved a tax of three zlotys for the restoration of the holy church that we purchased in the village of Nadiiv beyond Dolyna."[74] This register also contains information about the painting of icons that have been preserved to this day in the confraternity church. It notes particularly that in 1666 the members of the confraternity "engaged a painter to paint the icons of the apostles … with the icons of the feast days and bishops for 300 zlotys."[75]

In the records of the village confraternity of Valiava (near Peremyshl), we find entries made by confraternity members concerning a payment made in 1749 to "Iurii Voitovych, resident of Sosnytsia, for carving the emblem of the confraternity" and to a "painter for a processional picture."[76]

73.   For a more detailed description, see Ia. Isaievych, "Dzherel'ni materialy z istoriï ukraïns'koho mystetstva XVI–XVIII st. v arkhivi L'vivs'koho bratstva," *Tretia respublikans'ka naukova konferentsiia z arkhivoznavstva ta inshykh spetsial'nykh istorychnykh dystsyplin: Druha sektsiia* (Kyiv, 1968), 99–111.

74.   LNB, Basilian monasteries collection, MS 267, f. 24.

75.   Ibid., f. 20.

76.   BKP, 2027, f. 3.

There are similar items in the accounts of other confraternities. Information contained in records concerning the patronage activities of confraternities is augmented by data occasionally found in notes inscribed on the walls of buildings, on icons, and in the margins of ancient printed or handwritten books.

A great portion of the expenses incurred by the confraternities consisted of payments for military units and taxes that were frequently levied in disproportionally large amounts. Thus, for the repayment of the Swedish army indemnity in 1704, the magistrate obliged the Lviv Confraternity to pay 10,000 talers, while the Roman Catholic archbishop had to pay only 2,000. That year the plundering of the Swedes and extortions of magistrates cost the confraternity 120,000 zlotys.[77] Plundering by the Polish army continued in subsequent years.

In the course of litigation undertaken to defend the "privileges" of the confraternities, it was impossible to avoid paying bribes to various individuals, beginning with office clerks and ending with ministers and the king himself. In 1621 the Lviv Confraternity, besides participating in a fund drive to purchase a gift "from the city" for Prince Władysław, gave him an additional "gift." That year the confraternity also had to provide a "gift" for King Sigismund III, "who was not kindly disposed toward our Ruthenian issues," and in 1676 for King John Sobieski III. Royal chancellors and clerks[78] also took gifts of money, as did the royal secretary, the famous jurist Paweł Szczerbic,[79] and papal nuncios and prefects of the "Ukrainian-Armenian" College of the Theatines. In Lviv, the confraternity was obliged to pay bribes not only to scribes and other employees of castle and magistracy offices, but also to the royal starosta and wealthy patricians, including such men of letters as Bartłomiej Zimorowic and Samuel Kuszewicz.[80] It was necessary to support the procurators ("protectors,"

---

77.   "Wiadomość o kontrybucyi włożoney przez Szwedów na duchowieństwo lwowskie r. 1704 (wyjęte z aktów klasztoru lwowskiego ww.oo. Dominikanów)," *Pamiętnik Lwowski* 3 (1818): 176.

78.   *AIuZR*, 11: 54–57, 526, 48, 412.

79.   *AIuZR*, 11: 28, 48, in the years 1577–83.

80.   TsDIAL 129/1/1065, f. 5, 8, 9; *AIuZR*, 11: 305, 413, 436.

"patrons"), i.e., the lawyers or legal consultants in various courts of Warsaw and, in the eighteenth century, in the Lviv consistory court, as well as in Rome.[81]

The Lviv Dormition Confraternity constantly made appropriations for book printing, repairs to the printshop, the school, and other buildings, and for the upkeep of impoverished pupils, as well as assistance to members and other persons. Extending interest-free loans and financial subsidies to poor confraternity members, widows, and orphans was one of the mandates of the confraternity as a charitable Christian institution. Assistance was also given to impoverished craftsmen who were not members of any confraternity, to the sick, orphans, and prisoners of war who were returning from captivity. Thus, in the confraternity's seventeenth-century records, we encounter entries concerning aid given to "Hanuska with two little children, a poor orphan," a "poor bookbinder for bread," and to foreign visitors—Greeks, Serbs, Moldavians, and Russians. For example, in the records from the 1690s, we read about alms given to "the Greek from Iaşi who was here in captivity," a "Wallachian prisoner," "two prisoners, a Muscovite and a Cossack," and so on.

In organizing a mutual aid network for the burghers, the confraternities also took on the responsibility of maintaining the *shpytali*—hospitals or, rather, shelters. References to hospitals at Orthodox parishes are found in records dated 1522 (the city hospital on Ruthenian Street in Lviv) and 1538 (the hospital on Potters' Street, near the Theophany Church).[82] But there is no doubt that they existed earlier. The hospital maintained by the Orthodox burghers was relocated at the end of the sixteenth century to the grounds of the St. Onuphrius Monastery. After 1592 the Dormition Confraternity constructed a building to lodge the hospital (in 1662 the confraternity erected a new masonry building for the hospital on this site). Three other Ukrainian hospitals were located at the Theophany, St. Nicholas, and Annunciation confraternities in Lviv, and a fourth was attached to St. George's Church.[83] The Stauropegion provided its hospital

---

81.   TsDIAL 1 129/1/445; 129/1/1044, f. 13; 129/1/1091, f. 30; 129/1169, f. 77.

82.   I. Kryp'iakevych, "Ukraïns'ki shpytali u L'vovi v XVI–XVII st." *Likars'kyi visnyk* (Lviv), 1930, no. 1: 15.

83.   *MCS*, 368; *AIuZR*, 11: 238; TsDIAL, f. 201, op. 4b, spr. 40, 83.

with supplies of wood and food and made repairs to the building. Besides feeble "old men and women of the hospital," the hospital housed the sick, especially pupils from the school dormitory.[84] Occasionally the confraternity provided them with money for drugs.[85] The confraternity library contained some medical texts. In his personal library the confraternity member Kostiantyn Mezapeta had works such as a "medico-chemical pharmacopoeia," Galen's works, the *Salerno School of Medicine*, and a herbal, while Roman Striletsky owned a copy of a medical treatise by Girolamo Cardano.[86] In this manner current medical knowledge could occasionally be applied in the confraternity hospital for the healing of the sick, but in general the hospitals were merely refuges for the disabled.

All the above-mentioned activities of the Lviv Confraternity were typical of other confraternities as well. They acted as institutions of mutual aid and philanthropy; often they ran hospitals, and occasionally even hostels for travelers. In organizing its hospital, the Kyiv Confraternity saw to it that Cossack veterans—"heroic people wounded in battles"— were given a place to live out their old age.[87] The number of hospitals in Right-Bank Ukraine increased greatly, expanding from there into Left-Bank Ukraine. According to data for the years 1740–47, in seven out of ten regiments of the Cossack Hetmanate there were 589 hospitals. In most cases they were maintained not by confraternities but by local communities. Similar institutions began to emerge, though less frequently, in Sloboda Ukraine.[88]

The confraternities engaged in financial transactions and owned a variety of real estate. Suburban confraternities in Lviv owned land that had earlier belonged to the churches and had been released from the jurisdiction of the town council. The confraternity attached to St. Nicholas's Church,

---

84.   TsDIAL 129/1/1041; Album, 406, 412; *AIuZR*, 11: 689.

85.   *AIuZR*, 11: 65.

86.   LNB, Ossolineum collection, MS 2170, f. 31, 35; *AIuZR*, 12: 35; J. Skoczek, *Lwowskie inwentarze biblioteczne* (Lviv, 1939), 392, 395, 419.

87.   *PKK*, 2: 605.

88.   P. Efimenko, "Shpitali v Malorossii," *Kievskaia starina* 5 (1883); Sumtsov, "Shpital' v m. Boromle," 309–10.

the oldest in Lviv, had retained its land, citing the privilege (now considered a forgery) bestowed on the church by Prince Lev Danylovych.[89] Burghers residing in the suburbs settled on lands owned by the confraternities of SS. Nicholas, Theodore, and Paraskeva paid the appropriate confraternity a small rent (residents on land owned by the St. Theodore Confraternity paid five zlotys per year).[90]

This led to the emergence of the *iurydykas* of the confraternities—that is, properties whose residents were partly subject to the jurisdiction of the confraternities, as they enjoyed the benefits of their landholdings.[91] The *iurydykas* of the Lviv suburban confraternities were long-lived: in the first half of the nineteenth century there was still a "united parish *iurydyka*" of the churches of St. Nicholas and St. Paraskeva that also included tenants of the former *iurydykas* of the Resurrection, Transfiguration, Nativity of the Theotokos, and St. Theodore confraternities. Similar *iurydykas* emerged on lands owned by the confraternities in several other towns, particularly in Drohobych and Lublin,[92] but they were rare.

Although many confraternities accepted the Lviv statute, there were differences in their organizational structure. In some confraternities, "every year four guardians and one secretary are elected"; in others, "four elder and two junior members"; and in others still, a single guild master (*tsekhmistr*). In the town of Iavoriv, two senior " church trustees" and two "hospital trustees" were elected. In the town of Kańczuga, besides elders, two treasurers and two "executors for counting marks" (to conduct the voting) were elected. Four elders, two secretaries, and several assistant bailiffs were elected in Zamostia.[93] Individual statutes contain certain organizational details that might apply to most confraternities, but were not

89.   TsDIAL 201/4b/69, f. 1; 64, f. 1.

90.   AGAD, Potocki Family Public Archive, file 341.

91.   For a description of the *iurydyka*'s socioeconomic character, see *Z istoriï Ukraïns'koï RSR*, vols. 6–7 (Kyiv, 1962), 12–14; *Czasopismo Prawno-Historyczne* (Poznań) 11, no. 1 (1959).

92.   J. Mazurkiewicz, *Jurydyki lubelskie* (Wrocław, 1956).

93.   LNB, NTSh collection, MS 136, f. 10; Taras Shevchenko Institute of Ukrainian Literature, National Academy of Sciences of Ukraine, Manuscript Division, Ivan Franko Archives/3/4833, f. 27; *AIuZR*, 10: 552.

reflected in the Lviv statute. Thus, the statute of the Olesko Confraternity provided that voting should be conducted by means of marks placed by the names of candidates: "whoever of the four obtains the most marks will be first; the one with the next largest number of marks will be second; and the last one, or someone apt for the purpose, should be the secretary of the confraternity."[94]

An important characteristic of the confraternities was their tendency to become independent of the state. The statute of the St. Nicholas Confraternity in a suburb of Peremyshl provided as follows: "If one member does harm to another member, no one should appeal to the secular authorities; the matter should remain within the confraternity." Members could appeal to "other authorities" only when the confraternity was unable to resolve a dispute.[95] Confraternities in the town of Bolekhiv and in the villages of Kamianka Lisna, Makhnivka, and others categorically forbade appeals of confraternity sentences to "the court" or "the castle," that is, to the lord. Thus one may observe a definite tendency toward self-government, independent of the authorities of the Polish-Lithuanian Commonwealth and local estate owners.[96]

Although the statutes of the larger and smaller confraternities generally resembled one another, the scope of activity of confraternities in small and middle-sized towns was immeasurably smaller than that of the Lviv Stauropegion or the Vilnius Confraternity. However, thanks to their mass appeal, confraternities in the smaller towns played a noteworthy role in everyday community life and helped create favorable conditions for the many initiatives undertaken by the most prominent confraternities.

As noted above, the statutes of many confraternities required that representatives of every social estate—noblemen, the urban elite, and "plebeians"—should be members of these

---

94.   TsDIAL 201/4b/3006.

95.   BKP, MS Akc. 2652, f. 13.

96.   Taras Shevchenko Institute of Ukrainian Literature, National Academy of Sciences of Ukraine, Manuscript Division, Ivan Franko Archives 3/4836, f. 29, and 3/4834, f. 25; I. Franko, "Do istoriï tserkovnykh bratstv v Halyts'kii Rusi," *ZNTSh* 21 (1898), Miscellanea, p. 3.

organizations. With few exceptions, the most active members of the confraternities were the burghers; later, this was also true of the peasantry in some regions. However, the very declaration of the need for a fraternal union of nobles, burghers, and peasants to achieve Christian and national goals was an achievement in itself. Such an attitude helped promote joint political initiatives on the part of burghers and Cossacks, as well as some Orthodox noblemen and magnates.

The Church of the Lviv Dormition Confraternity (built 1591–1631) and the Korniakt Tower (1578).

Charter of Patriarch Jeremiah of Constantinople confirming the Lviv Dormition Confraternity's right to run a press and a school (document preserved at the TsDIAL).

Portrait (18th c.) of a member of the church confraternity in Sokal (original in the Lviv Historical Museum).

Above: The church (built in the 1630s) of the Lutsk Confraternity of the Elevation of the Holy Cross. Graphic reconstruction by Bohdan Kolosok.

Below: The 17th-c. Church of St. George and its campanile in Drohobych.

The Lublin Orthodox confraternity's church, built in the first half of the 17th c.

Portrait of Bishop Hedeon Balaban of Lviv.

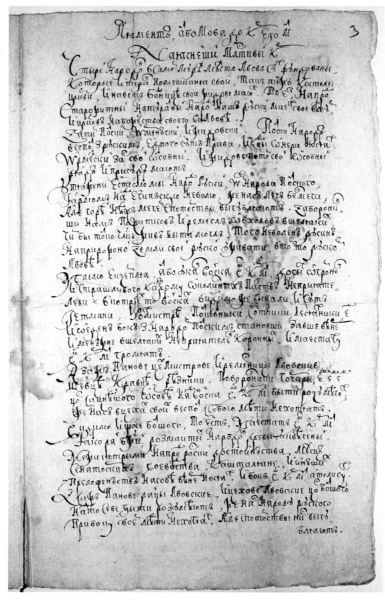

Letter of complaint from the Lviv Dormition Confraternity to the Polish king regarding the oppression of the Orthodox burghers (original preserved at the TsDIAL).

Icon of St. John the Evangelist by Matvii Domaratsky, a town councillor and member of St. Michael's Confraternity in Komarno (original in the Lviv Museum of Folk Architecture and Folkways).

Icon of St. Volodymyr the Great (painted ca. 1696–99) by Ivan Rutkovych, a member of the Zhovkva Confraternity (original in the National Museum in Lviv).

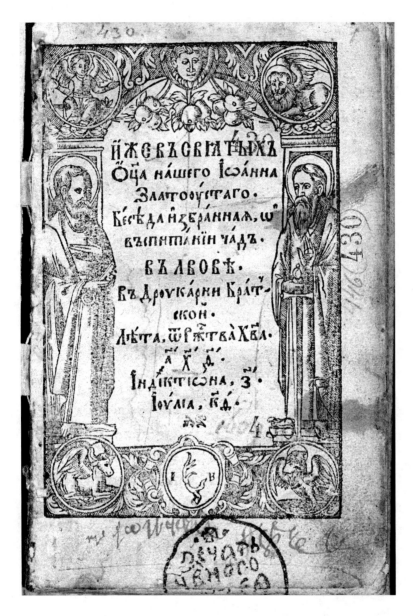

Title page of St. John Chrysostom's On the Education of Children, *published by the Lviv Dormition Confraternity Press on 29 July 1609 (copy preserved at the National Museum in Lviv).*

Seal of the Lviv Dormition Confraternity.

III

The Confraternities in Public Life and Religious Conflicts

I n the life of the Ukrainian-Belarusian community, religious, cultural, and political elements were so closely interwoven that in many cases they can scarcely be differentiated. The traditional church was the main national institution and the principal vehicle for the maintenance and development of cultural identity. Thus, the defense of religious rights was linked with the ethnically oriented cultural and political movement. If in historical studies these aspects are often analyzed separately, in real life they were virtually a single process. This also holds true for the activities of the confraternities.

More often than not, the cultural background influenced political decisions. This makes it necessary to begin with a discussion of those aspects of the cultural situation that determined the nature of the confraternities' involvement in religious and social conflicts. First, it is important to stress both the similarities and the differences in the development of Ukraine and Belarus on the one hand and their Eastern and Western neighbors on the other. Polish culture, or at least higher culture in Poland, was part of the "Latin" (that is, in religious terms, connected with Roman Catholicism, and later also with Protestantism) cultural sphere, while the character of Russian culture to the end of the seventeenth century was essentially determined by Eastern Orthodox Christianity in its specific post-Byzantine version. By contrast, Ukrainian and Belarusian culture began fairly early to develop a distinct character influenced by both the Eastern and Western Christian worlds. One manifestation of this was the comparatively swifter "Westernization" of Kyivan Orthodoxy and, later, the appearance of the Catholic Church of the Eastern rite. As a result, in some important cultural areas Ukraine and Belarus remained in the post-Byzantine Orthodox tradition, along with Russia, the Orthodox South Slavic nations, Romania, and Greece, while other aspects of Ukrainian and Belarusian culture were determined by contacts with Catholic and, later, also Protestant communities. The situation was further complicated by influences from Oriental cultures and, in the case of Russia, by contacts with the indigenous populations of Northern Europe and Asia. Since these contacts (particularly evident on the level of popular culture) will not be discussed here, it is essential at least to note the importance of this channel of cultural exchange.

Until the mid-seventeenth century, links between Ukrainians and Belarusians remained so close that in many spheres their cultures were inseparable. Both Ukrainian and Belarusian authors contributed to the development of the "plain Ruthenian language" (*prosta rus'ka mova*), which functioned as the Middle Ukrainian written language in Ukraine and as the Middle Belarusian written language in Belarus and Lithuania. Without a doubt, among the educated strata of society in both Ukraine and Belarus, there was a sense of a common Ruthenian ethnic and cultural identity. Initially, Belarus played the leading part in this common cultural sphere, as evidenced by the pioneering activities of Frantsysk Skaryna and the outstanding achievements of Belarusian cultural centers in Vilnius, Navahrudak, and elsewhere. Only later was that role assumed by Ukrainian educational centers in Ostrih, Lviv, and Kyiv. For a long time, differences between Ukrainian and Belarusian cultures remained mainly on the level of popular culture and spoken language. Among other factors, the transfer of most of Ukraine from the Grand Duchy of Lithuania to the Kingdom of Poland and the emergence of the Ukrainian Cossack tradition contributed to the further divergence of the two cultures (notwithstanding the active participation of many Belarusians in the Cossack movement). In the second half of the seventeenth century, the existence of the autonomous Ukrainian Hetmanate and the acceptance of the Cossack tradition in Ukraine as a whole promoted the further development of distinctive features in Ukrainian culture. The Ukrainian people, especially those residing in the

Hetmanate, became known in the West as a Cossack nation.

Ukrainians and Belarusians, together with Poles, Lithuanians, and, to a lesser degree, other ethnic minorities (mainly Germans, Jews, and Armenians) contributed to the emergence of the common cultural heritage of the Polish-Lithuanian Commonwealth. This culture is often referred to simply as Polish, but it was multiethnic in character, and only in time was it Polonized, at least ideologically and, to some degree, linguistically.[1] The "Commonwealth culture" took part in many European cultural movements, such as humanism, the Protestant Reformation and the Catholic Counter-Reformation, and the baroque trend in literature and the arts. The influence of the multiethnic Commonwealth as a whole on such neighboring countries as Russia, Romania, and Hungary was perhaps even more important than influences exerted by its constituent parts.

If the Western-oriented aspects of Ukrainian and Belarusian culture were intrinsically connected with cultural innovation, their Eastern contacts developed mainly in the context of traditional cultural models. The concept of "Slavia Orthodoxa" as a supranational spiritual community, most clearly formulated by Riccardo Picchio, has readily been accepted by most Slavists studying medieval and early modern literature.[2] It should of course be understood that Orthodox Slavdom was only part of the broader spectrum of Byzantine and post-Byzantine culture (the so-called *Byzance après Byzance*). Moreover, the term "Slavia" is not fully adequate, for it was not only Slavic peoples but Romanians as well who used Slavic languages—namely, Church Slavonic, Middle Ukrainian, and Middle Bulgarian—in literature and administration. Nor is the word "Orthodoxa" precise, since Catholics of the Eastern rite retained not only the Church Slavonic liturgy, but also Byzantine traditions in theology, church organization, architecture, painting, and music. The

---

1.   A transitional phenomenon was the appearance of individuals, mostly in the nobiliary milieu, who combined political loyalty to the Polish state with attachment to "all-Commonwealth" culture and their Ruthenian cultural heritage. See Sysyn, *Between Poland and the Ukraine*, 210–13.

2.   R. Picchio, *Letteratura della Slavia ortodossa (IX–XVIII sec.)* (Bari, 1991), 7–83.

whole sphere of activity of the European Eastern-rite churches can perhaps be defined as the area where Cyrillo-Methodian traditions remained vital in church life and in all cultural activities connected with the church. Literary genres and artistic styles described as belonging to the Old Rus' culture were in many cases characteristic of this whole area. It should be added that the second (linguistic) South Slavic influence, which affected the whole East Slavic region to various degrees, contributed greatly to increasing cultural uniformity among the Orthodox Slavic peoples.

The "Slavia Orthodoxa" was divided into two realms, those of the Southern and Eastern Slavs. Each of the three East Slavic peoples emerged mainly as a result of the consolidation of several tribes or, rather, tribal unions. As far as the Ukrainians are concerned, their forerunners were such early Slavic groups as the Polianians, Siverianians, Dulibians, Ulychians, Tivertsians, Derevlianians, and probably also the Eastern Croats. At the same time, the culture of all the East Slavic nations was imbued with common features within the framework of the Kyivan Rus' state. The Kyiv Metropolitanate, which remained the only religious center for this whole area until the early fourteenth century, provided essential uniformity of ecclesiastical organization. The heritage of Kyivan Rus' is erroneously styled "Russian" by historians who remain under the influence of the so-called "traditional scheme of Russian history."[3] Even now, many historians underestimate the degree to which many distinctive features of Belarusian, Russian, and Ukrainian culture originated during the Kyivan Rus' period and even earlier.[4]

---

3.   M. Hrushevs'kyi, "Zvychaina skhema 'russkoï' istoriï i sprava ratsional'noho ukladu istoriï skhidnoho slov'ianstva," first published in Ukrainian in *Stat'i po slavianovedeniiu* (St. Petersburg, 1904). For English translations, see *Annals of the Ukrainian Academy of Arts and Sciences in the USA* 2, no. 2 (1952): 355–64 and *From Kievan Rus' to Modern Ukraine* (Cambridge, Mass., 1984), 1–355–1–364. Cf. A. E. Presniakov, *The Formation of the Great Russian State* (Chicago, 1970), 6–35.

4.   See Ia. Isaievych, "Pochatky derzhavnosti i ranni etapy formuvannia skhidnoslovians'kykh narodiv," in *Etnichna svidomist': natsional'na kul'tura*, ed. H. A. Skrypnyk (Kyiv, 1991), 78–82.

The direction of cultural links and the nature of political activity in the late medieval and early modern periods were determined not only by cultural traditions but also, no less importantly, by the political situation in Eastern Europe. Early modern Russian culture developed under the protection of the independent state known in the West as Muscovy. Although its cultural relations with East and West never ceased completely, the ideologically motivated policy of the Muscovite state was one of cultural isolationism. By contrast, Ukrainians and Belarusians were deprived of their own statehood. The vast majority of them were Orthodox Christians, but the Ukrainian and Belarusian nobility gradually converted to the Roman Catholicism of the dominant Polish culture and, consequently, was becoming Polonized. Burghers, Cossacks, and those nobles who remained Orthodox considered the maintenance of their "fathers' faith" crucial to the preservation of their religious and ethnic identity. Cultural contacts within the Slavia Orthodoxa helped them defend that traditional cultural heritage, which they perceived as a link with the golden age of the nation.

At that time, the only independent Orthodox country was Russia, while the small principalities of Moldavia (the Volokh Land, Voloshchyna) and Wallachia (Multany, Muntenia, Țară Românească) remained semi-independent. It is quite natural that in countries where Orthodox Christianity was persecuted (or, at the very least, humiliated), the Orthodox clergy treated Orthodox rulers as their protectors. On the other hand, for Orthodox rulers to support their coreligionists living in heterodox states was not only the fulfillment of their Christian duty but also a tool of state policy. During the Polish and Swedish intervention in Russia at the beginning of the seventeenth century, Orthodoxy provided the ideological justification for a patriotic movement. Shortly thereafter, however, the slogan of "the defense of Orthodoxy" began to serve the expansionist policy of the Russian tsars. The worsening condition of Orthodoxy under non-Orthodox administrations could not but provoke the emergence of political forces seeking the protection of Orthodox monarchs, or even their full sovereignty. In most cases, the identity or similarity of faith (or, rather, of rite) was the main cause of such movements, not their "external manifestation," as many Soviet historians suggested. As will be discussed later, several influential parish confraternities, including those of Lviv and Kyiv, initiated contacts with Russia as a counterweight to Poland. At the same time, some hierarchs and other public figures, more or less associated with the confraternity movement, oscillated between subordination to the Kingdom of Poland and sympathy for the Orthodox Russian state. Their contradictory declarations of loyalties confuse modern historians, who are inclined to take at face value those declarations that are in agreement with established scholarly conceptions. What remains unappreciated is that in many cases, contacts with Russian authorities helped Orthodox public figures exert political pressure on the Polish authorities, or at least raised their political prestige.

During the initial stages, cultural contacts within the Slavia Orthodoxa developed mainly in the religious sphere, while contacts of Orthodox peoples with the heritage of Western culture were more extensive in the secular domain. Manuscripts, icons, and various artifacts circulated in Ukraine, Belarus, and Russia, as they did throughout the Slavia Orthodoxa. Most of the circulating manuscripts were liturgical books, but canonical and apocryphal religious literature, sermons, and hagiography were also a very important part of this exchange. Original literary works, including chronicles, letters, and secular texts of a practical character, were less numerous, but nonetheless interesting as evidence of cultural creativity. The nature of the exchange of traditional texts was determined mostly by the activities of monasteries, episcopal sees, and other ecclesiastical structures. The same may be said of exchanges in the realm of religious art. While church architecture developed quite independently, the export of icons from Russia to other Orthodox countries was an important influence.

Cultural contacts in the secular sphere developed mainly in the context of economic and political relations. Studies written in the 1980s suggest that some linguistic parallels reflect the character of cultural contacts. For example, the

Russian word *gosudarstvo* ("state," derived from *gosudar'*, "sovereign") derives from the Ruthenian *hospodar(stvo)* (then meaning "sovereign," "state"). Earlier, the title of the grand dukes of Lithuania, *hospodar i dědič*, was probably established under the influence of the identical titles of the princes of Galicia and Volhynia (*dominus* and *haeres* or *hospodar i dědič*).[5] The study of contacts and influences in the spheres of public administration, law, manners, and customs is only in its initial stages. Cultural interchange between Russia and the Orthodox provinces of the Polish-Lithuanian state received a new impetus from intellectuals who fled to the Belarusian, Lithuanian, and Ukrainian lands in order to escape Muscovite persecution: the *starets* (monastic elder) Artemii in 1554 or 1555; a group of Muscovite heretics in the late 1550s; Prince Andrei Kurbsky in the mid-1560s.[6] These people contributed to the popularity of the work of Maksim Grek and writers of his circle. The Muscovite émigré Ivan Fedorov was instrumental in establishing the first printshops in Ukraine in the cities of Lviv and Ostrih.

Changes in cultural patterns contributed to the appearance of new forms of cultural contact and to the narrowing of the gap between religious and secular culture. This process began much earlier in Ukraine and Belarus than in Russia. Initially, Latin-oriented and traditional cultures developed there mostly along parallel lines. The reciprocal modification of both traditions facilitated their coexistence, and to some degree mutual tolerance, in a milieu where East met West. The movement toward a synthesis of traditional cultural values with the new social and cultural trends developed in the framework of new institutions such as the confraternities and formal schools of the new type.

The Westernization of Ukrainian Orthodoxy was viewed with suspicion in Russia as long as the cultural orientation of the tsarist state was determined almost exclusively by

5. A. Zoltan, "K predystorii russkogo *gosudar'*," *Studia slavica* (Budapest) 29 (1985).

6. M. Dmitriev, *Pravoslavie i Reformatsiia: Reformatsionnye dvizheniia v vostochnoslavianskikh zemliakh Rechi Pospolitoi vo vtoroi polovine XVI v.* (Moscow, 1990).

conservative circles. Later, when modernizing trends in Russia took firmer hold, the attitude toward Ukrainian and Belarusian innovations became more sympathetic. Direct Russian contacts with Catholics and Protestants were instrumental in promoting the slow processes of cultural secularization. Innovations in religious affairs proved much more palatable when introduced not directly but through the intermediacy of the Ukrainians and Belarusians, who had already modified foreign cultural models and adapted them in some measure to Orthodox traditions. The secular and religious spheres cannot, of course, be neatly separated, and direct as well as mediated contacts can be traced in both spheres.

The contacts of Ukraine and Belarus with Russia bear some typological similarities to their contacts with Moldavia. Early in its history, the Moldavian principality inherited some of its social and political institutions and cultural models from the principalities of Galicia and Volhynia. The Middle Ukrainian language of Moldavia's charters was a continuation of the language of western Ukrainian administrative documents. Ukrainian manuscripts were disseminated in Moldavia, and the code of canon law used in Moldavia and other Romanian lands was adopted from Volhynia. Later, the situation was reversed when Moldavian princes (hospodars) assumed the role of protectors of western Ukrainian church institutions. Illuminated manuscripts from Moldavian scriptoria became very popular in Ukraine. Balkan stylistic trends in art and literature often reached Ukraine through Moldavia. At the same time, Ukraine continued to play the role of intermediary in the advancement of Western influence in Moldavia.[7]

The explosion of political and cultural activity in Ukrainian and Belarusian communities in the late sixteenth century was accompanied by an intensification of all the cross-cultural contacts described above. Quite naturally, the confraternities were deeply involved in these processes. Although the public activities of the confreres developed in response to the major socioeconomic challenges raised by the changing political and

---

7.   Ukrainian influence on Moldavian cultural life again became more intense after the cultural revival that began in Kyiv in the 1620s.

cultural landscape, on a personal level they were motivated by sincere religious feeling—a desire to fulfill the principal duties of a Christian life. This general perspective remained, but priorities in the form and content of confraternal public activity could not remain unchanged. When the oldest confraternities tried to establish some form of self-government within their congregations, the clergy did not oppose them: the weakness of Orthodoxy required consolidation rather than conflict within the national church. After the initial successes, however, when a degree of stability had been achieved, rivalry between the laity (at least, its most influential representatives) and the clergy became possible and even inevitable.

The scholarly literature, in concord with the texts of early modern religious writers, often begins with an exposition of the changes that occurred in religious life, focusing on the critical state of the church in the second half of the sixteenth century. The decline of morals, the dissolution of ecclesiastical structures resulting from unfavorable external circumstances, and even the degeneration of the structures themselves gave a certain impetus to the struggle for rebirth. However, the issue can be posed in different terms. It appears certain that in the first half of the sixteenth century the state of the Orthodox Church was better than in the second half, when there was a graver threat from other religions and the main issue was the consolidation of forces capable of resisting decline. Those forces began to issue warnings and mobilize public opinion for action. That is why dazzling descriptions of the decline began to appear only at that time, even when such a decline had been noted in earlier years. In Ukraine and Belarus there now arose a question that had been discussed earlier in Western and Central Europe, namely: who should spearhead the reform of religious life—the clergy or the laity? This raised the further question of whose influence should be dominant in the evolution of culture. As in the West, confraternity activists justified their desire for more influence in religious matters by indicating clerical abuses, especially on the part of the bishops.

The confirmation of the stauropegial rights of the Lviv Dormition Confraternity took place against the background of a confrontation between the Lviv Orthodox burghers, whose powers had been augmented by the confraternity, and Bishop Hedeon Balaban, who wielded more influence than his predecessor. The conflict was not local in scope: the burghers of Lviv supported the burghers of such towns as Rohatyn and Holohory. There was a similar situation in several towns of the Peremyshl eparchy. On the other hand, Hedeon Balaban, who came from an Orthodox noble family, enjoyed the support not only of the nobles, but also of burghers who avoided confrontations with the clergy.

Balaban's yearning to renew ecclesiastical and cultural life is apparent from his support of the establishment of a permanent Orthodox printing house in Lviv. At this time he believed that cultural development should be spearheaded by the social elite, first and foremost by the church hierarchy. The activists of the Lviv Confraternity were undoubtedly exaggerating when they included Balaban among those "priests and bishops who censure scholarship and forbid people to study, cursing those who study and excusing those who do nothing and despise learning, saying, blessed is every simple soul, for many books lead to folly." But there were pretexts for such a view. When a confraternity was founded in the town of Holohory, Balaban referred to its most educated members, Vasko Babych and Nechypor Sahaidachnyk, who had asked him to explain certain theological questions, as "simple fellows." "You have just crawled out of the manure," the bishop was quoted as saying, "and you learned about manure. What business do you have with Holy Scripture?"[8] Balaban's statements on this question were not just his personal opinions, but reflected the views of other church hierarchs. Ipatii Potii later declared that the main opponents of the Union were not members of the clergy but common people—craftsmen who, "having abandoned their trade (shoemaker's thread, scissors, and awl) and appropriated pastoral authority, are flaunting the Word of God, subverting and transforming it into blasphemous and false calumnies, and are reproaching, dishonoring, and defaming their own pastors."[9] The struggle

---

8.   *MCS*, 140–41, 155.

9.   *Pamiatniki polemicheskoi literatury*, vol. 2 (St. Petersburg, 1882), 116–17.

of the confraternities for the right of the laity to read and comment on theological works was undoubtedly analogous to that of activists of the Protestant Reformation.

The movement to limit the power of the bishop and other sociopolitical actions undertaken by the confraternities were led by the Lviv burghers Ivan Krasovsky and Iurii Rohatynets, as well as by a teacher at the confraternity school, Stefan Zyzanii. Well educated for their time and possessing considerable literary talent, they initiated a vigorous propaganda campaign among the broadest circles of the Ukrainian population, not only in Galicia, but also beyond its borders. From Balaban's letter of 3 February 1586 we learn that the bishop threw Krasovsky into prison for deprecating him in Lviv and other localities, composing some sort of agitational verses against him, and writing a letter to Kamianets in an attempt to muster those opposed to him. Later, Balaban also complained that Krasovsky, Luka Huba, and the whole confraternity were disseminating "libelous articles," letters, and verses against him.[10] The higher clergy feared that such protests would give rise to a broad social movement. On 30 April 1586, Balaban wrote the following about the activities of the Rohatynets brothers: "Confusion is being sown among the people by the saddlers Iurko and Ivan by means of new teachings of some kind that are leading to the spread of heresy, as well as to discord and threats to health among the ignorant, with the possibility of bloodshed causing great offense to the holy faith and the rights and privileges of the clergy, as well as our own episcopal ones." "In order to prevent the spread of heresy among the simple folk, as well as conflict, hatred, and bloodshed among them," the bishop excommunicated Iurii and Ivan Rohatynets from the church, "together with their pupils and adherents, subverters of the holy law."[11]

The bishop's anathemas did not intimidate the confraternity activists or put a halt to the confraternity movement, which had begun to spread not only in the towns, but also in some villages. In 1588, in a letter to the Cholhansky, Suliatytsky,

---

10. *MCS*, 133, 185.
11. Ibid., 136.

Vytvytsky, Hoshovsky, and Svarychovsky families and other petty Ukrainian nobles, Balaban complained that "at the devil's urging" the Lviv burghers were spreading "new and unusual teachings of some kind, contrary to holy law, that attract and tempt many simple people and are arousing disturbances, rebellions, and conflicts among the simple folk of the towns and certain villages.... " The bishop indicated further that the aim of the confraternities was to set the "simple folk" against the interests of the bishops and the "Orthodox knighthood," i.e., the nobility. "In order to support those teachings of theirs in a more secure and powerful manner and to stand by them, they have sworn to band firmly together, so that each one will be subordinate in religious and legal affairs to their Lviv Confraternity and remain under its authority."[12] We have cited extensively from the bishop's accusations, as they clearly demonstrate the anxieties of the church hierarchy concerning the social movement abetted by the confraternities, which was firmly taking root among the masses.

In 1590, some of the Orthodox burghers of Lviv (Ivan Bidlaha, Ivan Myntsovych, Khoma Kushnir, and Senko Lutsky) and residents of the suburbs (Semen Korunka, Ivan Morokhovsky et al.) supported Bishop Balaban. They declared that Iurii and Ivan Rohatynets had "long been causing ... revolts and disturbances in the Greek faith."[13] In warning against the possibility of bloodshed, the bishop's supporters claimed that since the founding of the confraternity, its members had been "refusing to subordinate themselves to the town council's authority, conducting their own trials and handing down sentences, and, by threatening people with eternal damnation, preventing them from appealing to the town council.... They are attempting to undermine church rites: they consider those craftsmen and servants who work for the Poles to be cursed ... and spit on them."[14] However, on 25 January 1591, "when all the people, both the clergy and the laity," convened before the metropolitan, the former opponents of the confraternity

---

12.   Ibid., 166–67.

13.   TsDIAL 9/347: 162–63; *MCS*, 241–53; *AIuZR*, 10: 63, 12: 532–34; LNB, Teky Zubryts'koho 1, no. 32.

14.   TsDIAL 52/3, vol. 20: 989.

recognized the authority of Metropolitan Mykhailo Rohoza of Kyiv (who was cooperating with the confraternity at this time) and asked for a reconciliation.[15] Many of them became members and activists of the confraternity.

One of the most popular leaders of the confraternity movement in the years 1586–93 was Stefan Zyzanii, a teacher at the Lviv school who is believed to have represented the radical wing of the national and religious movement. Later, Metropolitan Rohoza noted that Zyzanii, "together with his assistants, sowed bloodshed in Lviv."[16] Sometime at the beginning of 1593, the Vilnius Confraternity asked Zyzanii and Iurii Rohatynets, as representatives of the Lviv Stauropegion, to help them. In Vilnius, both of them conducted a "mighty and great war" against the Roman Catholics.[17] Rohatynets soon returned to Lviv, while Zyzanii remained in Vilnius. Metropolitan Rohoza and the king of Poland issued a number of edicts against Zyzanii, forbidding him to preach. At this time, the Lviv Confraternity members regarded him as one of their leaders and sent him reports about their activities. Although Zyzanii was not registered as a member of the confraternity and no longer even resided in Lviv after 1593, the confraternity called him its "beloved brother."[18] Even Rohatynets, who thought it expedient to adopt more moderate methods in certain questions, took Zyzanii's opinions into consideration and explained the motives for his actions to him. As may be seen from Rohatynets's letter to Zyzanii and the members of the Vilnius Confraternity (November 1599),[19] the differences of opinion between Zyzanii and Rohatynets pertained only to questions of tactics, while both were in agreement on the goals of the confraternity movement.

The actual leaders of the Lviv Confraternity in the late sixteenth and early seventeenth centuries were Iurii Rohatynets, Ivan Krasovsky, and Ivan Rohatynets. In 1588, Bishop Balaban addressed a letter to the confraternity as follows: "To the

---

15.   MCS, 247–75, 278.

16.   AZR, 4: 41, 105.

17.   "Barkulabovskaia letopis'," 10.

18.   MCS, 736–38.

19.   Ibid., 835–37.

shopkeeper Ivan Krasovsky and the saddlers Iurko and Ivan Kuzmych, burghers of Lviv, together with your assistants, whom you have taken into your midst." Metropolitan Rohoza's letter of 1589 is addressed to "Master Ivan Demydovych Krasovsky and Master Iurii Kozmych Rohatynets and other superintendents of the confreres."[20] Those election protocols that are extant (1604, 1608, 1611, 1612, 1616) indicate that Krasovsky was consistently the first of four elders to be elected by the confraternity.[21] At the beginning of the seventeenth century Ipatii Potii, by then a Greek Catholic metropolitan, complained in a letter to the superior of the Ruthenian province of the Dominican Order that the people of Lviv were not submitting to his authority or to that of the Orthodox bishop, and noted: "In Lviv, Rohatynets is a patriarch and a doctor. Whatever he commands, the priests babble in their sermons." Potii further noted that Rohatynets and the confraternity often disseminated their adverse opinions of him, "verbally and in writing," and wrote with exasperation about "instructions from the confraternity," recalling, in particular, some verses and a "heretical" book published by the confraternity printshop. The Orthodox hierarchy had an equally negative attitude toward the leaders of the confraternity.[22] Metropolitan Ioannes Sēmulas of Suceava, who was not dependent on the members of the confraternity and less obliged to reckon with the opinions of its members than the Ukrainian hierarchs, could express himself more openly. In September 1599, he wrote to the confraternity that his work was superfluous and that the members of the confraternity deserved the misfortunes that had befallen them, for they were not living in accordance with the teachings of the holy fathers, obeyed neither the bishop nor the metropolitan, and chose laymen as their leaders: "They have Krasovsky instead of the patriarch, Iurko Rohatynets instead of the metropolitan, and Ivan Rohatynets instead of the bishop."[23]

---

20.   Ibid., 170, 213.

21.   *AIuZR*, 11, 67, 72, 73, 78, 81.

22.   LNB, Teky Zubryts'koho 1, no. 39; Russian State Library, Moscow, Manuscript Division, Collection of the "Obshchestvo istorii i drevnostei rossiiskikh" 274, no. 3 (Sokolov, no. 895), f. 5.

23.   *MCS*, 826.

The conflict between the Lviv Confraternity and Hedeon Balaban lasted throughout 1586. At the end of that year a kind of truce was established, but in October 1587 the bishop renewed his hostile actions, and hostilities continued for almost fifteen years. The confraternity later declared that the "inhuman torments" caused by the bishop "should be recorded not only in ink, but in the blood and sweat of our brethren who have been tormented to death."[24] The episcopal synods held in Brest in 1590, 1591, and 1593 supported the confraternity, while a synod held in the spring of 1594 even revoked Balaban's episcopal status.[25] Apparently, at this stage the confraternity was able to take advantage of dissension within the hierarchy as a majority of bishops prepared to proclaim the Union.

It was only in January 1602, through the mediation of the high Moldavian official Luca Stroich (Stroici), that the Stauropegion signed an agreement with the bishop, who pledged to honor the confraternity statute and agreed to the free election of his successor, having given up the royal privilege providing for the inheritance of the episcopate by his nephew Ivan (Isaia). The confraternity adopted this agreement in the interest of consolidating the Ruthenian church, then threatened by a schism between the Orthodox and the adherents of the Union.

Although Isaia Balaban renounced all claims to the Lviv episcopate by signing the agreement of 1602, after the death of Hedeon Balaban he took over the bishop's seat with the help of an armed detachment. The confraternity lodged a resolute protest against the new pretender to the episcopal see.[26] Prince Kostiantyn Ostrozky demanded that the confraternity reconcile itself with Isaia,[27] but it continued to reject him and managed to effect the election of Bishop Evstafii (Ieremiia) Tysarovsky. By playing a key role in the election of a new bishop against the wishes of so influential a magnate as Ostrozky, the confraternities, headed by the Lviv Stauropegion, manifested

---

24.   *MCS*, 442; TsDIAL 129/1/1035.

25.   *MCS*, 538–48, 769–70.

26.   LNB, Teky Zubryts'koho 1, no. 32.

27.   *AZR*, 4, no. 170: 258; Ia. F. Holovats'kyi, "L'vovskoie Stavropihiiskoe bratstvo i kniaz' Ostrozhskii," *Vremennik Instituta Stavropihiiskoho* (Lviv, 1867), 79–81.

their strength. Mindful of this, neither Bishop Evstafii (Ieremiia Tysarovsky, 1607–41) nor his successors, Arsenii Zhelyborsky (1641–63) and Atanasii Zhelyborsky (1663–69), sought openly to thwart the confraternities. A certain weakening of the confraternities' initial fervor also favored the establishment of a compromise of sorts between them and the bishops.

More than other hierarchs, Patriarch Theophanes of Jerusalem, who had restored the Orthodox hierarchy in Ukraine in 1620, had to take into consideration the opinions of broad segments of the population, particularly the Cossacks. He bestowed stauropegial rights not only on the Lviv and Vilnius confraternities, but also on those of Kyiv, Lutsk, and Slutsk.[28] In 1624 Meletii Smotrytsky, then the Orthodox bishop of Polatsk, acting in the interests of the entire episcopate, visited the Eastern patriarchs and obtained an edict from Patriarch Cyril Lukaris (Kyrillos Loukaris) of Constantinople abolishing the stauropegial rights of all the confraternities.[29] However, on 15 December 1626, after an energetic protest launched by the most powerful confraternities, Lukaris was obliged to issue a new edict stating that the previous one did not affect the Lviv and Vilnius confraternities.[30]

The extensive rights of the confraternities aroused resistance on the part of the bishops and even the metropolitans. Even the former rector of the Lviv Confraternity School, Ivan (Iov) Boretsky, after being named metropolitan of Kyiv, expressed his dissatisfaction with the Lviv Confraternity for excluding the clergy from the school and other public affairs.[31] Later, notwithstanding their respect for Metropolitan Petro Mohyla's educational activities, the members of the Lviv Confraternity vigorously protested his interference in their internal affairs and refused to recognize his jurisdiction over them. In the eighteenth century, the Lviv Confraternity opposed all attempts by Iosyf Shumliansky and successive bishops (by now Greek Catholic ones) to subordinate the confraternities

---

28.   *PKK*, 1: 8–9, 2: 397–99.

29.   Hrushevs'kyi, *Istoriia Ukraïny-Rusy*, 8: 6–8. Cf. P. Kraliuk, *Dukhovni poshuky Meletiia Smotryts'koho* (Kyiv, 1997), 146.

30.   Golubev, *Kievskii mitropolit Petr Mogila*, 1: suppl., 287–89.

31.   Ibid., 290–91.

to their authority. The confraternity also refused to change its attitude toward the parish clergy. In 1779 Ivan Gudz, the representative of the Lviv bishop, wrote that the members of the Lviv Stauropegion Confraternity were "not allowing the priests to make any administrative arrangements, saying that priests should only serve Mass and that they themselves will carry out the administrative work."[32]

As mentioned earlier, demands for limitations on the rights of the clergy emanated not only from the Stauropegion, but also from numerous confraternities in other towns that had adopted its statute. To offset these confraternities, Hedeon Balaban, and later Metropolitan Iov Boretsky of Kyiv and other hierarchs began to establish confraternities of a different type that were subordinate to the clergy. At the demand of the members of the Lviv Confraternity, the synod of Brest (1591) condemned such confraternities and forbade the bishops to sow dissension in the confraternity movement.[33] But Balaban continued to establish confraternities subject to his authority, not to the Stauropegion. In 1602 he confirmed the charter of the Theophany Confraternity in Lviv, without mentioning that it had been established as early as 1591 by a statute similar to that of the Stauropegion.[34] Obviously, Balaban hoped to establish a new confraternity that would be obedient to him.

The Holohory and Rohatyn confraternities were also in conflict with Balaban. In 1588 the bishop wanted to dissolve the confraternity that had been established in Holohory and modeled on the Lviv Confraternity. In its place he wished to proclaim another confraternity subordinate to episcopal authority. According to the burghers of Holohory, Balaban said of their statute: "This confraternity is superfluous and should not be retained. I will give you a better confraternity [statute], but burn this one: it is from Lviv, from the heretics, and not from me. Simple people like you should not inquire into scholarly matters."[35] One of the initiators of the Holohory

---

32.   TsDIAL 408/1/388, f. 259.

33.   *AIuZR*, 10: 121–25.

34.   Ibid., 71–72; *MCS*, 279–81.

35.   *MCS*, 154–55.

Confraternity was the priest Vasko, a Jew who had converted to Orthodoxy and had been ordained by Balaban himself. This Vasko later wrote: "Since I was accustomed to order among the Jews and could not tolerate disrespect from the Jews who laughed at the disorder among us Christians, I asked the Lviv Confraternity to establish order in its parish."[36] Displeased by the founding of the confraternity, in 1592 Bishop Balaban pronounced an anathema against Vasko.[37] Later, during Vasko's visit to Rohatyn, Balaban had him arrested and ordered him to be bound with chains and thus "dragged him from the city; and imprisoned him for four days in a pit in the village of Striatyn." Later on, the Lviv Confraternity repeatedly and vigorously protested this act of cruelty.[38]

In Rohatyn, a confraternity took form in a milieu of educated burghers who, by 1587, were already in conflict with Bishop Balaban.[39] The conflict became particularly acute in the years 1589–90. Balaban, "tormenting the confraternity with imprisonment and beating schoolteachers, expelled the confraternity from the town." Later he appointed a priest, Fedir Kruten, who "refused to leave not only the confraternity, but also the hospital and the school, in peace."[40] Looking askance at the bishop and his adherents, the Rohatyn Confraternity made common cause with the Lviv Confraternity, of which it considered itself a collective member. It also continued to restrict the interference of the clergy in its affairs. In 1627, Metropolitan Boretsky of Kyiv demanded that the confraternity allow the priest to attend its meetings, noting that there is "great disrespect to the clergy" in the confraternity "because of the coarseness of some (members)."[41]

Similar relations between bishops and confraternities that did not want to submit to episcopal authority are known from other towns. Thus, in 1592–93 the Horodok Confraternity, which had contributed much to the development of public

36.   LNB, Teky Zubryts'koho 1, no. 35.
37.   TsDIAL 129/1/160.
38.   MCS, 423, 463, 522; AIuZR, 11: 99.
39.   DS, 52–53.
40.   MCS, 540; AIuZR, 12: 521.
41.   Vestnik Iugo-Zapadnoi i Zapadnoi Rossii, 1862, no. 3: 103–7.

school education and was one of the first to accept the statute of the Lviv Confraternity, was in open conflict with Bishop Mykhailo Kopystynsky of Peremyshl and the senior priest of Horodok, Hryhorii Popil, who "cursed them, and called their confraternity a heresy."[42] Between 1611 and 1663, a protracted struggle was waged in the Drohobych parish of the Elevation of the Holy Cross between the confraternity and priests of the Demko family, who wished to retain their hereditary authority over the parish. The confraternity eventually gained the upper hand and obtained recognition of its right to select priests freely. In 1619, even Terletsky, the wealthy priest of St. George's Church, was forced to transfer the church and all its possessions to the confraternity and agree that it was "to manage all affairs."[43] Despite clerical resistance, the principle of the election of priests became established practice in all Drohobych churches. In the eighteenth century, candidates for ordination had to give pledges to the confraternities that they would not take fees for baptisms, weddings, or funerals that exceeded the fixed rate, nor would they interfere in the affairs of the confraternities.[44] Confraternities in other towns and villages obtained similar rights. Thus, for example, the confraternity of the village of Kolekhovychi (Kholm Land) signed a contract with the local priest concerning the apportionment of parish income.[45] The confraternities also hired and discharged cantors, some of whom were teachers.[46] Documents concerning parish property were often signed jointly by priests and representatives of the confraternity.[47] During the seventeenth and eighteenth centuries, bishops usually supported those parish priests who wanted to restrict

42.   TsDIAL 9, vol. 348, f. 1076, 1138, 1153, 1421–23, 1593.

43.   Library of the Polish Academy of Sciences (Cracow), Manuscript Division, no. 262; TsDIAL 14, 101: 777; NM, Teky Podolyns'koho, f. "Drohobych."

44.   TsDIAL, 3: 232–35, 6: 21, 398–400.

45.   Ibid. 129/1/643. Modest (Strel'bitskii), "Svedeniia o sostave tserkovno-arkheologicheskago muzeia pri Kholmskom Sviatobogorodichnom bratstve po oktiabr' 1882 goda," *Kholmsko-Varshavskiia eparkhialnyia vedomosti*, 1882, no. 2: 384–85.

46.   Kórnik Library, Polish Academy of Sciences, MS no. 1211 (entry dated 19 December 1744 in the Sataniv municipal records).

47.   Ibid., entries of 1738.

confraternity activities. This is apparent from episcopal edicts, which frequently underscored that the confraternities should not violate the rights of the clergy.[48] Occasionally, exploiting the declining activity of the confraternities during the eighteenth century, the clergy managed to extract promises from members of the confraternity "to obey all spiritual authority"[49] and incorporate them into the statutes. In order to expand this practice, some eighteenth-century bishops (e.g., those of Lutsk, Kholm, and Lviv) printed blank statutes that provided for the dependence of future confraternities on the clergy.[50] In many cases, clergymen eventually succeeded in submitting disputes among members of confraternities to the authority of the episcopal consistories.[51] However, numerous confraternities in the cities and towns of Galicia, Volhynia, the Kholm region, Podlachia, and Podillia managed to defend their independence from the clergy throughout the seventeenth and eighteenth centuries. In 1886, Mykhailo Drahomanov commented positively on this aspect of confraternity activity, noting that it was "not a reaction in favor of Orthodoxy, but the beginning of a kind of reformation."[52] In present-day church historiography, one may encounter critical remarks to the effect that throughout the eighteenth century the confraternities, "in attempting to gain the upper hand over the priests, introduced the Protestant thesis that the faithful should govern themselves."[53]

Certain historians have explained the Reformational tendencies in the ideology of the confraternities as a result of West European and Polish Protestant influence. Panteleimon Kulish wrote that by interfering in the affairs of the bishops, the confraternities were imitating the Protestants and adopting

---

48.   TsDIAL 129/3/67.

49.   Taras Shevchenko Institute of Ukrainian Literature, National Academy of Sciences of Ukraine, Manuscript Division, Ivan Franko Archives/3/4835, f. 80.

50.   LNB, Division of Old Imprints, nos. 54318, 59512 and others.

51.   TsDIAL 201/4b/64, 129/1/775.

52.   *Materiialy dlia kul'turnoï i hromads'koï istoriï Zakhidn'oï Ukraïny*, vol. 1 (Kyiv, 1928), 156.

53.   V. Figol', "Tserkovni bratstva Halyts'koï hreko-katolyts'koï provintsiï XVIII st.," *Bohosloviia* 15 (1938): 247; 16 (1938): 231.

the Protestant way of thinking.[54] Occasionally Catholics, attempting to discredit the Orthodox, would also ascribe Protestant tendencies to them; sometimes such accusations, leveled even at activists very far removed from Protestantism, were taken at face value.[55] But the whole course of Ukraine's development in the sixteenth and seventeenth centuries shows that the Reformational trends gaining currency there cannot be reduced to a simple borrowing of ideas from the West. There is no doubt that some individual members of the confraternities were conversant with the ideology of the Protestants and read their works. Some confraternity members also had personal contacts with Protestants. But the nature of confraternity activities was determined not so much by external influences as by the situation in Ukraine itself. The fact that the ideology of the confraternities shared certain traits with the Western Reformation may be explained by the presence of similar phenomena in the Orthodox Church during the second half of the sixteenth century and in the Catholic Church on the eve of the Reformation, as well as by the all-European character of certain processes of social and cultural development. To summarize, the ideology and practical civic activism of the Stauropegion and confraternities under its influence were characterized by the following:

1. Sharp criticism of clerical abuses, especially those of the higher clergy. It is well known that Jan Hus, Martin Luther, and other founders of the Reformation movements also began by criticizing clerical abuses.
2. The application of the principle of election of the clergy by communities of laymen and the subordination of the clergy to those communities. The confraternities' ideal was expressed in the phrase "it is not the clergy that is directing the people, but the people who are directing the clergy"

---

54. *Chteniia v Obshchestve istorii i drevnostei rossiiskikh* 11 (1888), third pagination, 26, 27.
55. Albrycht Stanisław Radziwiłł believed that even Petro Mohyla was "infected" by heterodoxy, inasmuch as he "kept Calvinist teachers at the Kyiv school, so that heterodoxy penetrated the students' minds together with knowledge." Cf. A. S. Radziwiłł, *Pamiętnik o dziejach w Polsce*, vol. 3 (Warsaw, 1980), 15.

(coined by Kasiian Sakovych, who criticized this state of affairs as contrary to church canons).

3. Facilitating access for the laity to the Bible and theological works translated into a language comprehensible to all, with the concomitant use of the Bible to justify social and political demands.

4. The tendency to minimize the significance of the sacrament of holy orders. Even Ivan Vyshensky, who was an ardent opponent of confraternity activists but agreed with them on this point, declared, "It is not the bishops or the metropolitans who will save you."

5. Calling laymen to meetings that their contemporaries likened to Protestant assemblies. Ipatii Potii threatened members of the confraternities with anathema for their refusal to attend church services and for "holding instead some kind of meetings in their homes in private heretical fashion."[56]

6. The desire to purge the religious cult of certain national or local rites for which there was no justification in Scripture (e.g., blessing the Easter bread).[57]

Naturally, this does not exhaust the range of questions whose resolution would indicate that confraternity members manifested certain Reformational tendencies and elements of a humanistic outlook. Because of fundamental differences in social conditions, these tendencies did not develop to the same degree in Ukraine as in some other European countries, and thus did not lead to the establishment of Protestant churches. The desire not to weaken the traditional church in the face of the expansion of those churches, which were perceived as foreign, also hindered the development of the Reformational movements. In Ukraine, Orthodoxy was not the state religion, which helped

56. *MCS*, 744.
57. The blessing of ritual bread and other foodstuffs as part of Easter celebrations was an old local custom that the Greek hierarchy unsuccessfully tried to suppress (see Gudziak, *Crisis and Reform*, 377). The agreement of reform-minded confraternity activists and patriarchs on this point probably helped establish better relations between them. The same applies to the worship of some types of icons that were not in use in Greek church communities.

prevent the spread of heretical church sects on Ukrainian territory, unlike in Russia. However, the existence of certain forms of Reformational currents in Ukraine cannot be denied. The members of the confraternities themselves called Western Protestants "heretics," permitting the formation of temporary alliances with them only as a tactical maneuver. Nevertheless, it is no accident that contemporaries hostile to the confraternities called their supporters "Luthers," accusing them of "wanting not only the laymen, but also the bishop with all the clergy to submit to their authority."[58] In 1590 adherents of Bishop Hedeon Balaban, noting that supporters of the confraternities regarded the blessing of bread, braided bread, and water as idolatry, declared: "They are beginning in the same way as Martin Luther, who began by criticizing the blessing of water, and later great heresies arose. For even they have launched an attack on other sacraments, saying that confession and communion are not needed, except in cases of severe illness or on the verge of death.... They already look with disfavour upon baptism, declaring that people should be baptized not in childhood, but at thirty years of age.... "[59] Even if such accusations are exaggerated, they reflect to some degree the mood of the most consistent and active representatives of the confraternity movement of the late sixteenth and early seventeenth centuries. All this seems to indicate that the ideology of the confraternities included certain Reformational views, which emerged largely as a result of local conditions, rather than as imitations of the West, although the ideological influence of Western currents of thought should not be excluded entirely.[60] If the extent of these elements of the Reformation was limited, the program of the confraternities was not restricted to them alone. This was just one aspect of the multifarious participation of the confraternities in public and cultural life.

---

58.   Ibid., 202, 167.

59.   TsDIAL 52/3/20: 989.

60.   On Protestantism in Ukraine and Belarus, see G. H. Williams, *Protestants in the Ukrainian Lands of the Polish-Lithuanian Commonwealth* (Cambridge, Mass., 1988) (reprinted from *HUS* 2, nos. 1–2; 3/4, pt. 2); Dmitriev, *Pravoslavie i Reformatsiia*.

The conflict between the leading confraternities and the hierarchy not only became more acute but acquired an entirely new dimension in the mid-1590s, after the metropolitan and most bishops of the Kyiv Metropolitanate decided to establish a church union. Kostiantyn Ostrozky supported the idea of a universal union—the unification on equal terms of the whole Catholic Church and the whole Orthodox Church, headed by the Eastern patriarchs.[61] Later, some confraternities (especially the Vilnius Confraternity) also supported this idea. However, at this time the majority of bishops agreed to a particular union involving the Kyiv Metropolitanate, that is, its subordination to the Roman popes on condition that the Byzantine-Slavonic rite be retained. Such was the genesis of the Ruthenian (Ukrainian-Belarusian) Catholic Church of the Eastern ("Greek") rite. Both Ruthenian churches, the Orthodox Church and, as history later showed, the Greek Catholic Church were moving toward a synthesis of the native heritage, based on the Byzantine-Ruthenian tradition, with developments in contemporary Western Christianity. It was not a question of whether reforms should be accepted, but how far one could proceed along the path of reform without losing one's national and cultural identity. Subsequent developments showed that assimilationist currents in both churches represented the main threat: the Latinizing tendency led to the Polonization of certain circles of the Greek Catholic Church, while the Russifying trend emerged in the Orthodox Church after its forcible subordination to the Moscow Patriarchate. However, both churches appeared strong enough to resist these assimilationist movements. Fortunately, the religious schism did not lead to cultural isolation: on the contrary, the resulting polemics impelled each side to improve and enrich itself by studying the teachings and cultural achievements of its opponent. It must be stressed, however, that all this becomes clear only in retrospect. At the moment the Union was proclaimed, most of the clergy, public figures, and educated laity regarded it as a betrayal of the nation, inasmuch as the initiators of the unionist campaign were Jesuits (notably Benedykt Herbest

---

61.   Chodynicki, *Kościół prawosławny*, 507.

in 1567 and Piotr Skarga in 1577), while the Union itself was planned with the aid of King Sigismund III of Poland.[62] It was hard to foresee that events would not develop according to the plans of Herbest or the king. At this time, it was believed that the bishops' disposition in favor of the Union was determined more by self-interest than by general national considerations. As so often happens in moments of tragic schism, each side refused to perceive any good in the other and sought in every way to exaggerate the genuine and imaginary defects of its opponent. As Ihor Ševčenko has noted, the polemicists did not seek truth: they were sure they possessed it from the very beginning. Their arguments were intended to strengthen the beliefs of their own supporters rather than to convince their adversaries. The true importance of the polemics did not lie in their literary or theological distinction but in their role as an intellectual stimulus in Ukrainian and Belarusian society.[63]

Given prevailing circumstances, it is clear that the local bishops, who, in acceding to the Union, demanded, among other things, that the confraternities be subordinated to the hierarchy, only strengthened the autonomism of the confraternity leaders, who were already sharply at odds with them. For the official proclamation of the Union in October 1596, King Sigismund III and Metropolitan Mykhailo Rohoza of Kyiv convened another synod at Brest. Besides the clergy and noblemen, the synod was attended by eight delegates from the Vilnius Confraternity, three from the Lviv Confraternity, and one representative each from Kyiv, Halych, Volodymyr, Lutsk, Kamianets, Bratslav, Pidhaitsi, Skala, Brest, Pynsk, Minsk, and Slutsk.[64] Earlier, on 26 September, the Lviv Confraternity had entrusted its envoys, Dmytro Krasovsky, the brothers Iurii and Ivan Rohatynets, and Mykhailo Dobriansky, with a document stating that the confraternity was firmly opposed to

---

62.   Ibid., 416–17.

63.   I. Ševčenko, "Religious Polemical Literature in the Ukrainian and Belarusian Lands in the Sixteenth and Seventeenth Centuries," *Journal of Ukrainian Studies* 17, nos. 1–2 (1992): 56.

64.   *Ekthesis abo krotkie zebranie spraw ktore się działy na partykularnym, to iest pomiastnym synodzie w Brześciu Litewskim* (Cracow, 1597), in *Pamiatniki polemicheskoi literatury*, vol. 3 (Kyiv, 1903), 357–58.

the bishops' plans and would never agree to subordinate itself to papal authority. "We lay down our body and soul for the truth," declared the confraternity.[65]

It is well known that there was not one synod at Brest, but two. The majority of bishops voted for union and signed the act of union on 18 October 1596.[66] At the same time, the representatives of the confraternities and some of the clergy and nobility categorically protested the signing, declaring that they did not support the actions of Metropolitan Mykhailo Rohoza and his followers. The Lviv Confraternity became one of the chief opponents of the Union, although after the Brest synod it did not break relations with its former ally, Rohoza.[67] On 19 May 1604 Ipatii Potii, who had become the Uniate metropolitan after Rohoza's death, traveled to Lviv to demand that the burghers recognize his authority. Threatening them with "the sword," he declared in a letter: "It is a dangerous matter to resist God-given authority."[68] The burghers of Lviv "paid no attention to the letter; on the contrary, they ignored it and started some disturbances," arming themselves against Metropolitan Potii's attempt to take over the cathedral.[69] In order to discuss further action, it was decided to call a meeting of all Lviv confraternities and the clergy, to be held in the Dormition Church on 26 May.[70] It was perhaps at this time that a letter was sent to Potii by representatives of the Lviv Orthodox Eparchy (it was preserved in the confraternity archives and obviously written by someone close to confraternity circles). The authors declared that they would not submit to the Greek Catholic metropolitan and noted that Christians had been persecuted during the reign of the Roman emperors Augustus, Tiberius, Nero, Diocletian, and others. Potii's utterances were compared to poison, and his language was deemed murderous. The letter has all the features of polemical

---

65.   TsDIAL 129/1/301.

66.   *AZR*, 4: 103, 258.

67.   Kapral', "Aktovi materialy," 129.

68.   Krylovskii, *L'vovskoe Stavropigial'noe bratstvo*, suppl., 20–22.

69.   Ibid., 22–23.

70.   Russian State Historical Archive, St. Petersburg/823/1/266 (the certified translation from Ruthenian into Polish of the announcement signed by Hedeon Balaban and attached to the door of the Dormition Church in Lviv).

publicistic writing: "Everyone flees from a murderer. Your Grace is inept as a hunter: first you frighten instead of luring; you harm instead of healing...."[71] Writing to the Dominican superior, Potii complained that before becoming a bishop, in letters sent to him he "was raised to the skies, and now that [he had] submitted to the pope, [he had been] cast down ... all the way to hell" and accused of apostasy.[72] Assessing the position of the Orthodox laity, Potii wrote: "Perhaps even the patriarchs would align themselves with the holy union, but their little sheep or, rather, little goats would not permit them to do this, for these schismatic people have in them some kind of innate stubbornness (*innatam pertinentiam*)."[73]

An important episode of interconfessional conflict was the lawsuit brought by the Vilnius Holy Trinity Confraternity against Metropolitan Ipatii Potii in 1605. The confraternity insisted that the Uniate hierarchy had no legal authority over the Orthodox. The Main Tribunal of the Grand Duchy of Lithuania, acting in accordance with opinions prevailing among the nobility, took the side of the confraternity and, notwithstanding the king's categorical objections, insisted that the metropolitan could not try the confreres himself but had to sue them before the patriarch.[74] After the Holy Trinity Confraternity accepted the Union, its main adversary became the Orthodox Holy Spirit Confraternity.[75]

At the end of 1614, the new Greek Catholic metropolitan, Iosyf Veliamyn Rutsky, and the bishop of Volodymyr, Ioakym Morokhovsky (the son of a member of the Lviv Confraternity), made an attempt to enter the St. Onuphrius Monastery, where the printshop of the Lviv Confraternity was located at that time. The adherents of the confraternity raised the alarm, "a

---

71.   *MCS*, 860, 862.

72.   LNB, Teky Zubryts'koho 1, no. 39.

73.   St. Petersburg Branch, Institute of Russian History, Russian Academy of Sciences, Archive, Denys Zubryts'kyi collection/32; Russian State Library, Moscow, Manuscript Division, Collection of the "Obshchestvo istorii i drevnostei rossiiskikh"/274, no. 3, f. 3.

74.   Hrushevs'kyi, *Istoriia Ukraïny-Rusy*, 6: 575. Cf. Ia. Golovatskii [Holovats'kyi], "Sprava Vilenskago tserkovnago bratstva s Grekovichem pered Vilenskim tribunalom," *Chteniia v Obshchestve istorii i drevnostei rossiiskikh*, 1859, no. 3.

75.   *Arkhiv uniatskikh mitrapalitaŭ*(Minsk and Polatsk, 1996), 30–32.

battle occurred," and the attackers were repulsed. For this, "the starosta imprisoned the suburban burghers and summoned the burghers to city hall, declaring that they had done violence to the monastery and wanted to kill Lord Rutsky."[76]

A little later, Metropolitan Rutsky associated the armed attacks on the Greek Catholic clergy with the emergence of the Kyiv Theophany Confraternity. "A great hindrance to the union," he wrote, "is the new confraternity founded in Kyiv three years ago by schismatics without the king's permission. There they conduct meetings and hold their deliberations.... If this confraternity is not abolished, it is hard to expect anything good." In a declaration submitted in February 1618 to the Main Crown Tribunal of Lublin, Rutsky accused the Kyiv burghers of refusing to recognize the metropolitan's authority and charged that the newly established confraternity was at the forefront of the struggle against the Union.[77]

The founding of a confraternity in Lutsk elicited the displeasure of a Lithuanian magnate, Prince Albrycht Stanisław Radziwiłł. When the local castle administrator wanted to prevent the confraternity from building an Orthodox church in Lutsk, even the magistrate supported the confraternity, while the carpenters threatened the administrator's servants with axes.[78]

In a letter to Rome, the Uniate episcopate complained that Orthodox burghers, "under the pretext of charity ... [were] founding confraternities in all the towns, drafting their laws, and appointing officials. First they established a general tax according to everyone's capacities, and then they vote additional taxes at their weekly meetings."[79] Therefore, "although people of an order considerably lower than noblemen belong to the confraternity," they were able to collect large sums of money. The bishops further stressed that the confraternities were organizing protests at the Diets and

---

76.   *AIuZR*, 11: 344, 345.

77.   *Osnova*, 1861, no. 8: 76; Russian State Historical Archive, St. Petersburg/ 823/412, f. 1.

78.   *AIuZR*, 6: 479; *PKK*, 1: 35.

79.   M. Harasiewicz, *Annales Ecclesiae Ruthenae* (Lviv, 1862), 257–58.

taking various measures to unite the efforts of the population of several towns in defense of the traditional faith.

In Podlachia, the Theophany Confraternity of Bilsk was a stronghold of Orthodoxy. After 1645, when it joined the Union, that role was assumed by the St. Nicholas Confraternity attached to the monastery of the same name.[80]

The second half of the seventeenth century saw a change in the balance of power between Right-Bank and western Ukraine. Many representatives of Orthodox noble families migrated to the autonomous Hetmanate on the Left Bank, and those Orthodox nobles who remained in the Polish-Lithuanian Commonwealth gradually lost their previous political importance. In 1676 the Commonwealth Diet banned, on pain of death, any contact on the part of the confraternities and other persons with the Eastern Orthodox patriarchs.[81] Representatives of the Stauropegion sought the abolition of this decree at the Diet, but were unsuccessful.[82] Although their actions were nominally punishable by death, the confraternities sporadically continued to cultivate their links with the East and considered themselves subordinate only to the patriarchs.[83]

In June 1692 one of the officials of the confraternity, Iurii Papara, a burgher of Greek ancestry, met in Lviv with the Russian resident in Poland, B. M. Mikhailov, and informed him that Bishop Iosyf Shumliansky was a secret Uniate, but was afraid to declare this openly because "the confraternity stands firmly."[84] In 1699 Kamianets was returned to the Polish-Lithuanian Commonwealth by the Ottomans, but the Diet did not allow non-Uniates to reside there. The papal

---

80.   A. Mironowicz, "Orthodox Centers and Organizations in Podlachia from the Mid-Sixteenth through the Seventeenth Century," *Journal of Ukrainian Studies* 17, nos. 1–2 (1992); idem, *Podlaskie ośrodki i organizacje prawosławne w XVI i XVII wieku* (Białystok, 1991), 185–99.

81.   *Volumina legum*, vol. 5 (Warsaw, 1738), 362.

82.   *AIuZR*, 12: 168.

83.   Russian National Library, St. Petersburg, Manuscript Division/F. IV 215, f. 669–678.

84.   M. P. Koval's'kyi, "Politychni zv'iazky zakhidnoukraïns'kykh zemel' z Rosiis'koiu derzhavoiu v druhii polovyni XVII st." *Pytannia istoriï SRSR* 6 (1957): 142.

nuncio appealed to the king to allow him found a Greek
Catholic eparchy in Kamianets, which would have deprived
Shumliansky of the churches of Kamianets; accordingly,
in the following year, he openly proclaimed the Union in
his eparchy. The new Greek Catholic bishop immediately
attempted to subordinate the Lviv Confraternity to his
authority. Bishop Shumliansky himself, Crown Grand Hetman
Stanisław Jabłonowski, officials of the town council, and
Roman Catholic priests entered the Dormition Church with
an armed detachment.[85] This aroused indignation not only
among the masses ("plebeians" and "common fellows," as
they are called in contemporary sources), but also among
the clergy under Shumliansky's authority.[86] The bishop even
transferred his episcopal chair to the Dormition Church. On 10
August 1700, the members of the confraternity gathered for a
meeting and, "in order to prevent any further evil," resolved as
follows: "We promise, record, and pledge to act unanimously
and consult with one another in all things, to stand firmly for
one another and defend ourselves until the end of our days."[87]
Shumliansky's actions even worried the Polish government,
which feared that Russia would exploit the episode as a
pretext for intervention. Finally, the king ordered Shumliansky
and Crown Hetman Jabłonowski to return the church to the
confraternity.[88]

In 1702 Samuil Krasuvsky, the confraternity's preacher,
wrote a letter to Syluian Ozirsky, the preacher of the Kyivan
Caves Monastery, affirming his unwavering adherence to
the Orthodox faith.[89] But within a few years the confraternity
saw fit to recognize the Union. The prefect of the "Ukrainian-
Armenian" College of the Theatines in Lviv, the Italian Stefano
Trombetti, who enjoyed the trust of the confraternity members,
played an important role in this event. He believed that their

---

85.   A. Theiner, *Vetera monumenta Poloniae et Lithuaniae*, vol. 4 (Rome,
1864), 9; *Opisanie dokumentov i del, khraniashchikhsia v arkhive Sviateishego
Pravitel'stvuiushchego Sinoda*, vol. 22 (1742) (St. Petersburg, 1914), 825.

86.   *Sbornik letopisei, otnosiashchikhsia k Iuzhnoi i Zapadnoi Rusi*, (Kyiv, 1888), 211–12;
AIuZR, 10: 404, 416.

87.   *IuSLS*, 1: 4.

88.   V. M. Zaikin, *Episkop Iosif Shumlianskii i Stavropigiia* (Lviv, 1935), 13.

89.   *AIuZR*, 12: 603.

condition of non-subordination to the bishops should be met, otherwise "this confraternity, which leads a significant portion of the people and has always been the most steadfast of the opponents of the Union," might return to the authority of the patriarchs of Constantinople.[90] At this time the leaders of the confraternity were hoping that if the Stauropegion were not subordinated to the bishops, then their direct dependence on the pope would be no more onerous than their earlier formal dependence on the patriarchs.[91] On 5 April 1709 Pope Clement XI issued a breve stating that the confraternity was to be placed under his direct jurisdiction and that its independence of the Lviv bishops would be recognized.[92] This was the turning point in the adoption of "the Catholic religion of the Greek rite, united with the Roman" (ritus Graeci Romano uniti) by the Ukrainians of Galicia and the greater part of Right-Bank Ukraine. The conversion of the confraternities in the smaller towns and villages of western Ukraine to the Greek Catholic rite occurred almost imperceptibly once their parish priests came to terms with the bishops' proclamation of the Union.

A small number of Orthodox centers remained here and there in the interior of Belarus and in its regions bordering on Ukraine, as well as in the eastern parts of Right-Bank Ukraine. At the end of the eighteenth century a number of confraternities in the Dnipro valley region (Shpola, Lebedyn), as well as certain confraternities in Polisia (Pynsk, Brest), remained Orthodox. The St. Nicholas Confraternity of Bilsk and the Transfiguration Confraternity of Dorohychyn continued to provide leadership and organization for the Orthodox communities of Podlachia.[93] One of the documents pertaining to contemporary religious conflicts is a complaint issued by a priest against the members of the confraternity in Bishankovichi (Belarus). The priest noted that according to the resolutions of the Synod of Zamostia (1720), confraternity

90.   IuSLS, 1: 15, 17.

91.   O. Kyrychuk, "Perekhid L'vivs'koho Stavropihiiskoho bratstva pid iurysdyktsiiu sv. Apostol's'koho Prestolu (za materiialamy TsDIA Ukraïny u L'vovi)," in Uspens'ke bratstvo, 97–98.

92.   Documenta Pontificum Romanorum historiam Ucrainae illustrantia (1075–1953), vol. 2 (Rome, 1954), no. 628, 9–11.

93.   Papkov, Bratstva, 215–16.

meetings were to be chaired by him. For the last twenty-eight years, however, the confreres had not given him a single report; they looked with disfavor on the Union, "teach their schismatic children to read and sing in the church ... but do not allow Uniate children the same," and so on.[94]

As mentioned earlier, in the eighteenth century there were also confraternities in some Orthodox parishes of Left-Bank Ukraine. At that time, both the Orthodox confraternities and those established by Greek Catholic bishops restricted their activities to their own parishes. In general, though, the Greek Catholic confraternities strengthened the tendency that stood for the preservation of their Byzantine cultural heritage and traditional rites. Even in the eighteenth century, the urban confraternities were able to enforce the principle whereby the laity elected the clergy. Moreover, throughout the eighteenth century the statutes of most confraternities relied on the authority of the Eastern patriarchs, with no mention of the pope.[95] This was a manifestation not so much of a conscious confessional orientation as of traditionalism bordering on inertia.

The Lviv Stauropegion, which was also known for its intense conservatism, found itself facing a singular dilemma. Contrary to the promises and obligations recorded in the papal breve, the nuncios immediately began to interfere in confraternity affairs. In 1712 the papal nuncio Benedetto Odescalchi accused the confraternity of engaging a "schismatic" monk to perform divine services at the church.[96] In response to the nuncio's continuing attempts to interfere with the confraternity, that year one of its elders, Stefan Liaskovsky, declared conclusively that elders must report on financial affairs at their meetings, and not to the nuncio.[97] Contrary to the demands of the nunciature, in 1710 and 1716 elections of bishops were held by the nobility, clergy, and representatives of the confraternity. In 1720, however, a synod

---

94.   St. Petersburg Branch, Institute of Russian History, Russian Academy of Sciences, Archive, Collection 13/301, III–16, f. 2–3.

95.   Taras Shevchenko Institute of Ukrainian Literature, National Academy of Sciences of Ukraine, Manuscript Division, Ivan Franko Archives/3/4833, f. 2; 3/4835, f. 33; 3/4830, f. 5.

96.   Kyrychuk, "Perekhid," 98.

97.   *IuSLS*, 1: 25, 28; *AIuZR*, 12: 623–26.

was held in Zamostia to bring about a significant convergence between the structure and rituals of the Greek Catholic Church and Roman Catholic churches. This could not but complicate the position of the confraternities, especially the Lviv Confraternity, inasmuch as they defended the preservation of the traditional Byzantine-Slavonic rite.

Contrary to all hopes and promises, discrimination against Ukrainians did not cease after the acceptance of the Union. Moreover, the members of the Lviv Confraternity wrote that in the first half of the eighteenth century the "Ruthenian nation" in Lviv was being oppressed more than in the past.[98] Exploiting feuds within the confraternity, in November 1723 the nuncio appointed a committee to examine the "abuses perpetrated by the confraternity." In 1725 its members familiarized themselves with the Stauropegion statute, concluding that the patriarchs' privileges were contrary to the principles of canon law and should be abolished, while the papal breve of 1709 was to be annulled.[99] In the committee's opinion, it was the confraternity's duty to submit completely to the bishop. That year the nuncio accused the confraternity of printing books that largely contradicted the dogmas of the Catholic faith and of admitting "schismatics or those suspected of schism" as members.[100] The bishop closed and sealed the printshop and its inventory of books. Although the decree issued by the Congregation for the Propagation of the Faith in Rome on 9 September 1727 recognized the confraternity as independent of the bishop, it nevertheless subjected confraternity activities to the control of commissioners appointed by the nuncio.[101] The commissioners were generally Italians who served as prefects of the Lviv "Ukrainian-Armenian" College of the Theatines: Giuseppe Maria Redanaschi (1723–35), Giacomo Costa (1735–38), Giorgio Lascaris (1738–41), Girolamo Moro (1741–60), and Ignazio Rosetti (1760–84). The confraternity regarded this

---

98.   TsDIAL 129/1/1169: 7.

99.   *IuSLS*, 1: 112.

100.   Ibid., 118.

101.   *Congregationes particulares Ecclesiam Catholicam Ucrainae et Bielarusjae spectantes*, ed. A. G. Welykyj, vol. 1 (Rome, 1956), 243.

decision as the lesser evil, for the bishop was forced to remove the sequester from the printshop. In actual fact, however, the former rights of the confraternity were forfeited, and the prefect Giacomo Costa conducted an especially unfavorable policy toward it. He declared that its members "reek[ed] of schism,"[102] forbade the confraternity to admit new members, and sought to expel existing members. From 1733 to 1741, the confraternity attempted to establish the post of archimandrite to chair meetings, verify confraternity accounts, and supervise the free elections of elders and the admittance of new members. In this manner, the Stauropegion Confraternity hoped to reduce the control of the church authorities, but it was not successful.[103] Throughout the eighteenth century, members of the confraternity were frequently accused of publishing "heretical schismatic books" and supporting "schismatic" students educated at the Kyiv Academy. The confraternity also protested the efforts of the superiors of the Basilian Order to subordinate the St. Onuphrius Monastery to their authority.[104] Its members even persuaded the dietine of the palatinate of Ruthenia to raise a demand at the Diet that Rome issue no new directives contrary to the ancient statutes of the Stauropegion Confraternity.[105] In a memorandum submitted to the Austrian government of Galicia in 1780, the Greek Catholic bishop-elect wrote that the confraternity had consistently opposed the Union, taking advantage of its independence of episcopal authority. Even in the mid-eighteenth century, the confraternity did not fulfill the directives of the Roman Congregation for the Propagation of the Faith and barred three priests from entering the church for fifteen months. The bishop further quoted a statement of the Greek Catholic metropolitan Kypriian Zhokhovsky (1674–93) to the effect that the confraternities wished to manage church property "without clerical supervision." The bishop indicated that only three members of the Stauropegion had fulfilled the injunction concerning the declaration of fidelity to the Catholic

---

102.   *IuSLS*, 1: 186–87.
103.   Ibid., 184, 195; Zubritskii, "Lětopis'," 148.
104.   TsDIAL 129/1/1169: 24.
105.   *AGZ*, 23: 403.

faith; the majority had refused to do so.[106] It is difficult to determine the validity of frequent accusations that members of the confraternity were crypto-Orthodox. We know that some Roman Catholics often regarded as "Orthodox" those who simply maintained their loyalty to the Byzantine rite. There is no doubt that the preservation of this rite by both Ukrainian churches encouraged the development of inter-cultural relations in the Ukrainian lands. In principle, the confraternities' fidelity to the rite and other national traditions, as well as their openness to forging contacts between East and West, conformed to the general development of Ukrainian religiosity.

Apart from their involvement in conflicts in the religious sphere, the confraternities waged campaigns to attain political equality for Ukrainians, irrespective of their religious affiliation. Given their social composition, the confraternities mainly initiated legal actions against economic and political restrictions on Ukrainian merchants and craftsmen; they also demanded the right of Ukrainian burghers to be represented on town councils and belong to guilds. Representatives of the Lviv Confraternity frequently submitted protests to the town council and the castle office. Although these actions could not force the municipal authorities to suspend their discriminatory policy against the Ukrainian burghers, the many "protestations" in the castle and municipal courts had a certain effect and helped consolidate all those who opposed restrictions on the political and economic rights of non-Catholics. In February 1595 Luka Kravets, Iurii Rohatynets, and Matvii Babych were accused of "reviving and inciting revolt and schism among people of the Greek religion" by registering protests in the name of the confraternity in court records.[107] In the course of their trial, the municipal council imprisoned the following confraternity activists: Dmytro Krasovsky and Luka Huba in 1593; Ivan Krasovsky, Luka Huba, and P. Maletsky at the beginning of 1595; Luka Huba, I. Zinkovych, Matvii Babych, and A. Bidlaha in February 1595.[108] Despite these repressions, the members of the confraternity

---

106. TsDIAL 201/4b/292, f. 13–14.
107. *MCS*, 578.
108. TsDIAL/9, vol. 349: 325; *MCS*, 569.

continued to demand the right of Ukrainian burghers to participate in the municipal administration and guilds, as well as freedom of activity for the school and printshop. They gave bribes and "gifts" to officials of various ranks, from petty clerks to the influential Crown chancellor and the king himself; occasionally they managed to obtain royal privileges and mandates that forbade the town council from excluding the Orthodox and, later, Uniates from the guilds and restricting their trade, and so on. But the town council and guild leaders had no intention of following such directives, while the state authorities did nothing to enforce them. Thus, their expectations that money would allow them to "purchase freedom" were not very realistic. But measures pertaining to the collection of funds for envoys, the discussion of their instructions, and meetings of confraternity envoys at the Diet with other representatives of the anti-Catholic camp all helped mobilize Ukrainian burghers for the defense of their civic and religious rights and gave them experience in public affairs.

In the closing years of the sixteenth century and at the very beginning of the seventeenth, social and political conflict became more acute. The refusal of the Ukrainians of Lviv to accept the Union became a pretext for new attempts to exclude all of them from the guilds and deprive them of the last remnants of their civil rights. Later they would write: "The Polish community[109] launched a lawsuit ... against the Ruthenian community in the year 1597, desiring to forbid us to engage in our trades."[110] In response to this, the suburban confraternities rallied around the Stauropegion. On 27 August 1599, representatives of the suburban confraternities came to a meeting of the Stauropegion Confraternity, "desiring ... to be admitted unanimously with one will into the confraternity in order to participate in the [legal] proceedings that are being conducted around the question of the freedoms of the entire Ruthenian nation in connection with the Polish community's prohibition on the Ukrainian community's access to offices,

---

109.   That is, the Roman Catholic elite that claimed to speak on behalf of the entire Polish population.
110.   *AIuZR*, 11: 40.

guilds, and trades of all kinds." At the same time, those present pledged "unanimously, faithfully, and indivisibly to stand together until the end of the trial, begrudging neither property, time, nor themselves." It was decided to consider everyone opposed to the "initiated undertaking" a traitor and "not to dine with such people—neither eat nor drink."[111] Within two days, representatives were dispatched to Warsaw: the burgher Semen Lutsky and the painter Lavrin Fylypovych, a resident of the suburb. That year a few more representatives were sent to the royal court and to the Diet. In the following year (1600), confraternity delegations set out for Warsaw on three occasions, with part of the necessary funds lent by the villagers of Holovsko.[112] During the years 1601–7, 1611–17 and later, burghers and residents of the suburbs dispatched representatives to the Diet and the royal court. Ivan Krasovsky and Iurii Rohatynets took part in these "missions," but most often the representatives were Senko Lutsky, the blacksmith Senko Krasovsky (dispatched by the St. Nicholas Confraternity and all the residents of the suburbs), Mykola Dobriansky and, later, Stefan Khomych, Roman Striletsky, and others.[113] Given the decentralization of the Polish political system, provincial dietines of noblemen (*sejmiki*) were often of decisive importance. The confraternities also sent their representatives to these dietines: to the general dietine of noblemen of the palatinate of Ruthenia in the town of Sudova Vyshnia, to the local assembly in Halych (the noblemen of the Halych Land), and to Lutsk (the dietine of the palatinate of Volhynia).[114] The matter was constantly deferred by the Diet courts to a later date.[115] The author of *Navity*, a Ukrainian anti-Catholic pamphlet of the seventeenth century, correctly noted that although the nobiliary tribunals "could resolve the matter in one hour … they postpone them for several decades, which is leading to the decline and destruction of our churches.… "[116]

---

111.   Ibid., 3–4.

112.   Ibid., 24–25.

113.   Ibid., 4, 7, 15, 20, 36, 38, 41–52, 85.

114.   Ibid., 11, 35, 45, 380.

115.   Ibid., 52; TsDIAL 129/1/445: 466.

116.   "'Navity'—nevidoma pam'iatka ukraïns'koï publitsystyky XVII st.," *Naukovo-informatsiinyi Biuleten' Arkhivnoho upravlinnia URSR*, 1964, no. 6: 62.

The confraternities' envoys carried out their duties conscientiously. Traveling to Warsaw in 1600, Ivan Krasovsky "proposed, out of the goodness of his heart, to travel on his own horse, with his own food supplies."[117] Often community representatives would risk grave dangers: in 1607, for example, the envoy Kapustka was thrown into prison.[118] Unfortunately, few details are available about the appearances of confraternity members at the Diet courts and the royal courts. The *Perestoroha* (Warning) contains a speech allegedly made by a representative of the Lviv Confraternity at the Diet of 1598 in which he condemns the actions of the bishops who adopted the Union.[119] Scholars have concluded that such a speech could not have been made at that particular Diet. Clearly, the author of the *Perestoroha* attributed the speech to a confraternity representative on the strength of his familiarity with the declarations of confraternity envoys at the courts of the Warsaw Diet. The nature of these speeches may be deduced from the instructions of the confraternities to their envoys signed on 2 February 1609 by the elders Ivan Krasovsky and Andrii Bidlaha.[120] The envoys were instructed to demand that the king grant Ukrainians the opportunity to obtain full burghers' rights and the right to join guilds on the recommendation of their elders; they were also to demand "separate jurisdiction" for the Ukrainians of Lviv, with the right of self-government and a court, as in Kamianets. If it proved impossible to attain this, they were instructed to demand at least the same rights for the Ukrainians as those enjoyed by the Armenian and Jewish communities and traders, particularly the right to a "Ruthenian court" and "two guilds for the management of craftsmen."[121] The instructions concluded with these sarcastic words: "And if, God forbid, they do not agree to bestow on us the same freedom that the Jews have,

---

117.   *AIuZR*, 11: 20.

118.   Ibid., 47, 45.

119.   M. Vozniak, *Pys'mennyts'ka diial'nist' Ivana Borets'koho na Volyni i u L'vovi* (Lviv, 1954), 17, 42.

120.   TsDIAL 129/1/421; text in Krylovskii, *L'vovskoe Stavropigial'noe bratstvo*, suppl., 32–35; for a description of the document, see M. Khudash, *Leksyka ukraïns'kykh dilovykh dokumentiv kintsia XVI–pochatku XVII st.* (Kyiv, 1961), 12.

121.   *AIuZR*, 11: 189.

then there is nothing to be done but request a protective edict allowing us to leave for Moldavia. This is a joke, but a bitter one." The final declaration is highly significant. It indicates that the representatives of the confraternity did not expect a favorable resolution of the matter by the court and wanted to emphasize that in Moldavia, under the rule of a "pagan" sultan, the Orthodox allegedly were less oppressed than in a Christian state ruled by a Polish king. A similar opinion was expressed more openly in an appeal published in 1608 and, in almost the same words, in the draft of a pronouncement that plenipotentiaries of the Lviv Confraternity planned to deliver before the Polish king. The text of the letter added to the "Instruction" of 2 February 1609 was entitled "Lamentation or Pronouncement before His Majesty the King." This document stressed that Ukrainians had been living in Lviv from time immemorial, since its founding, which made their inequality all the more painful. "We, the Ruthenian nation, are oppressed by the Polish nation by a yoke heavier than Egyptian slavery. They destroy us and our descendants without a sword, but with something even worse than the sword, having denied us profits, handicrafts, and various commerce. Ruthenians in their native land, in this Ruthenian Lviv are not free to do anything whereby a man might sustain himself."[122] The speech is written in vivid, eloquent language. The author of the "Lamentation" and of the "Appeal" of 1608 may have been Ivan Krasovsky.

The "Instruction" cited documents dating from the years 1484–1510 about Ukrainian tailors being guild elders. Backed by historical data and citing the act of the Union of Lublin (1569), which guaranteed the Orthodox equal rights with the Catholics, the confraternity headed a movement of Ukrainian craftsmen against the discriminatory actions of guild elders. As mentioned earlier, from the end of the sixteenth century the protests of the confraternities in the municipal courts and at the Diet were closely associated with the craftsmen's movement against the guild leadership. On 20 March 1599 the tailors Lukash Kravets, Fedir Postava, and Mykola Dobriansky (a dedicated participant in confraternity activities) drew up a protest against the tailors'

122.   Krylovskii, *L'vovskoe Stavropigial'noe bratstvo*, suppl., 30; *PBSh*, 34–36.

guild. They claimed that "the Armenians and Jews of Lviv do not have such relations with the Poles as does our Ruthenian nation, yet they are enjoying their rights." They also asserted that Catholics, "having come to us Ruthenians, do not wish to live with us Ruthenians in Ruthenia according to the ancient rights, statutes, customs, and mores ... their courts deprive us of our rights, or, more exactly, tear them away from us." Within a short time the tailors submitted a complaint against the mayor, Przeździecki, who had unjustly imprisoned them. Later, notably in 1604, the tailors (including Luka Bortnykovych) complained that they and their Ukrainian apprentices were not being admitted to the guild on the grounds that they, as Orthodox, had been "anathematized by the Catholic Church." The confraternity also gave the tailors material assistance, making donations "for their lawsuit."[123]

In 1599 the tanners also declared that the guild leadership had refused to admit Ukrainian apprentices or bestow the rights of masters on those apprentices who worked for Ukrainians.[124] Ukrainian craftsmen, by no means newcomers to their native land, were indignant about being deprived of their ancient rights, noting that "even under pagan rule, a Christian nation does not experience such deprivation of freedom as is forced on us by the gentlemen councillors of Lviv under pious Christian rule.... "[125] Similar sharply worded protests were repeated for a number of years, with all non-guild craftsmen protesting against the ruling circles of the guilds together with guild members who were being excluded from their trade corporations.[126] In 1604, Orthodox furriers initiated a lawsuit against their forcible expulsion from the guild (a copy of one of these protestations has been preserved in the archives of the confraternity).[127]

Most Ukrainian craftsmen lived in the Cracow suburb on territory subject to the royal starosta rather than the city

---

123. TsDIAL 9/1, vol. 353: 1815, 2142–43; vol. 359: 744.

124. Ibid. 9/1, vol. 353: 2187–91.

125. Ibid., 353: 2268–70, 2333, 354: 2700.

126. I. Kryp'iakevych, "Borot'ba netsekhovykh remisnykiv proty tsekhiv u L'vovi," Z istoriï zakhidnoukraïns'kykh zemel' (Kyiv), no. 1 (1957).

127. TsDIAL 9, vol. 359: 777; Krylovskii, L'vovskoe Stavropigial'noe bratstvo, suppl., 24.

council. Although the starostas were keen on attracting as many craftsmen as possible to their neighborhoods, they, too, had a hand in the processes that led to the inequality of non-Catholic craftsmen, although they did not discriminate as systematically as the city council. In 1619 the blacksmith Senko Krasovsky, a participant in several confraternity missions, and other residents of the suburbs registered a complaint in the municipal records against the well-known magnate and starosta Stanisław Mniszek. Although legal proceedings against "the guild masters of the Polish nation" had been continuing for many years with no decision from the crown, according to the complaint, the starosta had ordered that Ukrainians in the Cracow suburb be barred not only from practicing their trades, but also from selling their various wares. In fulfilling these orders, the municipal guilds, "with the help of the starosta administration, are driving them out of the workshops, confiscating all sorts of wares, and beating them."[128] Despite these adverse conditions, some craftsmen demonstrated great steadfastness in the struggle for their rights. In 1620, Ukrainian cobblers opened forty booths outside the Cracow Gate and established a separate Ukrainian guild in the suburbs.[129] In 1635, the Catholic guild found it necessary to sign an agreement of union with the Ukrainian guild, with equal rights for both national groups; there was also to be an equal number of new members.[130] Later, the rights of Ukrainian cobblers continued to be violated,[131] but they had better opportunities for self-defense. Craftsmen of other specializations also defended their right to engage in their crafts, but the constant conflicts and legal actions adversely affected their economic status.

In the second half of the seventeenth century, the Lviv Stauropegion Confraternity also found it necessary to dispatch its representatives to the dietines in order to protest

---

128. TsDIAL 9/1, vol. 372: 1232.

129. Ibid., 374: 637, 372: 632.

130. Ia. F. Golovatskii [Holovats'kyi], "Akty otnosiashchiesia k istorii Iuzhnozapadnoi Rusi," *Literaturnyi sbornik Galitsko-russkoi Matitsy* (Lviv, 1870), 102.

131. *AGZ*, 1: 71 (Ukrainian cobblers' complaint of 1679).

discrimination against the non-Catholic population. In the late sixteenth century and throughout the seventeenth, the confraternity repudiated the ban forbidding Ukrainian burghers from owning houses outside the perimeter of Ruthenian Street and neighboring back streets. Individual Orthodox burghers "illegally" purchased masonry houses on other streets[132] and tried to avoid selling houses to people of other faiths; they were assisted in this by the confraternity.[133]

The Lviv city council remained completely in the hands of a small number of patrician families, although the "common people" (*pospil'stvo*, the *communitas*) struggled insistently for the right to participate in the municipal administration. In 1579, the city council established a representation of the *communitas* called the *quadragintaviratus*, i.e., a board of forty men. The first *quadragintaviratus* included Lesko Maletsky and Khoma Babych.[134] Later, throughout the seventeenth century, at its election meetings the confraternity would choose two representatives of the Ukrainian community to the *quadragintaviratus*—"delegates to city hall." In 1633, the senior confraternity officials Hryhorii Romanovych and Mykola Dobriansky were among the members of the *quadragintaviratus*; later, rank-and-file members of the confraternity were assigned to this body.[135] At the elections of 1686, it was decided that Kypriian Kyselnytsky and Petro Kurtevych "must go to city hall, and when a motion harmful to the nation is pending there, they should report on this at the meetings of the confraternity."[136] At the beginning of the seventeenth century an organization of "estates and nations" was formed in Lviv.[137] Most probably, the representatives of the Ukrainian burghers in this organization were also members of the *quadragintaviratus*. In their conflict with the council, the

132.   Sribnyi, "Studiï," *ZNTSh* 111 (1912): 11, 19–20; TsDIAL 201/4b/83, f. 32, 24–27; 52/3, vol. 77: 1073.

133.   Ibid., 18–19; TsDIAL 52/3, 20: 630; *AIuZR*, 11: 59.

134.   D. Zubrzycki [Zubryts'kyi], *Kronika miasta Lwowa* (Lviv, 1844), 204.

135.   *AIuZR*, 11: 89, 123, 147–48, 161; TsDIAL 129/1/1169, f. 68.

136.   *AIuZR*, 12: 171.

137.   J. Ptaśnik, "Walki o demokratyzację Lwowa od XVI do XVIII w.," in *Księga pamiątkowa ku czci prof. Oswalda Balzera*, vol. 2 (Lviv, 1925), 249.

confraternity as a whole supported the representatives of the "common people," particularly in the years 1576–77 and 1603–7.[138] Owing, however, to the influence of the dominant religion, the *quadragintaviratus*, together with the city council, repudiated the demands of the Ukrainian citizens. In 1643, with the support of the *quadragintaviratus*, the city council apportioned taxes without the participation of representatives of the Ukrainian community. The council members "taxed none of their number, but imposed an intolerably high sum on our Ruthenian nation, including obviously impoverished people, widows, and orphans ... and ordered them to pay the tax on pain of a double fine."[139] In 1669 the *quadragintaviratus* upbraided Ukrainians who, "although they had their assigned perimeters and enjoyed the use of one street," were purchasing buildings in the market and on other streets.[140]

The promises of the state authorities and the Roman Catholic clergy that ethnic persecution would cease after the acceptance of the Union were not fulfilled. Ukrainian burghers continued to be induced to convert to the Roman Catholic faith and were frequently barred from joining the town councils and guilds.[141] Thus, in 1743, the urban confraternity in Sambir protested the violation of the rights of the Ukrainian Uniate burghers. As in the past, religious inequality was particularly apparent in Lviv. In 1712 the members of the Dormition Confraternity and members of the suburban confraternities of St. Nicholas, St. John the Theologian, St. Paraskeva, the Theophany, the Resurrection, St. Theodore, and the Elevation of the Holy Cross assembled for a joint meeting. It was decided to initiate a joint lawsuit to obtain representation on city council. Two members of the Stauropegion were elected delegates to the Warsaw courts—the "seniors of the nation" Stefan Liaskovsky and Semen Hrebenka—while Demian Kostevych was elected from among the members of the suburban confraternities. In order to sustain the funding of

138.   Ibid.

139.   St. Petersburg Branch, Institute of Russian History, Russian Academy of Sciences, Archive, Denys Zubryts'kyi collection/32.

140.   TsDIAL 52/3, vol. 77: 1063–66.

141.   Dobrianskii, *Istoriia episkopov*, period III, 37; Harasiewicz, *Annales*, 559.

legal proceedings against the city council, which lasted from 1713 to 1722, fund-raising was conducted six times, and nearly 21,700 zlotys were spent on court costs.[142]

In 1740, the Stauropegion Confraternity once again sent its representatives, this time Iakiv Rusianovych and Iurii Kotsii, to Warsaw. The letter entrusted to them stressed that the Ukrainian burghers often paid more taxes than the Catholics, even though the Ukrainian burghers, who considered themselves the original residents of the city, were excluded from city council and their trade was restricted.[143] The legal proceedings renewed by the confraternity lasted a few more years. The city council published a brochure entitled *Status causae* that accused the Ukrainian population of Lviv of having sympathized with Khmelnytsky's army during the Ukrainian-Polish war of the mid-seventeenth century. Its authors sought to demonstrate the "perniciousness" of granting the Ukrainian burghers political equality. The confraternity replied with a brochure of its own.[144] This polemic did not play a decisive role in the matter; rather, it was the payment of bribes that helped sway the royal chancellor and the bishop of Cracow to the confraternity's side. With their assistance, representatives of the Ukrainian burghers obtained a decree in 1745 giving them access to the municipal administration. By a royal mandate of 28 September 1746, they were guaranteed half the seats on city council. Iurii Kotsii became a member of council; Iakiv Rusianovych and Mykhailo Horoshko joined the judicial board (*lava*), while Mykhailo Liaskovsky and seven other representatives of the Ukrainian burghers became members of the *quadragintaviratus*.[145] The Ukrainian burghers were then to send their representatives to city council to replace Catholic members whose terms of office were ending, so as to obtain an equal number of seats with the Roman Catholics. In 1749, however, the Roman Catholic members of city council held

---

142.   *IuSLS*, 1: 26–27, 59, 62, 77, 98.

143.   TsDIAL 129/2/8: 29–31.

144.   Ptaśnik, "Walki o demokratyzację," 252; St. Petersburg Branch, Institute of Russian History, Russian Academy of Sciences, Archive, Denys Zubryts'kyi Collection/44; *IuSLS*, vol. 1, 196–98.

145.   Ibid.; TsDIAL 129/1/1169: 91.

separate elections, inasmuch as they considered the Ukrainian members "representatives of a nation" rather than officers with equal rights. They devised a plan to conduct the next election behind closed doors in order to prevent the election of Ukrainian burghers. The members of the *quadragintaviratus* were undermined and intimidated, which resulted in further violations of the rights of Ukrainian burghers.[146] It was only in 1755 that the confraternity managed to obtain a mandate whereby half the envoys of the city of Lviv to the Diet and the provincial dietines were to be Ukrainians.[147] During the second half of the eighteenth century, quite a few Ukrainian confraternity members were members of city council. Vasyl Iliashevych was a councillor and later a magistrate, and Mykhailo Horbachevsky was a city attorney.[148] However, given the impoverishment of the Ukrainian burghers, they never attained parity with the Poles.

The protests of the Lviv Confraternity against discrimination by the Roman Catholic patriciate, which were entered in municipal and castle records in the late sixteenth century and throughout the seventeenth and eighteenth centuries, found an echo in other towns as well. Castle records were a partial substitute for the press, and their contents were often intended to influence public opinion. The confraternity was also engaged in direct agitation, especially in western Ukrainian towns. It sent envoys to raise funds and acquainted the people with its activities. Special appeals were written exhorting people to support litigation for religious rights. One such appeal was written from the Lviv prison on 13 March 1593 by members of the Lviv Dormition Confraternity. The letter recounts the latest wave of persecutions, whose aim was to "subordinate the city of Lviv ... people, guilds, and craftsmen to papal authority." It mentions that in the previous year Ivan Krasovsky, Luka Huba, and Prokip Popovych had been imprisoned for six days; Luka Huba, Ivan Zinkovych, Matvii Babych, Andrii Bidlaha, and Luka Bortnykovych were imprisoned at the time the letter was written. The confraternity sent the prisoners'

---

146.   *IuSLS*, 1: 232, 233.
147.   Ptaśnik, "Walki o demokratyzację," 255.
148.   *AIuZR*, 12: 480–487; *IuSLS*, 1: 238.

letter to neighboring towns[149] in order to enlist the aid of other
confraternities in the struggle for the defense of their rights. An
entry in the confraternity's expense accounts concerning the
payment of a fee to a "junior scribe, who had written letters to
cities, towns, and the nobility,"[150] attests to the forwarding of
similar proclamations to various localities.

In sending its representatives to the Diets, the Lviv
Confraternity also took measures to ensure that representatives
from all parts of Ukraine and Belarus would appear there.
In November 1599, Iurii Rohatynets wrote a letter to Stefan
Zyzanii stating that a Diet session was to convene in February,
and "representatives from both the nobility and the burghers
of every district should be present to make our grievances
public." "For that purpose it is necessary," continued one of
the leaders of the Stauropegion, "to collect funds promptly
in the towns and elect representatives. Make haste, one and
all!"[151] Of particular importance was an appeal published in
1608.[152] It stresses the lack of true justice ("we are oppressed
… by the yoke of the unspeakable woes of Egyptian slavery")
and expounds the program of the confraternity's cultural and
educational activities, focusing on the need to maintain the
school and printshop.

A wealth of sources makes it possible to elaborate on the
public activities of the Lviv Dormition Confraternity, but other
confraternities also played an important role in the development
of the national movement in the late sixteenth and seventeenth
centuries. Thus, as early as 1590, the confraternity in the town of
Horodok decided to adopt the statute of the Lviv Confraternity
and manage the town hospital. In time, as discussed earlier, it
waged an energetic action against the abuses of the Peremyshl
bishop and his appointed priest. In 1611, the Catholic patricians
(members of the town council and guild masters) of Horodok

---

149.   *AIuZR*, 10: 89–92.

150.   Ibid., 11: 48.

151.   *MCS*, 832.

152.   *AIuZR*, 12: 526–29. The proclamation was wrongly dated by Denys
Zubrytsky (*PKK*, 3: 53) and by Anton Petrushevych (A. S. Petrushevych, *Svodnaia
Halychsko-russkaia lětopys' s 1600 po 1700 h.*, vol. 1 [Lviv, 1874], 8–10; *Dopolneniia k
Svodnoi Halychsko-russkoi letopysy s 1660 po 1700 h.* [Lviv, 1891], 56).

accused the leaders of the confraternity—Mykhailo Kurylovych, Hryts Maliar, Hryts Kunashchyk, Pavlo Zakharchych, and Ivan Kravetsky—"and the whole confraternity and community professing the Ruthenian religion" of attempting to gain seats on the town council by holding "secret councils and revolts," as well as meetings, at first secretly, at night, and then openly. As stated in the declaration registered in the municipal records, "the whole community supported the rebels, except for one Stetsko Hlibovych, who remained loyal to the municipal council."[153]

The confraternity in Krasnostav, one of the oldest in Ukraine, adopted the Lviv statute and actively disseminated it. In 1620 this confraternity sent its representatives to the Stauropegion with a letter describing the abuses ("misfortunes and persecutions and griefs and imprisonment") perpetrated by Atanasii Pakosta, the Greek Catholic bishop of Kholm. Lukash Pelchynsky, a senior brother, and Mykola Marymukha requested aid from their Lviv confreres on behalf of the entire Trinity Confraternity.[154]

Ukrainians waged a prolonged struggle for their rights in the town of Liubachiv (Lubaczów). In 1621 the town council and community complained about the Roman Catholic priest, Marian Dobrostański, who had led an attack on the church and seized its property.[155] In the years 1640–46 the Lubaczów burghers continued their protests against those who had organized the attack on their church and (with the help of two noblemen, Jan Bębnowski, the administrator of the county head office, and Stefan Rykaczowski, the deputy county chief) appointed Greek Catholic priests for it.[156] In connection with these protests, in February 1646 the Lviv Confraternity decided "to give the Lubaczów Confraternity 20 zlotys in support of their church affairs." At the same time, 80 zlotys were donated to the Sokal Confraternity.[157]

In 1641, the burghers and priests of Sniatyn sent a letter by courier to Lviv describing "the occurrence of an unendurable

153. TsDIAL 9, 365: 2404, 2459.
154. TsDIAL 129/1/479.
155. TsDIAL 1 (Belz city records), 206: 292–93.
156. Ibid., 226: 485–86, 230: 295–96, 233: 104–9.
157. AIuZR, 11: 160.

and sad event for a poor town." Three Roman Catholic priests sent from Lviv had ordered the Orthodox church to be closed and had forbidden all baptisms and funerals. "Therefore, we, who have never been under the authority of their pastor (and we have no reliable information from our own bishop), are overwhelmed by great sorrow and appeal to you, our gracious friends, to help us with your kindness and Christian love and inform us by letter whether we and our churches should tolerate this.... "[158]

The Trinity Confraternity of Peremyshl also tried to organize a united effort of neighboring confraternities. Thus, in 1627, it sent a letter to confraternities in other towns with a request for material assistance in order to launch legal proceedings in the Diet. A letter was sent from Peremyshl to the Drohobych Confraternity, which sent money to Peremyshl and then passed the letter on to the Stryi Confraternity, and so on.[159] Documents dating from 1633, 1669, and 1680 attest that the Peremyshl burghers, particularly the Trinity Confraternity, continued efforts to secure the right of non-Catholics to participate without restriction in the town council, guilds, and trade.[160] Throughout the second half of the seventeenth century, the burghers and confraternities of Stryi, Drohobych, Sianik, Sambir, Staryi Sambir, and Stara Sil also engaged in protest actions against the Greek Catholic bishop of Peremyshl, Atanasii Krupetsky, and refused to recognize priests appointed by him. The urban Confraternity of St. Nicholas played a great role in the preservation of the traditional faith in Zamostia.[161]

The question of ties between the confraternities and the Cossacks deserves particular attention. In all probability, the educational work of Kyiv as a cultural center, initiated to a significant degree by activists of the confraternity movement, influenced the formulation of the Zaporozhian Cossacks' political program.

---

158.   TsDIAL 129/1/553, f. 2.

159.   Golubev, *Kievskii mitropolit Petr Mogila*, 1, suppl.: 295.

160.   TsDIAL 13 (Peremyshl castle records): 431, 367–69, 372–76.

161.   Ibid., 328: 994–1001, 1421, 1424; A. Prochaska, *Historia miasta Stryja* (Lviv, 1926), 99; Budilovich, *Russkaia pravoslavnaia starina*, 153.

The establishment of direct links between the confraternities and the Cossack Host may be attributed to the activity of Iov (Ivan) Boretsky and Hetman Petro Konashevych Sahaidachny. As a leader of the confraternity movement, Boretsky cooperated closely with the officers of the Zaporozhian Host, primarily with Sahaidachny. The support of the Zaporozhians ensured favorable conditions for the activities of the Kyiv Confraternity and its school.

After the hetman's death, Kasiian Sakovych, the rector of the Kyiv Confraternity School from 1620 to 1624, recounted that Sahaidachny had provided much material assistance to the Kyiv Confraternity and had become one of its members, together with the whole Zaporozhian Host. Petro Konashevych Sahaidachny, wrote Sakovych, was buried near the Kyiv Confraternity Church," ... which he joined with the whole Host and on which he expended great sums of money."[162]

The fact that the Cossacks had signed the Kyiv Confraternity's register was also mentioned in a memorandum to Rome from Uniate bishops who were seriously disturbed by cooperation between the confraternity leaders and the Zaporozhians.[163]

The Cossacks' public admission into the ranks of confraternity members was extremely significant, for by joining, they demonstrated their solidarity with the program of the confraternity and their intention to act in unison with it. The support of the Cossacks made possible the confraternity's contribution to the development of Kyiv as a major center of the religious and cultural revival.

The cooperation of the Kyiv Confraternity with the Zaporozhian Cossacks led to the restoration in 1620 of the Ukrainian Orthodox hierarchy, which was of great significance for continuing opposition to the Union. The visit to Ukraine of Patriarch Theophanes of Jerusalem, who was on his way

---

162.   K. Sakovych, *Virshi na zhalosnyi pohreb zatsnoho rytsera Petra Konashevycha Sahaidachnoho, hetmana voiska ieho korolevskoi mylosty Zaporozkoho* (Kyiv, 1622). For a reprint, cf. Kh. Titov, *Materiialy dlia istoriï knyzhnoï spravy na Vkraïni v XVI–XVIII v.* (Kyiv, 1924); V. Krekoten', ed., *Ukraïns'ka literatura XVII st.*, 220–38.

163.   Harasiewicz, *Annales ecclesiae Ruthenae*, 260.

home from Moscow, was utilized for this purpose. Theophanes spent almost a year on the premises of the Kyiv Confraternity. At first he feared to endorse the appointment of Orthodox bishops and then agreed to it only because of pressure exerted by representatives of the Zaporozhian Cossacks, who had promised him their protection. In the Kyiv Confraternity Church, Theophanes ordained the abbot of the confraternity monastery, Isaia Kopynsky, as bishop of Peremyshl; Iov Boretsky as metropolitan of Kyiv; and Meletii Smotrytsky, Boretsky's successor as rector of the confraternity school, as bishop of Polatsk.[164] The growth of the role of the confraternities during this period is apparent from the fact that during his sojourn in Kyiv, Theophanes not only ratified the Kyiv Confraternity but also endowed it with stauropegial rights. Such rights were also granted to the confraternities of Lviv and Lutsk, as well as of Slutsk in Belarus.[165] In addition, the patriarch confirmed the legal status of other confraternities, including the Minsk Confraternity.[166] Indeed, patriarchal charters were prepared with no mention of locality or confraternity name and sufficient blank space for appropriate additions,[167] indicating that the patriarch's hosts were planning to expand the network of confraternities.

After being designated metropolitan, Boretsky continued to encourage the expansion of confraternities and the development of confraternity schools, while Sahaidachny continued to assist him in this endeavor. His studies in the Ostrih Collegium, acquaintance with Ivan Boretsky and other cultural activists, and association with the Kyiv Confraternity enabled Sahaidachny to familiarize himself with the state of education in Ukraine. He understood that significant sums of money were required to engage qualified teachers so as to ensure a high level of instruction in the confraternity school.

---

164.   P. Orlovskii, "Uchastie zaporozhskikh kazakov v vosstanovlenii ierusalimskim patriarkhom Feofanom pravoslavnoi zapadnorusskoi tserkovnoi ierarkhii v 1620 godu," *TKDA*, 1905, no. 8: 642–50.

165.   Hrushevsky, *History of Ukraine-Rus'*, 7: 338.

166.   *Chteniia v Obshchestve istorii i drevnostei rossiiskikh*, 1896, no. 1 (176), *smes'*, 11–15.

167.   NBUV, Manuscript Institute, fond 18, no. 47.

Kasiian Sakovych wrote the following about Sahaidachny:

> He saw the Lviv Confraternity, although it is far away,
> He gave generous gifts to the town church,
> He bequeathed large sums of money to the confraternity,
> Insisting that learning take place there.

Sakovych was referring here to Sahaidachny's will, drawn up on 5 (15) April 1622, a few days before his death from wounds suffered at the Battle of Khotyn. By this act, Petro Sahaidachny bequeathed 1,500 zlotys "to the Lviv Confraternity School, for the teaching of little children," a sum that generated an annual income for the upkeep of "a learned teacher, an expert in the Greek language." The hetman was buried "at the church of the Slavonic school located in the Podil in a house belonging to the church confraternity."[168]

The restoration of the Ukrainian-Belarusian hierarchy, achieved during the rule of Hetman Sahaidachny, led several activists associated with the confraternities to publish works in praise of the historic achievements of the Cossacks. Thus, in a book entitled *Elenchus* (Pendant) published by the Vilnius Confraternity Monastery in 1622, the role of the Zaporozhian Cossacks in the defense of the traditional religion and culture was stressed.[169] The courage of the Zaporozhian Host was extolled in a poem dedicated to the Mahilioŭ Confraternity entitled "The Labyrinth" (Cracow, 1625) by Khoma Ievlevych, who soon became rector of the Kyiv Confraternity School.[170]

Bohdan Khmelnytsky's siege of Lviv in 1648 was a significant event in the history of the city. There is considerable evidence indicating that the Ukrainian population of Lviv helped the Cossacks, notwithstanding the threat of brutal reprisals. Allegedly, a Ukrainian painter showed the Cossacks the best approach for an attack on the fortifications

---

168.   S. T. Golubev, "Drevnii pomenik Kievo-Pecherskoi lavry," *Chteniia v Istoricheskom obshchestve Nestora letopistsa* 6 (1892), suppl., vi.

169.   A. Anushkin, *Na zare knigopechataniia v Litve* (Vilnius, 1970), 186.

170.   For the Polish text and Ukrainian translation, cf. V. Krekoten', "Z istoriï ukraïns'ko-bilorus'koho literaturnoho spivrobitnytstva: Poema Khomy Ievlevycha 'Labirynt,'" in *Ukraïns'ka literatura XVI–XVIII st. ta inshi slov'ians'ki literatury* (Kyiv, 1989), 253–85.

of the Carmelite monastery—through the homes of "schismatic" burghers, from the side of their church.[171] Even in the following century, the Lviv Confraternity was charged with having incited hostility toward Polish rule during the sieges of 1648 and 1655.[172] In 1648, its representatives of the confraternity met with Ivan Vyhovsky, the general secretary of the Zaporozhian Host, as well as with Khmelnytsky's personal chaplain, Ivan Hoholivsky. The latter donated a psalter to the confraternity school and an *Octoechos* to the Monastery of St. Onuphrius; he, in turn, received a gift of six books from members of the confraternity.[173] A book entitled *Prologue for the Month of March* donated in 1648 by the Cossacks to the confraternity in the village of Verbytsia made its way to the library of the St. Onuphrius Monastery.[174] Iannis Mazaraki, a member of the Stauropegion, served Khmelnytsky, while his son, Demian, served as a standard-bearer in the Cossack Host, and his daughter, Hanna, married the colonel of Lubny, Vasyl Svichka.[175]

In the mid-seventeenth century and later, the Lviv Confraternity had contacts with the Kyiv metropolitan and the Hetman government of Ukraine. Among its members was a prosperous Greek from Lviv, Theodosios Tomkevych, who was Bohdan Khmelnytsky's exactor (customs duty collector) and carried out many missions of a diplomatic and economic nature. In the years 1657–58 he was an intermediary between Hetman Ivan Vyhovsky and the Polish government, and, together with Pavlo Teteria, took part in preparations for the Union of Hadiach.[176] The confraternity instructed Tomkevych to remind

171.   *Sbornik letopisei, otnosiashchikhsia k Iuzhnoi i Zapadnoi Rusi* (Kyiv, 1888), 241.

172.   W. Łoziński, *Patrycjat i mieszczaństwo lwowskie w XVI i XVII wieku* (Lviv, 1892), 321.

173.   *AIuZR*, 11: 184 (LNB, Manuscript Division, Ossolineum collection 2391, f. 44).

174.   LNB, Manuscript Division, Ossolineum collection/2391, f. 44.

175.   V. Antonovych, "Prilutskii polkovoi osaul Mikhailo Movchan i ego zapisnaia kniga," *Kievskaia starina* 11 (1885): 69–70.

176.   K. I. Stetsiuk, *Narodni rukhy na Livoberezhnii i Slobids'kii Ukraïni v 50–70–x rokakh XVII st.* (Kyiv, 1960), 143, 171.

the hetman's court of the "tyranny" of Prokop Khmilevsky (Chmiliewski), the Greek Catholic bishop of Peremyshl.[177]

In 1659 the Lviv Stauropegion Confraternity dispatched two of its confreres, Mykhailo Sliozka and Vasyl Korendovych, to Metropolitan Dionisii Balaban of Kyiv with instructions to inform him of "our yoke and all manner of repressions and constraints imposed by the lords of the city council."[178] It should also be noted that Hetman Ivan Vyhovsky and his opponent, Pavlo Teteria, signed the register of members (Album) of the Lviv Confraternity after their terms of office ended.[179] They were clearly calculating on increasing their popularity among the Orthodox population.[180] Conversely, wealthy members of the confraternity also made use of their connections with the Cossack officers in order to obtain their patronage in various matters. In 1659, the confraternity leaders welcomed Ivan Briukhovetsky to Lviv (he was then the envoy at the talks with Poland and quartermaster-general of the Zaporozhian Host), and in March 1664 they welcomed Iurii Khmelnytsky, the former hetman.[181]

In 1669 or 1670 the Stauropegion presented a book entitled *Polustavets'* (a kind of prayer book), issued by the confraternity printshop, to Metropolitan Iosyf Tukalsky of Kyiv, who had been a close ally of Hetman Petro Doroshenko.[182] One of the sources of information on the confreres' commercial missions is a passport issued by Hetman Ivan Mazepa to a confraternity member named Mykhailo Savych, granting him the right to travel to Hetman Ukraine (including "to us in Baturyn in need") and bring in goods duty-free.[183]

Confraternity members often carried out a variety of political commissions during their commercial trips. Individual

177.   *AIuZR*, 11: 180–81.
178.   Ibid., 12: 572.
179.   Album, 155, 157.
180.   M. Andrusiak, "Pavlo Teteria i L'vivs'ka Stavropihiia," *ZNTSh* 151 (1931): 183.
181.   TsDIAL 129/1/1077: 17–18; *AIuZR*, 11: 173.
182.   TsDIAL 129/1/1098, f. 5.
183.   TsDIAL 129/1/1216.

members of the Stauropegion traded in all parts of Ukraine, traveling frequently to the towns of Podillia (Kamianets, Bar, Terebovlia, Ternopil, Iazlivets),[184] Bukovyna, Volhynia, and the trans-Dnipro region. Even in the second half of the seventeenth century and throughout the eighteenth, by which time Left-Bank Ukraine and Kyiv were divided by a state border from Right-Bank Ukraine, the members of the Lviv Confraternity took an active part in trade with these lands.[185]

The members of the Stauropegion were also active in economic and political contacts between Lviv and non-Ukrainian lands; they visited Poland (Cracow, Lublin, Gdańsk), frequently serving as intermediaries in the exchange of goods between Europe and the Middle East. As for contacts with a political shading, the most systematic were those with the Moldavian principality. Shared cultural traditions favored the cultivation of such links. In the past, the Moldavian lands had belonged to the Galician-Volhynian Kingdom. After the creation of a Moldavian state, many Ukrainians lived there, and the number of boyars of Ukrainian descent was considerable. But the most important feature of these relations was that both sides were interested in maintaining them. The Ukrainians sought the patronage of rulers of a state professing the same religion, while the Moldavian elite viewed the intermediacy of the Ukrainians as an additional channel for developing contacts with the Polish-Lithuanian Commonwealth. Having established its own state, Moldavia was also able to preserve those elements of a common cultural heritage that had been lost in Ukraine. For their part, starting earlier and proceeding in a much more consistent manner, the Ukrainians began the process of fusing the Eastern and Western elements of their culture with local tradition. In Moldavia, which was moving in the same direction, Ukrainian leaders could more easily establish rapport with the local elites than in any other country. This is apparent from the edicts issued by Moldavian princes that have been preserved in the archives of the Lviv Confraternity. Most are in the Ukrainian version of the

---

184.   F. Sribnyi, "Studiï," *ZNTSh* 115 (1913): 42.
185.   TsDIAL 129/1/1216.

Ruthenian written language, while others are in Old Church Slavonic. The Dormition Church, whose construction was completed in 1559, was built largely with funds donated by the Moldavian prince Alexandru Lapuşneanu. A considerable portion of the funds required for the construction of the new Dormition Church, which is still standing today, was donated by the princes Ieremia and Simeon Movilă (Mohyla) and by Ieremia's widow, Ielysaveta.[186] The members of the Lviv Confraternity often traveled to Moldavia in connection with construction projects, while representatives of the princes and their families frequently journeyed to Lviv. The confraternity also maintained ties with other Moldavian magnates, including Luca Stroich (Stroici), Nestor Ureche, and Isak Balyka. The Moldavian government's support helped strengthen the Lviv Ukrainians in their struggle against national and religious discrimination. Diverse relations with Moldavia were favorable to cultural exchanges. Ukrainian manuscript books circulated in Moldavia, while books of Moldavian origin were distributed in Ukraine.[187] In 1605, Prince Ieremia Mohyla asked the confraternity to provide assistance to his representative in Lviv, who was instructed to purchase paper and find precentors (diaky) who could copy books.[188] The Lviv Confraternity printshop had a positive influence on the evolution of printing in Moldavia. Certain documents also contain references to assistance (money or books) for Romanians from Wallachia and Moldavia.[189] At the end of the seventeenth century Dosoftei (Dositheus), the metropolitan of Suceava and a noted Romanian writer, spent time in Ukraine. He had various contacts with the Ukrainian communities of the towns in which he lived, especially Stryi and Zhovkva. The Lviv Confraternity gave the exile one

---

186.   IuILS, no. 82; AIuZR, 11: 637–38, 673, 376; Krylovskii, L'vovskoe Stavropigial'noe bratstvo, suppl., 89–95.

187.   P. P. Panaitescu, Manuscrisele slave din Bibliotecă Academiei RPR (Bucharest, 1959), 38–40; LNB, Manuscript Division, Ossolineum collection, nos. 368, 369.

188.   IuILS, no. 49.

189.   TsDIAL 129/1/1131, f. 12; 1119: 13, 29; I. Sharanevych, Nykolai Krasovs'kyi (Krasuvs'kyi) (Lviv, 1885), 112.

of its publications and lent him money.[190] Certain relations
with Moldavia were maintained in eighteenth century; of
particular note is the confraternity's sale of Greek type and the
delivery of printing paper.[191] The three emblems of Moldavia
and only one of Russia engraved on the interior of the cupola
of the confraternity church in Lviv may be regarded as a
unique symbol of the significance of Moldavia's support. The
residents of Lviv, well aware of the provenance of the funds
for the construction of this church, long referred to it as the
Volos'ka tserkva (Moldavian Church).[192]

The confraternities' relations with Russia began later
than with Moldavia, and at first they were only sporadic.
The confraternity itself considered those relations important,
and even greater importance has been assigned to them by
historiography. In Soviet publications from the 1950s to the
early 1980s, the very existence of such relations was exploited
for propagandistic purposes. More often than not, neither the
specific character of Russo-Ukrainian relations in the context
of the Slavia Orthodoxa nor the political aims espoused by the
Russian government have been taken into account. Initially,
contacts between the Lviv Confraternity and the Russian
government were promoted by Greek and South Slavic
hierarchs, who had already obtained "charity" from Russia.
In 1591, the confraternity asked Patriarch Jeremiah to write
a letter to the rulers of Moldavia, Wallachia, and Russia for
material assistance to the burghers of Lviv.[193] Finally, in the
summer of 1592 the confraternity sent its envoys, Luka Huba,
Mykola Dobriansky, Ivan Piatnytsky, and the priest Mykhailo
to Moscow. They carried with them the founding charters of
the confraternity, letters from the confraternity to Tsar Fedor
Ivanovich and the court functionary A. Ia. Shchelkanov,
letters of introduction from Dionysius, the bishop of Tŭrnovo,

---

190.   TsDIAL 129/1/1119: 29, 8.

191.   I. Svientsits'kyi, *Pochatky knyhopechatannia na zemliakh Ukraïny* (Zhovkva
and Lviv, 1924), plate CXIV.

192.   In ethnic terms, the adjective *volos'kyi* referred to Romanians (or
Moldavians) in general; in the political sense it meant the Moldavian principality,
where numerous Ukrainians resided along with Romanians.

193.   *Chteniia v Istoricheskom obshchestve Nestora letopistsa* (Kyiv), 5 (1891): 181.

to the tsar, Tsarina Sofia, and Boris Godunov, and Prince Kostiantyn Ostrozky's letter to the tsar. Describing the difficult situation of the Ukrainian population in the Commonwealth, the confraternity asked for help with the construction of a church and hospital, as well as for books, among them the *Psalter with Extensive Commentaries* and the homilies of St. John Chrysostom on St. Paul's epistles.[194] From Tsar Fedor's letter it is known that the confraternity obtained a sum of money from the Russian government for the construction of a church, "for the priests, deacons, and servants," and for the hospital. Although the envoys from Lviv carried with them patriarchal decrees confirming the establishment of the confraternity, the Russian government knew nothing about it, and the tsar's letters describe the representatives of the confraternity as "the priest Mykhailo with his escort" or "the priest Mykhailo with his servants."[195]

The Kyiv Confraternity also had contacts with Russia. In 1624, its envoys were detained on the Russian border in Putyvl, where they received forty sables sent from Moscow for the construction of a church. In the following year the confraternity dispatched the monk Fedir and the novice Ivan Matviiovych to ask the tsar to provide funds for a roof and icons for the newly constructed five-cupola church. Besides a letter addressed to the tsar, these envoys were to transmit a letter to Patriarch Filaret and the *dumnyi diak* Ivan Gramotin. The latter was particularly requested to explain the meaning of the term "confraternity" to the tsar: "And should His Majesty the tsar desire to learn what a confraternity is, explain this to him.... " The letter to Gramotin indicated further: "A confraternity is made up of Orthodox Christians living among people of other faiths, among Uniates and accursed heretics, desiring to separate themselves from them and have nothing in common with them, who join together lovingly with one another, register their names jointly, and call themselves confreres in order to repel the pressure of

---

194.   *IuILS*, nos. 90–96.
195.   Ibid., nos. 99, 100.

those of other faiths more strongly and quickly."[196] In January 1626 the Kyiv Confraternity transmitted another letter to the tsar through Opanas Kytaichych, a monk at the Kyivan Caves Monastery. Noting that Kyiv, renowned in the past, was now "full of various calamities and misfortunes caused by foes," the leaders of the confraternity recounted the founding of their school and again requested assistance for the decoration of the new church with icons and other embellishments.[197] It is not known whether the confraternity received any subsidy at this time. Metropolitan Iov Boretsky, the former rector of the confraternity schools of Lviv and Kyiv, played an essential role in developing further contacts with Russia. His letters indicate a certain ambiguity: in his letters to the tsar, Boretsky requested not only assistance but also patronage, whereas in his letters to Polish and Lithuanian magnates he expressed loyalty to the Commonwealth.[198] Taken together, his missives give the impression that this balancing act was intended to raise his political status. Boretsky's contacts with Russia forced the Poles to treat him with greater consideration, while his contacts with influential Poles increased his authority in the eyes of Russian governing circles. This is also true of Petro Mohyla, who did not sever his contacts with the tsar, although his loyalty to the Commonwealth was significantly stronger. The same could be said, to a certain degree, of individual leaders of the Lviv Confraternity in the second half of the seventeenth century, who maintained contacts with Russian diplomats and occasionally lent them money and exchanged information; conversely, on their journeys to Russia they would carry out the instructions of Polish governing circles. But this pertains more to individuals than to the confraternity as a whole, which could not have had a well-established political orientation at the time. For the most part, the confraternities' contacts with Russia were based on pragmatic considerations, although it was quite natural that the Polish threat would lead them to seek alliances with people of the same faith. As we

---

196.   *AluZR*, 6: 553–54 (*PKK*, 2: 404).

197.   *AluZR*, 6: 573–74.

198.   Main Archives of Older Records, Warsaw, Radziwiłł Family Archive, file II/745.

have seen, however, the Russians were not familiar with civic organizations such as the confraternities, and thus were not inclined to give them as much systematic aid as they did to monasteries and individual hierarchs in the Balkans.

In the second half of the seventeenth century, cultural interaction between Russia and Ukraine became more regular, but the role of the confraternities diminished. It is well known that the Kyiv Mohyla Academy, which was a continuation of the Kyiv Confraternity School, exerted a tremendous influence on the ecclesiastical life and educational system of Russia. Only some aspects of this influence, such as academic courses of rhetoric and poetics and school theater, have been studied in detail.[199] The activities in Russia of people educated in Ukraine helped disseminate the achievements of the Ukrainian cultural centers. While official circles invited contemporary Ukrainian scholars and educators to work in Russia, the Old Believers were interested in the legacy of the Ukrainian and Belarusian thinkers of the late sixteenth and early seventeenth centuries, many of whom (such as Stefan Zyzanii) were associated with the confraternities.[200] This is evident from the numerous copies and translations of their works.

During the late seventeenth and eighteenth centuries, the cultural map of Eastern Europe changed considerably. Russia's upper classes were superficially Westernized, almost by force, through the policies of Emperor Peter I and his followers. Left-Bank Ukraine gradually became subject to official policies intended to promote Russification, such as the subordination of the Kyiv Metropolitanate to the Holy Synod, the ukases of the 1720s forbidding Ukrainian publishers to print any texts that differed from Russian printed books, and the centralizing mandates of Catherine II and her administration. In Right-Bank Ukraine and Belarus the nobility was ultimately Polonized, and the Ruthenian language gave way to Polish in many spheres of public life and culture. Nevertheless, the Kyiv Mohyla Academy continued to influence the development of culture throughout

---

199.   P. Lewin, "The Ukrainian School Theater in the Seventeenth and Eighteenth Centuries: An Expression of the Baroque," *HUS* 5, no. 1 (1981): 54–65.

200.   A. Robinson, *Bor'ba idei v russkoi literature XVII veka* (Moscow, 1974).

Ukraine and in parts of Belarus. Conversely, not only Ukrainians but Belarusians were involved in cultural activities in Russia. As already mentioned, many Ukrainians and Belarusians were instrumental in promoting Petrine reforms.

Most Russian historians of a pro-Western orientation have assessed the Ukrainian and Belarusian impact on Russian culture of the seventeenth and eighteenth centuries very favorably. Other Russian scholars, notably those of a Eurasian or neo-Slavophile orientation, have considered the Ukrainian and Belarusian influences disastrous for the identity of "Holy Russia." For example, George Florovsky wrote that "Mohyla's internal toxin" was "far more dangerous than the Union" with Roman Catholicism. He condemned Stefan Iavorsky, St. Dymytrii of Rostov (Dmytro Savych Tuptalo), and other clerics educated in Ukraine not only for their acceptance of Catholic theological ideas and the Latin language, but also for their affinity with the European baroque. In consequence, Father Florovsky deplored the fact that, to use the words of Prince N. S. Trubetskoi, the culture of post-Petrine Russia was in many respects a continuation "not of Muscovite tradition, but of Kievan Ukrainian culture."[201]

If Russian historiography is divided on this point, Ukrainian and Belarusian historians are almost unanimous in their enthusiasm for the role played by Ukrainians and Belarusians in the so-called "Europeanization of Russia." In most cases, they underestimate the extent to which the Ukrainian influence on Russian culture made subsequent Russification much easier. The Ukrainian and Belarusian cultures were most vulnerable to Russification when their development lost momentum, mainly as a result of unfavorable political conditions.[202] Imperial discrimination against Ukrainian and Belarusian culture was devastating not only because of its direct effects, but also because it provoked cultural isolationism and populist provincialization of the cultural life of the submerged nations.

---

201.   See F. Sysyn, "Peter Mohyla and the Kiev Academy in Recent Western Works: Divergent Views on Seventeenth-Century Ukrainian Culture," *HUS* 8, nos. 1–2 (1984): 164, 167.

202.   Z. Kohut, *Russian Centralism and Ukrainian Autonomy: Imperial Absorption of the Hetmanate, 1760s–1830s* (Cambridge, Mass., 1988).

The Russian government policy of establishing bureaucratic control over all spheres of public and cultural life was also fatal to such institutions initiated by confraternities as community schools and hospitals.

Ukrainian contacts with Orthodox peoples in the Balkan and Danubian lands and, sporadically, with Orthodox Arabs also developed within the "post-Byzantine" cultural zone. South Slavic monks, mainly Bulgarians and Serbs, visited Ukraine, and some of them received assistance from the confraternities. Extremely important were the contacts of early confraternities with Greek Orthodox hierarchs such as Arsenios of Elasson, the patriarchs Jeremiah Tranos, Meletios Pēgas, Cyril Lukaris, and people from their milieu. Some Greek members of Ukrainian confraternities had contacts with Crete, which was then a major center of Greek culture.[203] Ukrainians involved in confraternity activities sometimes visited Greek communities in northern Italy, as is apparent from the panegyrical verses of Iakiv Sedovsky in honor of Hryhorii Kernytsky.[204] Contacts with the Arab world were much weaker. It should be recalled that Patriarch Joachim, credited with confirmation of the "model" confraternity statute, was a speaker of Arabic and even issued a charter for the confraternity in Arabic during his stay in Lviv.[205] In 1602 "a merchant from Araby, that is, from Antioch, Ferhat of Haleb," donated 15 zlotys to the Lviv Stauropegion Confraternity.[206] Some Ukrainians visited Palestine, where they became acquainted with local residents. Such contacts were certainly personal rather than institutional.

Owing to the corporative mentality of members of urban confraternities, the psychological climate was not favorable to the consolidation of burghers from various cities and towns for joint action. Only in the late sixteenth and early seventeenth centuries did the Lviv Confraternity attempt to coordinate the actions of other confraternities. Even then, the burghers did

---

203.   See Ia. Isaievych, "Greek Culture in the Ukraine: 1550–1650," *Modern Greek Studies Yearbook* 6 (1990): 97–122.

204.   K. Studyns'kyi, "Try panehiryky XVII st.," *ZNTSh* 12 (1896).

205.   For the original, see TsDIAL 129/1/68; *MCS*, 113–19.

206.   *AIuZR*, 11: 369; Sribnyi, "Studiï,"*ZNTSh* 108 (1912): 34.

not form stable national or regional structures similar to those developed by the nobility. Until the mid-seventeenth century, contacts among confraternities and groups of confraternities remained sporadic, centering on Orthodox deputies in the provincial nobiliary dietines. The subsequent political activity of confraternity members developed on an individual basis rather than within confraternal associations.

During the early period of their history, confraternities did not hesitate to innovate and attempted to create completely new institutions. With the passage of time, they became more conservative and limited themselves to the regeneration of customs and rituals inherited from their ancestors. After passing from professional educational and general national activities to the sphere of folk culture, parish confraternities still continued to exist, and their efforts, though limited, manifested an instinct for the self-preservation of Ukrainian and Belarusian cultural identity.

IV

The Confraternities and Education

Church confraternities were essentially educational institutions, for their members' primary task was the inculcation of the principles of Christian life. Thus, it is no wonder that "learning" is so often praised in the confraternities' declarations of goals and in the prefaces to their publications: this word meant mainly the acquisition of religious truths. At the same time, the mentality of confraternity members became increasingly rationalistic: faith, for them, was founded on knowledge. Quite naturally, the obligation to instill Christian moral norms in children became inseparable from the desire to furnish them with a certain degree of cultural refinement, as well as skills needed in public and economic life.

Providing the Ukrainian and Belarusian people with the best available educational opportunities was perceived as an urgent task by those interested in maintaining the prestige of their religion and nation. This could not be achieved by means of the traditional models of home or monastery instruction. Thus, as the confraternities were consolidated on the basis of new statutes, their leaders decided to organize "regulated" schools with their own statutes called, significantly, "pedagogical rules." This approach had become popular much earlier in Western Europe, where humanist educators were engaged in reorganizing schools according to rationally elaborated principles. The title of Johannes Sturm's school statute, "Leges scholae bene ordinatae," clearly reflects this way of thinking: school reform had to be introduced from above on the basis of certain "most rational" principles of "good order." The attitude of educators associated with the confraternities was very similar. Their educational achievements were the result of conscious and concerted action.

The Lviv and Vilnius confraternity schools founded in the 1580s were the earliest Orthodox institutions to combine elementary instruction with studies at a much higher level. Subsequently, schools also began to appear in other Ukrainian and Belarusian communities, first in the western provinces of Ukraine and the Grand Duchy of Lithuania and then in other regions. While noting the importance of this reform, we must not forget that individual parish schools had existed previously. A school at the Theophany Orthodox Church in the Halych suburb of Lviv is mentioned as early as 1546.[1] Books copied there provide evidence that this suburban school served as a kind of cultural center, small but active. The priest Anton Irynkovych, who proudly called himself a native of Lviv, contributed to its dynamism. Archival records and contemporary manuscripts also yield information concerning schools associated with Orthodox churches in Peremyshl (1548), Krasnostav (1550), Sianik (1551), Volodymyr, Tysmenytsia, and other towns.[2] These schools presumably maintained the traditional curriculum of elementary education: precentors instructed children in reading, writing and, in some cases, church music. In the Latin school of the Lviv Roman Catholic cathedral and in schools at some Roman Catholic churches, most students were children of foreign settlers, but gradually the number of Ukrainian students increased. Some Ukrainians studied at Western universities, but only a small portion of the documentation related to this is extant.

The first Ukrainian Orthodox institution of higher education was established in the magnate-owned town of Ostrih (Ostroh) in Volhynia at the end of 1576 or in 1577.[3] Owing to its influence on confraternity schools, a brief outline of the curriculum and history of this school is in order here.

---

1.   Kryp'iakevych, "L'vivs'ka Rus'," 37.

2.   K. Kharlampovich, *Zapadnorusskie pravoslavnyia shkoly XVI i nachala XVII veka* (Kazan, 1898), 199; I. Kryp'iakevych, "Z istorii halyts'koho shkil'nytstva XVI–XVIII st.," *Ridna shkola*, 1933, no. 2: 25; Ia. Isaievych, *Dzherela z istorii ukrains'koi kul'tury doby feodalizmu XVI–XVIII st.* (Kyiv, 1972), 51–53; V. Aleksandrovych, "Persha zhadka pro ukrains'ku shkolu v Peremyshli," *Zhovten'*, 1986, no. 9: 104.

3.   I. Myts'ko, *Ostroz'ka slov'iano-hreko-latyns'ka akademiia* (Kyiv, 1990), 28–29.

The beginning of educational activity in Ostrih is sometimes interpreted as an Orthodox reply to the founding in January 1577 of the Athanasian Greek College in Rome, whose task was to promote Catholicism among Greeks and other Orthodox peoples.[4] Be that as it may, the short preface on the title page of the parallel Greek-Church Slavonic Primer (Azbuka) printed in Ostrih by Ivan Fedorov (Fedorovych) mentions the Ostrih school as existing as early as 18 June 1578. According to the preface, the printshop and school in Ostrih were founded by Prince Kostiantyn Ostrozky, who gathered scholars "experienced in Divine Scripture, as well as in Greek, Latin, and, specifically, Ruthenian. Thus the book that is called Alpha-vita in Greek and Az-buki in Ruthenian was published for the elementary education of children."[5] As may be seen from the text of this primer, there "Ruthenian" was understood to mean Church Slavonic rather than the Ukrainian-Belarusian written language, which was then known as "common Ruthenian." Thus, three languages were to be studied—Greek, Latin, and Church Slavonic. The primer was intended for the elementary level, but the school also provided for higher levels of instruction. Contemporaries sometimes called it an academy or a "lycaeum trilingue."[6] The concept of the trilingual lyceum was advanced by Erasmus of Rotterdam and put into practice most successfully by Cardinal Francisco Jiménez in Alcalá de Henares (Compluto).[7] For Erasmus and Jiménez, the three languages were of course Hebrew, Greek, and Latin, while the Ostrih scholars substituted Church Slavonic for Hebrew. Their purpose, however, was very similar: to promote the knowledge of three sacral languages, to develop the textual study of the Bible and its translations on that basis, and, finally, to publish scholarly editions of the Bible,

4.　I. Myts'ko, "Ostrozhskii kul'turno-prosvetitel'nyi tsentr," Fedorovskie chteniia 1981 (Moscow, 1985), 57–59.

5.　There is a good facsimile edition of the Ostrih Greek-Church Slavonic Primer of 1578: see E. L. Nemirovskii, ed., Ostrozhskaia Azbuka Ivana Fedorova (Moscow, 1983). See also Ia. Isaievych, Literaturna spadshchyna Ivana Fedorova (Lviv, 1989), 111ff.

6.　The Ostrih school was termed a trilingual gymnasium and a trilingual lyceum in Szymon Pękalski's poem De bello Ostrogiano (Cracow, 1600).

7.　B. Hall, "The Trilingual College of San Ildefonso and the Complutensian Polyglot," Studies in Church History, 1969, no. 5.

which both institutions subsequently accomplished: the famous *Biblia Polyglotta* of Alcalá was published in 1514–17, and the first printed Church Slavonic Bible appeared in Ostrih in 1581.

Although most sources stress that the Ostrih school provided instruction in three languages, in some instances it is simply called "the Greek school."[8] This fact evinces the importance of Greek studies and their symbolic role in a school whose purpose was to promote Orthodoxy as the "true Greek faith." "It is well known that for a long time there have been Greeks in Ostrih," declared the author of *Perestoroha*, a pamphlet emanating from the milieu of the Orthodox lay confraternities.[9] It is known from various sources that in the late 1570s and early 1580s Ostrih was visited by Dionysius Rhalis-Paleologos, bishop of Cizycus (later of Tŭrnovo); Eustathatios Nathanael of Crete; Emmanuel Moschopoulos; Theophanes, bishop of Meglena; and Timotheos, bishop of Pula. There is evidence that most of them took part in the editing of the Bible and were involved in teaching Greek in the school. Later, teachers of Greek in Ostrih included the protosyncellus of the patriarchate of Constantinople, Nikephoros Kantakuzinos-Parasches (presumably for a short time in 1596) and the future patriarch Cyril Lukaris (1594–95 and 1597).[10] Zakhariia Kopystensky stressed in his well-known *Palinodia* that in Ostrih "there were orators equal to Demosthenes and Sappho and other philosophers as well. There were famous teachers trained in Greek, Slavonic, and Latin, and there were excellent

---

8.   The book *Otpys na lyst Ipatiia Potiia*, published in Ostrih in 1598 under the pseudonym "Kliryk Ostroz'kyi," contains a postscript "Written in the Ostrih Greek school." See *Pamiatniki polemicheskoi literatury*, vol. 3 (St. Petersburg, 1903), 432.

9.   Vozniak, *Pys'mennyts'ka diial'nist' Ivana Borets'koho*. For an English translation of the quotation, see J. Krajcar, "Konstantin Bazil Ostrozskij and Rome in 1582–1584," *Orientalia Christiana Periodica* 34 (1968): 200.

10.   Some authors maintain that Lukaris was rector of the Ostrih school and not the school in Vilnius: see G. Hering, *Ökumenisches Patriarchat und europäische Politik 1620–1638* (Wiesbaden, 1968), 158. Lukaris may, in fact, have served as rector in both Ostrih and Vilnius, but only documentation concerning his rectorship in the Vilnius Confraternity "academy" is extant. See Kharlampovich, *Zapadnorusskie pravoslavnye shkoly*, 265; Cyril Lucaris, *Sermons 1598–1602*, ed. K. Rozemond (Leiden, 1974), 7.

mathematicians and astrologers."[11] Although the Ostrih college was sometimes called an "academy," it was nonetheless understood that it had to raise its level of instruction in order to become a true institution of higher education. In 1603 the Uniate metropolitan, Iosyf Rutsky, wrote that the palatine of Kyiv (Ostrozky) "wanted to found an academy in Ostrih and had looked for professors in Greece."[12]

After the death of Kostiantyn Ostrozky in 1608, the Ostrih school began to decline. By the time of its final suppression in the 1620s, the "Academy" did not differ greatly from an elementary school. Short-lived though it was, the Ostrih school had a significant impact on the development of culture in Ukraine and other Slavic Orthodox countries. Although it could not be termed a true university, it had begun to evolve in that direction. The prototype of the trilingual "Greco-Latin-Slavonic" school was created there.[13] Its very name reflected not only the languages studied but also a more general tendency toward synthesizing native culture with the Greek and Latin cultural heritage. A "trilingual" program was later adopted by the Kyiv Mohyla Academy. Although that program was not fully realized there, it was through the Kyivan Academy that the concept of the "Greco-Latin-Slavonic" school found its way to Moscow.

Among the students and teachers of the Ostrih school were burghers, some of whom had studied in Lviv. The "Greco-Latin-Slavonic" school in Ostrih undoubtedly influenced the decision of the Ukrainian burghers of Lviv to found a similar institution in their own city. This was undertaken by a group of burghers who dedicated themselves wholeheartedly in the early 1570s to improving the educational system. As early as 1572, "representatives of the entire Ukrainian community of burghers and residents of the suburbs" of Lviv obtained from the king the right to send their sons to study the "liberal arts"

---

11.   *Lev Krevza's "A Defense of Church Unity" and Zaxarija Kopystens'kyj's "Palinodia,"* trans. B. Strumiński, HLEUL, English Translations, vol. 3, pt. 1 (Cambridge, Mass., 1995), 865.

12.   Golubev, *Kievskii mitropolit Petr Mogila*, 1: suppl., 180.

13.   I. N. Golenishchev-Kutuzov, *Gumanizm u vostochnykh slavian (Ukraina i Belorussiia)* (Moscow, 1963), repr. in his *Slavianskie literatury* (Moscow, 1970).

in the gymnasiums and schools of Lviv and other cities. This permission was confirmed by the Crown authorities in 1574 and 1577. It is apparent, however, from the edict of 21 June 1578 signed by King Stefan Batory that the city council did not abolish the earlier educational restrictions.[14]

For a certain time "Stefan" was the rector of the local Ukrainian school. Attesting to this is a royal confirmation in the Lviv municipal records, dated 23 September 1578, of a decree issued on 25 March 1577 by Prince Kostiantyn Ostrozky concerning the granting of the Magdeburg law to the town of Bazaliia. This decree was translated from Ukrainian into Polish by the rector, Stefan, who may safely be identified as Stefan Zyzanii. Considering his educational level and creative gifts, a significant role in the educational endeavors of the contemporary Ukrainian citizenry may be attributed to him. Finally, by the 1580s, the Ukrainian burghers of Lviv were able to establish a school distinguished by a higher level of organization and learning.[15] The measures they adopted in connection with the founding of the school, the purchase of the printshop belonging to Ivan Fedorov, a former collaborator of the Ostrih circle, and the organization of the Dormition Confraternity were closely interrelated. Patriarch Joachim's decree of 15 (25) January 1585 states that "the burghers of Lviv wish to found a school for the instruction of Christian children of every degree who would study the Holy Scriptures in Greek and Slavonic, so that their Christian race might not be left as if without a voice for lack of learning. And they also bought a printshop required for this school.... " If Joachim wrote that a printshop was established at the school, somewhat later Bishop Hedeon Balaban stressed the desire "to fund a Greek school at this printshop in the city of Lviv for the teaching of our piety."[16] Thus, the link between the school and the printshop was reciprocal. In order to ensure an appropriate

14.   MCS, 59, 67, 73, 76, 77.

15.   On the Lviv Confraternity School, see Ia. F. Holovats'kyi, "Poriadok shkol'nyi ili ustav stavropihiiskoi shkoly v L'vovi 1586 hoda," *Halychanyn: Literaturnyi Sbornyk* 2 (1863): 69–79; Hrushevs'kyi, *Istoriia ukraïns'koï literatury*, 6: 143–57.

16.   MCS, 120, 142; *Pryvileï natsional'nykh hromad mista L'vova*, 505. Cf. Gudziak, *Crisis and Reform*, 63.

level of instruction, textbooks had to be printed. Moreover, the printshop greatly benefited from its connection with the school, which attracted educated people who could become authors and editors of its publications. In Western Europe, prominent scholars frequently collaborated with printshops (the Aldine Academy in Venice is but one example). Some members of the Ostrih group of scholars and writers also taught at the Ostrih school and worked at the printshop. Similarly, prominent Ukrainian cultural activists in Lviv were grouped around the printshop and school for a longer period.

Certain historians have erroneously maintained that the Lviv school was established in 1586, "following the reorganization of the confraternity according to the statute ratified by Patriarch Joachim."[17] It is apparent from Joachim's decree, however, that there was already ("in the flesh") a confraternity with a hospital and school of its own;[18] hence the school was established no later than the end of 1585. Its initiators were Ukrainian burghers[19] who, according to a Greek teacher (clearly Arsenios of Elasson), had expended great efforts in order to introduce the Greek and Slavonic languages into the curriculum.[20]

During its first two years of activity, the school was directed by "the Ruthenian teacher," Stefan Zyzanii (Kukil), and "the Greek teacher," Bishop Arsenios of Elasson and Dimonika, who remained in Lviv from June 1586 until the spring of 1588. Arsenios was born in the village of Kaloriana near Trikkala. He studied in Trikkala at a school established by Jeremiah Tranos, then bishop of Larissa.[21] Subsequently, when Jeremiah became patriarch of Constantinople, he elevated Arsenios to the dignity of priest at the patriarchate and in 1584 to that of bishop of Elasson. Arsenios of Elasson taught Greek in Lviv for only two years, after which he went to Russia and was no

---

17. I. Wlasowsky, *Outline History of the Ukrainian Orthodox Church* (New York, 1956), 227.

18. *DS*, 37.

19. Sribnyi, "Studiï," *ZNTSh* 108 (1912): 105.

20. *DS*, 19.

21. Ph. Dēmētrakopoulos, *Arsenios Elassonos (1550–1626). Bios kai ergo* (Athens, 1984), 35–47.

longer involved in teaching. Even after his residence in Lviv, his grasp of Slavonic languages remained weak,[22] and he was not conversant with local customs. Consequently, Stefan Zyzanii, who was already a recognized authority in the eyes of the Lviv burghers, familiar with the traditions and requirements of the school system in Ukraine, could play a larger role in the organization of the Lviv Confraternity School.

From its inception, the most striking feature of the confraternity school was its democratic openness to all classes. The confreres stressed that the school had been founded "for the teaching of children of every degree."[23] Fees for instruction were comparatively low, and parents were to pay only "according to their capacity."[24]

Public figures and educated individuals close to the confraternities set a high value on the civic significance of a school education. In 1609 the confraternity printshop published the anthology *O vospitanii chad* (On the Education of Children), which is extant in two copies preserved in the Lviv National Museum and the National Library in Sofia (Bulgaria).[25] The main part of the anthology contains a Church Slavonic translation of the teachings of the fathers of the church, primarily St. John Chrysostom. Some scholars believe that the compiler was Ivan Boretsky, a teacher at the confraternity school who selected quotations corresponding to his personal views and convictions.[26] The most interesting part of the book is a verse introduction in the contemporary Ruthenian written language, the author of which was possibly the compiler of the anthology. It emphasizes that "everything that is good proceeds" from learning, as though from a spring, and that the Ukrainian nation's neglect of school education causes "disorder and all evil." Similar thoughts were expressed a little earlier in the famous *Perestoroha*,

---

22.   A. Dmitrievskii, "Arsenii, arkhiepiskop Èlassonskii (Suzdal'skii tozh) i ego vnov' otkrytyia istoricheskiia memuary," *TKDA* 17 (1898): 17.

23.   *DS*, 120; *IuILS*, no. 85.

24.   *AIuZR*, 11: 69.

25.   *PBSh*, 49–55.

26.   F. I. Naumenko, *Pedahoh-humanist i prosvitytel' I. M. Borets'kyi* (Lviv, 1963), 22.

whose author believed that the establishment of schools and printshops was of greater significance for the Ukrainian nation than the construction of churches.[27]

Proceeding from such views on the importance of school education, the confreres and educators who collaborated with them attempted to create a model school. According to various sources, instruction in the school concentrated on "Ukrainian studies" (*studii Ruthenici*). Moreover, the school retained the name "Greco-Slavonic" even after the teaching of Latin was introduced. A student roster dating from the end of the sixteenth century[28] lists 61 pupils, mainly from the city of Lviv and the Halych and Cracow suburbs. The names of a few children from other towns and villages are also given: the son of Sylvestr Shelest from the suburban village of Solonka, a cobbler's son from the village of Liubyn, an orphan from the town of Iavoriv, a widow's son from the town of Horodok, and a priest's son from the village of Sykhiv. Historians utilizing this register for research have not taken into account that it contains the names of only a fraction of those studying at the elementary level, since only portions of the register are extant. But the confraternity school was not limited to the elementary level and offered higher-level courses as well. Pupils at the elementary level were "urban sons" whose tuition was paid by their parents, while poor children ("paupers") were exempted from paying tuition. Most of the "paupers," including the singers of a children's choir, lived in the school dormitory. Poor adolescents and youths also resided there, helping the precentors "in service to the church" and carrying out various instructions from the confraternity: they copied and translated documents, acted as letter couriers, and carried books and type from the printshop to the storehouse. Besides the "boys" at the elementary level, the

---

27.   Vozniak, *Pys'mennyts'ka diial'nist' Ivana Borets'koho*, 17, 25–26; Krekoten', ed., *Ukraïns'ka literatura XVII st.*, 26.

28.   TsDIAL 129/1/116a (according to the old system of numeration, file 1120, folios 17–19). Most of the entries in this register are not dated. The main section obviously refers to the years 1587–88, but there are also entries for 1590 and 1595. In the published version (*AIuZR*, 10: 57–60), some entries are unjustifiably omitted, having been crossed out in the sixteenth century, probably in order to indicate that those entries had been transferred from the rough copy to the fair one.

confraternity school included *spudeï*, or higher-level students. Aside from studying (initially at the confraternity school and, from the second half of the seventeenth century, at other secondary and higher institutions in Lviv), they served as tutors ("pedagogues") of the "boys" in the elementary school. The educational level of the students was such that some of them were invited to become teachers of Slavonic, Greek, and Latin in other towns and were appointed confraternity preachers.[29] Indeed, the synthesis of various levels of instruction in a single educational institution was typical of medieval and early modern education in Western Europe. Reading and writing was taught even at certain universities.[30]

What was the general nature of the curriculum at the confraternity school? In the royal privilege granted in 1590 it was called "a school for engaging in the liberal arts." These consisted of the trivium (grammar, rhetoric, and dialectics) and the quadrivium (arithmetic, geometry, music, and astronomy), which were the subjects taught in medieval secondary schools. In the introduction to the *Octoechos* published by the confraternity in 1630, and in some archival records, the confraternity school holds the title of gymnasium.[31] Gasparino Barizza, a noted Italian pedagogue of the Renaissance, used the same term for his school. The curriculum of the humanist gymnasium, developed in the humanist schools of Italy in the fifteenth and sixteenth centuries, was adopted by the Protestant schools and Jesuits colleges,[32] and later by the Kyiv Mohyla Academy. In keeping with the foundations of this tradition, instruction in the gymnasium consisted of three classes in grammar (infima, media, and suprema or syntax) and classes in poetics and rhetoric. These subjects were also taught during the first years of study in certain institutions of higher education, which generally combined two levels

---

29.   *MCS*, 363, 371–73, 282.

30.   P. F. Grendler, *Schooling in Renaissance Italy: Literacy and Learning, 1300–1600* (Baltimore and London, 1989), 23–25.

31.   *Oktoikh* (Lviv, 1630), folio 4 (of the first foliation).

32.   F. Paulsen, *Geschichte des gelehrten Unterrichts auf den deutschen Schulen und Universitäten vom Ausgang des Mittelalters bis zur Gegenwart*, vol. 1 (Leipzig, 1919), 210, 292; Grendler, *Schooling in Renaissance Italy*, 140–41, 378, 405 and passim.

of instruction—secondary (gymnasium, college) and higher (academy, university)—until the sixteenth and seventeenth centuries. Philosophical and theological studies were offered only at a few gymnasiums with an expanded curriculum, which had the potential to evolve into academies (higher educational institutions).

The Kyiv Mohyla College was a case in point. At first the founders of the confraternity school in Lviv intended to introduce subjects typical of a higher educational institution, primarily philosophy. The "Poriadok shkil'nyi" (Pedagogical Rule) adopted on 8 October 1586 already provided that teachers were to lecture on the texts of "philosophers, poets, historians, and others" and that students were to study grammar and "advance toward the greater subjects of logic and rhetoric, the textbooks of which, translated into the Slavonic language, are available at the Lviv school."[33] The Greco-Slavonic grammar *Adelphotēs*, published for use in the confraternity school, also emphasizes that the study of grammar is "the key that opens the door to understanding the Bible: through grammar, the industrious ascend as though on the rungs of a ladder toward dialectics, rhetoric, music, arithmetic, geometry, and astronomy, and on the basis of these seven subjects ... we can acquaint ourselves with philosophy and medicine, and proceed to the most perfect subject of theology."[34] The path of learning thus proceeds from grammar through the seven liberal arts to subjects characteristic of the higher educational establishment of those days—philosophy, medicine, and theology. Similarly, Lavrentii Zyzanii, a teacher at the Lviv Confraternity School, emphasized that Slavonic grammar was the "key to understanding" that made it possible to comprehend rhetoric, philosophy, and the whole "indivisible union of the arts."[35] In November 1589 Patriarch Jeremiah Tranos of Constantinople confirmed the right of the confraternity printing house "to print ... not only breviaries, psalters, the Acts and Epistles, Menaions and Triodions, missals, Synaxaria, the Gospels, Metaphrasts, and Chronicles, and other

---

33.   *DS*, 26, 29.

34.   K. Studyns'kyi, "'Adel'fotes'— hramatyka vydana u L'vovi v r. 1591," *ZNTSh* 7 (1890): 5.

35.   Krylovskii, *L'vovskoe Stavropigial'noe bratstvo*, 253.

books of the theologians of our Christian church, as well as those books required by the school, i.e., grammar, poetics, rhetoric, and philosophy."[36] If the confraternity was planning to publish philosophical works deemed necessary for the school, then it clearly intended to introduce the teaching of philosophy. Certain conservative-minded burghers initially protested (in 1590) against the "teaching of grammar, dialectics, and rhetoric" in the confraternity school.[37] Thus, by contemporary standards, the confraternity school was a secondary school,[38] but, by introducing the teaching of philosophy, it attempted to go beyond that level and thus constituted a transitional stage in the formation of a higher educational institution. The teaching of Greek helped make it an important educational center for all countries in which the Orthodox Church was dominant and the Greek language considered paramount. In point of fact, scholars of West European education have indicated that attempts to raise the level of pre-university education there and the founding of schools which prepared people for the universities were germane to humanist pedagogy.[39] Patriarch Meletios Pēgas of Alexandria appealed to the confraternity on two occasions (in May and July 1597) to establish an institution of higher education, as he himself was unable to do so "in captivity," under the sway of the Ottoman Porte.[40]

In 1658, in accordance with the terms of the Treaty of Hadiach between Ukraine and Poland, the Cossacks obtained the Polish government's agreement to the founding of two Ukrainian academies, one of which was to be located in Kyiv.[41] This aroused great anxiety among the Jesuits, who suspected that the second Orthodox university ("academy") would be established in Lviv on the foundations of the confraternity "gymnasium."[42] Under that pretext, in 1661 they managed to

36.   *PKK*, 3: 17.

37.   *MCS*, 241.

38.   I. Kryp'iakevych, "350–littia seredn'oï shkoly u L'vovi," *Zhyttia i znannia*, 1936, no. 1: 281–82.

39.   S. Schindling, "Schulen und Universitäte im 16. und 17. Jh.," in *Ecclesia Militans* (Paderborn, 1988), 563.

40.   *MCS*, 797, 799.

41.   *Volumina legum*, 2d ed., vol. 4 (St. Petersburg, 1860), 12.

42.   F. Jaworski, *Uniwersytet Lwowski*(Lviv, 1912), 12.

obtain a royal mandate that converted their own Lviv college into an academy[43] (no city could have more than one academy). Following the abdication of King John Casimir, representatives of the Right-Bank Cossack officers demanded at the Diet elections of 1669 that Orthodox academies be established not only in Kyiv, but also in Hoshcha and Mahiliou̯, and that the Jesuits be barred from founding schools in those cities.[44]

The schemes of the Jesuits, harassment by the city authorities, and the departure of the best scholars for the Kyiv Mohyla College led to a decline of educational standards at the Lviv school, as well as at the Vilnius and Brest schools and others by the 1620s,[45] especially from the second half of the seventeenth century. Until 1592, several eminent professors could be found teaching at the gymnasium at any one time. By the seventeenth century there were, as a rule, two teachers, and by the eighteenth century there was often only one paid teacher. Although some students living in the confraternity dormitory also acted as teachers, the level of instruction at the confraternity school was certainly in decline.

Between 1589 and 1592 the urban Dormition Confraternity in Lviv obtained several privileges according to which its "universal" school was to be the only school in the city, and other "unofficial" schools were to be banned. However, in the first half of the seventeenth century there were several schools attached to churches in the suburbs of Lviv.[46] In the eighteenth century, schools housed in residences for teachers and students were established at several confraternities on the outskirts of Lviv. These included the parishes of the Annunciation, St. Nicholas, St. Theodore Tyron, St. Paraskeva, the Resurrection, the Theophany, "at the Tarnavka" (Nativity of the Theotokos), and St. George.[47] Students of the Jesuit academy lived in some

43.   *Antemurale* (Rome) 6 (1960–61), 102–3.

44.   *Congregationes particulares*, 1, no. 45: 58.

45.   M. Smotryts'kyi (Smotrzyski), *Paraenesis* (Cracow, 1629), 32 (repr. HLEUL, Texts, 1: 661).

46.   On teachers in Lviv schools, see Myts'ko, "L'vivs'ki sviashchenyky ta vchyteli," 16–17.

47.   TsDIAL 9/1, vol. 354: 2859; NM, general visitation of 1743, folios 5–32, MS 21082 (124), f. 10.

of these residences.[48] In practice, the Stauropegion did not initiate any activities to the detriment of the suburban schools. Early in the seventeenth century the Dormition Confraternity decided to establish a school at the St. Onuphrius Monastery, with the proviso that its precentor be subordinate to the rector of the urban school.[49]

According to the statute adopted in 1589, the Vilnius Confraternity was obliged to provide tuition-free instruction in its school in the "Ruthenian, Greek, and Polish languages to the children of confraternity members and to poor children." In its day, it was one of the leading schools established by Belarusian burghers and clergymen. The Lviv Confraternity maintained relations with this school, sending it fifty copies of its Greco-Slavonic grammar. At the request of the Vilnius Confraternity, the Lviv confreres dispatched qualified teachers, Kyrylo Trankvilion-Stavrovetsky and Stefan Zyzanii, to the Vilnius school. In 1617, the Vilnius Confraternity once again asked the Stauropegion to send a teacher for "Latin studies."[50] For their part, two graduates of the Vilnius school, Sylvestr Kosiv and Isaia Kozlovsky-Trofymovych, eventually became teachers at the Lviv Confraternity School.

At the request of the confraternities, the Lviv Stauropegion dispatched teachers to schools in Peremyshl, Brest, Rohatyn, and other towns.[51] A teacher from Lviv taught at the Stryi school in 1591.[52] In 1596, Peter Arcudios wrote that the confraternity school in Brest was "like a seminary, modeled on those ratified by Patriarch Jeremiah."[53] This was clearly a reference to the schools of the Lviv and Vilnius confraternities, whose founding documents had been confirmed by the patriarch. Under the influence of the Lviv school, schools

---

48.   Archives of Cracow Province and the city of Cracow, Wawel Division, Schneider portfolio, file 965.

49.   Cf. Album, 407–8.

50.   "Barkulabovskaia letopis'," 10 (sixth pagination); *AZR*, 4: 43, 44; *MCS*, 340.

51.   *MCS*, 288, 363, 370–73, 463. The Rohatyn confreres even called their institution "the school of Lviv teaching."

52.   Sventsits'kyi, *Opys'*, 13.

53.   Cited in Bieńkowski, "Organizacja Kościoła Wschodniego w Polsce," 834.

in Horodok, Halych, Komarno, Bilsk, and other towns were established or reorganized.[54]

Soon after its foundation in 1617, the Lutsk Confraternity also established a school for higher education and constructed a brick building to house it in 1620. A manuscript collection that belonged to the Lutsk school contained two documents dating from 1624 governing the character and structure of this school: "Articles of the Rules of the Lutsk Greco-Slavonic School" and the "Pedagogical Rule"—a copy of the Lviv statute.[55] Kostiantyn Kharlampovych referred to the latter document as the first statute of the Lutsk school and the "Articles" as its second statute, adopted somewhat later under the influence of the Jesuit college statute.[56] In the opposing opinion of Evgenii Medynsky, the "Articles" were the first statute, but shortly after its introduction, the burghers, dissatisfied with the preponderance of Jesuits, abolished them and adopted a "second, more democratic statute," the "Pedagogical Rule," modeled on the Lviv statute.[57]

Neither Kharlampovych nor Medynsky, in attempting to determine which of these "two statutes" was the earliest, was justified in counterposing the "Pedagogical Rule" to the "Articles." Both documents could have been in force simultaneously, without contradicting each other.[58] The "Pedagogical Rule" was a basic document pertaining to school organization, while the "Articles," which substantiated and elaborated on individual points of the statute, functioned as student regulations.

The "Articles" focused on maintaining discipline in the student body. Prior to registration at the school, every student

---

54.   TsDIAL 9/1, vol. 349: 897, vol. 354: 3511; *AZR*, 4: 70; Kharlampovich, *Zapadnorusskie pravoslavnye shkoly*, 365–68.

55.   *PKK*, 1: 44–54.

56.   Kharlampovich, *Zapadnorusskiia pravoslavnyia shkoly*, 343.

57.   Ie. Medyns'kyi, *Brats'ki shkoly Ukraïny i Bilorusiï v XVI–XVII st.* (Kyiv, 1958), 48–55.

58.   In point of fact, the records of confraternities located in villages and small towns sometimes contained two or three statutes adopted from other confraternities. Disregarding minor differences, the confraternities were governed in such cases by the features common to all the statutes entered in their records.

had to undergo a three-day probation. Given the variety of subjects and languages taught in the school, each student's course of study was determined by the school's directors, who took age, interests, and capabilities into account.

The high level of instruction at the Lutsk Confraternity School is confirmed by the fact that both students and faculty not only recited poetry in class, but also composed verses in the contemporary Ukrainian language. Thus, an anthology of funeral poems compiled by Davyd Andreievych and published in 1628 contained the "Lamentation of Poor Students of the Lutsk Confraternity School." It was written or recited by Hryhorii Somynovych, the school penitarch (a student charged with maintaining discipline in class). Stepan Polumerkovych, the author of an occasional poem on the funeral of Vasylysa Iatskivna, probably was also associated with the confraternity school.[59]

The teachers of the Lutsk school were monks from the confraternity monastery—Ielysei Ilkovsky (director of the school in 1628, also known as a composer); Pavlo Bosynsky (a teacher in 1634); the hegumen Avhustyn Slavynsky (a lecturer of rhetoric and philosophy in the mid-seventeenth century); and, possibly, Zosym Sohnykevych and the icon-painter Iov Kondzelevych.[60] The students included children of burghers and noblemen, as well as poor children who collected alms by singing on city streets.

The curriculum was similar to that of the Lviv school. Slavonic, Ruthenian, and Polish books were used. Sources refer in particular to Greek and Slavonic grammars and to a Latin dictionary. Singing was taught at an advanced level, and students sang polyphonic arrangements for six, eight, or more voices. The Lutsk school suffered considerably from interference by malicious Roman Catholic nobles, as well as by students and teachers of the Jesuit college. In 1627 Jesuit students attacked the Lutsk school, beating children, tearing textbooks out of their hands and destroying them. Similar attacks occurred in later years.[61]

---

59.   *PKM*, 1, nos. 170, 175.
60.   *AIuZR*, 6: 593, 687; *PKK*, 1: 124; S. Kurganovich, *Dionisii Zhabokritskii, episkop Lutskii i Ostrozhskii* (Kyiv, 1914), 11.
61.   *AIuZR*, 6: 593–94, 687, 753.

Inasmuch as the Ukrainian schools of Kyiv were under the protection of the Cossacks, they were able to develop more freely than those of Lviv and Lutsk. Some scholars still maintain the mid-nineteenth-century view that the school of the Kyiv Theophany Confraternity already existed at the end of the sixteenth century and was converted from a humble confraternity school into a college by Patriarch Jeremiah in 1588–89.[62] However, a number of documents attest that both the confraternity and the school were established in Kyiv in 1615–16. Its first rectors were Ivan Boretsky and Meletii Smotrytsky, followed by Kasiian Sakovych in the years 1620–24.[63] In a letter written in 1625 to the Russian tsar concerning their motives for founding a school, the confreres wrote: "We organized a school for Orthodox children at great cost for the teaching of the Slavonic-Ruthenian and Greek languages and (the subjects taught) by other teachers, so that the children would not drink the fatal poison of schism from an alien source and would not stray into the darkness of the Roman faith."[64] The school was confirmed by a decree of Patriarch Theophanes of Jerusalem granting stauropegial rights to the Theophany Confraternity. From the autobiographical notes of Ihnatii Ievlevych it is known that the Kyiv Confraternity School had elementary classes, as well as classes in grammar and syntax,[65] clearly indicating that the school was founded on principles that reached Ukraine from Western and Central Europe.[66] The Kyiv school also held poetry recitals: some occasional poetry published on the death of Hetman Petro Konashevych Sahaidachny is extant.

In 1627 Petro Mohyla was named archimandrite of the Kyivan Caves Monastery. He planned to establish a school there, but on a larger scale than the confraternity school. In so doing, he was imitating Western models. The possibility

---

62.   I. Stus, "The Early Years of the Kievan-Mohylian Academy," in *Millennium of Christianity in Ukraine, 988–1988,* ed. O. W. Gerus and A. Baran (Winnipeg, 1989), 139–40.

63.   Hrushevs'kyi, *Istoriia ukraïns'koï literatury,* 6: 162–72; Hrushevsky, *History of Ukraine-Rus',* 7: 323.

64.   *AIuZR,* 6: 573.

65.   *Universitetskiia izvestiia* (Kyiv) 26, no. 5 (1886): 75.

66.   I. Ševčenko, "The Many Worlds of Peter Mohyla," *HUS* 8, nos. 1–2 (1984): 11.

of competition between the confraternity school and the new school, which would be completely under the control of the monks, caused dissatisfaction in Kyiv.[67] In his will, Metropolitan Boretsky, the former rector of the confraternity school, ordered Petro Mohyla and the bishop of Lutsk, Isaakii Boryskovych, on pain of forfeiting his blessing, to "fund the school only under the aegis of the confraternity, and nowhere else." The will was signed on 1 March 1631, and by 11 March Mohyla had enrolled as a senior brother and trustee of the confraternity.[68] By formally enrolling in the confraternity, the ambitious archimandrite wished to nullify the confreres' opposition to his plan of establishing a school of higher education at the Caves Monastery, rather than at the confraternity, as Boretsky had planned. While spending some time in Lviv in June of that year, Mohyla invited Isaia Kozlovsky-Trofymovych and Sylvestr Kosiv of Lviv to be teachers in Kyiv. Shortly afterwards, a school was established at the Kyivan Caves Monastery; Trofymovych was appointed rector and Kosiv became a prefect. As is apparent from panegyrics to Mohyla ("Eucharisterion") written by students in the class of rhetoric, the "seven liberal arts" were taught at the school.[69] Owing to pressure exerted on behalf of the confraternity by Ukrainian nobles of the Kyiv palatinate, clergymen headed by Metropolitan Isaia Kopynsky, and the Zaporozhian Host,[70] Mohyla was forced to agree not only to merge the monastery school with the confraternity school, but also to establish it in the Podil on the site of the former confraternity school. In exchange for Mohyla's compliance, the confraternity granted him the status of elder brother and founder of the school.

In this manner, by means of a compromise, the issue was formally closed, but in fact Mohyla completely realized

---

67.   *PKK*, 2: 407.

68.   Ibid., 390, 410–11.

69.   Cf. facsimile (with an introduction by I. Ševčenko), *HUS* 8, nos. 1–2: 251ff. For an analysis of the text, see N. Pylypiuk, "Eucharisterion. Albo, Vdjačnost': The First Panegyric of the Kiev Mohyla School. Its Content and Historical Context," ibid., 45–70.

70.   *PKK*, 2: 412–21.

his goal.[71] While the institution was often called the Kyiv Confraternity School (College), there is no evidence that the confraternity had any influence on its activities after 1632. Records dating from 1632 to 1786 indicate that the school (first a college and later an academy) functioned at the Theophany Monastery,[72] which, according to tradition, retained the name of a "confraternity" monastery even after the lay confraternity ceased to exist.

Along with "Kyiv Confraternity School," the name "Kyiv Mohyla College" (later "Academy") was also widely used. But the tradition of attributing the origins of the Kyivan Academy to the secular confraternity school remained vital even when the essence of the confraternity's activities was long forgotten in Kyiv. In 1764, when the Left-Bank Cossack officers requested the consent of the empress to the founding of a university in Kyiv and Baturyn, the petition signed by Hetman Kyrylo Rozumovsky stated: "The first of these universities, comprising four faculties, can be in Kyiv, on the site of the present-day Kyiv Confraternity Monastery, from which the monks should be removed, and on this site buildings for teachers and students should be erected, for when the Kyivan schools were founded by my predecessor, the Little Russian hetman Petro Konashevych Sahaidachny, and later by the Kyivan metropolitan, Petro Mohyla, there was no monastery, but only a confraternity, that is, a place in which clerical and lay people who were studying could live."[73] This quotation makes it apparent that by the 1760s no one could recall the true nature of the former Kyiv Confraternity; it was even forgotten that Mohyla had not founded a confraternity school but a Lavra (monastery) school. What was remembered was the main point, namely, that the oldest institution of higher learning in Kyiv, which laid the foundations for the Academy, was a secular establishment.

71.　A. Sydorenko, *The Kievan Academy in the Seventeenth Century* (Ottawa, 1977), 29–31; Pylypiuk, "Eucharisterion," 59.

72.　*PKK*, 2: 468, 469, 465. The monastery was closed in 1786.

73.　"Proshenie Malorossiiskago shliakhetstva i starshin vmeste s getmanom o vosstanovlenii raznykh starinnykh prav Malorossii, podannoe Ekaterine II v 1764 godu," *Kievskaia starina*, 1883, no. 6: 344.

Although the Kyivan College (1632–1701) and the Academy (1701–1817) cannot be regarded as confraternity schools, they not only preserved but extended the significant accomplishments of their predecessor, the confraternity school, which was in existence from 1615 to 1632. The sons of burghers from all parts of Ukraine comprised a significant percentage of its student body. The Kyivan Academy became an all-Ukrainian institution of higher learning open to all social strata, attracting eminent churchmen, educators, scholars, and writers. Thanks to the activities of the Academy and the Caves Monastery printshop, Kyiv became the foremost cultural center of Ukraine.

The history of the Kyivan Academy and its predecessor requires further study.[74] Here we shall limit ourselves to examining its relations with the confraternities, which were manifold. The confraternity schools provided elementary education to future entrants of the Kyivan Academy, whose graduates were often engaged as teachers by the confraternities. The importance of the academy for western Ukraine increased during the late seventeenth and eighteenth centuries in connection with the (previously mentioned) decline in the level of instruction at the Lviv Stauropegion School. In the eighteenth century it was even called a "trivial" school.[75] Dormitory residents studied at the trivial school and, having completed their studies, taught their younger colleagues. Some of them studied concurrently at the Lviv "public schools," especially the Jesuit

---

74.   See the anthology of articles entitled *The Kiev Mohyla Academy* (*HUS* 8, nos. 1–2, 1984) including bibliographic surveys by Frank Sysyn, Paulina Lewin, Omeljan Pritsak, and Oksana Procyk. A series of Ukrainian translations of courses in philosophy offered at the Kyiv Mohyla Academy was prepared and partially published by the Institute of Philosophy and the Institute of Ukrainian Studies of the National Academy of Sciences of Ukraine. Ukrainian translations of philosophical works by Teofan Prokopovych, Stefan Iavorsky, Hryhorii Skovoroda and others have been issued by the Naukova Dumka Publishing House. For recent discussions of the history of the Kyiv Mohyla Academy, see *Kyievo-Mohylians'ka akademiia v imenakh, XVII–XVIII st.: Entsyklopedychne vydannia*, comp. Z. I. Khyzhniak (Kyiv, 2001); *Kyievo-Mohylians'ka akademiia: Materialy do bibliohrafichnoho pokazhchyka literatury z fondiv Naukovoï biblioteky NaUKMA*, issue 1, comp. T. Shul'ha, intro. Z. I. Khyzhniak (Kyiv, 2002); Z. I. Khyzhniak, *Rektory Kyievo-Mohylians'koï akademiï, 1615–1817* (Kyiv, 2002).

75.   TsDIAL 408/1/388: 35. The adjective "trivial" is derived from "trivium."

Academy.[76] Even earlier, there were cases of Orthodox students studying at Catholic schools. As early as 1616, a Ukrainian from Ostrih was enrolled at the papal Greek College in Rome; he expressed hostility toward the Uniates, calling them Poles and stressing that he was a true Ukrainian, unlike them—*se esse verum Ruthenum non illos*.[77] Quite a few Orthodox Ukrainians studied at the Zamość (Zamostia) Academy. At least some of them lived on the premises of the Zamostia Confraternity and taught at the confraternity school. Hryhorii Butovych, a student of the Kyivan Academy and the author of a panegyric to Arsenii Zhelyborsky published by the Stauropegion, had contracts with the Zamostia Confraternity, particularly in 1640–42, as did Petro Sozonovych Balyka of Kyiv and Mykhailo Hunashevsky, the owner of an important manuscript anthology including the text of the *Perestoroha*, in 1645–46.[78] Ukrainians—not only Uniates, but also Orthodox—also comprised no less than thirty percent of the general enrollment of about 700 students at the Jesuit Academy in Lviv.[79] In 1691 the Russian diplomatic resident, Volkov, citing one of the confraternity leaders, Iurii Papara, recounted that the Jesuits allowed the Ukrainians, after completing their studies of rhetoric, to attend courses in philosophy for only one year: "they do not allow us to study philosophy for more than a year, and then command us to be Uniates."[80] Occasionally, students had to assume an alias in order to complete their courses. Nevertheless, throughout the eighteenth century Ukrainians frequently attended the Lviv Academy. Among them were the former Kyivan Academy students Iakym Bohomolevsky, Mytrofan Slotvynsky, Petro Kos (Kuliabko), Iosyf Rudensky, and Vasyl Hryhorovych-Barsky.[81] Students from Kyiv often resided at the Lviv Confraternity and served as tutors at the confraternity school. At the beginning

76. NM, general visitation, 15, 4; *Congregationes particulares*, 161.

77. *Epistolae aliaque scripta Metropolitarum Kioviensium H. Potij et J. Velamin Rutskyj (1596–1637)* (Rome, 1955), 30.

78. Budilovich, *Russkaia pravoslavnaia starina*, 82.

79. S. Bednarski, "Dzieje kulturalne jezuickiego kolegium we Lwowie w XVIII wieku," *Pamiętnik Literacki* 23 (1936).

80. RGADA 79/1, vol. 237, folio 173.

81. P. Kudriavtsev, "Osvitni mandrivky vykhovantsiv Kyïvs'koï akademiï za kordon u XVIII st.," *Kyïvs'ki zbirnyky* (Kyiv) 1 (1930–31): 287.

of 1725, the nuncio appointed a commission to scrutinize confraternity activities that included the Lviv Roman Catholic vicar, Feliks Szaniawski; the Lviv canon, Tomasz Józefowicz; and the archimandrite of the Miltsi Basilian monastery, Inokentii Pikhovych. The commission categorically demanded that the confraternity forbid Orthodox students to reside in its dormitory, particularly those who had earlier studied in Kyiv, unless they adopted the Catholic faith.[82] It should be noted that at various times, there were quite a few students from Lviv at the Kyivan Academy. In the eighteenth century these included, in particular, Oleksander (Sofronii) Myhalevych, who became a professor in Kyiv and later rector of the Moscow Academy; a burgher's son, Anton Myhanetsky; Vasyl Konashevych; and Ivan Blonsky. An even greater number of Kyivan Academy students came from the environs of Lviv,[83] and some of them studied in Lviv before leaving for Kyiv. Occasionally the confraternity provided assistance to its students who intended to continue their education in Kyiv. Thus, on 8 November 1691, 30 zlotys were issued to Bazylevych and Susalsky, "students who are going to Kyiv"; in 1692, 15 zlotys were given to the student Terletsky for his journey to Kyiv. In 1697 the confraternity sent money to the student Charnetsky, who was studying in Kyiv.[84] Some of the students sent to the Kyiv Mohyla Academy later returned to Lviv to teach at the confraternity school. For example, the above-mentioned Bazylevych was a teacher at the confraternity no later than 1694. The Kyivan Academy's relations with Lviv are also corroborated by the existence in the library of the Kyiv Mohyla Academy of lecture notes taken at the Lviv Jesuit Academy.[85]

Many of those who studied at the Lviv and Kyiv academies in the late seventeenth and eighteenth centuries and rallied around the Lviv Confraternity during their stay in Lviv later made their careers in ecclesiastical and educational

82.   IuSLS, 1: 113.

83.   Akty i dokumenty, otnosiashchiesia k istorii Kievskoi akademii (Kyiv, 1904), section 2, vol. 1: 41, 63, 285, vol. 5: 297, 527.

84.   TsDIAL 129/1/1119: 13, 29; Sharanevych, Nykolai Krasovs'kyi, 115.

85.   N. I. Petrov, Opisanie rukopisnykh sobranii, nakhodiashchikhsia v gorode Kieve, vol. 1 (Moscow, 1891), 233–43, 280; NBUV, Manuscript Institute, MS I-6232, 2.

institutions, not only in Ukraine but beyond its borders. There is evidence that Teofilakt Lopatynsky, who completed his education at the Kyiv Mohyla Academy, was born and studied in Lviv. In 1706–8 he was rector of the Slavonic-Greco-Latin Academy in Moscow. Ianuarii Zablotsky, who studied in Kyiv, Mohyliv, and Lviv, entered the St. Aleksandr Nevsky Monastery in St. Petersburg in 1717, serving as director of its library in 1732.[86] Mytrofan Slotvynsky, mentioned earlier, was a graduate of the Kyivan Academy, a teacher of philosophy and a prefect at the Kharkiv Collegium and, in 1737, rector of the Moscow Academy. After his studies in Kyiv and Lviv, Iakym Bohomolevsky taught briefly in Russia.[87] Iosyf Zahorovsky, who had studied rhetoric in Lviv, was transferred in 1733 from the Kyivan Caves Monastery to the St. Aleksandr Nevsky Monastery. In 1736 Andrii Chaikovsky was summoned from Kyiv to take a post at the Vologda seminary. He had studied in Lviv in 1715 and later completed his studies in Kyiv, where he taught at least until 1742. Andrii (Amvrosii) Zertis Kamensky, who taught at the Nevsky Seminary in St. Petersburg from 1736 to 1748 and was later appointed rector of the Moscow Academy, studied in Lviv, Kyiv, and Moscow. The former Greek Catholic Pafnutii Zakharzhevsky studied in Lviv, then in Kyiv, and finally in one of the Polish colleges. In 1739 he was defrocked for "disloyal speech" while serving in Russia; from 1730 to 1741 he taught children of clergymen in Samara and later at the Kolomna seminary. Graduates of Lviv schools sometimes obtained posts in the Russian civil service. For example, the nobleman's son Ivan Tarnovsky studied in the lower classes of the Lviv Jesuit Academy (up to rhetoric). Having mastered several languages (Ukrainian, Latin, and Russian), he became a translator for Voznitsyn and Volkov, Russian diplomatic representatives in Poland. He arrived in Moscow in 1694 with his uncle Polikhronii, the hegumen of the Krekhiv Monastery.[88]

---

86.   K. Kharlampovich, *Malorossiiskoe vliianie na velikorusskuiu tserkovnuiu zhizn'*, vol. 1 (Kazan, 1914), 590, 629, 650, 817.

87.   *Akty i dokumenty, otnosiashchiesia k istorii Kievskoi akademii*, section 2, vol. 1: 288.

88.   Kharlampovich, *Zapadnorusskiia pravoslavnyia shkoly*, 579, 618, 621, 629, 713, 797.

In the eighteenth century, students affiliated with the Stauropegion school could also attend lectures in the school at St. George's Cathedral. A manuscript copy of the philosophy course from the mid-eighteenth century contains the following notation in Latin: "On 9 September 1748, a course in dialectics was begun at St. George's Cathedral in Lviv and completed on 7 October of the same year under the Rev. Vasyl Boryshkovych.... "[89] As a result of the activities of this school and other monastery schools, many manuscript copies of courses in rhetoric, poetics, logic, philosophy, natural science, and other subjects were collected in monastery libraries.[90] From 1711, an insignificant number of Ukrainians also studied at the "Ukrainian-Armenian" College of the Theatines, which was established in 1665.[91]

During the seventeenth and eighteenth centuries, besides higher educational institutions (such as the Kyiv, Lviv, and Lutsk schools, and possibly the Vinnytsia school and others), elementary schools maintained by local residents sprang up in many regions of Ukraine: those in central and eastern Ukraine were maintained by "the community,"[92] while confraternities managed those in the western Ukrainian lands. Also very active were major confraternity schools in the palatinate of Podlachia, namely the school of the St. Nicholas Confraternity in Bilsk and that of the Transfiguration Confraternity in Dorohychyn. In 1699 a commission appointed in the name of the Polish king prohibited the Orthodox confraternity school in Bilsk from enrolling Uniate and Roman Catholic students.[93] Some confraternity statutes stated explicitly that the confraternity managed the affairs of the school[94] or that

---

89.   Petrov, *Opisanie rukopisnykh sobranii*, 234–35.

90.   LNB, Basilian monasteries collection, MSS 158, 251, 466, 506, 541, 720 et al.

91.   E. Tryjarski, "Studia nad rękopisami i dialektem kipczackim Ormian polskich, 3," *Rocznik Orientalistyczny* 24, no. 1 (1960): 45.

92.   I. Pavlovskii, *Prikhodskie shkoly v staroi Malorossii i prichiny ikh unichtozheniia* (Kyiv, 1904, repr. from *Kievskaia starina*), 23; A. Lazarevskii, "Statisticheskie svedeniia ob ukrainskikh narodnykh shkolakh i gospitaliakh v XVIII veke," *Osnova*, 1862, no. 5: 82–89.

93.   A. Mironowicz, *Podlaskie ośrodki i organizacje prawosławne w XVI i XVII wieku* (Białystok, 1991), 209, 220.

94.   Statute of the confraternity in Kamianka Strumylova; text in B. Faliński, *Źródła dziejowe starostwa i parafii Kamionka Strumiłowa* (Kamianka Strumylova, 1928), 74, 76.

some of its funds were to be expended on the teacher's salary,[95] and confraternity elders were instructed to "make efforts on behalf ... of the school."[96] According to the statute of the confraternity in the village of Strashevychi near Staryi Sambir, members were obliged to ensure that "poor children be taught in the confraternity school, and nothing be exacted from them, in accordance with the rules of the confraternity school."[97] But even confraternities whose statutes made no mention of this often maintained schools. For example, during the eighteenth century there were no fewer than three schools in Drohobych: at the confraternities of St. George, the Holy Trinity, and the Elevation of the Holy Cross.[98] Teachers at these schools were known as *bakaliary* (from the Latin *baccalaureus*) or *director scholae*. The larger and medium-sized towns had several schools (there were three in Brody and three or four in Stryi),[99] while the smaller towns and many villages had one each. Itinerant students and teachers who transferred from one school to another became commonplace. As early as the end of the sixteenth century, Varfolomii Zhashkovsky of Halych, the son of impoverished parents who later became servants in Lviv, "lived as a student in Ruthenian schools in various towns."[100] From approximately 1645 to 1649, the precentor Fedir Vyshniansky taught in Rohatyn, Stryi, Drohobych, and later in Stryi once again. Vyshniansky was an educated man with a library of his own. Besides him, Demian Babychenko from the town of Khorol, Kostiantyn Bekyshevych, and other "bachelors" who had arrived from various towns of Galicia (Buchach, Rohatyn, Uhniv, Drohobych), Podillia (Vyshnevets, Bar), and sometimes even from the trans-Dnipro region, taught in Stryi during the seventeenth century. During the second half of that century, Hryhorii Voloskovych, Luka

95. Statute of the confraternity in Olesko (TsDIAL 201/4b/3006).

96. Statute of the suburban St. Nicholas Confraternity in Peremyshl (National Library, Warsaw, Special Collections Division, MS 2652, f. 19).

97. *Visnyk Narodnoho Doma*, 1911, no. 9: 154–56; nos. 11–12: 169–78.

98. *Narodna tvorchist' ta etnohrafiia*, 1963, no. 4: 94.

99. Kryp'iakevych, "Z istoriï halyts'koho shkil'nytstva," 24; V. Zalozetskii, "Neskol'ko svedenii o gorode Strye," *Chervonaia Rus'* (Lviv), 1890, no. 44: 1–2.

100. Dobrianskii, *Istoriia episkopov*, period II, xiv–xv.

Noselevych, Panteleimon Tyshivetsky, and others taught at the confraternity school in Zamostia.[101] In the records of various town councils and in the margins of some manuscript and printed books still preserved in churches one may find references to such itinerant precentors who earned their living not only as teachers but also as copyists of books, and who would hire their students on occasion to perform these tasks. Thanks to them, centers for the copying of books were established at some of the confraternity schools. Thus, books copied in the late sixteenth and early seventeenth centuries by the teachers Ivan Berevych, Vasyl Bohonosyk (two books), Symon, a relative of Bishop Makar Tuchapsky, and others were preserved in the town of Stryi. It should be noted that one of the graduates of the Stauropegion school was a precentor from Transcarpathia, Ivan Iuhasevych (1741–1814), who, upon returning there, copied and designed more than thirty manuscript anthologies.[102]

Books used in the urban schools contain a variety of marginal notations in Church Slavonic and Latin, as well as in Ukrainian. It is clear that not only some of the teachers, but also the most able students knew Latin. As a rule, the quality of instruction in the urban confraternity schools was considerably higher than in the rural schools. As noted in the description of the Drohobych region compiled by an Austrian government official in 1774, "villagers who wanted to provide their children with a better education than the fourteen days of teaching given by the village priest" sent them to study in Drohobych.[103] Other towns also served as educational centers for neighboring villages.

The large number of schools established through the initiative of the confraternities helped increase the demand for textbooks. In the late seventeenth and early eighteenth centuries, primers were published in relatively large editions.

---

101.   TsDIAL 13, 376: 1194, 371: 1630; Zalozetskii, "Neskol'ko svedenii o gorode Strye," 44–49; Budilovich, *Russkaia pravoslavnaia starina*, 81.

102.   Ia. P. Zapasko, *Ornamental'ne oformlennia ukraïns'koï rukopysnoï knyhy* (Kyiv, 1960), 108, 112; É. Baletskii, "Ėgerskii rukopisnyi irmologii," *Studia slavica* (Budapest) 4, fasc. 3–4 (1958): 302.

103.   LNB, Kozłowski portfolio, 76, 15, f. 27.

Six hundred copies were published of the Lviv primer of 1662; the primer of 1692 was published in 1,987 copies, and primers published between 1698 and 1722 appeared in press runs of 5,900 to 7,000 copies. During a period of 22 years (from 1698 to 1720), 24,900 copies of primers were printed, approximately equaling the number of copies of other publications that appeared during those years.[104] As compared with other books, primers sold briskly: for example, 643 copies of primers were sold in Lviv between 1738 and 1740.[105] There was also a great demand for other schoolbooks.[106] The Lviv Confraternity maintained numerous elementary schools by supplying them with textbooks. In so doing, the Stauropegion rendered a great service, for these rural and urban schools played a significant role in the cultural and educational development of Ukraine. In the so-called "Plan for the abolition of the Union" (the exact date is not known, but the document probably dates from the late seventeenth or early eighteenth century) we read: "the most recalcitrant ones and those who most encourage disobedience in others are the Ukrainians from the common people (plebs) who know how to read in their language. The cause of their recalcitrance must therefore be eradicated, and then it will cease on its own. And we Poles can achieve this easily if we forbid those sons of peasants to study in the schools attached to the churches, and, by so doing, we shall avoid the harm that we are often obliged to suffer at the hands of the serfs. For a peasant schooled in a simple village school, fleeing several dozen miles from his master, seeks his freedom.... The noblemen of the palatinates of Ruthenia, Volhynia, Podillia, and Bratslav, along with neighboring lands, complain of this. Therefore, instructions given to estate administrators must oblige them to keep careful watch to ensure that peasant children become accustomed not to books but to the plow, hooked plow, hoe, and flail!"[107] A

---

104.   For an enumeration of the various editions of primers, see *PKM*, 1–2 (indexes in 1: 128 and 2, pt. 2: 114).

105.   TsDIAL 129/1/1170, f. 1–2.

106.   Of all the publications of the Lviv printshop, the most frequently reprinted were the *chasoslovy* or breviaries (eleven editions were printed between 1602 and 1739).

107.   Harasiewicz, *Annales ecclesiae Ruthenae*, 160–61.

number of historians believe that the "Plan" was drafted by
an exponent of the views of the Polish nobility, while others
assume that the author was a Ukrainian who, in creating a
literary mystification, deliberately exaggerated the situation
so as to expose the attitude of the Roman Catholic nobility
toward the Uniate Church. Whatever the case, this document
shows that the link between educational level and propensity
to social activism had been recognized, attesting yet again to the
immense sociopolitical significance of the educational activity
conducted by the confraternities.

* * *

The most detailed monument of early modern Ukrainian
pedagogical thought is the Lviv Confraternity School statute.
Entitled "Poriadok shkil'nyi" (Pedagogical Rule), it may also
very well reflect the experience of the Ostrih school. The
Pedagogical Rule was later adopted by the Lutsk Confraternity
School, and possibly by other schools as well. An examination
of this document is therefore useful for understanding the
pedagogical philosophy of the confraternity movement
as a whole. The oldest copies of the Pedagogical Rule are
two Ukrainian texts from Lviv: the first was ratified by the
confraternity and affixed with its stamp on 8 October 1586,[108]
while the second was slightly altered after 1588 and copied
into the confraternity's Album.[109] A Greek version has also
survived in two copies (in a separate notebook without a seal,
as well as in the Album).[110] It is somewhat shorter than the
Ukrainian text and was most probably translated from the
Ukrainian original.[111]

The Pedagogical Rule provided for close cooperation between
school and home. A parent or guardian who wished to send his
child to the confraternity school was first required to familiarize

---

108.   DS, 21–29; PBSh, 37–43; TsDIAL 129/1/87. In the following text, articles of
this version are cited in parentheses.

109.   DS, 30–34; Album, 448–54. Articles of this version are not numbered.

110.   DS, 21–29; Album, 445–53. Articles of the Greek version are not
numbered.

111.   I am indebted to Professor Ihor Ševčenko for an assessment of differences
between the Ukrainian and Greek texts.

himself with the Rule so that he would understand "in what manner his son will be taught." He was forewarned that he would be expected "to help the school in every possible way" (article 1). The confraternity required that registration of students take place in the presence of parents, a teacher, and one or two witnesses.[112] The Rule cites as a model the trade-guild custom of craftsmen publicly registering apprentices and publicly testing their skills at the end of an apprenticeship. "And from this practice, the master receives great satisfaction" (articles 1, 19).[113]

In the evenings, students were required to read and explain their homework to their parents or to the landlords at their places of residence. One of the responsibilities of teachers and caretakers of the school, as enumerated in the Rule, was to remind parents and guardians that children were to behave at home according to the "rules of school education." The Rule stipulated that a student's failure at school had to be accounted for (obviously, by the confraternity), whether it was due to the negligence of teachers or to parental interference with the child's "studies and acquisition of good manners" (article 18).

Instruction was to begin and end at a time determined by the teacher (article 6). It was the teacher's responsibility to ensure that every student attended school, to ascertain the reason for absences and, in the case of chronic absenteeism, to expel the child (articles 7, 17). In the morning, students were questioned on "yesterday's work," and their written homework was checked (article 10). After the midday meal, students were required to "write by themselves the lessons assigned by their teacher on their slates, except the younger pupils, for whom the teacher himself must write out the exercises" (article 11). The Greek grammar textbook compiled at the confraternity school also specified that students were to write out on their slates the conjugations of verbs according to paradigms given to them.[114]

---

112. There are known cases of students registering on their own. The late sixteenth-century list includes the following entry: "Fedor Dionisiievych asked to be taught and gave four groszy" (TsDIAL 129/1/1116a, f. 4).

113. Betsy B. Price discusses noticeable similarities between the rituals of inception in medieval Western craft guilds and universities. Cf. "Master by Any Other Means," *Renaissance and Reformation* 13, no. 1 (1989): 115.

114. *Adelphotēs* (Lviv, 1591); cf. reprint, ed. O. Horbatsch (Frankfurt am Main, 1973), 137.

The Rule suggested that students test each other on difficult words as they walked to and from school (article 11). A review of the week's work was conducted on Saturday mornings. After lunch came arithmetic, study of the church calendar, singing, and a discussion of a moral theme (the study of "good habits"). Repetition was generally considered the most efficient technique of study. In the preface to one confraternity publication, the human mind is compared to a slate that is "blank and naked when it knows nothing and understands nothing." However, "when a subject is mastered, whether it be philosophy, theology, astrology, mathematics, arithmetic, rhetoric, or some other subject, then, as on a slate, this knowledge is written on the human mind."[115]

As evidenced by a number of points in the Rule, its compilers were well aware that student progress largely depended on the pedagogical expertise of the teacher (*dydaskal* or *daskal*), assisted by the best students—the *protoskholy*. The teacher was required to serve as an example of moral behavior. If a teacher or student was found to be a thief, drunkard, slanderer, or "money lover," not only was he forbidden to teach, but he was not allowed to live on the confraternity premises in order to prevent him from setting a bad example (preamble and article 19).

Students were to be punished "not tyrannically, but in a manner befitting a teacher" (article 12). The system of rewards is also interesting: outstanding students were given an honored place in the classroom, on the principle that "He who is more able should sit higher, even if he is very poor" (article 3).

In keeping with the democratic character of the confraternity schools, the Rule emphasized that "wealthy students are not to be given preference or privilege over indigent students" (article 4), and "the teacher must teach and love every child alike, whether he be the son of a rich man or a destitute orphan who begs on the street for his daily bread" (article 5).

Every week, two to four students were assigned to keep order in the school; none could refuse "when his turn came." It was their responsibility to come early to school to sweep,

115.   *Apostol* (i.e., Acts and Epistles in Church Slavonic) (Lviv, 1666), preface.

light the stove, sit by the door and "note well" who entered and left, taking note of those who had not studied or misbehaved (article 16). A "penitarch" and "censors," chosen from among the students, helped maintain discipline.[116] A later document indicates that some students who lived in the dormitory (*bursa*) were selected as "officials" to help the choir director (whom the confraternity appointed to supervise the dormitory). There was an "awakener" who had to rouse his fellow classmates from sleep, two "window guards" who made sure that windows and walls were clean and that no one used coal to write on the walls, and two "pacifiers" who swept the yard and were responsible for general order. There was also someone assigned to tend the sick, as well as a paid guard (*philax*) who locked the gate, gave out meals to dormitory residents, and washed the dishes.[117]

A characteristic aim of humanistic pedagogy was to prepare students for participation in civic life (*formazione alla vita civile*).[118] Thus, in confraternity schools students held various elective offices of "self-government," while older students had to study not only under the guidance of an instructor, but also independently. The application of humanistic techniques to the study of ancient Greek and Latin, initiated by Petrarch, was further elaborated in the fifteenth and sixteenth centuries. Students copied quotations, aphorisms, examples, and anecdotes (*loci communes*) into a special notebook, and to facilitate its use, they compiled alphabetical indexes.[119] In the seventeenth and eighteenth centuries, students and teachers in Ukraine compiled similar manuscript collections of various study materials, proverbs, short stories, and so forth. There is evidence that individuals associated with the confraternity schools were among the first in Ukraine to apply these methods of teaching and research.[120]

---

116. *AIuZR*, 11: 288, 399.

117. P. Kryvonosiuk, "Stavropihiis'ka bursa v 1751 r.," *Istorychnyi visnyk* (mimeographed journal edited by history students at the Lviv Ukrainian Underground University), 1923, nos. 2–3: 28; I. Kryp'iakevych, "Deshcho zi zvychaïv u l'vivs'kii shkoli ta bursi," *Zhyttia i znannia*, 1934, no. 6: 168–69; *DS*, 111.

118. E. Garin, *L'educazione in Europa, 1400–1600* (Bari, 1957).

119. Ibid.

120. Some such collections are preserved among the manuscripts from the Lviv Stauropegion library.

Evgenii Medynsky has suggested that the confraternity schools of Ukraine and Belarus influenced Comenius's pedagogical system.[121] He even finds parallels between specific sections of confraternity school statutes and sections in the works of the great Czech pedagogue. However, the similarities between Comenius's ideas and those expressed in the statutes of confraternity schools are limited to regulations that were common to most humanist schools.[122]

Before examining the curriculum of the confraternity schools, it is worth noting which textbooks were used. To help satisfy educational needs in Ukraine, Ivan Fedorov published a primer in 1574. It was probably reissued in Lviv later in the sixteenth century or in the first half of the seventeenth, but no copy has been found. From archival sources we can ascertain that confraternity editions of the primer appeared in 1671, 1692, 1698, 1701, 1720, and 1754. Those that have survived (published in 1671, 1692, and 1710) have the same text and title: *A Primer of Useful Guidance in Reading and Writing the Slavonic Language for Those Who Wish to Study*. All the primers begin with the material found in the Fedorov primer: the alphabet, syllables of two and three letters, punctuation, and a short reader of prayers and religious songs.[123] After finishing the primer, students studied reading and writing from the breviary and psalter. Ukrainian printshops issued both books in abbreviated inexpensive editions especially "for the education of small children." In the printshop records they are called "school breviaries" and "little psalters" (*psaltyrky*). For the study of musical notation, the schools used "irmologions," first in manuscript and, from 1700, in printed form as well.[124]

---

121.   E. Medynskii, *Bratskie shkoly Ukrainy i Belorussii v XVI–XVII st. i ikh rol' v vossoedinenii Ukrainy s Rossiei* (Moscow, 1954); cf. Ukrainian translation (Kyiv, 1958).

122.   Cf. Ia. Isaievych, "Ian Amos Komens'kyi i Ukraïna," *UIZh*, 1967, no. 3: 129–31.

123.   On the other versions of the Church Slavonic Primer, cf. R. Cleminson, "First Slavonic Primers to 1700," *Australian Slavonic and East European Studies* 2 (1988): 1–27.

124.   Iu. Iasynovs'kyi, *Ukraïns'ki ta bilorus'ki notoliniini Irmoloï XVI–XVIII st.* (Lviv, 1996), 78, 87–88.

In 1591, the confraternity published a Greco-Slavonic grammar under the title *Adelphotēs* (Greek for "confraternity"). The book, written by Arsenios of Elasson and his Lviv *spoudeioi* (students), was based mainly on the Greek grammar by Constantine Laskaris, but in some chapters the authors express original thoughts.[125] It is believed that Ukrainian students checked the Slavonic grammatical terminology, which later had a great influence on grammars of other Slavic languages. Both the Greek and the Slavonic sections of the grammar were highly esteemed in Ukraine and abroad, not only at the time of its composition but also in later centuries.

When its printshop was established, the Lviv Confraternity announced a plan to publish not only grammars but also textbooks of poetics, rhetoric, and philosophy, as well as chronicles. Various difficulties prevented the fulfillment of the project. Of the books planned for the higher levels of education, only the Greco-Slavonic grammar was published. Other textbooks of "higher learning" were kept in the library.

Presumably, the library was used at least occasionally by students and teachers of the confraternity "gymnasion." A brief survey of the contents of the "educational" section of the library[126] may give some idea of the subjects studied not only in the Lviv school but also in other schools of its type. The core holdings consisted of textbooks for the study of classical Greek and Latin. As early as 1601, the library had a Latin dictionary; in 1619 it acquired a "dictionary in folio" and a "quadrilingual dictionary"; and in 1688 it possessed a "dictionary of the Latin language," a Latin-Greek-German dictionary, a Polish-Latin-Greek dictionary by Cnapius (Knapski), and a "Lexicon of Turkish, Arabic, and Persian." In 1601, we find a Greek grammar manual by Nicolas Cleynaerts (Clenardus), Latin grammar manuals by Cornelius Valerius and Manuel Alvarez, and a textbook for the study of classical Latin phraseology by Aldus Manutius

---

125. Studyns'kyi, "'Adel'fotes'"; N. P. Kiselev, "Grecheskaia pechat' na Ukraine v XVI veke," *Kniga: Issledovaniia i materialy* 7 (1962), 187; Dēmētrakopoulos, *Arsenios Elassonos*, 123.

126. The most complete publication of the Stauropegion library catalogues has been prepared by Vira Frys (forthcoming).

the Younger. For the study of classical languages, students of confraternity schools could turn to the original works of Greek and Latin authors. Greek literature was represented in the Lviv library by authors from the main periods of its development: Classical (Aesop, Pindar, Euripides); Hellenistic (Heliodorus, Appolonius of Alexandria, "Alexandria" by Lycophron of Chalcis); Greco-Roman (Lucian); and Byzantine (Photius's *Bibliotheca*; a commentary on the Iliad by Bishop Eustathius of Thessalonica). There were also texts of the main representatives of Greek political rhetoric of the classical era (Demosthenes, Isocrates), a collection of *Speeches of Ancient Orators* (in Greek), epigrams by Greek poets, a Greco-Latin edition of the Apocrypha, and various other books. Among the theological books in Greek, mention should be made of the critical edition of St. John Chrysostom's commentaries on the Acts of the Apostles and on the Pauline Epistles published at Eton in 1612 by Sir Henry Savile.[127] Roman literature was represented by Virgil, Horace, Ovid (three editions were held in 1688), and the speeches of Cicero (including an edition with commentaries by Cellius). Of the Italian humanists, the library held such Latin works as Petrarch's *De remediis utriusque fortunae* and Pico della Mirandola's *Flores poetarum*. In the second half of the seventeenth century, the library acquired many historical works, among them those of Xenophon, Thucydides, Dionysius of Halicarnassus, Plutarch, Appian of Alexandria, and Justinus. As early as 1601, the library held the *Hungarian Chronicle*, the Polish chronicle of Marcin Bielski, and a book by the Venetian historian Marco Antonio Sabellico (1436–1506). Also represented were Ukrainian historical works in manuscript: two chronicles and several collections of copies of historical documents.

Of the philosophers, Aristotle seems to have been considered most important. In 1601, the library had only his *Organon*, but by 1688, it held nine Greek and Latin editions of his works: three copies of the *Organon*, the *Ethics*, the *Rhetoric*, etc. It also possessed the *Textbook of Peripatetic Logic*, a complete edition of Plato, an introduction to dialectics by Porphyry

---

127.   *Pershodrukar*, 145.

Isagogus, the *Enchiridion* of Epictetus, the *Institutionum Dialecticarum* by Pedro Da Fonseca, and various other books on philology and theology.[128]

The collection of the Stauropegion library does not, of course, fully reflect the course of study at the higher levels at the confraternity school. Some of the books in the library were not acquired deliberately but were received as gifts, and part of the collection was not catalogued. Moreover, students certainly made use of the private libraries of instructors. If a little-known figure such as Pafnutii Kuntsevych had a hundred books of his own, then scholars of the level of the Zyzanii brothers or Pamvo Berynda may have possessed many more. Only a small number of books have survived from the rich library of Lavrentii Zyzanii, who taught at the Lviv Confraternity School. These include his own Church Slavonic edition of the commentary on the Apocalypse by Andrew of Caesarea (for which Zyzanii used the Greek original of the work) and a copy of the Suda *Lexicon* in the Milan edition of 1499.[129] The library of the confraternity member Roman Striletsky, who died in 1651, consisted of twenty-three books, among them nineteen in Latin and two in Greek. Not surprisingly, the library of a Greek member of the confraternity, Kostiantyn Mezapeta, included many more books in Greek. A catalogue compiled by the owner in 1651 listed Greek grammars by Gretser and Vergara and a Greek edition of Demosthenes.[130] The libraries of Striletsky and Mezapeta were bequeathed to the confraternity.

The holdings of the confraternity library give only a very general idea of the school curriculum. Further details are known from the Pedagogical Rule. Study in the lower grades began with "letters and syllables" based on the primer, breviary, and psalter. The technique of learning syllables and using them to develop reading skills, common in ancient Greece and Rome, was also accepted by Renaissance teachers

---

128.   Ia. Isaievych, "Biblioteka L'vivs'koho bratstva," *Bibliotekoznavstvo i bibliohrafiia* (Kharkiv) 3 (1966).

129.   A. G. Boner, "So znakom vladel'tsa," *Voprosy bibliotechnogo dela, bibliografii i istorii knigi v Sibiri i na Dal'nem Vostoke* (Novosibirsk, 1975), 184.

130.   *Fedorovskie chteniia 1976* (Moscow, 1978), 70–71.

in Italy and elsewhere.[131] It may have come to Ukraine from the Byzantine tradition, as well as from European schools. In the nineteenth century, this method, common in elementary schools throughout Ukraine, was ridiculed as archaic, but it had certain advantages and was considered particularly suitable for languages with a phonetically oriented orthography.[132]

As is apparent from the Rule, students were divided into three groups: "the first will learn to recognize and put together words, the second will learn to read and memorize, and the third will learn, by reading, to explain, discuss, and understand" (article 9). Thus the first group learned reading and writing, while the second and third went on to more advanced skills.

It is quite understandable that the study of Greek was prominent in the schools founded by the Lviv and Vilnius confraternities. For Ukrainian students, it was a way of learning about the roots of their Orthodox identity, while for their Greek colleagues it was also a means of promoting their native culture, which was important to the Greek community both in Ukraine and beyond its borders. The Rule confirms that the study of Greek, Church Slavonic, and common Ruthenian proceeded along parallel lines. Some of the recommended methods may seem strange today, but their purpose is quite clear. For example, students were requested to ask questions of one another in Greek. When asked in Greek, they were to answer in Church Slavonic, and when asked in Church Slavonic they had to answer in the "common" language. They were not to converse in the vernacular, but exclusively in Greek and Church Slavonic.[133]

Some scholars have maintained that the study of Greek began in Lviv ca. 1604. However, as early as 1592 students of the Lviv Confraternity School were already being invited to become teachers of Greek, Latin, and Church Slavonic in Peremyshl.[134] Even in the early years of the confraternity school, the level of

---

131.   Grendler, *Schooling in Renaissance Italy*, 156–57.
132.   Ibid., 157, 160–61.
133.   *DS*, 29.
134.   *MCS*, 363.

instruction in Greek was so high that students translated not only from Greek into Church Slavonic but also from Ukrainian into Greek, and even wrote Greek verses. Greek charters and letters of the Eastern Orthodox patriarchs were kept in the archives of the Lviv Confraternity along with their Ukrainian translations, the latter presumably produced at the confraternity school.[135] During his visit to Ukraine in 1589, the patriarch of Constantinople, Jeremiah II Tranos, was greeted in Greek in the town of Ternopil by a teacher of the Lviv Confraternity School named Kyrylo. It has generally been assumed that this Kyrylo, also mentioned in other documents, was Kyrylo Trankvilion-Stavrovetsky.[136] However, discovered documents identify a hieromonk named Kyrylo Ivanovych as an expert in the Greek language,[137] whereas Kyrylo Trankvilion-Stavrovetsky used the works of Dionysius the Pseudo-Areopagite in Latin translation.[138] This would indicate that Kyrylo Ivanovych, rather than Kyrylo Stavrovetsky, was the monk Kyrylo of the Lviv Confraternity School.[139]

Later, teachers of the Lviv school included such experts on Greek philology as Cyril Lukaris, his protosyncellus Joseph (who also taught in Kyiv and Halych), Fedir Kasianovych, Ivan Boretsky, and probably Havrylo Dorofeiovych as well. In 1604, Ivan Boretsky signed a contract with the confraternity, agreeing to serve as rector and teacher of Greek and Latin for the modest annual salary of forty zlotys. Later he became rector of the Kyiv Confraternity's "Helleno-Ruthenian" school,

---

135.　B. L. Fonkich, *Grechesko-russkie kul'turnye sviazi v XV–XVII vv.* (Moscow, 1977). For descriptions of the Greek parchment charters now in the Central State Historical Archive of Ukraine in Lviv, cf. O. Kupchyns'kyi and E. Ruzhyts'kyi, *Kataloh perhamentnykh dokumentiv Tsentral'noho derzhavnoho istorychnoho arkhivu URSR u L'vovi, 1233–1799* (Kyiv, 1972).

136.　S. I. Maslov, *Kirill Trankvillion-Stavrovetskii i ego literaturnaia deiatel'nost'* (Kyiv, 1984).

137.　Ia. Isaievych, "Novye materialy ob ukrainskikh i belorusskikh knigopechatnikakh pervoi poloviny XVII veka," *Kniga: Issledovaniia i materialy* 34 (1977), 149–51.

138.　K. Trankvilion-Stavrovets'kyi, *Perlo mnohocěnnoje*, ed. with commentary by H. Trunte, vol. 2, *Kommentar* (Cologne and Vienna, 1985), 356–59.

139.　Ihor Myts'ko has suggested that Kyrylo may be identified with Hieromonk Kypriian of Ostrih. Cf. I. Myts'ko, comp., *Materialy do istoriï Ostroz'koï akademiï, 1576–1636: Bio-bibliohrafichnyi dovidnyk* (Kyiv, 1990), 37.

and subsequently Orthodox metropolitan of Kyiv. There is no doubt that it was he who persuaded the Cossack hetman Petro Konashevych Sahaidachny to bequeath a large sum of money to the Lviv Confraternity in 1622, with the stipulation that the interest be employed to maintain a "qualified master, expert in Greek." The executors of Sahaidachny's will were Boretsky himself and the new hetman, Olyfer Holub, "together with the whole Zaporozhian Host."[140] It is not surprising that Boretsky thought it essential to ensure a stable income for a preceptor of Greek: the future of Greek studies was already in question, even though the influence of ethnic Greeks had never been so strong in the Lviv Confraternity. It would appear, however, that even the hetman's legacy was of no avail, for in the 1630s the teaching of Greek was discontinued for lack of instructors. Nevertheless, the study of Greek remained in high esteem, and in the second half of the seventeenth century there were periods when it was taught, though not on such a high a level as before. Prayers in Greek printed in Cyrillic were included in some Lviv editions of primers.[141] As late as 1686, a former pupil of the Lviv Confraternity School, Pavlo Nehrebetsky, maintained in his memorandum on the advantages of Greek studies over Latin that "among White Ruthenians" the study of Greek was being maintained only in Lviv, while elsewhere there were Latin higher schools alone.[142] Generally speaking, however, in the late seventeenth and eighteenth centuries, instruction in Lviv was offered in the "Ruthenian language" (that is, Ukrainian and Church Slavonic), as well as in Latin. It is interesting to note that the Lviv school was sometimes called "Greco-Slavonic" even after the introduction of Latin into the curriculum: evidently the two "Orthodox" languages were considered more significant from an ideological viewpoint.

   In the opinion of humanistically minded pedagogues, the aim of education was the mastery of rhetoric, which contributed to the intellectual development and moral elevation of students and society in general.[143] The transition from medieval to

---

140.   Krylovskii, *L'vovskoe Stavropigial'noe bratstvo*, suppl., 76–77.

141.   *PKM*, 1: 86, 103, vol. 2, pt. 1: 25.

142.   Kharlampovich, *Zapadnorusskiia pravoslavnyia shkoly*, 308–423.

143.   Paulsen, *Geschichte*, 64–65, 292.

Renaissance education in Italy was marked by a revival of classical rhetoric and the elevation of poetics to the status of a separate discipline.[144] At every level of instruction, students were taught the theoretical bases of disciplines (first grammar and then rhetoric, poetics, and dialectics), proceeded to the study of literature, primarily ancient, and finally prepared their own compositions based on the models they had studied.[145] This scheme, worked out in Italy in the first half of the fifteenth century and characteristic of humanistic schools in general, influenced the method of instruction in Ukrainian confraternity schools. In studying rhetoric, students acquainted themselves not only with classical prose models (Isocrates, Demosthenes, Cicero), but also with Ukrainian rhetorical prose. Manuscript textbooks of rhetoric and poetics were to be found in the Stauropegion library, as well as in the libraries of other confraternities. On the basis of their investigation of Kyivan manuscripts, Hryhorii Syvokin and Paulina Lewin have shown that Ukrainian poetics of the seventeenth century were a significant phenomenon in Ukrainian literary life.[146] A byproduct of the study of poetics was the composition of poems that made their way into confraternity publications and manuscript collections.

Students learned the essentials of philosophy by reading Aristotle and his disciples and commentators. They also studied manuscript courses in philosophy, logic, and dialectics. A few of these manuscripts catalogued in the confraternity library probably belonged to teachers of philosophy.

Like all schools of the time, the confraternity schools taught the fundamentals of theology. However, Ivan Vyshensky criticized the Lviv Confraternity for what he considered insufficient attention to these matters. A former confraternity teacher, Lavrentii Zyzanii, was reproved in Moscow for including information in his catechism "about the heavenly spheres and planets, about the zodiac, eclipses of the sun, thunder and lightning ... earthquakes ... comets and

---

144. Grendler, *Schooling in Renaissance Italy*, 205, 236.
145. Paulsen, *Geschichte*, 345.
146. Lewin, "Ukrainian School Theater"; H. Syvokin', *Davni kyïvs'ki poetyky* (Kharkiv, 1960), 106.

other stars" on the grounds that this information was "taken from Greek magicians and idol worshippers."[147] Presumably, during his tenure as a teacher in Lviv and elsewhere, Zyzanii also included something about natural history and astronomy in his lectures. As a rule, philosophy courses afforded some acquaintance with nature and medicine. In addition, elements of astronomy were taught in connection with the study of the calendar, as were arithmetic and fractions. A collection of arithmetical exercises dating from 1609 that originated in a Ukrainian school (perhaps the Ostrih School) provides evidence that besides the four arithmetical operations, elementary textual problems were also solved.

Occasionally, students had the opportunity to gain some knowledge of the fine arts. Among the teachers in Lviv, for example, was the engraver Vasyl Ushakevych. The curricula of the Lviv and Lutsk confraternity schools included "musical instruction." In the Lviv Confraternity School's first year of existence, the confraternity managed to obtain a charter from Patriarch Jeremiah permitting "vocal music, with the use of notes" during church services.[148] In January 1591, students greeted Mykhailo Rohoza with choral singing in twelve voices—the oldest known performance of polyphonic vocal music in Ukraine.[149] A church deacon usually served as director of the children's choir. From 1604, this function was performed by Fedir Sydorovych.[150] An instruction probably dating from the late seventeenth century to Ruzkevych, a teacher at the confraternity school, specified that the student choir was to consist of four voices: bass, alto, tenor, and descant.[151] The confraternity provided indigent students in the choir with clothing, caps, and boots. Members of the choir and other students studied polyphonic choral music and were acquainted with the rudiments of music theory. The confraternity library

---

147.   N. P. Kiselev, "O moskovskom knigopechatanii XVII veka," *Kniga: Issledovaniia i materialy* 2 (1960), 129.

148.   TsDIAL 129/1/6, f. 12.

149.   M. Antonovych, "Polifonichna muzyka v ukraïns'kykh tserkvakh u dobi kozachchyny," in *Intrepido Pastori* (Rome, 1984), 596.

150.   B. Kudryk, *Ohliad istoriï ukraïns'koï tserkovnoï muzyky* (Lviv, 1937), 18, 19.

151.   *DS*, 112.

had a copy of Johann Spangenberg's *Quaestiones musicae*. A member of the confraternity, Kostiantyn Mezapeta, owned a book on harmony, a "tablature" (notes for polyphonic instrumental music), and scores, both manuscript and printed, for part singing. Students of the confraternity school probably also used scores from Mezapeta's library. In 1633, Mezapeta and a confraternity secretary, Vasyl Bunevsky, were engaged by the confraternity to supervise the improvement of musical performance at the confraternity church.

In 1637, after the death of Hryhorii Romanovych, his heirs donated scores of eight-part and twelve-part compositions to the school, and these were passed on to the teacher Atanasii.[152] A register of music notebooks (dating from 1697) used by students comprises 87 volumes. These included 372 choral works (predominantly motets, also known in Ukraine as "concerts") for three to twelve voices. The register gives the first word or title of each motet, often with the surname of the composer. Among them were Shavarovsky, Byshchovsky, Chernushyn, Lakonenko, Koliadchyn, Pikulynsky, Mazuryk, Iazhevsky, and Mykola Dyletsky (well known as the author of the *Musical Grammar*).[153] The composer Zavadovsky may be identified with the deacon Ievstafii Zavadovsky, a well-known engraver in contact with cultural circles in Kyiv and Lviv. The confraternity paid the composer Havalevych, also a deacon, five zlotys on 20 April 1694 "for motets in three parts." On the same day, Bazylevych was paid six zlotys for motets for three church services and four zlotys for four-voice motets, while the "bassist" was paid 15 groszy for transcribing two canons.[154] It is important to note that Bazylevych had earlier studied in Kyiv, where he evidently learned composition.

Putting their knowledge of music and poetry to practical use, indigent students went from house to house reciting poetry and asking for donations. In summer they were allowed to support themselves in this manner until 1:00 a.m., and in winter until 3:00 a.m.[155] As Ivan Pankevych has noted,

---

152.   *AIuZR*, 11: 91, 351.

153.   Ibid., 12: 62–71.

154.   TsDIAL 129/1/1119: 37.

155.   *MCS*, 112 (night hours were reckoned from sunset).

this custom, which was current in Lviv as early as the sixteenth century, eventually spread throughout the country, including Left-Bank Ukraine and Transcarpathia. It contributed to the appearance of a new genre of itinerant student verses and songs similar in many respects to those of the Western *vagantes*.[156] Students also took part in public processions organized by the confraternity, even though the Catholic hierarchy occasionally prohibited them to do so.[157]

Another typical phenomenon of the humanistic school was the student theater, which developed in Lviv, Lutsk, Kyiv, and other larger towns. Confraternities in Ukraine were not involved in organizing religious dramatic performances to the same extent as in some Western cities.[158] The Stauropegion published a series of dramatized declamations and dialogues that were performed by students of the confraternity school, including *Prosphonēma* (1591), Christmas verses by Pamvo Berynda (1616), *Christos Paschon* by Andrii Skulsky (1630), and *Meditations on the Passion of Christ* by Ioanikii Volkovych. *Christos Paschon* is a Ukrainian reworking of a tragedy compiled in Byzantium in the eleventh and twelfth centuries from the tragedies of Euripides, Aeschylus (*Prometheus Bound*; *Agamemnon*), and Lycophron, as well as from the Gospels and the Apocrypha. Volkovych's *Meditations* is the first datable attempt to stage a performance on the theme of the Passion of Christ in Ukraine.[159] The surnames of some student performers are included in the text published in 1630: Bunevsky (probably the son of the confraternity clerk), Langish, and Herhiievych. As Oleksander Biletsky wrote, "it is entirely possible that the Lviv Confraternity and its school were the cradle of old Ukrainian drama."[160] In the early seventeenth century,

---

156.   I. Pan'kevych, "Pidkarpatorus'ka zapyska students'koï virshi z 1751 r." *Podkarpatska Rus'*, 1928, no. 3: 1.

157.   *AIuZR*, 12: 545.

158.   Particularly well known is the Confraternity of the Passion, which had a tremendous influence on French theatre and literature. See also R. Blasting, "The German Bruderschaften as Producers of Late Medieval Vernacular Religious Drama," *Renaissance and Reformation* 13, no. 1 (1989): 1–14.

159.   V. Riezanov, *Drama ukraïns'ka*, vol. 1 (Kyiv, 1925), 20.

160.   O. Bilets'kyi, "Zarodzhennia dramatychnoï literatury na Ukraïni," *Pratsi v 5–ty tomakh*, vol. 1 (Kyiv, 1965), 306.

Ivan Vyshensky even accused confraternity members of not wanting "to work for the church; they only stage and perform comedies."[161] In the late seventeenth and eighteenth centuries, students in Lviv also staged dramatic performances. On 17 April 1765, the confraternity paid a teacher the considerable sum of 15 zlotys for instruction in "dialogues."[162] Before holidays, the confraternity would hire carpenters and painters to build sets for Nativity plays (*vertepy*) to be performed in the church. In 1743, during an inspection of the church by diocesan officials, a strict prohibition was issued against "meetings and fables (*confabulationes*), especially those not conforming to Christian doctrine and sometimes even offensive to it ... so that the house of God not be turned into a theater."[163]

* * *

The archives of the Stauropegion provide many details about the school's operation and material status. Although this information relates to a particular school, it gives an idea of school life in general.

The confraternity elected "school wardens" to supervise the school. Their primary responsibility was to ensure suitable premises for classes. At first the school was located in a house owned by a confraternity member, Ivan Mynets,[164] until its own building (begun as early as the 1580s) was finished. In the first decades of the seventeenth century, the confraternity had at its disposal two school buildings: a "little wooden school" with a "school kitchen" and a "big school" built of brick. The old printshop burned to the ground in 1630 and was relocated in the school no later than June of that year. This resulted in a "great lack of space," prompting the confraternity to add a second floor to accommodate the printshop in 1633–34. The first floor was then used for the school and for the instructor's residence.[165] The old wooden school building was transferred

161.   I. Vyshens'kyi, *Tvory* (Kyiv, 1959), 191.
162.   TsDIAL 129/1/1138: 9.
163.   *NM*, general visitation, no. 15, f. 4.
164.   TsDIAL 129/1/1044: 7.
165.   *AIuZR*, 11: 345, 350, 376, 379, andothers.

to the grounds of the St. Onuphrius Monastery and rebuilt as
a residence.

School furniture consisted of a "large blackboard," tables, and
benches. The confraternity provided food and firewood for the
school dormitory, where choir members and indigent students
lived. In 1733, the wardens reported that annual expenditures
for the support of poor students and for the hospital amounted
to 700 zlotys.[166] Toward the end of the eighteenth century, there
were thirty boys living in the dormitory.[167] Teachers' salaries
came from quarterly installments paid by the students' parents,
a portion of the "bell tax," and profits from the production and
sale of candles. Teachers had the right, according to established
custom, to be provided with their midday meal by their students'
parents, with each family taking its turn. Occasionally the
confraternity assigned a certain additional sum toward material
assistance for teachers. It was not uncommon for wealthy
individuals to leave bequests to the Stauropegion Confraternity,
with the stipulation that a small portion be assigned to the
school. Such was the case with the estate of Constantine Korniakt
in the village of Zboiska, registered in 1604.[168] As noted earlier,
Hetman Petro Konashevych Sahaidachny of the Zaporozhian
Host left a special bequest for the teaching of Greek at the Lviv
Confraternity School. In announcing this gift, the executors of the
hetman's will, Ivan Boretsky and the new hetman, Olyfer Holub,
"together with the whole Zaporozhian Host," spoke of "this
foundation of the honorable Petro Konashevych Sahaidachny, a
man worthy of every honor and eternal remembrance, with the
efforts of the entire knighthood of the Zaporozhian Host made
through the mediation of myself, Iov Boretsky, the Orthodox
metropolitan of Kyiv, for the school or, rather, for the instructors
(*dydaskaly*), so that instruction at the confraternity school may
continue from now on without interruption for all time, with no
decline in quality or cessation.... " It was further stipulated in
the name of the new hetman and the whole Zaporozhian Host

---

166.   TsDIAL 129/1/1169: 6.
167.   TsDIAL 129/1/1012: 4.
168.   Album, 402, 405.

that if the confraternity applied the interest toward anything other than the school, it would be required to double the sum, and if it should persist in failing to carry out the terms of the will, it would be required to return six times the amount to the fund.[169] On 29 July, a confraternity messenger brought from Kyiv "a gift from Petro Sahaidachny—250 talers" and a "half-purple" mantle of the hetman's that was sold in Constantinople for 120 zlotys.[170] From this sum, the confraternity lent money to its members on condition that they pay the school eight percent annual interest. The borrower's real estate served as collateral. From 1630 to 1690, Sahaidachny's bequest was in the hands of the Affendyk family (Ianii and then Petro), who had to pay 160 zlotys yearly to the school. In 1690, the confraternity lent 2,000 zlotys to Kurtovych, with Iurii Papara as guarantor. From that time until the 1770s, the interest was paid by the owners of the Kurtovych (and later the Papara) residence.[171] The hetman's bequest contributed greatly to the maintenance of the Ukrainian school in Lviv. During the seventeenth century, the school occasionally suffered periods of decline. In 1658 and 1676, the confreres demanded that the level of instruction be improved, as Sahaidachny's bequest had been made for that express purpose. In appreciation of his efforts, they referred to the hetman as "Sahaidachny, worthy of eternal memory," or "of glorious memory."[172]

The confraternity school often had to operate under difficult conditions. Initially, it faced resistance from an influential segment of the Orthodox hierarchy, which "disparaged and hindered instruction."[173] For example, it is known that in 1590, Bishop Hedeon Balaban's servants drove a group of schoolboys away from the Lviv Confraternity School and imprisoned four students. Two years later, the bishop "sent to the school" his brothers Adam and Ivan and their friend Vasylkivsky, who threatened the teachers.[174] When reproached for this incident,

---

169. Krylovskii, *L'vovskoe Stavropigial'noe bratstvo*, suppl., 76–77.
170. *AIuZR*, 11: 362, 365.
171. *AIuZR*, 12: 345, 223, 224; TsDIAL 129/2/802, f. 41.
172. *AIuZR*, 11: 209, 12: 580.
173. *MCS*, 141.
174. Ibid., 234, 235, 416; *AIuZR*, 10: 66–67.

Balaban replied that he supported education, but "according to the old customs."[175]

Later, the Orthodox clergy made even more determined efforts to take control of the school and reduce the influence of laymen on school instruction to a minimum. In 1614, Patriarch Cyril Lukaris proposed that the school be run by two or three individuals and that the rest of the confreres not interfere in school matters. For the office of school director, he recommended Havrylo Dorofeiovych, an opponent of the confraternity and a supporter of the higher clergy.[176] Patriarch Theophanes of Jerusalem was more categorical, demanding that the management of the school and printshop be entrusted to the monks of St. Onuphrius Monastery.[177] Even Ivan (Iov) Boretsky, upon becoming metropolitan, indicated the Vilnius Confraternity, where monks had gained control of the confraternity school and printing press, as an example to the Lviv burghers.[178] A letter of 1633 from the hieromonk Leontii was written in a similar vein. Criticizing the "disorder" in the confraternity, he advised that a preacher (*kaznodii*) be invited to teach at the school and that the St. Onuphrius Monastery be supervised by a monk who was expert in printing and could manage the printing press. Leontii also noted the example of the Vilnius Confraternity, where secular people "never meddled" with church income. He recommended the ordination of those who would serve the confraternity (clearly, in the school and printing house).[179]

All these clerical demands and admonitions show that the Lviv Confraternity maintained control over educational activity. The management of the school remained in the hands of laymen, which contributed to the increasingly secular nature of the curriculum and established the prevailing attitude toward education. Ivan Vyshensky reproached the confraternity members for their fascination with "rhetorical fables." According to him, "he who once manages to read a

---

175.　　MCS, 876; TsDIAL 129/1/219.

176.　　Golubev, *Kievskii mitropolit Petr Mogila*, 1, suppl.: 200–201.

177.　　AZR, 4: 508.

178.　　Golubev, *Kievskii mitropolit Petr Mogila*, 1: 290–91.

179.　　Ibid., 2, suppl.: 33.

line from a fable by Aristotle becomes ashamed to read the
Psalter, and other church rules mean nothing to him, as he
considers them simple and stupid."[180]

Quite naturally, the attitude of the municipal authorities
toward non-Catholic schools was by no means favorable. Again,
the Lviv Confraternity School serves as the prime example, for it
is much better documented than other educational institutions.
The king's initial recognition of the confraternity's right to
teach the "liberal arts" (dated 15 October 1592) immediately
aroused the suspicions of Roman Catholics in Lviv. The rector
of the Catholic Cathedral School, Krzysztof Kącki, who held
this post after the death of the previous rector, Adam Burski,
sent his students to attack the confraternity school. At 1:00 a.m.
on 7 December, they assaulted the students Pavlo and Makar,
who were soliciting donations at the time, and brought them
to their own school, where they beat them and held them in
chains until the following day. Then they attacked a student
named Maksym, and on the night of 9 December, the rector
again dispatched a large gang of students. At 2:00 a.m. they
attacked the poor students of the confraternity school, taking
the donations they had gathered and "tearing their clothes,
beating them until they bled, and injuring them so that they
barely escaped with the help of good people." During the
same night, Roman Catholic students allegedly again set upon
the same students with sabers, guns, and other weapons,
wounding some of them. In response to these events, the
elders of the confraternity and the rector of the confraternity
school, Stefan Zyzanii, immediately issued a strong protest.[181]
That did not halt the violence. In the early spring of 1595, the
Orthodox princes Kyryk Ruzhynsky and Adam Vyshnevetsky
lodged a formal protest in the name of the confraternity against
Roman Catholics of Lviv who "beat schoolchildren and poor
students on the street, dragging them to their own school,
beating them, holding them and committing various injustices
against them.... "[182] In 1599 Iurii Rohatynets wrote to Vilnius

---

180.   Vyshens'kyi, *Tvory*, 189, 190.
181.   *MCS*, 407–9; TsDIAL 9/347: 798.
182.   *MCS*, 609.

that the Catholics wanted to forbid the confraternity entirely from teaching Ukrainian children.[183] In January 1649, the confraternity instructed its envoys to the Diet to do everything in their power to prevent any obstruction to the confraternity's teaching activities.[184] According to a letter of 7 April 1694 from the king to the city council, a few days earlier a large gang of students of the cathedral school had forced their way into the confraternity school on orders of their rector, snatching books out of the hands of younger children and harassing the teachers. The letter stated that if the gates had not been closed in the nick of time, a riot would have been unavoidable. The king therefore ordered that henceforth students no longer be hindered in their studies. He may not have been motivated solely by good will: at that time, the Russian diplomatic resident Mikhailov was visiting Lviv, and the king did not want to provide him with an occasion for interference.[185] In 1730, the confraternity complained to the court of the Roman Catholic chapter against the rector of the Latin Cathedral School, Zadniewicz, whose students had been harassing the confraternity school. Such incidents, even if they occurred only sporadically, contributed to an atmosphere of instability and unease around Ukrainian educational institutions.

To summarize, the confraternities' involvement in educational affairs evolved according to changes in their social status. After the Ostrih Academy, the confraternity schools of Lviv, Peremyshl, Lutsk, Kyiv, Kremianets, and other towns were the earliest Ukrainian institutions of secondary education. Incorporating both Eastern and Western medieval models, as well as those of the Renaissance, they contributed to the formalization of educational patterns. Eventually the Kyiv Mohyla Academy and its affiliated schools inherited the curricular and pedagogical innovations of the confraternity schools.

---

183.   Ibid., 837; *AZR*, 4: 202.

184.   *AIuZR*, 10: 188.

185.   According to the king's letter, the incident occurred "in the presence of a foreign diplomat, who can easily make an elephant out of a fly" (TsDIAL 139/1/1034).

As we have seen, the major confraternities, especially that of Lviv, initially sought to restrict clerical influence on education. They succeeded to some extent in the late sixteenth and early seventeenth centuries, but then the situation was reversed. As time went on, the confraternities could no longer ensure institutional and financial stability for their schools. This was achieved only by the church when it founded such well-organized schools as the Kyiv Mohyla Academy, Orthodox colleges in Chernihiv and Pereiaslav, or the Basilian colleges in Right-Bank and western Ukraine. The Ostrih Academy and the confraternities provided the initial impetus for the modernization of higher education, but the decisive reforms were accomplished by the church hierarchy and monasteries.

More durable, perhaps, was the impact of the confraternities on elementary education. The network of elementary schools administered by confraternities or communities promoted the cross-fertilization of popular and elite culture in the seventeenth and eighteenth centuries. In many regions of Ukraine, schools run by precentors (*diakivky*), which evolved directly from the elementary confraternity schools, survived until the mid-nineteenth century or even later. It was an archaic village school that gave Taras Shevchenko his first exposure to the heritage of Ukrainian medieval and early modern culture.[186] Without such schools, very properly called "popular," he and other peasant children would have been unable to take their first steps toward higher education. Thus, by establishing a link between traditional and modern culture, the confraternities helped maintain the continuity of cultural development in Ukraine.

---

186.   Cf. *ZNTSh* 221 (1990): 49–52.

Pages from the register of children enrolled at the Lviv Dormition Confraternity School (original preserved at the TsDIAL).

"The Teaching of Children," part of the icon (2d half of the 15th c.) of SS. Cosmas and Damian from the Lemko village of Iablonytsia Ruska (original in the National Museum in Lviv).

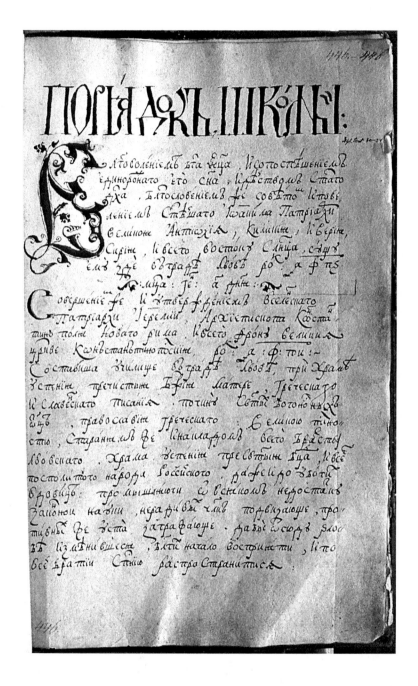

Copy of the Lviv Dormition Confraternity School Statute adopted in 1586.

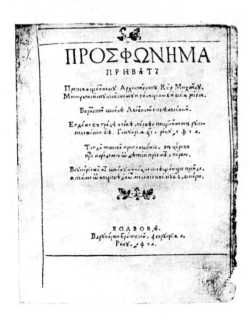

Title page of the Gospel published by the Lviv Dormition Confraternity Press on 20 Aug. 1636.

The 17th-c. building of the Lviv Dormition Confraternity Press. Drawing by Frantsysk Kovalyshyn, 1903.

Title page of the Leitourgikon *published by the Lviv Dormition Confraternity Press on 14 Apr. 1759. Etching by Jan Filipowicz (Ivan Fylypovych).*

Title page of the Artykuly *(statute, written on 24 Sept. 1681) of the St. Nicholas Confraternity on the outskirts of Peremyshl.*

ПОМЕНИКЪ

Emblem and verses from the 1677 Pom'ianyk *(commemorative register of deceased members) of the Lutsk Confraternity of the Elevation of the Holy Cross (copy preserved at the National Library in Kyiv).*

Printer's mark (17th c.) of the Lviv Dormition Confraternity Press.

V

The Publishing Activities of the Confraternities

Some major confraternities, both Ukrainian (Lviv, Lutsk, Peremyshl, and Kremianets) and Belarusian (Vilnius and Mahilioŭ), were involved in publishing activities and owned printshops. The most productive publishing enterprise was owned by the Lviv Stauropegion Confraternity.

The importance of confraternity printing can best be evaluated against the background of the general history of Ukrainian book printing. While the role of the printed book in Europe was a natural continuation of that of the manuscript book, the latter did not disappear immediately but, on the contrary, coexisted with the printed book for some time. Such was also the case in Ukraine; indeed, the golden age of the Ukrainian manuscript book almost coincided with the initial period of book printing. Many important manuscripts were produced in the second half of the sixteenth century, among them copies of the Gospels and theological treatises, as well as chronicles and literary works. Even in this period, book writing was in the hands of numerous scribes dispersed throughout towns and villages, and comparatively large scriptoria were rare exceptions.[1] Sometimes books, especially liturgical ones, were produced at the request of the confraternities. Often confraternities contributed funds to purchase books for use in parish churches.

Printed books were known in Ukraine soon after the invention of printing. A copy of the *Provinciale Romanum*, a previously unknown Gutenberg edition, was found in 1935 by Borys Zdanevych in the Library of the Academy of

---

1.   Ia. Zapasko, *Pam'iatky knyzhkovoho mystetstva. Ukraïns'ka rukopysna knyha* (Lviv, 1995); idem, *Mystets'ki rukopysni pam'iatky Ukraïny* (Lviv, 1997).

Sciences of the Ukrainian SSR in Kyiv.[2] Most probably, this copy reached Ukraine only in comparatively recent times, but there is little doubt that, as early as the last two decades of the fifteenth century, printed books were not a rarity in large Ukrainian cities. According to some accounts, the famous Nuremberg publishing and bookselling firm of Anton Koberger had contacts with Lviv. The first known printed book by a Ukrainian author, Iurii Drohobych's *Iudicium pronosticon anni currentis*, was published in Rome in 1483.[3]

The import of books and manuscripts from abroad was one of the factors stimulating indigenous book printing in Eastern Europe and the Balkans. The first book printed in Glagolitic, one of the two specifically Slavic alphabets, was a missal published in 1483, presumably in Venice. The other Slavic alphabet, Cyrillic, was used by all Orthodox Slavic peoples and Romanians. The appearance of book printing in that alphabet was a response to the cultural needs of the Ukrainian, Belarusian, Russian, and Romanian lands. The first books mainly for readers in Ukraine and Belarus, however, were printed not on their native territory but in Cracow, the capital and largest city of the Kingdom of Poland. The emergence of a nation's printing tradition outside its ethnic territory was a rather typical phenomenon for ethnic communities with no state of their own. For example, the first Armenian books were printed in Venice, Constantinople, and Lviv;[4] Venice was also the first major center for South Slavic book publishing.

The choice of Cracow as the site of the first printing enterprise using Cyrillic type may be explained by the availability of qualified craftsmen there, as well as by the fact that the existing ethnic and religious inequality of people of the Orthodox faith was perceived less acutely in the capital of the kingdom than in its provinces. In addition, the

2.   See a reproduction in B. Zdanevych, *Kataloh inkunabul*, comp. H. Lomonos-Rivna (Kyiv, 1974), 181–200.

3.   See *Iurii Drohobych: Bibliohrafichnyi pokazhchyk*, comp. Ia. Isaievych and M. Vavrychyn (Lviv, 1983).

4.   Ia. Dashkevich, "Pervyi armianskii knigopechatnik na Ukraine Ovanes Karmateniants," *Patma-Banasirakan Handes (Istoriko-filologicheskii zhurnal)*, 1976, no. 1: 221–36.

Orthodox diocese of Peremyshl was situated comparatively near to Cracow. Along with Poles, there were also Germans, Lithuanians, Belarusians, Ukrainians, Italians, Hungarians, Czechs, and other ethnic groups in Cracow, which contributed significantly to the city's role as a major center of intercultural contacts. It is quite understandable, in this context, that the first Cyrillic Church Slavonic books were published in Cracow and that the technical management of the Cyrillic printshop was in the hands of a printer of German origin, Shvaipolt Fiol (Schweipolt Veyl).[5] Fiol printed four liturgical books, two of them dated 1491 and two undated. The Ruthenian language of their colophons, as well as the use of dating from the birth of Christ (*po Bozhiem narozheniem*), indicates that these books were printed for a Ukrainian and Belarusian readership. In Russia, dating reflected the Byzantine tradition and was standardized according to the presumed date of the creation of the world, 5508 B.C. Within a short time of their publication, Fiol's imprints became known in Russia as well, as may be seen from Russian inscriptions in copies of these books; the oldest of these are dated as early as 1517 and 1536.[6] Copies of the earliest Cyrillic printed books were imported into Russia from Ukraine and Belarus in particularly large numbers in the seventeenth and eighteenth centuries, when cultural interchange among the three East Slavic countries became more intense.[7]

The design, texts, and language of the books printed by Fiol reflect many aspects of the influence of the South Slavic manuscript tradition on the literature of the East Slavic peoples. In general, the imitation of manuscripts is a well-known feature of early printed books. In this respect, the first Belarusian printed books published by Frantsysk Skaryna were quite exceptional, as they contained many bold

---

5.   On the possible initiators of this enterprise, see *Pershodrukar*, 19–20, 2d ed. (Lviv, 1983), 17–18. See also M. Bośnjak, *A Study of Slavic Incunabula* (Zagreb and Munich, 1968).

6.   E. L. Nemirovskii, *Opisanie izdanii tipografii Shvaipol'ta Fiolia* (Moscow, 1979).

7.   This circumstance does not allow us to agree with E. Nemirovsky's suggestion that the Cracow Cyrillic printing shop was established in order to export books to Russia. Cf. Nemirovskii, *Nachalo slavianskogo knigopechataniia* (Moscow, 1971).

innovations, along with more traditional features. Scholars are correct in discerning Renaissance influence in the content of Skaryna's prefaces to his publications, as well as in his language, enriched with vernacular influence, and his brilliant book design.[8] Skaryna's books were equally important for Belarusians and Ukrainians, whose cultural development in that period is best viewed as a single process. Even so, it may have been no accident that the first publisher to establish a printing enterprise in Eastern Europe was a Belarusian rather than a Ukrainian. Ethnic and religious inequality was less acutely experienced by the Orthodox population in the large cities of the Grand Duchy of Lithuania than it was in western Ukraine, where the major Ukrainian cities were situated. The Belarusian Orthodox burghers were more influential than their counterparts in Ukraine, where conditions for the development of new cultural trends were less favorable at the time.

If one discounts the small "anonymous printshop," whose activity was mainly episodic,[9] the continuous development of the printing industry in Russia began with the activity of Ivan Fedorov and Petr Mstislavets at the Moscow state-owned printing house (1563–65). In Ukraine it commenced with the activity of Ivan Fedorov (who called himself Feodorovich and was also called Khodorovych or Khvedorovych during that period of his life) in his own shop in Lviv (1573–74) and at the printshop of Prince Kostiantyn Ostrozky in Ostrih (1578–81).[10] Both the Lviv and Ostrih printshops had strong

8.   See *Belorusskii prosvetitel' Frantsisk Skorina i nachalo knigopechataniia v Belorusii i Litve* (Moscow, 1979); *Frantsysk Skaryna: Zbornik dakumentaŭ i materyialaŭ*, ed. V. I. Darashkevich (Minsk, 1988); *Frantsysk Skaryna i iaho chas: Èntsyklapedychny davednik* (Minsk, 1988; Russian edition: Minsk, 1990); E. L. Nemirovskii, *Frantsisk Skorina* (Minsk, 1990).

9.   There is strong evidence that anonymous editions were published for the Russian market, most probably in Moscow. A. E. Viktorov and Iu. A. Labyntsev have suggested that some of these editions were printed in Vilnius, and I have suggested that their printer had Belarusian connections. Cf. Iu. Labyntsev, "Pervoe izdanie Ivana Fedorova i Petra Timofeeva Mstislavtsa v sobranii GBL," *Kniga: Issledovaniia i materialy* 47 (1984), 172, 178, 218–19; *Pershodrukar*, 29–30.

10.   Following his departure from Moscow and prior to his arrival in Ukraine, Ivan Fedorov worked in the Belarusian town of Zabludaŭ as a master at the printing press owned by an Orthodox magnate, Ryhor Khadkevich. See E. L. Nemirovskii, *Vozniknovenie knigopechataniia v Moskve: Ivan Fedorov* (Moscow, 1964); idem, *Ivan Fedorov v Belorussii* (Minsk, 1979); *Pershodrukar*, 10–16, 28–35, 48–54.

connections with those Lviv burghers who were involved in the reorganization of the Lviv Dormition parish association into a regular confraternity.

The subject range of the first printed books was largely influenced by previous cultural development. Studies on the history of the Russian book stress that printing was important to the government and to the Orthodox Church hierarchy as a means of achieving uniformity of liturgical texts in accordance with the official policy of centralization. In Ukraine, contrary to the hierarchy's aspirations, book printing took on a polycentric structure. Nevertheless, the Orthodox Church in Ukraine also tried to use book printing as a means of ensuring the greater uniformity and broader circulation of liturgical texts. This was very important for the consolidation of Orthodoxy, which had come under pressure from the Counter-Reformation and, especially in the early stages, from Protestantism. The significance of the introduction of book printing was not, of course, limited to the needs of the church. Contributing to the spread of literacy, the printed book was a prerequisite of development in every sphere of cultural life.

In the 1970s, several studies dealt with Ivan Fedorov's role in book publishing[11] and book design,[12] as well as with his literary output.[13] It was no accident that Fedorov's literary talent became apparent mostly in Lviv, for it was there, with the assistance of a group of local Ukrainian burghers and clergymen, that he became an independent publisher. The circumstances of his activities in Zabludaŭ and Ostrih were different in many respects. On the one hand, Fedorov had to reckon with the opinions of the enterprise owners who published or commissioned the books that he printed. On the other hand, his excellent reputation as a specialist was unquestionable; hence the publishers and their advisors were ready to take his opinions and experience into account.

11.　　E. L. Nemirovskii, *Ivan Fedorov, okolo 1510–1583* (Moscow, 1985). See also Nemirovskii's other studies and his bibliography: *Nachalo knigopechataniia v Moskve i na Ukraine. Zhizn' i deiatel'nost' pervopechatnika Ivana Fedorova: Ukazatel' literatury, 1574–1974* (Moscow, 1975).

12.　　Ia. Zapasko, *Mystets'ka spadshchyna Ivana Fedorova* (Lviv, 1974).

13.　　Isaievych, *Literaturna spadshchyna Ivana Fedorova.*

Accordingly, Fedorov's Zabludaŭ and Ostrih imprints often reflect a compromise with local intellectual circles. In contrast to the famous afterword to the Lviv *Apostol*, the texts of the prefaces and afterwords of the earlier Zabludaŭ editions and of the later Ostrih editions were nearer to models accepted in the South Slavic and East Slavic manuscript book. At the same time, Fedorov introduced elements taken from the Western printed book, among them the title page, heraldic verses, and prefaces. The Church Slavonic Bible printed by Fedorov and his assistants in Ostrih in 1581 is rightly considered a masterpiece of Ukrainian book printing.[14]

More often than not, traditional historiography has depicted the founders of printing in various countries as solitary inventors isolated from society or even opposed to it. As far as Ivan Fedorov is concerned, such views have been justly criticized.[15] The undeniable personal achievements of Fedorov and other founders of printing in East Slavic countries were made possible only by their involvement in the social and cultural movements of their times.[16]

Before organizing his publishing enterprise, Fedorov sought financial support "from the rich and noble," but, in his own words, "neither Ukrainians nor Greeks" helped him, "except for some minor clergy and some insignificant people from the laity," whose assistance was "like that of the poor widow who had offered two mites."[17] Documents confirm that Fedorov had business dealings mostly with Lviv burghers and clergymen, some of whom later became associated with the Lviv Dormition Confraternity. It is known that Leontii, a hegumen at the St. Onuphrius Monastery, which was supervised by the Dormition Confraternity, bought forty

14.   See *Fedorovskiie chteniia 1983* (papers read at a conference devoted to the 400th anniversary of the Ostrih Bible held in Lviv and Ostrih in September 1981). Facsimile editions of the Ostrih Bible were published in Winnipeg in 1981 and in Moscow in 1988. See also R. Mathiesen, "The Making of the Ostrih Bible," *Harvard Library Bulletin*, 1981, no. 1: 71–110.

15.   Hryhorii Tysiachenko (pseudonym of Hryhorii Salyvon), "Kazkovyi i real'nyi obraz pershodrukaria," *Bibliolohichni visti*, 1924, nos. 1–3: 172–73.

16.   See *Pershodrukar*, 8–14.

17.   See Ivan Fedorov's epilogue to the *Apostol* of 1574. For a reproduction, see Isaievych, *Literaturna spadshchyna*, 96.

copies of Fedorov's *Apostol* at a discount price of two zlotys per copy.[18] Ivan Mynets, a confraternity member, visited Lublin with Ivan Fedorov's son, known as Ivan Drukarovych (Ivan, the son of the printer). The latter was associated with burghers who opposed the authority of Bishop Hedeon Balaban, provoking a conflict that eventually led to Drukarovych's death. A complaint of the Dormition Confraternity against the bishop alleged that he had thrown "Ivan, the printer's son, into a cellar, where he died of hunger."[19] A well-known painter, Lavrin Pylypovych Pukhala, who cooperated with Ivan Fedorov, was sent in 1599 as a representative of the Lviv confraternities to the Warsaw Diet court "in the matter of the liberties of the Ruthenian nation."[20]

Ivan Fedorov died on 15 December (5 December, according to the Julian calendar) 1583 in the house of Senko Sidliar (Senko the Saddler) and was buried at the St. Onuphrius Monastery. His printing equipment was seized by his creditors, one of whom was Foltyn Bertoldo, a Cracow burgher, from whom two of Fedorov's presses were acquired by Satsko Senkovych, the son of Senko Sidliar, and Senko Korunka, a painter. They planned to organize their own printing enterprise, but later sold the press and other equipment to Kuzma Mamonich, a well-known Belarusian publisher in Vilnius and a member of the Vilnius Orthodox Confraternity. As early as 1579, Ivan Fedorov pledged his Lviv printing press as security against money he had borrowed from Israel Iakubovich. As he was unable to repay the borrowed sum, the equipment remained in the hands of the creditor. The founding members of the Dormition Confraternity then began to collect funds in order to redeem the equipment. The last installment was paid in 1597, but by November 1585 Ivan Fedorov's press was already in the church repository.[21] The fund-raising campaign was part of the confraternity's program in the early stages of its activity,

18.   TsDIAL 129/1/1034.

19.   *Pershodrukar*, 80–82; TsDIAL 129/1/1183, f. 64, 68.

20.   On the staff of the Lviv Confraternity printshop, see H. Koliada, "Knigoizdatel'stvo L'vovskogo bratstva v XVI veke," *Uchenye zapiski Stalinabadskogo ob"edinennogo pedagogicheskogo i uchitel'skogo instituta im. T. G. Shevchenko*, Filologicheskaia seriia, issue 1 (1952): 200, 211.

21.   See *Pershodrukar*, 112–13.

coinciding with the reorganization of the confraternity and the founding of its school.

In January 1585 the confraternity informed Patriarch Joachim of Antioch about its plans to erect a building for the printing press, and in 1590 members of the confraternity stated that the building was under construction.[22] Fedorov's equipment was insufficient for this new printshop. In 1585 Lesko Maletsky, a founder of the confraternity, bequeathed metal utensils from his home to be used for founding type.[23] Some Cyrillic and Greek type was made by Konrad Forster, a Cracow typefounder. In a letter of 1593, Szymon Szymonowicz wrote to Jan Zamoyski, the chancellor of the Kingdom of Poland, that Forster had cast type for Cracow, Wrocław, and Frankfurt printshops, as well as for "a Rutheno-Greek printing press in Lviv."[24]

The establishment of the Lviv Confraternity printshop was facilitated by the availability of qualified staff in Lviv. A prominent role in organizing the press was played by the monk Myna. In 1579–80, together with Ivan Fedorov's friend Senko Sidliar, he corresponded on theological matters with Prince Andrei Kurbsky, and in 1585 he was active in the fund-raising campaign for the press. In a document of 2 July 1588, he is mentioned as "a printer" (*impressor*), while in another document generally considered to have been written in 1591, he is given the title of "learned printer" (*uchonyi drukar*).[25]

The leaders of the Lviv Confraternity declared that they had founded their printshop in order to publish "very accurately and with great diligence the sacred church books, not only Books of Hours, Psalters, Acts and Epistles, Menaions and Triodions, Rituals, Synaxaria, Gospels, Lives of the Saints, Torzhnyky, Chronicles and other books of theologians of our church of Christ, but also books needed by the school, i.e., books of grammar, poetics, and philosophy."[26]

---

22.   *Pershodrukar*, 82; *IuILS*, 60.

23.   TsDIAL 52/2/20: 631.

24.   J. Ptaśnik, *Cracovia impressorum XV et XVI saeculi* (Lviv, 1922), 385.

25.   *Pershodrukar*, 98; *MCS*, 165, 418.

26.   *MCS*, 135–36.

The earliest publication of the Lviv Confraternity printshop is a leaflet, or rather a kind of small poster, that was printed on 23 January 1591 and contained the text of two charters, one issued by Patriarch Jeremiah and the other by the metropolitan of Kyiv, Mykhailo Rohoza. The patriarch's title was printed in Greek at the head of the first charter. Church Slavonic translations of the title and the text followed; at the end, the signature and title appeared in Greek only.[27]

Only a week later, on 1 February 1591, a small book of eight leaves in quarto appeared under the Greek title *Prosphonēma*,[28] containing Church Slavonic verses on the emblem of the city of Lviv. A "Preface by the Children" and the text of the first chorus were printed in Church Slavonic and Greek, while the second and third choruses appeared only in Church Slavonic, with numerous Ukrainisms.[29] The publication is important as the earliest paratheatrical text of the Orthodox school.

In 1591, the Lviv Confraternity also published a book entitled *Adelphotēs: Hrammatika dobrohlaholivaho ellinoslovenskaho iazyka* (Brotherhood: A Grammar of the Good-Sounding Helleno-Slavonic Language).[30] The curious title was perhaps an attempt to show that Slavonic and Greek are so close as to be considered

---

27.   Only two copies of this leaflet are known, one in the Lviv National Museum and another in the Russian National Library (formerly the Imperial Public Library) in St. Petersburg. Cf. *PKM*, 1: 29, no. 21. For a reproduction of the patriarch's charter, see Kiselev, "Grecheskaia pechat'," plate between 180–81.

28.   N. P. Kiselev believed that only one copy of *Prosphonēma* had survived, that in the State Library in Moscow. Today two more copies are known: one in NBUV (acquired as part of the Pavlo Popov collection) and one in the Russian National Library in St. Petersburg. Cf. Kiselev, "Knigi grecheskoi pechati v sobranii Gosudarstvennoi biblioteki SSSR im. V. I. Lenina," *Kniga: Issledovaniia i materialy* 26 (1973), 143–44; *PKM*, p. 30, no. 23.

29.   There are several descriptions and publications of the text of this edition: *Pamiatniki polemicheskoi literatury*, vol. 3 (1903), *Primechaniia*, cols. 61–75; *Die älteste ostslawische Kunstdichtung, 1575–1647*, vol. 1, ed. Hans Rothe (Giessen, 1976), 15–26; *Ukraïns'ka poeziia: Kinets' XVI–pochatok XVII st.*, ed. V. Kolosova and V. Krekoten' (Kyiv, 1978), 137–44, 377–78.

30.   Although *Adelphotēs* is not particularly rare, it remained unknown to Émile Legrand. Copies of it are to be found in many libraries, not only in Ukraine but in other countries as well. The Russian State Archive of Ancient Acts in Moscow has as many as 42 copies, while a total of 68 copies are documented in the preliminary list prepared by the editorial board of the Union Catalog of early Cyrillic printed books. Cf. *V pomoshch' sostaviteliam Svodnogo kataloga staropechatnykh izdanii kirillovskogo i glagolicheskogo shriftov* (Moscow, 1982), 34.

two aspects of a linguistic unit.[31] This was a further development of Constantine Kostenecki's notion of the intimate proximity of the Greek and Church Slavonic languages.[32] The book could not, of course, be a grammar of a nonexistent "Hellenoslavic" language, but actually consisted of two separate grammars, the first of which served as a model for the second. The text of the Greek grammar appears either on the left-hand page or at the top of the page, while the corresponding Church Slavonic text appears on the right-hand page or at the bottom of the page. As noted previously, the Greek grammar was compiled by Arsenios of Elasson on the basis of various Greek printed grammars, especially that of Constantine Laskaris. The parallel Church Slavonic text is attributed to Arsenios's Ukrainian students.[33]

Shortly after the founding of the Lviv Confraternity printshop, the Orthodox hierarchy made an attempt to bring all publishing activities in Ukraine and Belarus under the control of its bishops. On 26 October 1591, a synod of bishops in Brest decided that the Lviv and Vilnius confraternity presses should print only texts that had received episcopal approval. The selection of books for printing was also to be a prerogative of the metropolitan of Kyiv and the bishops. Funds collected to finance book printing were to be sent to the bishop of Lutsk, Kyrylo Terletsky, who alone was to disburse them to the Vilnius and Lviv confraternities.[34] Had these provisions been implemented, the bishops would have monopolized publishing activity, with the confraternities acting as mere executors of their commissions.

In order to avoid episcopal control, the confraternities tried to maintain direct contact with the Eastern patriarchs. In 1593 the Lviv Confraternity published a book containing the Greek

31.   N. P. Kiselev believed that the word *Adelphotēs* ("brotherhood" in Greek) was not part of the title, but designated a "collective author." See Kiselev, "Knigi grecheskoi pechati," 44.

32.   Cf. O. Strakhova, "K voprosu ob otnoshenii k grecheskomu iazyku v slavianskoi pis'mennosti (XI–XVII vv.)," in *Ėtnogenez, ranniaia ėtnicheskaia istoriia i kul'tura slavian*, ed. N. I. Tolstoi et al. (Moscow, 1985), 39; H. Goldblatt, *Orthography and Orthodoxy: Constantine Kostenecki's Treatise on the Letters* (Florence, 1987).

33.   Studyns'kyi, "'Adel'fotes,'" 1–40.

34.   *Pershodrukar*, 104.

and Church Slavonic text of a work by Patriarch Meletios Pēgas of Antioch entitled *Per tēs Christianon eusebeias pros Ioudaious apologia* (Apology for Christian Piety against the Jews).[35] The text had been brought to Lviv by Emmanuel Mezapeta, a Greek from Crete and an active member of the Lviv Dormition Confraternity. The verso of the title page contains both the Greek original and a Church Slavonic translation of a poem by Emmanuel Axillios praising the author.[36]

The Greek type used in the confraternity's bilingual publications was the same as that made for the Ostrih printshop. Both Nikolai Kiselev and Janina Czerniatowicz have stressed the originality of its design as compared with the type found in books from other printshops.[37] In the past few decades it has been shown that Greek fonts based on the handwriting style of the best manuscript copyists of the Cretan-Venetian school of calligraphy served as models for this font. Specifically, Boris Fonkich examined letters used by Robert Estienne in Paris and by some German printers in Germany who imitated the handwriting of the famous Greek calligrapher Angelos Vergikios, as well as the letter design of Venetian publications that imitated the writing of other representatives of the same school, especially Antonios Episcopoulos.[38] It cannot be ruled out that models for some letters were also found in local manuscripts influenced by the above-mentioned calligraphic style.

As far as the orthography of the Greek texts of the Lviv Confraternity bilingual publications is concerned, they may be divided into two groups. The Grammar of 1591 and the treatise by Meletios Pēgas published in 1593 share such orthographic features as the interchange or omission of accentuation marks

---

35.   É. Legrand, *Bibliographie hellénique ... XVe et XVIe siècles*, vol. 2 (Paris, 1885), 88–89.

36.   Today two copies are known to exist, one in the Library of the Russian Academy of Sciences in St. Petersburg and another in the Czartoryski Library in Cracow.

37.   N. P. Kiselev, "Grecheskaia pechat'," 175–76; J. Czerniatowicz, *Książka grecka średniowieczna i renesansowa* (Wrocław, 1976), 301, 322.

38.   B. L. Fonkich, "Grecheskie teksty Ostrozhskoi Biblii," *Fedorovskie chteniia 1981* (Moscow, 1985), 110–11.

and errors reflecting modern Greek pronunciation.[39] These features make them noticeably different from West European scholarly publications of Greek texts of the same period, but very similar to books published in Venice and elsewhere for the use of Greeks themselves. On the other hand, the Greek texts in Jeremiah's charter, published in 1591, and in the Prosphonēma[40] contain many more grammatical and orthographical errors. The composition of these texts, as well as of Greek fragments in the Ostrih Bible, was the work of someone who had a very limited knowledge of Greek manuscripts and printed books and had mastered only colloquial Greek.[41] One of the typesetters of the Greek texts was probably Fedir Kasianovych.[42]

Printing in the Greek language by the Lviv Confraternity press was a short-lived phenomenon. Although only a limited number of titles containing Greek texts were published, their importance to the cultural life of the region was considerable. Émile Legrand included in his famous bibliography only books whose texts were fully or partly Greek, published "in Greek by Greeks." Commenting on the importance of these books for Greek culture, Kiselev suggested that it would be more precise to define them as published "for Greeks" as well.[43] Using that formula, we can say that in Lviv, just as earlier in Ostrih, Greek texts were published by *both* Greeks and Ukrainians for *both* Greeks and Ukrainians. Greek printing in Ukraine, then, belongs to the cultural history of both peoples. It had repercussions in Belarus, Russia, and Romania. The same may be said, to some extent at least, about "joint ventures" in the field of education.

---

39.   Ibid., 112.

40.   Linguistic and stylistic divergences occurring in various portions of the Greek text of the *Prosphonēma* may be explained by assuming that there were at least three different authors. See H. Trunte, "Die zweisprächigen Teile des 'PROSPHONEMA.' Zu Autorschaft und Entstehung des lemberger Panegyrikos vom 1. Februar 1591" in *Studien zu Literatur und Kultur in Osteuropa. Bonner Beiträge zum 9. Internationalen Slawistenkongreß in Kiew*, ed. H.-B. Harder and H. Rothe (Cologne and Vienna, 1983), 347–49.

41.   Fonkich, "Grecheskie teksty," 113–14.

42.   *Kniga: Issledovaniia i materialy* 7 (1962), 205.

43.   Kiselev, "Knigi grecheskoi pechati," 132.

Studying the typographical layout of the Lviv Confraternity bilingual editions of 1591–93, Kiselev noted the consistent use of Greek capital letters as opposed to Cyrillic ones in the Church Slavonic texts. In some titles, whole lines were printed in the Slavonic language, but with Greek capital letters. As a result, some text fragments are very similar in general appearance and in some details to the contemporary "civil" (*grazhdanka*) forms of Cyrillic. They look more modern than the "civil" fonts that were introduced in Petrine Russia and later accepted by all other Orthodox Slavic countries. To some extent, this attempt to simplify the design of Cyrillic letters presages later developments.[44]

Meletios Pēgas voiced his high appreciation of the Lviv Confraternity's publishing activity in one of his letters to Tsar Fedor Ivanovich.[45] He sent several letters to the confraternity, urging that they be printed "in Greek and in Ruthenian, and if possible also in Latin." This could not be accomplished, for just then the confraternity suspended its publishing activity for more than a decade. During this period, confraternity members rendered assistance to other Ukrainian and Belarusian printshops, namely those of the Vilnius Confraternity and the Ostrih Academy and, after their reconciliation with Bishop Hedeon Balaban of Lviv, also to his printshops in the villages of Striatyn and Krylos. Although the Ostrih and Striatyn printing presses were short-lived, they had considerable influence on the further development of Ukrainian book publishing. The Ostrih center began the publication of Church Slavonic translations of those monuments of Byzantine patristics that were especially popular in all East Slavic and South Slavic lands. The earliest Orthodox polemical works to be printed were also published in Ostrih. In December 1596, one of leaders of the Lviv Confraternity, Iurii Rohatynets, wrote to the confraternity that Prince Kostiantyn Ostrozky had asked it "for a loan of Greek and Slavonic type to publish the proceedings of the Brest synod." The plan was not fulfilled, and a book containing a

---

44.   Kiselev, "Grecheskaia pechat'," 196–98.
45.   W. Regel, ed., *Analecta Byzantino-Russica* (St. Petersburg, 1891), 104–6; *MCS*, 392.

description of the Brest synod, titled *Ekthesis* (Exposition), was published in Cracow in Polish only. In July 1596, Prince Ostrozky asked the Lviv Confraternity to send "some three boxes of Greek type" to Ostrih, because he wanted to publish Pēgas's book "against heretics ... in Greek and Ruthenian."[46] As Iurii Rohatynets wrote, the prince also asked the confraternity to dispatch Fedir Kasianovych, "who is well acquainted with our [i.e., the confraternity's] Greek type and experienced in setting it."[47] The prince was probably referring to the *Dialogue on Faith*, which was published in Greek in Vilnius (1596). A Ukrainian translation prepared by a certain Nykyta is known only in manuscript form, although an old catalog mentions the Derman edition of 1603 (the Derman printshop was affiliated with the Ostrih cultural center).[48]

The Lviv Dormition Confraternity resumed its publishing activity in 1608, when the Ostrih press was in decline and the Striatyn press had discontinued its activities. The printshop was located in the St. Onuphrius Monastery. An important role in the activities of the press was played by learned monks, such as Pafnutii Kulchych and Pamvo Berynda. The confraternity leaders Iurii Rohatynets, Ivan Krasovsky, and Havrylo Iaroshevych were also active as supervisors of the press.[49] Among the confraternity publications of this period were St. John Chrysostom's *O vospitanii chad* (On the Education of Children, 1609), the same author's *Kniha o sviashchenstvi* (Book on the Priesthood), with its documentary supplement *Sobor v bohospasiemom hradi Vilni byvshii* (Synod in the Divinely Protected City of Vilnius, 1614).[50] Verses were also published, such as *Plach albo liament na smert' Hryhoriia Zhelyborskoho* (Plaint or Lamentation on the Death of Hryhorii Zhelyborsky, 1615), and *Na rozhstvo ... virshi* (Christmas Verses, 1616) compiled for the confraternity school by Pamvo Berynda. The confraternity also

46. *Pershodrukar*, 127.

47. Ibid., 113, 114.

48. K. Koperzhyns'kyi, "Ostroz'ka drukarnia v Ostrozi ta v Dermani pislia Beresteis'koï uniï (1596), ïï vydannia ta diiachi," *Bibliolohichni visti*, 1924, nos. 1–3: 81.

49. *Pershodrukar*, 113, 114; Isaievych, *Bratstva*, 197.

50. *Istorychni dzherela ta ïkhvykorystannia* (Kyiv), issue 1 (1964): 179–80.

began to carry out its program of publishing revised editions of texts for ecclesiastical use. The afterword to the *Chasoslov* (Book of Hours), published in 1609, affirms that "This book of hours has been checked against many other books of hours." It was stressed that the order of services had been changed as compared with editions that began with the midnight service (*polunoshchnitsa*). In keeping with an ancient tradition reflected "in numerous old manuscript books of hours," the vesper service was placed at the beginning. In Russia, Patriarch Nikon introduced a similar change as late as 1653. The Lviv Psalter of 1615 was corrected by the hieromonk Kyrylo, who knew Greek well.[51] Pavel Stroev was right to stress that Lviv and Kyiv publishers had practiced the correction of liturgical texts long before Patriarch Nikon's reform in Russia.

Another pause in the Lviv Confraternity's publishing activity began in the year 1616. That same year saw the appearance of the first book printed in Kyiv—a small book of hours for school use issued by the printshop of the Kyivan Caves Monastery. Some professionals on the staff of the monastery printshop had gained their qualifications at the Lviv Confraternity press or at least had been associated with it. The Kyivan Caves Monastery printshop was founded by Archimandrite Ielysei (Ivan before monastic vows) Pletenetsky, the son of Khoma, deacon of the Lviv Confraternity church. An important role in Kyiv book publishing was played by the former Lviv Confraternity School rector Ivan (Iov) Boretsky, as well as by Pamvo Berynda, who had worked at the printshops of Hedeon Balaban in Striatyn and of the Stauropegion Confraternity in Lviv. Also involved was Tymofii Oleksandrovych Verbytsky, who presumably learned the art of printing in Ostrih and later served as printer to Kyrylo Trankvilion-Stavrovetsky in Pochaiv and Rokhmaniv. The equipment and type from Balaban's Striatyn printshop were used in publishing the first books in Kyiv. The rapid rise of printing in Kyiv owed much to the previous achievements of printers from western Ukraine, especially those of Lviv.

---

51.   Perhaps he can be identified with Kyrylo Ivanovych, and not with Kyrylo Trankvilion-Stavrovetsky, as has been generally assumed. See Isaievych, "Novye materialy ob ukrainskikh i belorusskikh knigopechatnikakh," 150.

With their experience and the financial resources of the Caves Monastery at its disposal, the Kyiv publishing center could afford to take on editorial projects of a kind that would have been unthinkable earlier.

Perhaps the finest achievement of the Kyivan scholars and printers was a volume of St. John Chrysostom's homilies on the fourteen Pauline epistles. The text had previously been translated by Kypriian of Ostrih and later checked by Lavrentii Zyzanii "against the best-known Greek archetype, excellently published in the town of Eton."[52] If the Eton edition, issued by Sir Henry Savile, was appreciated in modern times as "the first work of learning on a great scale published in England,"[53] then it must be acknowledged that the Ukrainian publishers took care to obtain the best sources for their editorial work. The *Homilies on Acts* (1625) were corrected on the basis of the same Eton edition, which was borrowed by the Kyiv editors from the library of the Lviv Stauropegion Confraternity.[54] This is but one example of the close cooperation of Kyiv book publishers with the confraternities, especially that of Lviv.

The next stage in the history of Ukrainian book printing began in the 1630s. The Caves Monastery publishing center retained its leading role under the patronage of the monastery's archimandrite, Petro Mohyla, who became metropolitan of Kyiv in 1633. The Lviv Confraternity resumed its publishing activity in 1630, but limited its scope almost exclusively to liturgical texts, as these were extremely significant for the further consolidation of the Orthodox Church. It is important to stress that at this time the confraternity publishers were very particular about the theological and philological correctness of translations. For example, the text of the *Octoechos* of 1630 was established after a comparison of various sources, such as printed books (the Moscow edition of 1630 and the Derman edition of 1604), an ancient "Serbo-Bulgarian"

52.   Titov, *Materiialy dlia istoriï knyzhnoï spravy*, 57.

53.   H. Hallam, *Introduction to the Literature of Europe in the Fifteenth, Sixteenth, and Seventeenth Centuries*, vol. 2 (New York, 1882), 363.

54.   For a more detailed account of the books printed in Ukraine in this period, see Isaevich, *Preemniki pervopechatnika*, 56–57 and passim; Ia. Isaievych, *Ukraïns'ke knyhovydannia: vytoky, rozvytok, problemy* (Lviv, 2002).

manuscript from the Neamṭ Monastery in Moldavia, and the "correct Greek text" obtained from Patriarch Cyril Lukaris of Constantinople. Some copies of the Gospels of 1636 have an "Explanation of Corrections" as a supplement.[55] It was stressed there that some passages lacking in the Slavonic editions were taken from "ancient" Greek texts; on the other hand, editors left some traditional Slavonic readings that did not occur in the Greek Gospels and in St. Theophilact's exegeses. Thus, Metropolitan Petro Mohyla was unjust in denouncing the Lviv Confraternity for the poor quality of its printed liturgical texts, alleging that the Lviv publishers were "laymen, ignoramuses, idiots, purveyors rather than censors of sacred books."[56] Mohyla's efforts to control the confraternity publications may be explained by his desire to consolidate the authority of the centralized church administration, as well as to restrict the activities of rival presses.[57]

By the 1630s, the confraternity's relations with hired printing specialists were already firmly established. Decisions on printing specific titles and on print runs of any edition were taken by general meetings of the confraternity members. Having made a decision, the confraternity signed a contract with a *maister* or manager of the press. It had to pay the manager an agreed price for every copy and supply him with printing equipment and paper. Managers themselves had to pay weekly salaries to apprentices and provide them with food, as well as with firewood for the winter. As further remuneration, the confraternity would allow the printing of additional copies besides those that were to be delivered to its storehouse, to be distributed among the staff "according to everyone's contribution."

In 1630–33 and 1641–43, the Lviv Confraternity engaged Andrii Skulsky as manager of its printshop; in 1634–37 and

---

55.   It was entitled *Ob"iasneniia ispravlenii s izvody starohrecheskimi městneobrětaiushchikhsia v ... slovenskikh izdaniiakh, na někh zhe městěkh izbyvaiushchikh, iazhe ne obrětaiutsia v hrecheskikh i tolkovanii s[via]taho Theofilakta, neotměnna zhe zdě s"stoiatsia.*

56.   *MUH*, 2: 250.

57.   V. M. Nichyk, *Petro Mohyla v dukhovnii istoriï Ukraïny* (Kyiv, 1997), 71; Turilov and Floria, "K voprosu ob istoricheskoi al'ternative," 21, 43.

1644–48, Mykhailo Sliozka was in charge. They both tried to become independent publishers, but only Sliozka succeeded. He printed books not only in Church Slavonic and Ukrainian, but also in Latin and Polish, for which he bought type from Jan Szeliga's successors. Periods of cooperation between Sliozka and the confraternity alternated with periods of open rivalry. It is interesting to note that Ivan Berezhansky, who was in charge of the Lviv Confraternity printshop in the early 1640s, made type molds for Greek letters for the printshop in Iaşi, the capital of the Moldavian principality.[58] Its only known Greek-language publication of this period was a synodal decree of Patriarch Parthenios I, published in 1642.[59]

In the Lviv Confraternity shop, two presses were usually at work simultaneously, each requiring four or five workers. For example, in 1645, ten printers were engaged: the manager, Andrii Skulsky; his assistant, Stepan Komarensky; four apprentices (typesetters Mykhailo and Matvii; pressmasters Ivan and Sevastian), four "boys" (Lesko, Tymko, Iarmola, and "a typesetter").[60] In 1645, Tymko is mentioned as an apprentice; by 1647 he is Tymofii the typesetter, while in 1646, in the text of inscriptions in a book that he sold, he calls himself "Tymofii Oleksovych Zhoratsky, printer in Lviv."[61]

Many printers who later worked at other presses began their professional careers at the Lviv Stauropegion Confraternity. Specialists from there were also active abroad. Andrii Skulsky worked in Wallachia between 1635 and 1637.[62] In 1643, Ivan Kunotovych worked in the Wallachian town of Cîmpolung (Dovhopole), where he printed an *Anfologion* modeled on the Lviv edition of 1638. In the following year, he and his companions published an *Exegetic Gospel* at the Dealul

---

58.   *Pershodrukar*, 199, 271–72.

59.   No copy of this publication has been preserved, but it is mentioned in the Latin translation published in Paris in 1643. See V. Kiriiak, *Cartea şi tiparul în Moldova în secolele XVII–XVIII* (Chişinău, 1977), 73; I. Bianu and N. Hodoş, *Bibliografia românească veche 1508–1830*, vol. 1 (Bucharest, 1903), 119; Legrand, *Bibliographie hellénique … XVe et XVIe siècles*, 2: 451.

60.   TsDIAL 129/1/1169: 78–79; 129/1/1170, f. 14, 17.

61.   Pushkin Institute of Russian Literature (St. Petersburg), Manuscript Division, no. 01319, f. 4–5.

62.   *Pershodrukar*, 180.

(Dial) monastery. Ivan Berezhansky, who produced a Greek font for the first Moldavian printshop in Iași, was in the service of the Lviv Stauropegion in 1643.[63]

The Lviv Confraternity press was administered by its lay members. This arrangement was sharply criticized by the clergymen, who urged that the shop be returned to the management of the St. Onuphrius Monastery, as it had been in the years 1608–16. Even the former rector of the confraternity school, Ivan (Iov) Boretsky, after becoming metropolitan, advised the Lviv burghers to follow the example of the Vilnius Confraternity, where the school and printing press were managed by monks. Later, Leontii, a hieromonk at the Maniava Hermitage, recommended that the shop be transferred to the supervision of the hegumen of the St. Onuphrius Monastery and again praised the Vilnius Confraternity, where printing and all others matters "were under the authority of the fathers, while laymen do not interfere."[64]

The Lviv Stauropegion Confraternity could afford independent management of its publishing activities, but this was scarcely possible for other confraternities. In 1633, the Theophany Confraternity, monastery, and hospital were founded in the Volhynian town of Kremianets. The founding charter allowed the confraternity to establish "a Ruthenian press for printing pious books."[65] The political leaders of the Volhynian Orthodox nobility, Lavrentii Drevynsky (a member of the Lviv Confraternity from 1603, and later an elder of the Lutsk Confraternity),[66] Danylo Malynsky, and Andrii (Atanasii) Puzyna (an elder of the Lutsk Confraternity and, from 1632, the

---

63. There were misunderstandings between the Lviv Confraternity and the Moldavian government. These were partly due to the fact that the Iași press was managed by Sofronii Pochasky, appointed by Metropolitan Petro Mohyla, who was in conflict with the Lviv Confraternity because of competition between its press and that of the Kyivan Caves Monastery (*Pershodrukar*, 199, 200).

64.   Golubev, *Kievskii mitropolit Petr Mogila*, 1, suppl.: 290–91; 2, suppl.: 33.

65.   N. I. Petrov, "Kremenetskoe pravoslavnoe Bogoiavlenskoe bratstvo," *TKDA* 3, no. 9 (1887): 126.

66.   Kasiian Sakovych wrote that Drevynsky provided assistance to many schools (*PBSh*, 340).

Orthodox bishop of Lutsk)[67] were instrumental in establishing these institutions. In 1636, Metropolitan Petro Mohyla allowed a school of liberal arts subordinate to the rector of the Kyivan College to open in Kremianets.[68] Soon afterwards, an abridged version of Meletii Smotrytsky's Church Slavonic grammar was published in that town in 1638.[69] An engraving with the emblem of the Theophany is sufficient evidence that the press was connected with the Theophany Confraternity or Monastery. In the same year, two more books were published in Kremianets: a pronouncement of Bishop Atanasii Puzyna at a diocesan synod (*Sinod vedle zvychaiu dorochnoho ... septevria 26 roku 1638 v tserkvi kathedral'noi Lutskoi ... otpravovanyi i v tom zhe roku v Krementsi dlia vědomosti vydrukovanyi*)[70] and *O tainakh ili misteriiakh*, a reissue of the *Dydaskaliia* by Sylvestr Kosiv (published at the Kuteino monastery in 1637).

The Kremianets Confraternity followed the model of Lutsk, where the leading role was played not by burghers but by the noblemen of the Volhynian palatinate and the monks of the confraternity monastery. This leads to the conclusion that the monasteries of Kremianets and Lutsk were also responsible for publishing activities. A printing press was donated to the monastery of the Lutsk Confraternity of the Elevation of the Holy Cross by an itinerant printer, the monk Sylvestr. In 1640, "the poor monastery of the Lutsk confraternity" (a quotation from the preface to their publication) managed to issue a book of modest appearance, the *Apostoly i evanheliia* (Acts and Epistles and Gospels), reprinted from the edition issued by Pavlo Domzhyv-Liutkovych.

---

67.   Contemporaries considered Atanasii Puzyna well-educated (E. Šmurlo, *Kurie a pravoslavný východ v letech 1609–1654* [Prague, 1928], 119). The preface to the Lutsk publication *Apostoly i evanheliia* (1640) states that Atanasii Puzyna, a stern defender of Orthodoxy at the Commonwealth Diet and at the provincial dietines, "shone with knowledge and rhetoric."

68.   Petrov, "Kremenetskoe pravoslavnoe Bogoiavlenskoe bratstvo," 126.

69.   *Hrammatiki ili pismennica jazyka sloven'skaho, Kremjanec', 1638: eine gekürzte Fassung der kirchenslawischen Grammatik von Meletij Smotryc'kyj*, ed. O. Horbatsch (Munich, 1977).

70.   Before World War II, Ivan Ohiienko found one hundred copies of this edition in the Warsaw Public Library. For a reproduction of the text, see his "Zahublenyi kremianets'kyi starodruk 'Synod Luts'kyi 1638 r.,'" *Elpis*, 1931, no. 5: 89, 92–95. No copy is known to exist today.

As mentioned earlier, the printing enterprise of the Kyivan Caves Monastery was founded with the active participation of professionals who obtained their qualifications at the Lviv Confraternity printshop. The two private printers operating in Kyiv, the Zaporozhian Cossack Tymofii Verbytsky and a burgher from Belarus, Spiridon Sobol, had good relations with intellectuals associated with the Kyiv Theophany Confraternity. In 1625–28, Verbytsky published in Kyiv all the books used for elementary education: the primer, the book of hours (two editions), and the psalter.[71] Spiridon Sobol, born in Mahilioŭ, had a printshop in Kyiv from 1628 to 1630. After that, he returned to Belarus, publishing books that gave Kyiv as a false address of his shop. One of his publications was a prayer book published in 1632, presumably in Kuteino. In 1633, the Russian border authorities confiscated from a merchant traveling to Moscow a book that they described as "the prayer book printed at the Kyiv Theophany Monastery, that is, in the confraternity."[72] Perhaps the Kyiv Theophany Monastery or the Theophany Confraternity were disseminating the Kuteino prayer book of 1632 or its prototype. Later, Sobol continued his publishing activities in Mahilioŭ, but finally went to Kyiv and became a monk, first at the Kyiv Confraternity Monastery and later at the Caves Monastery. Sobol died in Wallachia in 1645. His printing equipment became the property of the Mahilioŭ Confraternity Monastery, and part of it was acquired by the St. Nicholas Confraternity in Sokal, western Ukraine.[73]

The charter of 1642 authorizing the founding of the monastery and church of St. John the Theologian in the Lviv suburb of Pidzamche included permission to run a printshop,[74] but the confraternity did not manage to undertake a publishing program. It is known also that the Trinity Confraternity in Peremyshl bought a small printshop from a local burgher, Andrii Piatysotnyk, but in 1683 it was resold to the Lviv

71.   For more details on him, cf. Isaevich, *Preemniki pervopechatnika*, 66–69.

72.   I. Kamanin, "Eshche o drevnosti bratstva i shkoly v Kieve," *Chteniia v Imperatorskom obshchestve istorii i drevnostei rossiiskikh* 9 (1895): 181.

73.   Isaevich, *Preemniki pervopechatnika*, 69–74; Isaievych, *Ukraïns'ke knyhovydannia*, 183–86.

74.   LNB, Ossolineum collection, MS 1087, 239.

Stauropegion Confraternity.[75] The most important centers of Belarusian publishing in this period were the Mamonichi firm in Vilnius and the Holy Spirit Monastery, which operated printshops in Vilnius and at the monastery's branch in Vievis (Ievie). It cannot be excluded that some books with Vilnius on their title pages were actually printed in Vievis.[76] Because the Holy Spirit Monastery was initially associated with the Holy Spirit Confraternity and retained the designation "confraternal monastery," scholars consider its publications to be part and parcel of confraternity printing.[77] There is no evidence, however, that the lay confraternity had any influence on the publishing activities of the monastery, and in this period the word "confraternal" in its name referred to the religious brotherhood of monks rather than to the lay confraternity connected with the monastery. In Mahilioŭ in the mid-seventeenth century, books were published on behalf of the Theophany Monastery, while in the late seventeenth and eighteenth centuries the same type was used by the printshop of the Theophany Confraternity.[78] Owing to lack of evidence, it is difficult to say whether there was a real shift of responsibilities or only a change in terminology.

Today, no less than 25 printing presses are known to have operated in Ukraine between 1574 and 1648. They were situated in 17 localities: seven in villages, the rest in cities and towns. Lviv alone had 12 presses at various times. Of 25 printing presses, 17 were owned by Orthodox Ukrainians and produced books mainly in Church Slavonic and Ukrainian (Ruthenian), 6 enterprises were owned by Polish Roman Catholics, one by Armenians, and one by Protestants.[79] In the Grand Duchy of Lithuania, which included the Belarusian and Lithuanian lands, at least 22 presses were active between 1569 and 1648 (11 Orthodox, 1 Uniate, 4 Roman Catholic, 3 Protestant, and 3 that published both Protestant and Catholic

---

75. State Archives in Przemyśl, Archives of the Greek Catholic parishes/124, f. 2, 5, 7, 10.

76. Ia. Isaevich, "Rol' bratstv v izdaniii i rasprostanenii knig na Ukraine i v Belorussii (konets XVI–XVIII vv.)," *Kniga i grafika* (Moscow, 1972), 127–36.

77. Halenchenka, "Bratskae knihadrukavanne," 269–73.

78. *Kniha Belarusi 1517–1917* (Minsk, 1986), 116, 169, 192.

79. For a list of printshops in Ukraine, see *PKM*, 1: 121; 2, bk. 2: 96.

books). Of these, 11 were located in Vilnius and the others divided among 14 towns.[80] Initially, the confraternity presses, mainly those of Lviv and Vilnius, played a very important role, but eventually they began to lose momentum.

The decentralized structure of Ukrainian and Belarusian printing largely contributed to the diversity of book production, especially in the early decades of the seventeenth century. At the same time, most presses, particularly those belonging to itinerant craftsmen, were very small. In Ukraine, Belarus, and Lithuania, only the largest printshops (those of the Kyivan Caves Monastery, the Vilnius Jesuit Academy, and a few others) could afford to have 12–15 workmen. For comparison, the following data are useful: in Prague, only the famous Melantrich firm had 15–20 workers, while all other printing enterprises maintained staffs of 2–3. In Paris and Lyon, printshops with 15–20 workers were considered large. Johannes Froben with 15–20 workers and Christophe Plantin with his 150–60 were rare exceptions.[81] In Ukraine, the vast majority of books were published by a few large enterprises. For example, between 1574 and 1648, 69.9 percent of the total was produced by four publishers (29.8 percent by the Kyivan Caves Monastery, 21.7 percent by the Lviv Confraternity, 12.1 percent by Prince Kostiantyn Ostrozky, and 6.3 percent by Mykhailo Sliozka). Books printed in Vilnius constituted 75 percent of all titles printed in the Grand Duchy of Lithuania between 1553 and 1660.[82] Only the largest cities, such as Vilnius, Lviv, and Kyiv, developed into important and lasting centers of the book industry and trade. The reasons for this were mainly economic: cities offered greater availability of qualified craftsmen and larger markets.

---

80.   For a list of printshops in the Grand Duchy of Lithuania, see *Drukarze dawnej Polski od 15 do 18 wieku*, fasc. 5: *Wielkie Księstwo Litewskie*, ed. A. Kawecka-Gryczowa (Wrocław and Cracow, 1959), 5–6; *Kniha Belarusi, 1517–1917*, 51–130, 514–18.

81.   For sources of figures given here, as well as further in this study, see Isaevich, *Preemniki pervopechatnika*, 122–25; Isaievych, *Ukraïns'ke knyhovydannia*, 300–301.

82.   M. B. Topolska, *Czytelnik i książka w Wielkim Księstwie Litewskim w dobie Renesansu i Baroku* (Wrocław, 1984), 119.

The advance of the Counter-Reformation, as well as the decline of the burghers' status and the economic stagnation of the cities, caused a further worsening of the fortunes of small and medium-sized private publishing firms. In the mid-seventeenth century, of the burgher-owned shops, only that of Sliozka remained. After his death, book publishing was long monopolized by the Lviv Stauropegion Confraternity and the monasteries. In the second half of the seventeenth century, 35 percent of all titles published in Ukraine came from the Kyivan Caves Monastery press and 25 percent from the monastery presses in the Chernihiv Orthodox Eparchy. On Belarusian territory, only a few printshops using Cyrillic type were active in the second half of the seventeenth century, among them those of the Orthodox burgher Maksim Voshchanka in Mahilioŭ, who published some books under his own name and others for the Theophany Confraternity (1693–ca. 1707), and of the Uniate Basilian monastery in Suprasl (1695–97 and from 1715 on). During the eighteenth century, the Mahilioŭ Confraternity published some religious books in Church Slavonic, namely the *Apologia* of St. Dymytrii of Rostov (Dmytro Savych Tuptalo) (1716), an *Octoechos* (four editions: 1730, 1740, 1747, and 1754), a *Breviary* (1735), a *Trefologion* (1748), and a *Book of Hours* (1771). To these books should be added several others printed in Mahilioŭ with no indication of the publisher's name.[83]

In the first half of the eighteenth century, the most productive Ukrainian printshops were those of the Kyivan Caves Monastery, the Chernihiv monastery, and the two Greek Catholic monasteries in Pochaiv and Univ. However, beginning in the 1720s, the Russian Orthodox Church introduced strict censorship of books published in the Ukrainian Hetmanate. This was in keeping with the centralizing policy of the Russian Empire aimed at the liquidation of Ukrainian political and cultural autonomy. The Kyiv and Chernihiv printshops were allowed to reprint old religious books only on condition that they not differ in text or even in orthography from censored Russian editions. This was a cruel blow to Ukrainian culture.

---

83.   *Kniha Belarusi, 1517–1917*, 134, 135, 138, 140–143, 149.

Having been forbidden to publish new texts, the Kyiv and Chernihiv printers applied their energy to improving the design of their publications. The engravings in many Kyiv editions attained very high standards.[84]

As far as the content of books was concerned, only printshops in western Ukraine and western Belarus remained relatively free. The most important of these were the printshops of the Pochaiv Basilian monastery in Ukraine and the Suprasl Basilian monastery in Belarus. The Lviv Confraternity tried to make use of its monopolistic privileges to ban the Pochaiv publishing house, but did not succeed.[85] It was in Pochaiv that the most important textbooks and literary works were published at this time. The Lviv Confraternity publishers of this period remained much more conservative. They printed mostly liturgical books, which, after the Zamostia synod, were subject to censorship by representatives of the Holy See.[86] As noted in the previous chapter, their most popular publications were primers. Only in the 1740s did the Lviv Stauropegion Confraternity resume the publication of literary texts. For example, in 1744–45 two works of Mykhailo (Manuil) Kozachynsky, the prefect of the Kyiv Mohyla Academy, were published in Lviv: the drama *Blahoutrobiie Marka Avreliia Antonina kesaria Rymskoho* (The Mercy of Marcus Aurelius Antoninus, Caesar of Rome) and *Filosofiia Aristoteleva* (Aristotle's Philosophy), which also included panegyrics to the Rozumovsky family. Both books were printed in Cyrillic, employing the type of the Lviv Confraternity, while the Latin type was from the Lviv Jesuit Academy, and the fine engravings were executed in Kyiv. Ironically enough, even a highly influential member of the Ukrainian establishment had to look abroad for a printer in order to publish books devoted to the Empress Elizabeth I and her favorite: evidently the Russian authorities did not wish to make any exemption to their comprehensive ban on original publishing in annexed Ukraine. Unfortunately, the Lviv Confraternity press did not

---

84.   Ia. Zapasko, *Mystetstvo knyhy na Ukraïni v XVI–XVIII st.* (Lviv, 1971); D. Stepovyk, *Ukraïns'ka hrafika XVI–XVIII stolit': Evoliutsiia obraznoï systemy* (Kyiv, 1982).

85.   *MUH*, 6: 70–71, 164.

86.   *MUH*, 5: 417.

fill the gap resulting from the Russian persecutions. Its most interesting publications of this period were reprints of books previously issued elsewhere: the 1752 and 1760 editions of *Bohosloviia nravouchytelnaia* (Didactic Moral Theology) followed the Pochaiv edition of 1751, while the *Ifika ieropolityka* of 1760 repeated the text of the Kyiv edition of 1712 devoted to Hetman Ivan Skoropadsky.

After the dissolution of the Lviv Confraternity by the Austrian authorities in 1788, the St. Onuphrius Monastery tried to acquire the confraternity printshop. The monks argued that the press had originally been in their possession.[87] As they failed to prove this, the printing equipment was assigned to the Stauropegion Institute along with other property of the confraternity.[88] It continued publishing until 1939. However, the Stauropegion Institute publishing house, formally a successor of the confraternity press, became an institution with quite different social and cultural functions. It would be inappropriate to include its activities in a history of confraternity printing.

To assess the cultural significance of confraternity publishing, it is necessary to take account not only of the thematic range but also of the design and language characteristic of their imprints. During the initial period of Ukrainian and Belarusian book printing, most titles published by the confraternity presses, as well as by other Orthodox publishing enterprises, were in Church Slavonic.[89] As in other Orthodox Slavic countries, Church Slavonic was initially received in Ukraine not as a foreign language but as the most elevated style of the native language. The language variant used in Ukraine differed from those used elsewhere mainly in pronunciation and accentuation.[90] Many elements of the "Middle Bulgarian" orthography were retained in confraternity editions during

---

87. Isaievych, *Dzherela*, 139–42.

88. Orlevych, *Stavropihiis'kyi instytut*, 16–17.

89. See Ia. Isaievych, "Der Buchdruck und die Entwicklung der Literatursprachen in der Ukraine (16.–1. Hälfte des 17. Jh.)," *Zeitschrift für Slawistik* 36, no. 1 (1991): 40–52; *Istoriia ukraïns'koi kul'tury*, vol. 2 (Kyiv, 2001), 198–201.

90. B. Uspenskii, *Arkhaicheskaia sistema tserkovnoslavianskogo proiznosheniia* (Moscow, 1968), 102.

the late sixteenth and early seventeenth centuries, and even later. Owing to the orthographic and lexical Bulgarisms, the language looked archaic, which endowed it with the dignity perceived as indispensable to a sacral language that symbolized the continuity of cultural development.

If in Russia books were long published only in the intentionally modernized Church Slavonic language, Ukrainian publishers, including confraternities, took another path and began printing in two different languages, the purest Church Slavonic (as they conceived of it) and the so-called "plain Ruthenian language" (*prosta rus'ka mova*) that constituted Middle Ukrainian in Ukraine and Middle Belarusian in the Grand Duchy of Lithuania. Notwithstanding its appellation, the latter was not a vernacular but rather a peculiar medium-level style of the written "cultural" language. Polonisms, Church Slavonic forms, and even artificial constructions were included in this "plain" language precisely in order to differentiate it from the true vernacular "spoken in the streets." Sometimes scholars attempt to determine the place where a given text was written or printed by identifying elements of the Ukrainian or Belarusian vernaculars or their dialects. Such a procedure can be helpful only in the case of less educated authors or scribes, for those with a better education generally tended to choose forms different from those of their native vernacular. In Ukraine, for example, writing "e" in place of the etymological "i" in legal terminology was one of the signs of the "more dignified" official language strongly influenced by Belarusian features of the documents and written law codes of the Grand Duchy of Lithuania. Conversely, in Belarus the pronunciation of "ѣ" as "i" in liturgical practice[91] was meant to emphasize the distinctiveness of the sacral language from the everyday vernacular.

The "plain Ruthenian" language was used for printing verses, school declamations, polemical pamphlets, and prefaces to liturgical and theological books. The broadening of the scope of texts translated from Church Slavonic into the

---

91. P. Zwoliński, "Psalmów kilka słowieńskich Łukasza Górnickiego i ich pierwowzór," *Slavia Orientalis*, 1963, no. 2: 259–62.

"common language" may be attributed, at least in part, to the influence of Reformation trends. Initially, as a rule, only books for domestic reading were translated, but the situation changed in the second quarter of the seventeenth century, when prayers and even parts of liturgical books began to appear in translation into the "common language." It is interesting that the publishing houses of the Ostrih Academy and the Kyivan Caves and Pochaiv monasteries introduced the "common language" more actively than the Lviv Confraternity press. Ukrainian scholars and writers associated with the confraternities probably wanted to stress the antique roots of Ukrainian culture in order to consolidate Ukrainian ethnic and political self-consciousness. Loyalty to tradition and the conservation of some archaic forms were considered useful in withstanding the denationalizing pressure of the social environment. This explains the puristic approach of editors of confraternity publications, especially liturgical ones, who wanted to rid the old texts of specifically Ukrainian elements. Another motive for using allegedly "pure" Church Slavonic for such publications was the desire to make them acceptable in other Orthodox Slavic countries.

There was also printing in the Latin alphabet, predominantly of books in Latin and Polish. The Cyrillic printing of the East Slavic peoples had much in common with the printing of the Romanians and the Orthodox Southern Slavs. On the other hand, the Latin-alphabet book production of Ukraine and Belarus was closely connected with the printing industry of central European countries. It is important to stress that Latin and Polish were used for writing and printing not only by the Polish minority in Ukraine and Belarus, but also by Ukrainian and Belarusian authors who defended their cultural and political distinctiveness. Here again, the confraternities appeared more conservative than Metropolitan Petro Mohyla and his cultural milieu. The Lviv Stauropegion had even acquired a Latin font, but sold it to the Kyivan Caves Monastery, which subsequently began printing in Latin and Polish. On the other hand, Mykhailo Sliozka used both Cyrillic and Latin in the publications of his private press. In the eighteenth century, Ivan Fylypovych (Filipowicz), a talented engraver and member of the Stauropegion Confraternity, established a press to publish Ruthenian (Church Slavonic and Ukrainian), Polish, and Latin books. To eliminate competition from him, the confraternity prevented him from printing Ruthenian books, and, as a result, from 1753 to 1767 Fylypovych printed only Polish and Latin books at his press, while the confraternity occasionally hired him to manage its Ruthenian press.

It should be added that the Jewish population of Ukraine and Belarus used Hebrew and Yiddish books published abroad. Not until 1697 did the first Hebrew-language press appear in the small town of Zhovkva in western Ukraine. During the eighteenth century, several small Jewish presses operated in Ukraine and Belarus. They were able to satisfy only a small part of the demand; hence most Hebrew books continued to be imported. Occasionally, the Lviv Confraternity press cooperated in technical matters with the Jewish printers of Zhovkva. For example, managers of the confraternity press were among the customers of the Jewish type founders there.[92]

In book design, Ukrainian publishers, including the managers of the confraternity presses, appeared more innovative than in their approach to the language of texts. They managed to combine Ukrainian manuscript traditions with the achievements of the Western graphic arts. In publications of the late sixteenth and early seventeenth centuries, elements of Renaissance art are discernible, but subsequently baroque influences became prevalent. Very common was the use of illustrations and emblematic compositions, and woodcuts appeared side by side with copper engravings.[93] Many illustrations in confraternity editions had their prototypes in Western graphic art, but in most cases this did not preclude a certain originality in book design. Printed books remained

92.   *Kniga: Issledovaniia i materialy 7* (1960): 232; V. Vuitsyk, "Novi dokumental'ni vidomosti pro ukraïns'koho hravera i drukaria XVIII st. Ivana Fylypovycha," *ZNTSh* 236 (1998): 457–63.

93.   Ia. Isaevich, "Pervye graviury na medi v knigakh tipografii Ukrainy," *Pamiatniki kul'tury: Novye otkrytiia, ezhegodnik 1978* (Leningrad, 1979), 301–307.

highly decorative and, in many respects, akin to the traditions of folk art.[94]

Studying the dissemination of confraternity publications is a very important scholarly task. The history of the book trade is much less studied than that of book printing, although its importance for economic and intellectual development can hardly be overestimated. The gradual conversion of books into commodities was a landmark in the cultural evolution of society. Before the establishment of indigenous printing, there were two major categories of books on the market: manuscript books of local and foreign origin and printed books, all of which were imported from abroad. After the introduction of printing in Ukraine, competition began between domestic and foreign books, which led to the delineation of their spheres of influence. The patterns of that delineation varied in particular countries, regions, and even cities according to their cultural traditions and models. The Orthodox confraternities contributed greatly to this process.

Confraternity printing emerged at the initial stage of book printing in Eastern Europe, when it was conducted more to achieve political and cultural goals than for profit.[95] As noted earlier, the Lviv Confraternity press printed school textbooks, poems by Ukrainian authors, and political pamphlets, and thus was not commercially oriented. This situation changed in the second quarter of the seventeenth century: when proceeds from donations were exhausted, a stable source of income became necessary, and the publication of books for ecclesiastical use was the most reliable way to assure the financial stability of the enterprise. The widespread dissemination and reprinting of the same titles generally indicates the popularity and spontaneous demand for literature of this kind. Because of the scarcity of liturgical books in many churches, parishioners and donors

---

94.   Zapasko, *Mystetstvo knyhy*; Stepovyk, *Ukraïns'ka hrafika XVI–XVII stolit'*; *Ukrainskie knigi kirillovskoi pechati XVI–XVIII vv.: Katalog izdanii, khraniashchikhsia v Gosudarstvennoi biblioteke im. V. I. Lenina*, comp. T. N. Kameneva and A. A. Guseva, vol. 1 (Moscow, 1978) (title page wrongly gives 1976).

95.   E. L. Keenan, "On Some Historical Aspects of Early Book Printing in the Ukraine," *Recenzija* 5, no. 1 (Fall–Winter 1974): 6.

were even willing to pay very high prices. For example, the production cost of the *Apostol* of 1639 issued by Sliozka's Lviv press was 3.5 zlotys, but the book was sold by the publisher at 12 zlotys per copy and resold by secondhand dealers for as much as 15–36 zlotys per copy. Manuscript copies of the same book sold for only 6–10 zlotys at this time.

The willingness of buyers to pay more for printed books than for manuscripts proves that they were already considered more authoritative and prestigious than handwritten volumes. The new was in higher esteem than the old, demonstrating, at least in this sphere, a system of values contrary to the one of the Russian Old Believers, who venerated all that bore the aspect of antiquity.

Owing to slow sales, even the very high prices of liturgical and prayer books could not provide publishers with sufficient returns to pay for large stocks of paper required for subsequent publications. This compelled printers to look for additional sources of earnings. For example, Mykhailo Sliozka traded not only in books, but also in cloth and other merchandise. The availability of large reserve funds not affected by market fluctuations eventually helped church institutions to oust burgher-owned enterprises from the scene.

Thus, the concentration of book production that was not achieved through directives of the church administration or the civil authorities occurred as a result of the gradual elimination of small publishers by the largest firms under worsening market conditions. Only initially, when the churches' demand for books had not yet been met, was there room enough for both large and small enterprises. Once the demand fell, only comparatively large or at least medium-sized printshops managed to hold their ground. To achieve their goals, the richest and most influential firms used not only economic mechanisms but also non-economic means of pressure. Disproportionately high retail prices could be maintained only when the largest printing presses enjoyed a semi-monopoly, which was related to the size of the market. Some church hierarchs, institutions, and private printers even tried to turn this semi-monopoly into a full monopoly: for example, the Lviv Confraternity, using bribes and "donations," obtained privileges from the Polish kings and the Orthodox hierarchy in order to eliminate other Ukrainian printers from the city. The Orthodox metropolitan of Kyiv, Petro Mohyla, excommunicated Sliozka for printing a missal before Mohyla sold out his edition of the same book. When competitors could not be eliminated, large publishers sometimes concluded agreements on dividing the market.

Only large publishers, such as the Lviv Confraternity and the Kyivan Caves Monastery, had regular bookstores attached to their printshops. Books from those stores were purchased by individual buyers, as well as by wholesale merchants who later sold them at higher prices. For virtually all such merchants, books were only secondary articles sold along with more profitable goods. Fairs played an essential role in the book trade, as they did in all commerce at that time. Not only liturgical texts but also sermons and religious books used in schools were sold in increasing quantities. Several merchants also sold non-religious books issued by Ukrainian and Belarusian publishers, but of these, only primers—owing to their great print runs—were of some economic significance.[96] Some non-religious books could be profitable for printers only because authors or their patrons covered production expenses. Panegyrics and books with panegyrical prefaces often brought rewards to authors or publishers from those to whom they were dedicated. Sometimes customers picked up only part of the press run, and the rest was sold by the printer. Nevertheless, for most publishers, returns on secular books were minimal as compared with those from liturgical texts and prayer books.

Those who bought liturgical books at the printshops resold them mainly to burghers, peasants, and communities who purchased the books in order to donate them to parish and monastery churches. Many copies of early imprints preserved in libraries, churches, and private collections are inscribed by buyers, owners, and donors. The usual formula was that of purchase and donation, whose text ran more or less as follows: "In the name of the Holy Trinity. I, ... , peasant of the village of

---

96.   In the late seventeenth and early eighteenth centuries, primers were published by the Lviv Confraternity in average press runs of 6,000 copies (see Isaievych, *Bratstva*, 150).

... , together with my family, bought this sacred book from ... with my own money (in most cases, the price was expressed) ... and donated this book to the church in the village of .... All priests and deacons of this church should pray for the salvation of my soul and those of the members of my family. Anyone who dares to remove this book from the aforesaid church should be anathematized and excommunicated."

The threat of excommunication could not stop those who wanted to sell books for profit. Liturgical books are not usually to be found in the churches to which they were donated. Many books contain inscriptions attesting to several consecutive sales, with the prices usually rising from one sale to the next. When inflation is taken into account, however, one must conclude that the real price of books was falling steadily.

Occasionally Ukrainian publishers, including the Orthodox metropolitan and bishops, accused one another of greed. At the same time, the confraternity publishers maintained that they were continuing to print books to serve the people and the church; it was only their competitors who were doing so out of "greed for profit." Some contemporary scholars take such declarations at face value, but the point is that the possibility of making a profit through this cultural activity demonstrated that society was capable of sustaining such activity. Profits from the publication of literature for which there was a popular demand enabled some publishers to subsidize the printing of other books for which demand had not yet ripened. Although the authorities continued to impose regulations and restrictions on the market, the attitude to books as merchandise was firmly established during the seventeenth century. In Ukraine and Belarus, as elsewhere, practice eventually showed that book publishing could develop, or at least achieve stability, only if commercial effectiveness was assured. For the development of publishing, to use the words of Elizabeth Eisenstein, "the mixture of many motives provided a more powerful impetus than any single motive (whether that of profit-seeking capitalist or Christian evangelist) could have provided by itself."[97] The

---

97.   E. L. Eisenstein, *The Printing Press as an Agent of Change*, vol. 1 (Cambridge, 1979), 456.

rate of secularization and commercialization was very slow throughout Eastern Europe, which is quite understandable in the given socioeconomic and cultural context. Only much later, mainly in the second half of the eighteenth century, did changes occur in most East European countries that, contrary to Gary Marker's view,[98] are comparable with the Western "printing revolution."

The profitability of liturgical book printing largely contributed to a change in the thematic composition of book production. In Ukraine between 1586 and 1615, liturgical texts constituted 13 percent of all titles published and 41 percent of all printed pages. During the next 30 years, from 1616 to 1645, the proportion of liturgical titles grew to 44 percent, and their page volume reached 66.7 percent of the total. This occurred mainly at the expense of educational and political literature. Similar trends were characteristic of Belarusian printing.

Because of these changes, the subject range of publications in Belarus and Ukraine became even more limited and, consequently, the activity of printers could not eliminate the manual copying of books. The number of titles of manuscript books was many times larger than that of the titles of imprints. The copying of books remained decentralized: manuscripts were copied by village priests and deacons, itinerant students and teachers, and sometimes also by burghers and even peasants. Many scribes were connected with local confraternities. In most cases, manuscripts were copied for the copyist's own use or on the orders of individuals, parishes, or confraternities. The sale of secondhand manuscripts was much more widespread than the sale of new ones. Not only manuscripts but printed books served as originals for copying. For example, Kyrylo Trankvilion-Stavrovetsky's *Zertsalo bohosloviia* (The Mirror of Theology), published in 1618 in Pochaiv and at the Univ monastery in 1692, was copied throughout the seventeenth and eighteenth centuries in various parts of Ukraine and even in Russia. No less than thirty handwritten copies of this book are known to exist, and

---

98. G. Marker, "Russia and the 'Printing Revolution': Notes and Observations," *Slavic Review* 41 (1982): 270.

that is only a preliminary figure.[99] This is but one example; more could be cited. The role of the confraternities in the production and dissemination of manuscripts and printed books has yet to be studied. Reliable conclusions can be drawn only after the completion of a computerized union catalogue of Ukrainian manuscripts and old imprints (now in progress at the I. Krypiakevych Institute of Ukrainian Studies in Lviv).

Cyrillic books in the Church Slavonic language, both manuscript and printed, were used in all countries of the Slavia Orthodoxa and in Romania. This facilitated the movement of such books from one country to another. Books written and printed in Ukraine and Belarus were exported to Moldavia, Russia, and other countries. In the 1620s, Patriarch Filaret of Moscow banned "Lithuanian" (i.e., Ukrainian and Belarusian) books, and some of them were even burned.[100] Such repressive measures were sometimes reiterated, but they did not stop the movement of books across the border of the Muscovite state. In the second half of the seventeenth century, the influx of books printed in Ukraine into Russia increased noticeably. On the other hand, liturgical books from the Moscow press were considered authoritative in Ukraine and Belarus, and some were even reprinted there. It is also known that manuscript books of South Slavic origin continued to circulate in Russia, Belarus, Ukraine, and the Romanian lands during the seventeenth century and even later. Most numerous were liturgical texts, as well as patristic and hagiographic works of Byzantine and South Slavic authors. Much more diverse were Latin-alphabet books, most of them written in Latin, imported into Eastern Europe from the West. After the so-called printing revolution in Western Europe, the range of books available to readers in Ukraine and Belarus increased tremendously, a fact whose significance can hardly be overestimated.

It is not easy to generalize about the importance of the publishing and book-trading activities of the confraternities, especially as special studies of the problem are only in their

---

99.   Ia. D. Isaievych and I. Z. Myts'ko, "Zhyttia i vydavnycha diial'nist' Kyryla-Trankviliona Stavrovets'koho" in *Bibliotekoznavstvo ta bibliohrafiia* (Kyiv, 1982), 62–65.

100.   Cf. Isaievych, *Preemniki pervopechatnika*, 145.

infancy. It is well known that in Eastern Europe the initial changes in book production and trade were extremely slow and confined primarily to the religious sphere. Nevertheless, the fact remains that the introduction of printing, with the active participation of the confraternities, set in motion significant social and cultural processes and accelerated others. In comparison with statistical data on Western European book publishing, the quantity of books published by the Ukrainian printing presses, including those of the confraternities, may appear small. Even so, their influence on the development of Ukrainian culture was far from negligible. Cyrillic book printing certainly contributed to the spread of literacy. Although the vast majority of the population remained illiterate, the number of literate and even well-educated individuals rose slowly but steadily. There were buyers and readers of books, mainly of religious content, not only among the nobility, clergy, and staff of local government and judicial institutions, but also among burghers and peasants. Of course, educated burghers were not numerous and literate peasants were the exception, but the very fact of such exceptions is notable. According to a statement of the Syrian traveler Paul of Aleppo, in the mid-seventeenth century there were numerous elementary schools in Ukrainian villages. Without printed books, the activities of those schools would have been very difficult, if not impossible. Theological works and some secular publications had an appreciable impact on the most active cultural figures who shaped the development of the Ukrainian cultural tradition. The printing of theological and other books was also crucial to the functioning of institutions of higher education.[101]

Confraternity book publishing at the very first stage of its history had a distinctly creative character. In the late sixteenth and early seventeenth centuries, economic development, along with the increasing social activity of townsmen and part of the nobility, promoted the assimilation of some elements of the Renaissance cultural heritage. Both indigenous traditions and cross-cultural contacts contributed to the distinctive features of Ukrainian book publishing.

---

101.   For more details on Ukrainian book publishing and printing, see Isaievych, *Ukraïns'ke knyhovydannia* (Lviv, 2002).

In the late seventeenth and early eighteenth centuries, conditions for Ukrainian book publishing grew steadily worse. In eastern Ukraine, the establishment of strict Russian censorship had a disastrous effect on printing as a tool of cultural progress. In western Ukraine (Galicia and the Right Bank), Polish was taking the upper hand in both education and printing. The Lviv Stauropegion remained the only Ukrainian confraternity that continued printing Church Slavonic and, to some extent, Ruthenian texts. Most numerous were liturgical books, also published by the Pochaiv, Suprasl, and Univ monastery presses. The network of minor confraternities in towns and villages was instrumental in creating a demand for these books throughout various parts of Ukraine and Belarus.

Books published by confraternities, primarily by those of Lviv and Vilnius, remained in use long after the confraternities' activities had ceased. They contributed to the longevity of the Ukrainian and Belarusian cultural traditions.

VI

The Archives of the Confraternities

While many confraternities maintained archival holdings, only the archive of the Lviv Dormition (Stauropegion) Confraternity was not dispersed but survived as an entity, with all its main components intact. It was inherited by the Lviv Stauropegion Institute (1793-1939) and formally organized as an archive under the institute's auspices in 1886. Currently the archives of the Dormition Confraternity and the Lviv Stauropegion Institute constitute fond 129 in the Central State Historical Archive of Ukraine in Lviv.[102] The manuscript and old imprint collections of the Stauropegion Institute Museum were moved to the Lviv Historical Museum. Study of the Lviv Confraternity archive helps explain the structure of the archives of other major confraternities; moreover, it contains materials on confraternities with which the Stauropegion cooperated. The importance of this archive was recently highlighted in the comprehensive studies of Iuliia Shustova,[103] who maintains that the archive in its entirety may be regarded as a textual continuum reflecting the activities and mentality of the confreres.

Confraternity members considered the founding and confirming charters ("privileges") obtained from the state authorities and the church hierarchy to be the most important documents in their archives. This is entirely understandable, as these documents were indispensable for the defense of the confraternities' legal rights. In their interpretation of such decrees, written in the name of patriarchs, bishops, or kings,

---

1.　P. K. Grimsted, *Archives and Manuscript Repositories in the USSR: Ukraine and Moldavia*, Book 1, *General Bibliography and Institutional Directory* (Princeton, N.J., 1988), 441, 469–70.

2.　Shustova, "Dokumenty L'vovskogo Stavropigiiskogo bratstva," 24–25; idem, "Arkhiv L'vovskogo Uspenskogo Stavropigiiskogo bratstva kak fenomen kul'tury" in *Tekst v gumanitarnom znanii: Materialy mezhvuzovskoi konferentsii* (Moscow, 1997), 94–97.

historians generally consider these eminent persons the "founders" or "initiators of the founding" of the confraternities. That was not always the case. Confraternity members would often obtain legal sanctions from the Eastern patriarchs, bishops, or the crown following the de facto establishment of their confraternities. In some cases they managed to obtain such sanctions with the aid of bribes, while in others they exploited differences between individual hierarchs. Confraternities that did not succeed in obtaining privileges of their own occasionally copied the texts of charters granted to other confraternities. Many confraternities in the western Ukrainian lands and in Right-Bank Ukraine used articles taken (directly or indirectly, through the intermediacy of other confraternities) from the statute of the Lviv Dormition Confraternity. Some adopted the statutes of the Vilnius or Kyiv confraternities, often with changes and additions. Most confraternities in the trans-Dnipro region had no statutes. A few confraternities considered grants of the Galician-Volhynian princes to be the foundation of their rights, in addition to the decrees that they obtained themselves. For example, the St. Nicholas Confraternity in Lviv based the rights to its landholdings on Prince Lev Danylovych's charter of 1292.[104] The Horodok Confraternity also considered its holdings to have been "granted by the Ruthenian princes."[105]

Quite often, founding decrees included the text of the statute ("articles," "rules") of a given confraternity, although confraternities frequently had separate decrees ratifying their statutes. The main function of the statute was to regulate a confraternity's organizational structure and help strengthen the discipline of its members. Many statutes contained identical requirements; on the other hand, statutes often complemented one another by focusing attention on various aspects of confraternity life. Some old statutes have pages missing or show the erasure of articles unpropitious for the clergy. Such statutes are a reminder that in the struggle for influence between the confraternities and the clergy, the balance of power did not shift in favor of the confraternities.

---

3.   AGAD/Lustracje/XIII/48. As noted by Denys Zubrytsky in the first half of the nineteenth century, Lev's decree is a later forgery.

4.   AGAD/Lustracje/48; BKP, 5512, f. 12.

Although the statutes are one of the most important sources for the history of the confraternities, researchers should be aware that very often the most significant aspects of confraternity life were reflected very weakly in them, if at all. For this reason, the conclusions of researchers who assess the general tendency of a particular confraternity's activities solely on the basis of its statute cannot be considered definitive.[106]

In the late nineteenth and early twentieth centuries, many decrees and statutes of the confraternities were gathered by regional ethnographers and collectors. Some of them were published in collections of documents and periodicals, particularly in eparchial newsletters (*eparkhial'nye vedomosti*), but the great majority of these documents remain unpublished. A number of statutes have been preserved in the library holdings of the Peremyshl Greek Catholic chapter, the manuscripts of which have been little studied by researchers.[107] Statutes of confraternities in western Ukrainian towns and villages may also be found in the manuscript division of the Vasyl Stefanyk Library, National Academy of Sciences of Ukraine (holdings of the Basilian monasteries and of the Shevchenko Scientific Society), the National Museum in Lviv, the Ivan Franko Archives (now held in the T. H. Shevchenko Institute of Ukrainian Literature, National Academy of Sciences of Ukraine), and certain other collections. Confraternity charters are also preserved in the holdings of state and church institutions and various archival collections (particularly in the Main Archives of Older Records in Warsaw and in the Central State Historical Archive of Ukraine in Lviv).

The decrees and statutes utilized by certain confraternities are known only from copies. Thus, for example, the original

---

5.   See, e.g., I. Velyhors'kyi, "Svidky nashoï kul'tury," *Nasha kul'tura*, 1936, no. 4: 311.

6.   In 1948, the manuscript collection of this library was transferred to the National Library (Biblioteka Narodowa) in Warsaw. For information on the collections of the Peremyshl cathedral library, see Ia. Isaevich, "Kirillovskie staropechatnye knigi v kollektsiiakh Pol's'koi Narodnoi Respubliki," *Kniga: Issledovaniia i materialy* 8 (1963), 292; E. Hrytsak, "Kapitul'na biblioteka v Peremyshli," *S'ohochasne i mynule* (Lviv), 1939, no. 1: 96–98; [B. Balyk], "Rukopysy Peremys'koï hreko-katolyts'koï kapituly v Narodovii Bibliotetsi u Varshavi," *Bohosloviia* 37 (1973): 193–213; 38 (1974): 237–43.

decrees pertaining to the Kyiv Confraternity are not extant. Fortunately, in 1773 Kasiian Lekhnytsky, a lecturer in philosophy at the Kyivan Academy, and Ieronim, a monk at the confraternity monastery, made copies of the records that the Kyivan Academy then had in its possession. At the beginning of the nineteenth century, these copies were recopied for Metropolitan Evgenii Bolkhovitinov.[108] The founding decrees of the Kyiv Confraternity were published on the basis of those copies.[109] The contents of the decrees, as well as their linguistic and stylistic features, prove beyond doubt that the publication is an adequate rendering of the text of authentic documents of the first half of the seventeenth century. Their authenticity is also confirmed by the discovery of almost identical texts of copies of some of the decrees obtained by the Kyiv Confraternity among documents of other confraternities.

Often confraternity members themselves would copy their founding decrees and statutes and, occasionally, the most important letters addressed to the confraternity into a special book. In many cases, such a book was combined with a roster containing the names of new confraternity members.[110] Thus, in the early seventeenth century, copies of the most important decrees were bound together with a list of the confreres of the Lviv Stauropegion Confraternity. Later, copies of new decrees dated up to 1649, inclusively, as well as privileges granted to the confraternity, library catalogues, an inventory of the property of the Dormition Church and the St. Onuphrius Monastery, and a ledger containing receipts signed by the confraternity's debtors were added to this book. It acquired the title *Album of the Stauropegion Confraternity*[111] and has often been used

---

7.   NBUV, St. Sophia collection, MS II-495, f. 69–70; collection of the theological academy, MS II-220, 133–35.

8.   *PKK*, 2 (Kyiv, 1846; 2d rev. and expanded ed., Kyiv, 1898).

9.   The roster was occasionally referred to as the "confraternity registry" (see the statute of the confraternity in the town of Kulykiv, dated 1725, in BKP, MS 2769, f. 2).

10.   The manuscript is preserved in the Lviv Historical Museum. The founding decree and those confirming the Lviv Confraternity, as well as the statutes of the confraternity and the confraternity school, were published in *DS* (Lviv, 1895) and in fuller versions by Myron Kapral in *Pryvileï natsional'nykh hromad mista L'vova (XIV–XVIII st.)* (Lviv, 2000) on the basis of originals now

by researchers of the history of confraternities. In the Lutsk Confraternity, copies of decrees issued to it, its most important resolutions, a ledger of documents, books, and articles of the confraternity, and resolutions pertaining to the election of elders were compiled into an anthology. This "Lutsk anthology" was the basis for the publication of the most important documents pertaining to the history of the confraternity.[112]

Besides their own privileges and statutes, confraternities frequently entered the privileges or statutes of other confraternities into their copy-books, assuming that the confirmation of the rights of one confraternity would attest to the legitimacy of analogous requirements made by other confraternities.

In the smaller confraternities, particularly rural ones, a book would contain not only a roster of members and copies of privileges (if any existed), but also entries concerning all other matters in which the confreres were engaged, such as resolutions on the election of elders and notes on income and expenses. In the larger confraternities, in addition to a roster, there were other types of books in which various matters were recorded. Typical of these are the archives of one of the Rohatyn confraternities (Nativity of the Theotokos), which contained the following documents in 1733: a statute, a roster ("confraternity books in which their names are recorded"), a ledger of resolutions passed by the confraternity ("decrees and sentences of the confraternity"), and a ledger of income and expenses.[113]

Besides the rosters, *pom'ianyky* or *subitnyky* also attest to the membership of the confraternities: these were little books containing the names of deceased members to be remembered at requiem services. A source of this type was first studied by Mykhailo Maksymovych, who published fragments of "A *Pom'ianyk* of the Lutsk Confraternity Church Begun in 1618" from a copy made in 1677–78 by Ieremiia Savytsky.

preserved in the Central State Historical Archive of Ukraine in Lviv (fond 129) and copies included in the Album. For a description of the Album, see DS, ii–iii.

11.   PKK, 1, 2d ed. (1898).

12.   NM, records of the general visitation, MS 11, f. 109.

The manuscript, which was considered lost, survived in the collection of the Manuscript Institute of the Volodymyr Vernadsky National Library of Ukraine in Kyiv. Aside from the portion copied by Savytsky, it contains later listings of members and monks who died between 1678 and 1793.[114] Similar *pom'ianyky* were compiled in villages, such as the one "recorded in the village of Kormanychi ... through the efforts of Their Graces the elder and young gentlemen of the confraternity."[115] The first pages of the *pom'ianyk* indicate that it was begun in 1685, when Ivan Kurochka and Stefan Koval headed the confraternity, and that Oleksander Smerechansky had begun inscribing the entries. In certain cases, registry entries are important for the light they cast on the biographies of activists connected with the confraternities. One example of this is the "Prototypon onoma," a ledger of a church that was under the supervision of the Zamostia Confraternity.[116]

In certain confraternities, such as that of Zamostia, the minutes contained only entries pertaining to the election of elders.[117] In others, resolutions adopted by the confreres and notes of discussions on various issues were also recorded. Unfortunately, the session minutes of the Kyiv, Lutsk, Rohatyn, and other leading confraternities are not extant. Of the confraternities located in large cities, we have the minutes of meetings (though by no means complete) of the Lviv Stauropegion Confraternity. In the early seventeenth century, its books of minutes were called "electoral ledgers," inasmuch as the minutes of electoral meetings were also recorded in them. In the eighteenth century, the books of minutes were known as books or acts of public meetings (*Liber sessionum, Acta sessionum publicarum*). In addition to the most important resolutions, these books contained notes on discussions and contents of some of

---

13.   The manuscript now has the shelf number NBUV, f. 30, no. 56. Cf. *Kievlianin*, 1841, 304–23; *PKK*, 1: 370; O. Biriulina, "Reiestr dukhovnykh osib Luts'koho brats'koho pom'ianyka" in *Pam'iatky sakral'noho mystetstva Volyni na mezhi tysiacholit'* (Lutsk, 2000), 34–38.

14.   BKP, MS 2967, t. 1–3.

15.   Budilovich, *Russkaia pravoslavnaia starina*, 83–96; *Pamiatniki russkoi stariny v zapadnykh guberniiakh Imperii izdavaemye P. N. Batiushkovym*, vol. 7, album (St. Petersburg, 1885), no. 17.

16.   Budilovich, *Russkaia pravoslavnaia starina*, 63–67.

the documents that had been discussed. The oldest extant book of minutes is the "electoral ledger" for 1599–1650.[118] It contains no entries for the years 1620–32, possibly because entries were copied into it from another book that is not extant. The minutes of the confraternities from the seventeenth century to the first quarter of the eighteenth were published by Amvrosii Krylovsky.[119] However, as a result of his oversight, the published books contain many incorrect readings, and no attempt has been made to restore either the original order of the entries or to separate the minutes from other texts.

In addition to the minutes of meetings, the so-called *Liber Plantationum* for the years 1686–1725[120] contains accounts of income and expenses, copies of outgoing correspondence, and a ledger of donations to the confraternities. Still unpublished is a book of minutes (*Acta sessionum publicarum*) dating from the mid-eighteenth century (for 1733, 1740–42, and 1749–58)[121] in which, in keeping with an adopted resolution, there are also copies of letters sent to and from the confraternity (except those considered confidential) and of letters read at meetings. Occasionally, through the scribes' oversight, minutes were recorded on an inappropriate page. Some books of the seventeenth and eighteenth centuries include notes explaining that the chronology of entries is disrupted by pages sewn out of order. Occasionally the books contain gaps, indicating a certain period of inactivity on the part of confraternity members or carelessness of the scribe.[122]

Researchers who make use of these minutes should be aware that they, too, do not reflect every aspect of the

17.   TsDIAL 129/1/1043; *AIuZR*, 11: 58–163.

18.   *AIuZR*, 11: 58–163.

19.   LNB, Manuscript Division, Ossolineum collection, MS 2125; *AIuZR*, 12: 164–352.

20.   TsDIAL 129/1/1169.

21.   One of the ledgers contains the following interesting entry (written in Ukrainian, but partly in the Roman alphabet): "Every year we must compile the names of the elders and give a record to the younger confreres up to the present day.... I have delayed this work, gentlemen confreres: this occurred not so much because of my neglect as owing to various impediments" (TsDIAL 129/1/1077: 73). When Amvrosii Krylovsky published the ledger, he omitted this fragment. See *AIuZR*, 11: 73–74.

confraternities' activity. Matters pertaining to ethnic and religious conflicts, in particular, often were not processed through the office: they were transmitted verbally to specific individuals so as to maintain confidentiality.

Besides minutes of meetings, an equally valuable source are ledgers of income and expenses, inasmuch as the financial management of the confraternities reflected their public and cultural activity. The ledgers were kept by elders and treasurers, who reported on these matters to the confraternity membership. In the eighteenth century, the Greek Catholic Church administration required that all confraternities keep ledgers of income and expenses, which were to be audited by the clergy. Thus, the statute ("articles") of the confraternity in the village of Viazivnytsia, issued by the bishop, provided as follows: "The confraternity should have a book made of white paper; in it they should record meetings, a list of income and expenses and annual accounts, and they should show this book to the protopresbyter during his visit to the church or during a general visitation."[123] A similar article was included in the statute of the Leżajsk Confraternity[124] and a number of others. However, few confraternities carried out the injunction to keep ledgers of income and expenses. In certain cases, this is to be explained primarily by the unwillingness of the confraternities to give the clergy control over their finances.

A whole series of ledgers of income and expenses of confraternities in cities, towns, and some villages, mostly in the western Ukrainian lands, is extant. Some of them contain references to expenses connected with school needs, which are a valuable source for the history of education.

At times it was stipulated that elders should calculate confraternity income and expenses in a rough copy and enter them into the "main ledger" only on the eve of making their reports. Thus, the seventeenth-century statute of the confraternity in the town of Oleshychi dictated that during their one-year term of office confraternity elders should not use "the main ledger, in which the confraternity treasure

---

22.   BKP, MS 2728, f. 6.
23.   BKP, MS 2868, f. 17.

is recorded," but "for the whole year they should write all matters, the income and expenses of the confraternity, in another ledger." Only a week before "submitting the accounts" were the elders to record "the whole matter and the entire wealth of the confraternity" in the main ledger.[125] The same requirement is included in the statute of the St. George Confraternity of Drohobych (1746), which makes reference to the "great" (main) ledger.[126]

Understandably, the leading confraternities located in the large cities had especially many administrative matters to keep track of, and therefore maintained more complex financial documentation. However, a substantial number of books pertaining to economic activity have been preserved only in the archives of the Lviv Stauropegion Confraternity. Among them are general ledgers of income and expenses, as well as particular ledgers associated with various aspects of confraternity activity. One of the oldest books, never published and rarely used by historians, is the "Ledger of Endowments for the Needs of the Monastery and Hospital" for 1594–95.[127] There are also separate ledgers of expenses pertaining to the construction of the school, the conduct of lawsuits, the upkeep of pupils in the dormitory of the confraternity school, and the hospital. These ledgers of income and expenses were kept for reporting purposes by confreres assigned to particular tasks.[128]

A valuable source is the ledger of expenses pertaining to the construction of the church in 1592. In it, several listings are extant in rough and clean copies. Individual pages are devoted to entries on costs connected with the purchase and transport of various building materials and to lists of expenses pertaining to the salaries of tradesmen: the master builder ("mason"), his apprentices, students, and, finally, laborers. There is even an index that facilitated the search for ledgers indicating particular types of expenses.[129]

---

24.   BKP, MS 2725, f. 7.
25.   BKP, Akc. MS 2906, f. 13.
26.   TsDIAL 129/1/1041.
27.   TsDIAL 129/1/1044, f. 5.
28.   Ibid., f. 1, 4, 26, 44–45.

The records kept by confraternity booksellers provide much material useful for studying the history of culture. Among them are lists of books transferred from the storehouse to the bookstore (with reports to the booksellers), ledgers pertaining to the sale of books and, lastly, ledgers of various payments made from funds acquired by the booksellers through their trade. The fact of the matter is that in the seventeenth and eighteenth centuries profits from the bookstore helped defray a variety of everyday expenses: the needs of the printing house, construction, the school and hospital, the conduct of lawsuits, and subsidies to individuals (including foreign guests). Accordingly, the ledgers of booksellers' expenses contain materials pertaining to various aspects of confraternity activities. Some of these ledgers were published by Amvrosii Krylovsky, though with certain omissions. Thus, in the ledger of book sales begun on 20 November 1649, the publisher omitted entries that he considered "of no historical interest." In reality, exceptionally interesting material was omitted, particularly information concerning a "strike" of printing-house workers and data on prices and measures, etc.[130] Most book-trade ledgers of the eighteenth century have never been published.[131]

Payments made by the confraternity to specialists who served its printing press were entered in separate books. Of particular value is a book containing the confraternity's contracts with printers for the period 1680–1757.[132]

The documentation of current expenses ceased to concern the confraternity once it had settled accounts with all interested parties and the reports of confreres supervising various matters had been approved. For example, a ledger pertaining to "all sorts of utensils, wood, cord, horses, oats, hay, wagons, and blacksmiths" has the following marginal note: "This ledger is no longer necessary." Nevertheless, a significant portion of the old records that were of no practical use to the confreres has been preserved in the Stauropegion archives.

---

29.   TsDIAL 129/1/1065, 1141, no. 1, vol. 1: 546–50.

30.   For example, the ledger of books sold by Ivan Chesnykivsky in the years 1733–41 (TsDIAL 129/1/1170) and by Khrystofor Deima in the years 1758–75 (ibid., spr. 1222).

31.   TsDIAL 129/1/1171; AIuZR, 12: 379–437.

It should be emphasized that individual categories of records often were not kept separate. In ledgers of expenses, in particular, one may encounter entries referring to decisions approved by the confraternity, which, by rights, should have been entered into the books of minutes.

Another valuable historical source is the correspondence among confraternities, as well as the letters written by confraternities to various public officials. Some confraternities had seals for the certification of their representatives' credentials, letters, and other documents. For example, the seal of the St. George Confraternity of Iavoriv depicted a horseman with a spear (St. George) encircled by the inscription: "Seal of the Iavoriv Confraternity."[133]

In the late sixteenth and seventeenth centuries, confraternity members and their opponents frequently entered their "protestations" (complaints) into the records of castle courts, particularly those of Lviv and Peremyshl. Some of them feature motifs characteristic of contemporary Ukrainian political writings. Their authors speak angrily of the downtrodden state of the Ukrainian nation in its native land. Both certified and uncertified copies of such complaints are preserved in confraternity archives.

Thus, the most significant documents pertaining to the history of the confraternities were collected in their archives. Given the exceptional importance of these archival materials, before proceeding to a survey of other sources, we shall examine the organization of bookkeeping and archive management in the confraternities and the structure of their archives. In this regard, the archive of the Lviv Dormition Confraternity contains unique materials. It is the only archive of a Ukrainian civic association of the sixteenth to eighteenth centuries that remains extant, not in fragments, but almost in its entirety, with all its component sections intact. Hence it is extremely important not only for the study of Ukrainian history, literature, and language, but also for the study of the history of archives in Ukraine.

---

32.   BKP, MS 2910, f. 5.

According to the system of record keeping adopted by the confraternity, from the end of the sixteenth century the following groups of documents were preserved in its archives: 1) various incoming documents, including privileges, letters to the confraternity, extracts from public records, etc.; 2) minutes of confraternity meetings; 3) rough copies and copies of outgoing documents; 4) ledgers of income and expenses and other materials pertaining to the confraternity's economic activities.

The confraternity "treasury" contained a "sack for privileges" to preserve the most valuable documents: charters issued by Eastern patriarchs, Kyivan metropolitans, Lviv bishops, kings of Poland, some notes on debts, and so on. Later, these documents were stored in a special chest containing the statute of the confraternity and documents transferred to the Stauropegion by associations of Ukrainian burghers in Lviv that predated it.

Privileges and other important but brief documents were kept folded to safeguard them. The content of each folded document was indicated on the spine in the form of a title or annotation, for example, "A protestation of furriers expelled from the guild." On the obverse of Greek-language decrees, there was occasionally a longer resume than usual for the benefit of those who did not read Greek. The obverse of a decree issued in the name of Patriarch Jeremiah, dated July 1592, concerning the abolition of the Stauropegion, bears a notation documented with sources to the effect that the document is a forgery committed by the Lviv bishop Hedeon Balaban with the help of Bishop Dionysius of Tŭrnovo.[134]

Some ledgers impart the contents of individual documents in considerable detail; occasionally they include opening sentences and a description of the external appearance of documents.[135] As a rule, later lists of charters are less detailed.[136] Some of them were compiled on the occasion of a general inspection of the archives, while others were prepared in connection with the transfer of records from one

33.   *MCS*, 361–62.

34.   Album, 382–91.

35.   *AIuZR*, 11: 169–70 (1648), 231–34 (1664); TsDIAL 129/1064 (1651), 129/1/837 (1724), 129/1/878 (1726), et al.

confraternity official to another. Most incoming documents, especially the numerous letters written by other confraternities and by Ukrainian public figures to the Stauropegion, were not recorded in the ledgers. The burghers' international relations are reflected in letters sent from other countries. Letters and notes written in Greek, Italian, Magyar, Czech, and other foreign languages are preserved in the archives of the Lviv Confraternity. They contain approximately seventy letters written by the Eastern patriarchs (in Greek or Church Slavonic) and seventy-six letters from princes and lords of Moldavia (most in Ukrainian and some in Church Slavonic).

Besides letters, many certified and uncertified extracts from record books (castle, municipal, and others) are to be found in the archives of confraternities. There are also numerous extracts from records of lawsuits concerning questions of property and, in particular, of inheritance and the sale of buildings belonging to the confraternity and its individual members. Fascicles of records grouped in thematic or chronological order, comprising incoming letters and various extracts, were occasionally compiled. Thus, an ancient ledger contains a "special fascicle" of letters received in 1591 from the towns of Halych and Holohory and various extracts pertaining to matters about which the confreres of those towns wrote.[137] There is also a fascicle entitled "Various original letters written ... to the confraternity from Rome and Warsaw from 1727 to 1730."[138]

Only an insignificant portion of the outgoing documents has been preserved in the archives of those institutions and of individuals who received letters from the confraternity. Individual rough copies and letters ready to be sent, but never posted for one reason or another (e.g., a letter to the burghers of Novokostiantyniv containing the text of a confraternity statute), have remained in the archives of the Lviv Confraternity.[139] Books containing copies of outgoing documents were also kept, but not on a regular basis.[140]

36.   Album, 385.
37.   LNB, Manuscript Division, Ossolineum collection, MS 2093.
38.   TsDIAL 129/1/423.
39.   TsDIAL 129/1/1035.

Records concerning internal affairs constitute the largest group of papers preserved in confraternity archives. These include correspondence between individual members with regard to confraternity issues, as well as various instructions and extracts. But most of the material recording the multifarious confraternity activities is in the form of books or unbound notebooks,[141] primarily the books of minutes and ledgers of income and expenses discussed above.

The archival materials compiled in the most orderly manner are those pertaining to legal affairs. Confraternity secretaries were responsible for daily record-keeping. Those active in the seventeenth century were known as *pysari*; those of the eighteenth century were called *sekretarii*. Among them, the following should be mentioned: Vasyl Ievstafiievych (elected to this post in 1604, 1608, 1611, and 1612), Vasyl Bunevsky (1616), Kostiantyn Mezapeta (1633), Vasyl Hryhorovych (1641), Pavlo Lavryshevych (1644), Vasyl Korendovych (1657), Ivan Liashkovsky (1666, 1669), Mykola Krasovsky (1690), Mykhailo Liaskovsky (1741, 1749, 1751), and Vasyl Iliashevych (1758). Occasionally, deputy secretaries were also elected. The secretary would enter resolutions adopted by the confraternity into its records and read his notes to those present. He also conducted correspondence, but the seal for the authentication of letters was usually kept by one of the confraternity elders. When many letters had to be prepared at once, students of the confraternity school would be engaged to help.

The archives were preserved in a special room containing an iron chest and cupboard.[142] In 1732 Petro Kos catalogued the confraternity archives, compiled two registers "of all its privileges, rights, and documents since its founding ... during the years 1522–1731," and wrote a memorandum entitled "Status confraternitatis" on the basis of these archival documents.[143]

---

40.   O. I. Kaluzhniatsky reckoned that the confraternity archives contained more than 200 fascicles, notebooks, and books (see *Trudy XIV arkheologicheskago s"ezda*, vol. 2 [Kyiv, 1910], 272). A survey of books in the confraternity archives was compiled by Volodymyr Mylkovych (published in Sharanevych, *Nykolai Krasovs'kyi*, 75–79, 87–93, 120–23, 162–63).

41.   TsDIAL 129/1/1169: 104, 94.

42.   LNB, Basilian monasteries collection, MS 132 (104), 4, 9.

Later, the confraternity elected archival directors (*archivi directores*). In 1751 Iakiv Gavendovych, Khrystofor Deima, Antin Levynsky, and Hryhorii Srokovsky were assigned to that task. The latter was an eminent archival specialist and expert in jurisprudence (who, like Mykhailo Slonsky, was an official in the castle registry).[144] They were instructed to classify the archives, compile registers of documents, and search for lost records. In order to improve the system for the preservation of documents, the confraternity issued an order (honored mainly in the breach) that elders and other officials of the confraternity consult archival materials only in the session room and not remove them from confraternity premises. When the need arose to take certain documents out of Lviv, confraternity messengers had to sign receipts for them.[145]

After the dissolution of the Lviv Confraternity (1788), its archives were transferred to the Stauropegion Institute. Scholarly research on the confraternity archives was initiated by Denys Zubrytsky, who served as director of the library and archive of the Stauropegion Institute from 1831 to 1847, with some interruptions.[146] Zubrytsky sent certain documents of the confraternity to scholars in Kyiv, St. Petersburg, and Moscow for publication. Several records were also transferred to the Ossoliński and Baworowski libraries in Lviv. In this manner, materials from the confraternity archives were incorporated into various archival collections.[147]

However, the great majority of materials of the former archive of the Lviv Confraternity remained in the possession of the Stauropegion Institute. A significant part of these documents was catalogued by Ilarion Svientsitsky.[148] His catalogue also includes quite a few records that did not

---

43. TsDIAL 129/1/1169, f. 103; *IuSLS*, 1: 242.

44. *AIuZR*, 11: 7, 10, 266.

45. Ia. Isaievych, "D. I. Zubryts'kyi i ioho diial'nist' v haluzi spetsial'nykh istorychnykh dystsyplin," *Naukovo-informatsiinyi Biuleten' Arkhivnoho upravlinnia URSR*, 1963, no. 1: 48.

46. LNB, Ossolineum collection, MS 2093, and Baworowski collection, "Teky Zubryts'koho," MS 2125; St. Petersburg Branch, Institute of Russian History, Russian Academy of Sciences, Archive, Denys Zubryts'kyi collection; State Historical Museum in Moscow.

47. Sventsits'kyi, *Opys'*, 89–174.

belong to the Lviv Confraternity but became the property of
the Stauropegion Institute, possibly during the organization
of the archaeological and bibliographic exhibition of 1888–89
(especially manuscripts donated by parishes). Svientsitsky's
catalogue did not include manuscripts in book form and
fascicles belonging to the confraternity archives.

In the early stages of its organization, the Central State
Historical Archive of Ukraine in Lviv acquired almost all
the extant archival materials of the Lviv Confraternity for
the period 1586–1788 (approximately 1,700 items) and of the
Stauropegion Institute for the period 1790–1939. These items
were merged into one fond, no. 129. Subsequent reorganizations
and classifications, as well as the loss of individual groups of
documents, have hindered the complete reconstruction of
the original contents and structure of the Lviv Confraternity
archive. However, even the extant materials convincingly
attest to the adequate level of archival practice in Ukraine in
the late sixteenth and seventeenth centuries.

As is apparent from individual extant documents,
the archives of other large confraternities were similarly
organized, even though the quantity of documentary material
was much smaller. Some confraternities in small towns
had their own archives, which, in addition to documents,
contained other valuable materials. Thus, the "secular
confraternity" in Potik had an "Archive for the safekeeping
of confraternity articles."[149]

Aside from archives, confraternity affairs were reflected
most fully in documents stored in the archives of church
institutions, both eparchial (episcopal, consistorial) and
parochial. For example, the archive of the Uniate metropolitans,
transferred by the Russian authorities to St. Petersburg
and now preserved in the Russian State Historical Archive,
contains some early documents on Belarusian and Ukrainian
confraternities.[150] Consistory archives include complaints
lodged by the clergy against the confreres and records of
confraternity activities. The eparchial court record-books of

---

48.   NM, records of the general visitation, 11, f. 92.
49.   *Arkhiv Uniatskikh mitrapalitaŭ*, 24, 30, 31, 32 et al.

the Kholm and Peremyshl eparchies contain materials on lawsuits initiated by clerics and laymen against confraternities and decisions rendered in cases of conflicts ensuing between various confraternities. Individual records pertaining to such matters have also been preserved.

Some information on confraternities is contained in the records of visitations, that is, descriptions of parishes written by representatives of eparchial administrations of the Greek Catholic Church.[151] Here one may encounter data on the holdings of confraternity libraries and occasional references to the existence of confraternity schools, as well as conflicts between rural confraternities and priests and owners of villages.[152]

Records of the visitations of deaneries in Right-Bank Ukraine are preserved in the above-mentioned archive of the Uniate metropolitans and the State Archive of Zhytomyr Oblast. Records of visitations of the Lviv-Kamianets Eparchy are preserved at the National Museum in Lviv; those of visitations of the Kholm Eparchy (in the Kholm Land, which was part of the palatinates of Ruthenia and Belz) are in the Lublin archives; those of the Peremyshl Eparchy are in the archives of Peremyshl and, finally, those of the Mukachiv Eparchy are in the State Archive of Transcarpathia Oblast. The contents of a number of visitations have been summarized in historico-statistical descriptions of parishes of Right-Bank Ukraine (Podillia, Volhynia, and the Kyiv region).

References to confraternities occur in letters and reports sent to Rome by papal nuncios and Greek Catholic metropolitans. A significant portion of these materials was published by Atanasii Velyky (Athanasius Welykyj) in a series of documents from the Vatican archives.[153]

---

50.   On visitations, see I. Skochylias, "Protokoly iepyskops'kykh i dekans'kykh vizytatsii tserkov Kyivs'koï uniats'koï mytropoliï XVIII st." in *Rukopysna ukraïnika u fondakh L'vivs'koï naukovoï biblioteky im. V. Stefanyka NAN Ukraïny ta problemy stvorennia informatsiinoho banku danykh. Materialy mizhnarodnoï naukovo-praktychnoï konferentsiï 20–21 veresnia 1996 r.* (Lviv, 1999).

51.   See, e.g., F. Dragomiretskii, "Mestechko Lantskorun'" in *Trudy komiteta dlia istoriko-statisticheskago opisaniia Podol'skoi eparkhii,* no. 2 (Kamianets-Podilskyi, 1878–79), 112–13.

52.   *Epistolae aliaque scripta Metropolitarum Kioviensium H. Potij et J. Velamin Rutskyj (1596–1637)* (Rome, 1955); *Epistolae Metropolitarum Kioviensium Catholicorum Raphaelis Korsak, Antonii Sielava, Gabrielis Kolenda (1637–1674)* (Rome, 1956).

He also published other sources important for the study of confraternities, including papal breves and bulls,[154] minutes of meetings of the Congregation for the Propagation of the Faith, letters and decrees published by this congregation,[155] and a number of others.

Books published by the confraternities are important for the study of their history. Quite often, a comparison of all extant copies helps establish facts pertaining to the publishing activities of the confraternities that cannot be found in any other sources. Of particular importance to historians are those copies on which manuscript annotations have been preserved, some of which pertain to the purchase of books by individuals or confraternities. For example, an annotation of 1747 made on a Triodion manuscript of the early seventeenth century from the village of Pidlyssia reads as follows: "This book, entitled *Paschal Triodion*, was purchased for twenty-five zlotys collected from the whole confraternity of Pidlyssia residents."[156] An annotation of 1695 on the *Paschal Triodion* of 1688 from Humenne contains one of the infrequent references to the existence of confraternities in Transcarpathia.[157]

For the study of urban confraternities, the records of municipal authorities and castle courts are very important sources. In some cases, particularly in deeds of purchase and sale of real estate, they contain materials about a network of confraternities. Confraternity officers and teachers at confraternity schools are mentioned in some contracts.

Certain aspects of confraternity activity are reflected in literature. A major source for the study of the ideology of the confraternity movement is the *Perestoroha* (Warning), a monument of Ukrainian political thought of the early seventeenth century. Other important sources are polemical

---

53.   *Documenta Pontificum Romanorum historiam Ucrainae illustrantia*, 2 vols. (Rome, 1953–54).

54.   *Acta S. Congregationis de Propaganda Fide Ecclesiam Catholicam Ucrainae et Bielarusjae spectantia*, 5 vols. (Rome, 1953–55); *Congregationes particulares Ecclesiam Catholicam Ucrainae et Bielarusjae spectantes*, 2 vols. (Rome, 1956–57).

55.   BKP, Akc. MS 2751.

56.   I. Pan'kevych, "Pokraini zapysy na pidkarpats'kykh tserkovnykh knyhakh," *Zbirnyk Naukovoho tovarystva "Prosvita"* (Uzhhorod) 6 (1929): 133.

works of Ukrainian writers, particularly Kasiian Sakovych, Meletii Smotrytsky, and the Greek Catholic metropolitan Ipatii Potii. The "Book of the History of the St. Onuphrius Monastery of Lviv," compiled in 1771 by Bonifatii Krovnytsky and recopied by Havryil Popil, may be cited as an example of the interpretation of the history of confraternities in later monastery chronicles.[158] It contains summaries of some records pertaining to the history of relations between the monastery and the Stauropegion Confraternity during the seventeenth and eighteenth centuries. The attitude of certain circles of the Ukrainian nobility in the conflict between the confraternities and the church hierarchy is reflected in the "Lives of Lviv Bishops of the Greek Rite," a historiographic monument discovered in one of the manuscript collections of the Lviv eparchial archive.[159]

Sources for the history of confraternities in various parts of Ukraine and in various periods of history are not equally distributed. The archives of many confraternities have perished. Among extant sources, those relating to confraternities in small towns and villages are poorly represented. The quantity of sources that illustrate particular problems in the history of confraternities does not correspond to the importance of those problems. All this must be considered when examining sources relating to the activities of the confraternities from the sixteenth to the eighteenth century. Assessing the place occupied by various confraternities in the public life and cultural activity of their time requires a comparative study of all types of sources that have been preserved.

---

57.   LNB, Basilian monasteries collection, MS 132 (104). After 1771, various individuals made additions to this chronicle until 1817, while in 1866 Modest Matsiievsky compiled a survey of events from the life of the monastery for later years.

58.   Ia. Isaievych, "Nevidoma pam'iatka ukraïns'koï istoriohrafiï druhoï polovyny XVII st.," *UIZh*, 1970, no. 2: 66–72; V. Kmet', "'Zhyttiepysy l'vivs'kykh iepyskopiv hrets'koho obriadu'—pam'iatka ukraïns'koï istoriohrafiï druhoï polovyny XVII st." in *Lwów: miasto, społeczenstwo, kultura*, vol. 4 (Cracow, 2002), 65–90.

Conclusion

The confraternity movement is a phenomenon that helps us comprehend the place of early modern Ukraine between Eastern and Western Christianity. Born in the early Christian East, confraternities functioned in medieval Western Europe as religious associations of laymen. The Orthodox and Greek Catholic confraternities of Ukraine and Belarus, sharing organizational principles with Roman Catholic ones, developed many distinctive features that allow us to see them as manifestations of what the major western Ukrainian writer Ivan Franko described as "the spiritual force of a nation that always needs to refresh itself by absorbing alien influences and, at the same time, putting up some resistance to those influences."[1]

Some historians consider the Ukrainian and Belarusian confraternities to be direct descendants of medieval fraternal associations (*bratchiny*), which, presumably, were genetically connected with early Christian brotherhoods or early medieval guilds. It is difficult to prove or refute this thesis, since information about the *bratchiny* is scarce. It cannot be ruled out that the latter were the nuclei out of which confraternities later developed. Nevertheless, the organizational structure of the Orthodox confraternities had much more in common with Western religious confraternities of laymen than with the archaic *bratchiny*, while the range of activities of Ukrainian and Belarusian confraternities was determined by local conditions rather than by foreign influences. Confraternities attached to Orthodox and later also Greek Catholic parishes developed primarily as a framework for the religious, social, and cultural activities of Ukrainian and Belarusian burghers, although at some stages of their history they also included noblemen and peasants.

The first reliable documents concerning legally sanctioned Orthodox confraternities date from the mid-sixteenth century.

---

1.   I. Franko, *Zibrannia tvoriv*, vol. 41 (Kyiv, 1984), 39.

Such documents include the statute of the Annunciation Confraternity (1542) and that of the St. Nicholas Confraternity (1544), both in the Pidzamche suburb of Lviv. Confraternal activity at that time was limited mostly to philanthropy and the upkeep of church property, although some confraternity members were involved in religious and social conflicts. The confraternities became much more active in political and cultural affairs with the founding or, more precisely, the reorganization of the brotherhood of parishioners of the Dormition Church in the inner city of Lviv. In January 1586 they proclaimed the founding of a confraternity and adopted a statute that included articles on the confraternity's authority over the clergy and the establishment of a school and a printshop. The founders of this confraternity belonged to the milieu of Orthodox artisans and merchants residing in the Ukrainian quarter of central Lviv. The most active of them were the saddlers Iurii and Ivan Rohatynets, the tailor Dmytro Krasovsky, and the shopkeepers Ivan Krasovsky, Lesko Maletsky, and Ivan Bohatyrets. Their close associate was the teacher, writer, and philologist Stefan Zyzanii (Kukil). In 1593 Patriarch Jeremiah II Tranos of Constantinople granted rights of patriarchal stauropegion (i.e., exemption from the authority of the local bishop and direct subordination to the patriarch) to the Dormition Church and the St. Onuphrius Monastery, which were under the patronage of the confraternity. After that, the Dormition Confraternity styled itself the Stauropegion Confraternity, frequently referred to in the documents simply as the "Stauropegion" (Stavropihiia). Although the Lviv Stauropegion Confraternity declared its direct subordination to the patriarch, the latter exerted no real authority over it.[2]

After this reorganization, the Dormition Confraternity soon became the most influential association of laymen in Ukraine and constituted a model for similar organizations in other cities, towns, and even villages. In Lviv alone there were confraternities in all suburban parishes. Also particularly active in the late sixteenth and early seventeenth centuries was the Belarusian Orthodox Confraternity of Vilnius (Vilna,

---

2.   *Epistolae Metropolitarum Kioviensium*, 326.

Wilno), which had a crucial impact on confraternities in the Grand Duchy of Lithuania. The Theophany Confraternity of Kyiv was founded as late as 1615, and the Confraternity of the Elevation of the Holy Cross was established in Lutsk in 1617. Perhaps the most impressive fact in the history of the confraternity movement was the enrollment of Hetman Petro Konashevych Sahaidachny, together with the whole Zaporozhian Host, in the Kyiv Confraternity. This was, of course, a political manifestation intended to demonstrate the involvement of the Zaporozhians in the national and religious revival of the period. In the late seventeenth and eighteenth centuries, confraternities were active in virtually every town and in numerous villages of western Ukraine and Belarus, as well as in many towns and villages of the eastern provinces.

Confraternities, like all voluntary associations, are characterized by their socially integrative functions, which may be exercised in various ways. Active members of most confraternities considered it their task to improve the discipline and cohesiveness of church communities. At the same time, in both Ukraine and Belarus, there were essentially two types of confraternities. The "rank-and-file" parish confraternities, which survived until recent times, took care of the local churches and were instrumental in socializing the parishioners in towns and villages. They also promoted the spiritual enlightenment of members through sermons and common prayer. In some towns, there were burgher confraternities that not only performed all the functions of ordinary confraternities but also opposed the supremacy of the hierarchy and devoted much attention to cultural and political activity, sometimes even trying to establish an organizational framework for the political representation of the Ukrainian and Belarusian communities. Such tasks were undertaken, specifically, by the major urban confraternities founded or reorganized in the late sixteenth and early seventeenth centuries. The statute of the Lviv Stauropegion Confraternity even proclaimed the right of lay congregations to dismiss inept priests and bishops. Many Orthodox historians explain such provisions as reflecting the exceptional situation of the period, when only extraordinary measures could stop abusive conduct by a corrupt hierarchy, but it should be remembered that the Protestant Reformation in the West also began with criticism of clerical abuses. The reality of such abuses should not, however, conceal the fact that for Reformation-minded laymen they constituted a good pretext for assuming greater influence in church affairs, which was in keeping with their growing political importance and self-consciousness.

The major confraternities that competed for influence with the hierarchy were also the ones most actively involved in defending the political and cultural rights of Ukrainians. Their role was especially important in the national and cultural revival of the late sixteenth and early seventeenth centuries. In Ukraine and Belarus, Roman Catholics constituted a small minority, but their religion was dominant, enjoying the support of the Polish-Lithuanian state and its social structures. Discrimination against the Orthodox and, later, the Uniate Church led to the deterioration of Ukrainian and Belarusian culture. Among Ukrainian and Belarusian noblemen there was a tendency toward integration with the ruling Polish nobility and, in consequence, a gradual loss of religious and national identity. Under such conditions, Orthodox townsmen and, later, Cossacks assumed the role of defenders of national political rights and cultural traditions. In many cities and towns, confraternities conducted political activity in defense of the civil rights of Orthodox burghers. They not only sent petitions and protests to the authorities but also distributed pamphlets and proclamations appealing to the Orthodox faithful for unity in defense of their civil and religious rights. Forbidding their members to bring their conflicts into the official courts of the Polish-Lithuanian state or the Catholic-dominated city magistracies, confraternities tended to become self-governing bodies of the Orthodox community. Although attempts at cooperation between confraternities remained sporadic, their activities may be seen as an attempt to establish alternative administrative structures for the Ukrainian majority population. These structures could draw charisma only from native religious institutions. In such a situation, it was extremely important to maintain the prestige of Orthodox churches so that they could compete successfully with Roman

Catholic churches. The magnificence of sacral architecture and the splendor of church services enhanced the self-esteem of local residents, which was an important factor in preserving their national identity. Confraternities therefore built new churches and repaired old ones, commissioning icons and mural paintings. The Lviv Dormition Church, built by the Lviv Stauropegion Confraternity, is a good example of how Renaissance models were combined with the traditions of Ukrainian architecture. The plan was adapted from local wooden churches, while the façade was embellished in complete accord with the principles of Italian Renaissance architecture.

Extremely important were the educational activities sponsored by the confraternities. As Ihor Ševčenko aptly observed, in contradistinction to the Ostrih center, with its rather short-lived school and press, the confraternities "did not represent isolated instances of cultural activity; they involved a whole social stratum of the burgher elite, which assumed the task and burdens of cultural patronage."[3] Confraternity members considered the maintenance of the "faith of their fathers" crucial to the national revival and the subsequent political upsurge. At the same time, being deeply influenced by cultural trends of Western origin, they consciously pursued a policy of accommodating traditional values to new social realities. Eventually, the orientation on "Greek" and "Latin" cultural models became a distinctive feature of the ideology of the Ukrainian national and cultural movement of the late sixteenth and early seventeenth centuries. In this respect, the situation in the Ukraine was similar to that in the Greek lands under Venetian rule, as well as in the Greek diaspora in Italy and other Catholic countries.

After the acceptance of the Union by most bishops of the Kyivan Orthodox metropolitanate, all major confraternities remained in the anti-Uniate camp and played an important role in it. This can be explained by the fact that the Union of Brest was promoted by the bishops and the Polish authorities and

---

3.   I. Ševčenko, *Ukraine between East and West* (Edmonton and Toronto, 1996), 140.

that its conditions were generally perceived as advantageous to them, rather than to the Ukrainian and Belarusian community. Confraternities introduced a spirit of competition into both the Ruthenian churches, Orthodox and Eastern-rite Catholic, which undoubtedly helped improve the general level of religious and cultural life. Consequently, despite the anti-Uniate orientation of the early Orthodox confraternities, their activities have been evaluated positively not only by Orthodox authors, but also by virtually all Catholic scholars.

In both the political and the cultural spheres of their activity, the confraternities participated in general European cultural and ideological trends. Speaking of Western Europe, Peter Burke noted that "in the late sixteenth and early seventeenth centuries there was a systematic attempt by members of the elites, mostly Protestant and Catholic clergy, to reform the culture and way of life of ordinary people."[4] Protestant and, perhaps to a lesser degree, Roman Catholic theology of that period postulated the elimination of those popular rituals that were proclaimed pagan or superstitious. Similarly, some Ukrainian Orthodox confraternities opposed such popular traditions as the Easter ritual of blessing bread, eggs, and other food, or the veneration of icons that were considered uncanonical. In combating such rituals, confraternities stressed their absence in Greece. Errors in liturgical books were also corrected on the basis of comparison with Greek models. Thus, Ukrainian confraternities may be seen as anticipating the reform of Patriarch Nikon in Muscovy. For several reasons, this "philological" activity did not provoke the kind of opposition that surfaced there. The attitude of the Ukrainian confraternities toward Greek models was more balanced: they borrowed only those Greek rites that they considered well-founded. Furthermore, the changes were not introduced as hurriedly as Nikon's reform, nor were they associated with government pressure.

The schools attached to Orthodox confraternities in some large towns were influenced by principles of European humanist and post-humanist education. Their level was especially high

---

4.   P. Burke, *Popular Culture in Early Modern Europe* (New York, 1978), 234.

in the late sixteenth and early seventeenth centuries, but later began to decline. In the Lviv Confraternity School during the first two years of its activity, the leading role belonged to the "Ukrainian teacher," Stefan Zyzanii, and to the "Greek teacher," Bishop Arsenios of Elasson and Dimonika, who resided in Lviv from June 1586 until the spring of 1588. Arsenios and Zyzanii may have been the principal authors of the Lviv school's bylaws, which incorporated several important principles of humanistic pedagogy. They strongly emphasized the equality of all students, the need for cooperation between home and school, and the role of education in preparing young people for participation in the community.

The school curriculum included rhetoric, poetics, logic, elements of theology, and church music. Among the teachers at the Lviv school were such prominent scholars and writers as Cyril Lukaris, Fedir Kasianovych, Ivan Boretsky, and probably Havrylo Dorofeiovych. Boretsky later became rector of the Kyiv Confraternal "Helleno-Ruthenian" School and subsequently Orthodox metropolitan of Kyiv. It was probably he who persuaded the Cossack hetman Petro Konashevych Sahaidachny to bequeath a large sum of money to the Lviv Confraternity in 1622 to support a teacher of Greek.

The first formal Orthodox schools in Vilnius, Kyiv, and Lutsk were also founded by confraternities. The Kyiv school is especially important as a predecessor of the famous Kyiv Mohyla College (later Academy), which emerged as a result of the fusion of the schools of the Kyiv Theophany Confraternity and the Kyivan Caves Monastery. Besides advanced schools in several cities, the confraternities maintained numerous elementary schools in towns and villages, especially in the western provinces of Ukraine and Belarus.

Some confraternities established their own publishing enterprises. The most famous and prolific among them were those of the Lviv and Vilnius confraternities. Printing presses were also owned by the Mahilioŭ Theophany Confraternity and the Peremyshl Trinity Confraternity. We do not know of any book published by the latter; perhaps its press was used only for the printing of engraved icons. During its initial period of activity, the Lviv Confraternity press served mainly educational and ideological purposes, publishing textbooks, political pamphlets, and literary works. From the second quarter of the seventeenth century, it published mainly liturgical texts, which were extremely important for the further consolidation of the Orthodox Church.

Generally speaking, the late sixteenth and early seventeenth centuries were the most creative and fruitful period in the history of the Orthodox confraternities. The upsurge of their political and cultural activities coincided. Scholars, writers, artists, and teachers connected with the confraternities attempted with some success to forge intellectual links between the traditions of the old Byzantine East and new cultural trends emanating from the West. For Zakhariia Kopystensky it was a matter of national pride to turn for his cultural roots directly to Greek original sources, rather than to their Latin reflections. At the same time, his own writings, as well as those of other Ukrainian authors of the period, were influenced by Renaissance and baroque models from the West. In addition, Ukrainian icons commissioned by the confraternities evince a highly original and creative blend of traditional motifs with those reflecting Renaissance and baroque aesthetics. The same may be said of the church choral singing cultivated in confraternity schools. The confraternities should be credited with the marked broadening of the social base of the cultural and educational movement in Ukraine.

Beginning with the second quarter of the seventeenth century, the situation began to change. The social mobility of the burghers flagged. This, as well as the desire to achieve greater consolidation of the defenders of Orthodoxy, led to the emergence of confraternities in which burghers and clergy cooperated closely. The most notable among them were the Vilnius, Lutsk, and Kyiv confraternities. This compromise between laity and clergy did not last long. The Orthodox hierarchy gradually consolidated its authority and succeeded in promoting reforms of its own—a process that may be described as an Orthodox Counter-Reformation. The more influential the hierarchy became, the less it was disposed to tolerate anticlerical attitudes among the principal confraternities. When Petro Mohyla united in his person the offices of archimandrite of the Kyivan Caves Monastery and metropolitan of Kyiv, there was no longer any place for the activities of the Kyiv Confraternity.

Mohyla did not manage to subordinate the Lviv Stauropegion Confraternity, nor did he even succeed in his efforts to control its editorial activities. Nevertheless, the political and economic decline of the towns contributed to a gradual loss of vitality in the Kyiv Confraternity and the confraternity movement as a whole. The Lviv Confraternity successfully defended its stauropegial status and did not allow the bishops to interfere in its internal affairs, but failed to retain its overall influence on the church. Most confraternities returned to the level of those medieval fraternal associations that limited their program to caring for churches, promoting devotion, and arranging mutual assistance. The "keeping of the light," i.e., providing candles for church services and funerals, was considered, as before, an especially important duty of members. The formalization of rituals led, perhaps, to an impoverishment of spiritual life. In seeking funds to "maintain the splendor" of church decorations and services, the confraternities did not hesitate to resort to usury.

Those scholars who stress that baroque culture was not specifically associated with the Counter-Reformation use as an argument the existence of baroque cultural forms in Orthodox countries. However, the intensification of baroque traits in literature and art coincided, as a rule, with the emergence of Counter-Reformational trends in the life and ideology of the Orthodox Church. Harvey Goldblatt has noted recently that a writer as apparently traditionalist as Ivan Vyshensky was influenced by post-Tridentine Roman Catholic concepts of sacral liturgical language.[5] Even some of the intellectuals employed by the confraternities criticized "excessive" confraternal interference in church affairs.[6]

The increasing influence of the clergy on culture was particularly evident in the educational system. If in the early confraternity schools most teachers were laymen, in the newly

---

5.   H. Goldblatt, "On the Language Beliefs of Ivan Vyšens'kyj and the Counter-Reformation," *HUS* 15, nos. 1–2 (1991): 21–34.

6.   Isaievych, *Bratstva*, 80–81.

founded Kyiv Mohyla College all professors were monks. The leading role in cultural life was assumed by the Mohyla College and its branches, as well as by the Kyivan Caves Monastery and subsequently also by some Basilian monasteries. The Kyiv Mohyla College was oriented on Counter-Reformational cultural models, and, as a result, the "Westernization" of Ukrainian culture proceeded one step further. Not only was the curriculum of the Mohyla College similar to that of most schools of a comparable level in Central Europe, but so were the forms of everyday life among students and teachers. Many of those forms were of medieval origin: it suffices to mention "itinerant students" collecting alms and serving as village teachers and cantors. Their customs, manners, and folklore bear astonishingly many resemblances to those of the medieval European *vagantes*.[7] Moreover, the Marian sodality of students of the Mohyla Academy was very similar to such sodalities in the Jesuit schools. If earlier confraternities managed to combine Eastern and Western cultural traditions and treated them as equally important, Mohyla and people of his generation changed the balance in favor of neo-Latin influences and even implanted into Orthodox theology some important elements of Catholic thought. Nevertheless, the degree to which the purity of Orthodoxy was contaminated is not so important: the adaptation of tradition to the new reality was the only way to survive while preserving links with traditional culture.[8] Ihor Ševčenko aptly entitled his profound and provocative study of the cultural patterns of this period "The Many Worlds of Peter Mohyla." He shows that one of those worlds remained the Greek one: Mohyla and those around him by no means wanted to sever contacts with their Greek Orthodox heritage.[9] Liturgical texts were corrected against Greek originals and contacts with Greek scholars were maintained. Orthodox church leaders

7.   Some of these customs were retained in the schools for training clergy, the famous *bursy*, until the early twentieth century. I leave aside the question of whether there were some reciprocal influences (as suggested by Gogol) between Cossack customs and those of the *bursa* pupils.

8.   A. Naumow, "Zmiana modelu kultury a kwestia ciągłości rozwojowej," *Zeszyty Naukowe KUL* 27, no. 4 (108) (1984): 31.

9.   Ševčenko, "The Many Worlds of Peter Mohyla," 18–20.

and most Greek Catholic ones continued to regard the Greek heritage as a distinctive feature of the "true Eastern faith." Such an orientation was shared by the confraternity leaders, even though they could not accept Mohyla's supremacy in cultural life. The achievements of the institutions established by Mohyla and other hierarchs were evidence that the new organizational structures were better adapted to the new situation than the confraternity gymnasiums. Incidentally, many teachers at the elementary schools maintained by confraternities or communities were former students of the Kyivan Academy. Their activities became an important bridge between the neo-scholastic culture of the educated clergy and the folkloric culture of peasants, rank-and-file Cossacks, and most townsmen.

The situation in the field of book publishing developed in the same vein as other spheres of cultural life. From about the third quarter of the seventeenth century, the Lviv Confraternity press remained the only publishing enterprise that managed to compete with monastery-owned presses. All private printshops owned by burghers had collapsed. Even the Lviv Confraternity press ceased to publish secular literature and switched definitively to the more profitable sphere of liturgical texts. Most of the confraternity's publications of this period were mere reprints of books published earlier. Primers were perhaps its most important products. The Kyivan Caves Monastery took over from the Lviv Confraternity the task of correcting liturgical books. The Belarusian confraternities of Vilnius and Mahilioŭ retained printing presses, but their publishing activities were minimal. The diminishing role of secular printing may be seen as additional evidence of the advance of antireform trends in the Ukrainian Orthodox Church.

In the late seventeenth and early eighteenth centuries, Greek Catholic bishops began to organize confraternities openly opposed to reform whose statutes stressed total subordination to the clergy. The wide diffusion of such confraternities is attested by the fact that statute forms were printed with blanks for the insertion of names of individual confraternities. The Orthodox confraternities that survived here and there, mostly along the right bank of the Dnipro and in Belarus, did not differ greatly from their Uniate counterparts. Although they lost their reforming fervor in the late seventeenth and early eighteenth centuries, both Orthodox and Uniate confraternities continued to function as conduits of socialization for burghers and, to some extent, for peasants as well. During this period, confraternities also contributed to the development of architecture, icon painting, and church music.

From the late eighteenth century on, confraternities lost significance in the development of higher culture. The decline of confraternities at this time was a general European phenomenon that may be explained by a variety of factors, among them the growing influence of the state on social life, as well as the gradual abatement of belief in salvation and in the need to pray for deceased confreres.[10] In more general terms, the decline of the confraternities was associated with the secularization of culture and public life that, in the last decades of the eighteenth century, was evident in Eastern Europe no less than in the rest of the continent. Change was so profound that the last years of the eighteenth century have much more in common with the next century than with the preceding decades. The development of secular culture in the late eighteenth and nineteenth centuries led to a break in the cultural development of social elites. At the level of the popular culture of peasants and, less overtly, of traditionalistic burghers, there was initially no abrupt break. Thus, the common people of the villages and small towns preserved many old customs, including those connected with confraternities. Such was the course of development in most Roman Catholic countries and in some regions of Ukraine and Belarus. Later, the situation was reversed. Peasant culture gradually began to lose its organic links with medieval tradition, while the resuscitation of such traditions was taken up by cultural elites. The idea of reviving confraternities was born in the milieu of certain public activists and even bureaucrats only after appearance of studies on old confraternities and their surviving remnants. As we have seen, the new associations that claimed to be continuators of the old confraternities had no direct links with them.

---

10.   G. De Rosa, "Le confraternite in Italia tra Medioevo e Rinascimento," *Ricerche di storia sociale e religiosa* (Rome), n.s. 17–18 (1980): 9.

The acme of cultural and political activity of the Ukrainian and Belarusian confraternities coincided with a period of crucial change in the social and cultural life of Ukraine. This fits the general pattern of development of voluntary associations, which are particularly active in societies experiencing rapid social change.[11] At the same time, the upsurge of Orthodox confraternities overlaps the first stages of the spread of baroque culture. It is now generally accepted that East European baroque culture also included notable elements of the Western medieval and Renaissance heritage.[12] The proportion of these elements was, of course, different at various stages of development. In the late sixteenth and early seventeenth centuries, the confraternity movement was initiated by unusually creative and self-confident individuals. For example, among the leaders of the Lviv Confraternity were the saddlers Iurii and Ivan Rohatynets, as well as the merchants Ivan Krasovsky and Lesko Maletsky, who were not only traders or craftsmen but also outstanding politicians, writers, and founders of schools. They displayed important elements of the individualistic and civic Renaissance mentality. Leaders of confraternities in the late seventeenth and early eighteenth centuries were men of a different stripe. They combined baroque piety with a medieval spirit of modesty and even humility (at least in the sphere of culture) and were not inclined to undertake the task of consciously changing traditional cultural and social models. In this regard they were quite different from the men of the previous period, whose drive for innovation was of the very essence of their psychology. While there were already some baroque influences on the curriculum of the early confraternity schools, in Ukrainian colleges of the later period baroque elements became dominant.

Ukraine and Belarus were the only countries in which Orthodox lay confraternities came into being. This may be attributed to the special position of these countries between the worlds of Western and Eastern Christianity. Although structurally connected to their Western counterparts, the Eastern-rite confraternities also developed their own original

---

11.   Anderson, "Voluntary Associations in History," 209.
12.   Krekoten', ed., *Ukraïns'ka literatura XVII st.*, 8.

features. It is important to note that in its internal development the indigenous church in Ukraine and Belarus passed through stages similar to those of the Western churches, from a lay reform movement to reform guided by the hierarchy. Only during the latter stage did the baroque culture fully mature. The fluctuation between periods of spiritual and cultural revival on the one hand and, on the other, periods of stabilization and formalization of new cultural models is also to be observed in the case of Ukraine and Belarus. Although more detailed study has yet to be undertaken, one may draw the preliminary conclusion that the revival of institutions of medieval origin, such as confraternities, did not exclude the retention of some important achievements of Renaissance culture, if only to a limited extent and in a very different cultural and social context. Later, the remnants of traditional confraternal ceremonies helped blend some elements of the baroque cultural heritage with traditional folk culture.

As we have seen, the confraternity movement played an important role as a catalyst and, in many respects, a prominent factor in the early stage of the Ukrainian and Belarusian national and cultural movement of the late sixteenth and early seventeenth centuries. Though any historical analogy leads to oversimplification, it is tempting for a historian to draw a comparison between the revival in which the confraternities were involved and later manifestations of national revival. Both in the late sixteenth century and in the second half of the nineteenth, a national movement was initiated by circles that may be described as intellectual elites. A very similar situation was observed in the 1920s and 1990s. In all these cases, the growth of popular support for pioneers of the respective revivals was more evident at the initial stages. Growth later slowed, and, when external conditions became less favorable, mass support for innovation faded almost entirely, at least to the superficial observer. Nevertheless, important achievements of the initial periods survived periods of stagnation or decline, providing an ideological basis for subsequent upsurges, even if these were to develop on a different social basis and in quite different political circumstances.

Bibliography

Unpublished Sources
Archive of Cracow Province, Cracow
  Wawel Division, Schneider portfolio, file 965.

Central State Historical Archive of Ukraine (TsDIAL), Lviv
  Fond 9 (Lviv Castle Office), section 1, vols. 338, 341, 347, 348, 349, 353, 354, 359, 365, 372.
  Fond 13 (Peremyshl Castle Office), vols. 371, 376, 431.
  Fond 14 (Peremyshl Land Office), vols. 101 32/2, 32/3, 32/4.
  Fond 29 (Magistracy of the City of Drohobych), vols. 2–4.
  Fond 52 (Magistracy of the City of Lviv), section 2, vols. 10, 11, 17, 20; section 3, vols. 20, 77.
  Fond 129 (Lviv Stauropegion Confraternity),[1] section 1, files 10, 14, 17, 71, 87, 93, 137, 160, 193, 219, 232, 260, 263, 267, 301, 391, 421, 423, 445, 466, 479, 553, 737, 775, 837, 878, 1012, 1034, 1035, 1036, 1037, 1041, 1043, 1044, 1064, 1065, 1077, 1091, 1098, 1104, 1106, 1119, 1131, 1135, 1169, 1170, 1183, 1191, 1261; section 2, files 15, 802, 941, 1005; section 3, files 67, 86.
  Fond 159 (Financial inspectorate of Galicia), section 8, vol. 863.
  Fond 201 (Consistory of the Greek Catholic Metropolitanate), section 4b, files 13, 14, 40, 64, 69, 83, 292, 3006.[2]
  Fond 408 (Greek Catholic Metropolitan Ordinariate), files 69, 388.

Institute of the Peoples of Asia, St. Petersburg
  Manuscript Division, MSS B. 1228, B. 1229.

---

1.   In the Ukrainian version of this book, files of this fond were quoted according to their previous shelf numbers. I am grateful to Vasyl Kmet for updating the numeration.

2.   This fond is currently being reorganized. As new shelf numbers have not yet been assigned to all files, I use the old numeration here.

Kórnik Library, Polish Academy of Sciences, Kórnik
Manuscript Division, no. 1211.

Library of the Polish Academy of Sciences, Cracow
Manuscript Division, no. 262.

Library of the Russian Academy of Sciences, St. Petersburg,
Manuscript Division
E. Kaluzhniatskii collection.

Lviv Historical Museum, Manuscript Division
MS 121 (Album of the Lviv Stauropegion Confraternity).

Main Archives of Older Records, Warsaw
Lustracje/XVIII/48.
Potocki Family Public Archive.
Radziwiłł Family Archive/II/745.

National Library, Warsaw, Special Collections Division
Akc. (provisional shelf numbers of MSS from the Peremyshl
Greek Catholic Chapter), MSS 2027, 2652, 2725, 2728, 2751,
2769, 2826, 2868, 2906, 2910, 2920, 2921, 2923, 2924, 2933,
2943, 5512.

National Museum, Lviv
MSS 11, 91, 120, 170, 21082.
General visitation, no. 11, no. 15.
Teky Podolyns'koho (Podolyns'kyi portfolio).

Pushkin Institute of Russian Literature, St. Petersburg
Manuscript Division, no. 01319.

Russian National Library, St. Petersburg
Manuscript Division, no. F. IV 215.

Russian State Archive of Ancient Acts, Moscow
Fond 79, section 1, vol. 237.

Russian State Historical Archive, St. Petersburg
Fond 823 (Archive of the Greek Catholic Metropolitans), section 1, files 168, 266, 412.

Russian State Library, Moscow, Manuscript Division
Collection of the "Obshchestvo istorii i drevnostei rossiiskikh," file 274, no. 3.

St. Petersburg Branch, Institute of Russian History, Russian Academy of Sciences,
Archive
Denys Zubryts'kyi collection, files 30, 32, 44.
Dobrokhotov collection, file 315.

State Archives in Przemyśl
Archives of the Greek Catholic Bishopric, charter no. Supl. 28.
Archives of the Greek Catholic parishes, file 124.

Institute of Ukrainian Literature, National Academy of Sciences of Ukraine, Manuscript Division
Fond 3 (Ivan Franko Archives), MSS 4830, 4833, 4834, 4835, 4836.

Vasyl Stefanyk Library, National Academy of Sciences of Ukraine, Lviv, Manuscript Division
A. S. Petrushevych collection, MS 449.
Basilian monasteries collection, MSS 132, 158, 251, 267, 466, 506, 541, 720.
Kozłowski portfolio, MSS 15, 76.
NTSh collection, MSS 15, 136, 258.
Ossolineum collection, MSS 368, 369, 1087, 2093, 2125, 2170, 2391.
Teky Zubryts'koho (Zubryts'kyi portfolio), files 32, 35, 39.

National Library of Ukraine, National Academy of Sciences of Ukraine, Kyiv, Manuscript Institute
Fond 18 (Consistory of the Greek Catholic Metropolitanate), nos. 8, 47.

St. Sophia Collection, II-495.

Theological Academy collection, MSS I-3957, I-6232, II-220.

Published Sources and Bibliographies

Acta S. Congregationis de Propaganda Fide Ecclesiam Catholicam Ucrainae et Bielarusjae spectantia. Analecta OSBM, ser. 2, sec. 3. Ed. A. G. Welykyj. 5 vols. Rome, 1953–55.

Adelphotēs. Die erste gedruckte griechisch-kirchenslavische Grammatik, L'viv-Lemberg 1591. Specimina Philologiae Slavicae, 2. Ed. O. Horbatsch. Frankfurt am Main, 1973.

Akta grodzkie i ziemskie z czasów Rzeczypospolitej Polskiej [= *AGZ*]. 25 vols. Lviv, 1868–1935.

Aktovyia knigi Poltavskago gorodovago uriada XVII veka. Vol. 3. *Spravy vechistye 1672–1680 gg.* Chernihiv, 1914.

Akty i dokumenty, otnosiashchiesia k istorii Kievskoi akademii. 5 vols. Kyiv, 1904.

Akty izdavaemye Vilenskoiu komissieiu dlia razbora drevnikh aktov. 39 vols. Vilnius, 1865–1915.

Akty, otnosiashchiesia k istorii Iuzhnoi i Zapadnoi Rossii, sobrannyia i izdannyia Arkheograficheskoiu komissieiu [= *Akty IuZR*]. 15 vols. St. Petersburg, 1863–92.

Akty, otnosiashchiesia k istorii Zapadnoi Rossii, sobrannyia i izdannyia Arkheograficheskoiu komissieiu [= *AZR*]. 5 vols. St. Petersburg, 1846–53.

Arkheograficheskii sbornik dokumentov, otnosiashchikhsia k istorii Severo-Zapadnoi Rusi. 14 vols. Vilnius, 1867–1904.

Arkhiv Iugo-Zapadnoi Rossii, izdavaemyi Vremennoiu komissieiu dlia razbora drevnikh aktov, pri Kievskom, Podol'skom i Volynskom general-gubernatore [= *AIuZR*]. Pt. 1. Kyiv, 1859–1904.

Arkhiv uniatskikh mitrapalitaŭ. Minsk and Polatsk, 1999.

"Barkulabovskaia letopis'." Ed. M. V. Dovnar-Zapol'skii. *Universitetskiia izvestiia* (Kyiv) 38 (1898), no. 12.

Bianu, I., and N. Hodoş. *Bibliografia românească veche 1508–1830.* Vol. 1. Bucharest, 1903.

Boniecki, A., comp. *Herbarz polski.* 16 vols. Warsaw, 1899–1913.

Congregationes particulares Ecclesiam Catholicam Ucrainae et Bielarusjae spectantes. Analecta OSBM, ser. 2, sec. 3. Ed. A. G. Welykyj. 2 vols. Rome, 1956–57.

Cyrillic Books Printed before 1701 in British and Irish Collections. A Union Catalogue. Comp. R. Cleminson, C. Thomas, D. Radoslavova, and A. Voznesenskij. London, 2000.

Diplomata Statutaria a Patriarchis orientalibus Confraternitati Stauropigianae Leopoliensi a. 1586–1592 data, cum aliis litteris coaevis et appendice [= DS]. Iubileinoe izdanie v pamiat' 300-litniaho osnovaniia L'vovskoho Stavropihiiskoho Bratstva, 2. Vol. 2. Lviv, 1895.

Documenta Pontificum Romanorum historiam Ucrainae illustrantia (1075–1953). Analecta OSBM, ser. 2, sec. 3. Ed. A. G. Welykyj. 2 vols. Rome, 1953–54.

Ekthesis abo krotkie zebranie spraw ktore się działy na partykularnym, to iest pomiastnym synodzie w Brześciu Litewskim. Cracow, 1597. In *Pamiatniki polemicheskoi literatury.* Vol. 3. Kyiv, 1903.

Epistolae aliaque scripta Metropolitarum Kioviensium H. Potij et J. Velamin Rutskyj (1596–1637). Rome, 1955.

Epistolae Metropolitarum Kioviensium Catholicorum Raphaelis Korsak, Antonii Sielava, Gabrielis Kolenda (1637–1674). Analecta OSBM, ser. 2, sec. 3. Ed. A. G. Welykyj. Rome, 1956.

Faliński, B. *Źródła dziejowe starostwa i parafii Kamionka Strumiłowa.* Kamianka Strumylova, 1928.

Frantsysk Skaryna: Zbornik dakumentaŭ i materyialaŭ. Ed. V. I. Darashkevich. Minsk, 1988.

Golovatskii [Holovats'kyi], Ia. F. "Akty otnosiashchiesia k istorii Iuzhnozapadnoi Rusi." *Literaturnyi sbornik Galitsko-russkoi Matitsy.* Lviv, 1870.

Grimsted, P. K. *Archives and Manuscript Repositories in the USSR: Ukraine and Moldavia.* Book 1, *General Bibliography and Institutional Directory.* Princeton, N.J., 1988.

Harasiewicz (Harasevych), M. *Annales Ecclesiae Ruthenae.* Lviv, 1862.

Hrammatiki ili pismennica jazyka sloven'skaho, Kremjanec', 1638: eine gekürzte Fassung der kirchenslawischen Grammatik von Meletij Smotryc'kyj. Ed. O. Horbatsch. Munich, 1977.

Hrets'ki rukopysy u zibranniakh Kyieva. Kataloh. Comp. Ie. Chernukhin. Kyiv, 2000.

Iaremenko, V., ed. *Ukraïns'ka poeziia XVI st.* Kyiv, 1987.

_____., ed. *Ukraïns'ka poeziia XVII st. (persha polovyna).* Kyiv, 1988.

Isaevich, Ia. "Kirillovskie staropechatnye knigi v kollektsiiakh Pol'skoi Narodnoi Respubliki." *Kniga: Issledovaniia i materialy* 8 (1963).

Iurii Drohobych. Do 500-richchia vykhodu pershoï drukovanoï knyhy vitchyznianoho avtora. Bibliohrafichnyi pokazhchyk. Comp. Ia. Isaievych and M. Vavrychyn. Lviv, 1983.

Kniha Belarusi, 1515–1917: Zvodny kataloh. Comp. H. Ia. Halenchenka et al. Minsk, 1986.

Kolosova, V., and V. Krekoten', ed. *Ukraïns'ka poeziia: Kinets' XVI–pochatok XVII st.* Kyiv, 1978.

Korshunaŭ, A., comp. *Pomniki starazhytnai belaruskai pis'mennastsi.* Minsk, 1975.

Krekoten', V., ed. *Ukraïns'ka literatura XVII st.* Kyiv, 1987.

Krettner, J. *Erster Katalog von Bruderschaften in Bayern.* Munich, 1980.

Kupchyns'kyi, O., and E. Ruzhyts'kyi. *Kataloh perhamentnykh dokumentiv Tsentral'noho derzhavnoho istorychnoho arkhivu URSR u L'vovi, 1233–1799.* Kyiv, 1972.

Kyievo-Mohylians'ka akademiia: Materialy do bibliohrafichnoho pokazhchyka literatury z fondiv Naukovoï biblioteky NaUKMA. Issue 1. Comp. T. Shul'ha. Intro. Z. I. Khyzhniak. Kyiv, 2002.

Legrand, É. *Bibliographie hellénique, ou, Description raisonnée des ouvrages publiés en grec [ou] par des Grecs aux XVe et XVIe siècles.* Vol. 2. Repr. Paris, 1962.

Lev Krevza's "A Defense of Church Unity" and Zaxarija Kopystens'kyj's "Palinodia." HLEUL, English Translations. Vol. 3, pt. 1. Trans. Bohdan Struminski. Cambridge, Mass., 1995.

Litopys rus'kyi za Ipats'kym spyskom. Trans. and ed. L. Makhnovets'. Kyiv, 1989.

Litterae nuntiorum apostolicorum historiam Ucrainae illustrantes. Analecta OSBM, ser. 2, sec. 3. Ed. A. G. Welykyj. Vols. 1–2. *1550–1593* and *1594–1608.* Rome, 1959.

Litterae S. Congregationis de Propaganda Fide Ecclesiam Catholicam Ucrainae et Bielarusjae spectantes. Analecta OSBM, ser. 2, sec. 3. Ed. A. G. Welykyj. 7 vols. Rome, 1954–57.

Lucaris, Cyril. *Sermons 1598–1602.* Ed. K. Rozemond. Leiden, 1974.

L'vivs'ki vydannia XVI–XVIII st. Kataloh. Comp. Ia. Isaievych. Lviv, 1970.

Marinelli, O. "Le confraternite di Perugia dalle origini al sec. XIX: bibliografia delle opere a stampa." *Annali della Facoltà di lettere e filosofia* (Perugia) 2–4 (1965).

Materiialy dlia kul'turnoï i hromads'koï istoriï Zakhidn'oï Ukraïny. Vol. 1. Kyiv, 1928.

Meletii Smotryts'kyi. Hramatyka. Ed. V. V. Nimchuk. Kyiv, 1979.

Monumenta Confraternitatis Stauropigianae Leopoliensis [= *MCS*]. Ed. W. Milkowicz. 2 vols. Lviv, 1895–96.

Nemirovskii, E. L. *Gesamtkatalog der Frühdrucke in Kyrillischer Schrift.* Vol. 1. *Inkunabeln (1491–1500). Die Druckereien von Schweipolt Fiol 1 (Krakau) und Djordje Crnojevic (Cetinje).* Bibliotheca Bibliographica Aureliana, 140. Baden-Baden, 1996. Vol. 3. *Die Prager Druckerei von Francisk Skorina (1513–1519).* Bibliotheca Bibliographica Aureliana, 155. Baden-Baden, 1998. Vol. 5. *Die Druckerei von Francisk Skorina in Wilna.* Bibliotheca Bibliographica Aureliana, 171. Baden-Baden, 1999.

_____.*Nachalo knigopechataniia v Moskve i na Ukraine. Zhizn' i deiatel'nost' pervopechatnika Ivana Fedorova: Ukazatel' literatury, 1574–1974.* Moscow, 1975.

Niesiecki, K. *Herbarz polski.* 10 vols. Leipzig, 1839–46.

_____. *Opisanie izdanii tipografii Shvaipol'ta Fiolia: Opisanie staropechatnykh izdanii kirillovskogo shrifta.* Issue 1. Moscow, 1979.

_____., ed. *Ostrozhskaia Azbuka Ivana Fedorova.* Moscow, 1983.

The Old Rus' Kievan and Galician-Volhynian Chronicles: The Ostroz'kyj (Xlebnikov) and Četvertyns'kyj (Pogodin) Codices. HLEUL, Texts. Vol. 8. Cambridge, Mass., 1990.

Opisanie dokumentov i del, khraniashchikhsia v arkhive Sviateishego pravitel'stvuiushchego sinoda. Vol. 22 (1742). St. Petersburg, 1914.

Pam'iatky polemichnoho pys'menstva. Pam'iatky ukraïns'ko-rus'koï movy i literatury, 5. Ed. Kyrylo Studyns'kyi. Vol. 1. Lviv, 1906.

Pamiatniki, izdannyia Kievskoiu komissieiu dlia razbora drevnikh aktov [= *PKK*]. 2d ed. Kyiv, 1897–98.

Pamiatniki polemicheskoi literatury. Vols. 1–3. St. Petersburg,

1845–1903.

Panaitescu, P. P. *Manuscrisele slave din Bibliotecă Academiei RPR.* Bucharest, 1959.

Patrologia latina. Comp. J.-P. Migne. 222 vols. Paris, 1844–64.

Patrylo, I. *Dzherela i bibliohrafiia istoriï Ukraïns'koï tserkvy.* 3 vols. Rome, 1975–95.

Pershodrukar Ivan Fedorov ta ioho poslidovnyky na Ukraïni (XVI–persha polovyna XVII st.): Zbirnyk dokumentiv. Comp. Ia. Isaievych, O. Kupchyns'kyi, O. Matsiuk, and E. Ruzhyts'kyi. Kyiv, 1975.

Petrov, N. I. *Opisanie rukopisnykh sobranii, nakhodiashchikhsia v gorode Kieve.* Vol. 1. Moscow, 1891.

Petrushevych, A. S. *Dopolneniia k Svodnoi Halychsko-russkoi letopysy s 1660 po 1700 h.* Lviv, 1891.

_____.*Svodnaia Halychsko-russkaia lětopys' s 1600 po 1700 h.* Vol. 1. Lviv, 1874.

Polnoe sobranie russkikh letopisei. Vols. 2 and 32. Moscow, 1962–75.

Pomniki dziejowe Przemyśla. Vol. 1. Przemyśl, 1936.

Porfirii, Episkop. *Vostok khristianskii: I.* Kyiv, 1846.

Prava, po kotorym suditsia malorossiiskii narod. Ed. A. F. Kistiakovskii. Kyiv, 1878.

Prava, za iakymy sudyt'sia malorosiis'kyi narod, 1743. Comp. Iu. Shemshuchenko. Ed. K. Vyslobokov. Kyiv, 1997.

"Proshenie Malorossiiskago shliakhetstva i starshin vmeste s getmanom o vosstanovlenii raznykh starinnykh prav Malorossii, podannoe Ekaterine II v 1764 godu." *Kievskaia starina,* 1883, no. 6.

"Protokul do zapysovania sprav potochnykh na rok 1690." *Chernigovskiia gubernskiia vedomosti 1852 goda,* nos. 36–45 (Chernihiv, 1852).

Pryvileï natsional'nykh hromad mista L'vova (XIV–XVIII st.). Comp. M. Kapral'. Lviv, 2000.

Radziwiłł, A. S. *Pamiętnik o dziejach w Polsce.* Trans. and ed. A. Przyboś and R. Żelewski. 3 vols. Warsaw, 1980.

Regel, W., ed. *Analecta Byzantino-Russica.* St. Petersburg, 1891.

Riezanov, V. *Drama ukraïns'ka.* Vol. 1. Kyiv, 1925.

Rothe, H., ed. *Die älteste ostslawische Kunstdichtung, 1575–1647.* 2 vols. Giessen, 1976–77.

Sbornik letopisei, otnosiashchikhsia k Iuzhnoi i Zapadnoi Rusi. Kyiv, 1888.

Shchapov, I. *Vostochnoslavianskie i iuzhnoslavianskie rukopisnye knigi v sobraniiakh Pol'skoi Narodnoi Respubliki.* 2 vols. Moscow, 1976.

Sheptyts'kyi, Metropolitan Andrei, comp. *Monumenta Ucrainae Historica.* Vol. 2. Rome, 1964.

Shynkaruk, V., V. Nichyk, and A. Sukhov, ed. *Pam'iatky brats'kykh shkil na Ukraïni. Kinets' XVI–pochatok XVII st.: Teksty i doslidzhennia* [= *PBSh*]. Kyiv, 1988.

Sribnyi, F. "Dva epizody z istoriï borot'by Hedeona Balabana z L'vivs'kym bratstvom." *ZNTSh* 117–18 (1913).

Supplicationes Ecclesiae Unitae Ucrainae et Bielarusjae. Analecta OSBM, ser. 2, sec. 3. Ed. A. G. Welykyj. 3 vols. Rome, 1960–62.

Sventsits'kyi, I. *Opys' Muzeia Stavropihiiskoho instituta, vo L'vově.* Lviv, 1908.

Theiner, A. *Vetera monumenta Poloniae et Lithuaniae.* Vol. 4. Rome, 1864.

Titov, Kh. *Materiialy dlia istoriï knyzhnoï spravy na Vkraïni v XVI–XVIII v.: Vsezbirka peredmov do ukraïns'kykh starodrukiv.* Kyiv, 1924. Repr. Cologne and Vienna, 1982.

Trankvilion-Stavrovets'kyi, K. *Perlo mnohocěnnoje.* Ed. with commentary by H. Trunte. Vol. 2, *Kommentar.* Cologne and Vienna, 1985.

Ukrainskie knigi kirillovskoi pechati XVI–XVIII vv.: Katalog izdanii, khraniashchikhsia v Gosudarstvennoi biblioteke im. V. I. Lenina. Vol. 1. *1574–pervaia polovina XVII v.* Comp. T. N. Kameneva and A. A. Guseva. Moscow, 1976. Vol. 2/1. *Kievskie izdaniia 2-oi poloviny XVII v.* Comp. A. A. Guseva. Moscow, 1981. Vol. 2/2. *L'vovskie, novgorod-severskie, chernigovskie, unevskie izdaniia 2-oi poloviny XVII v.* Comp. A. A. Guseva and I. M. Polonskaia. Moscow, 1990.

V pomoshch' sostaviteliam Svodnogo kataloga staropechatnykh izdanii kirillovskogo i glagolicheskogo shriftov. Moscow, 1982.

Volumina legum. Vol. 5. Warsaw, 1738.

Vyshens'kyi, I. *Tvory.* Kyiv, 1959.

Zastyrets', I. *Hramota iepyskopa H. Balabana, osnovuiucha bratstvo tserkovne peredmishchan adamkovets'kykh v Berezhanakh.* Lviv, 1905.

Zdanevych, B. *Kataloh inkunabul.* Comp. H. Lomonos-Rivna. Kyiv, 1974.

Zizanij, L. *Hrammatika slovenska: Wilna, 1596.* Ed. and intro. G. Freidhof. 2d ed. Frankfurt am Main, 1980.

Secondary Literature

Aleksandrovych, V. "Maliari-chleny Uspens'koho bratstva, kinets' XVI–persha polovyna XVII st." In *Uspens'ke bratstvo i ioho rol' v ukraïns'komu natsional'no-kul'turnomu vidrodzhenni.* Lviv, 1996.

_____. "Persha zhadka pro ukraïns'ku shkolu v Peremyshli." *Zhovten'*, 1986, no. 9.

_____. "Pryvilei peremys'koho iepyskopa Antoniia Radylovs'koho dlia drohobyts'koho Khrestovozdvyzhens'koho bratstva z 1556 r." In *Drohobyts'kyi kraieznavchyi zbirnyk* 4 (2000).

_____. *Zakhidnoukraïns'ki maliari XVI st.: Shliakhy rozvytku profesiinoho seredovyshcha.* Lviv, 2000.

Alekseev, A. A., ed. *Ostrozhskaia Bibliia. Sbornik statei.* Moscow, 1990.

Anderson, R. T. "Voluntary Associations in History." *American Anthropologist* 73, no. 1 (1971).

Andrusiak, M. "Pavlo Teteria i L'vivs'ka Stavropihiia." *ZNTSh* 151 (1931).

Angelozzi, G. *Le confraternite laicali.* Brescia, 1978.

Antonovych, M. "Polifonichna muzyka v ukraïns'kykh tserkvakh u dobi kozachchyny." In *Intrepido pastori.* Rome, 1984.

Antonovych, V. "Prilutskii polkovoi osaul Mikhailo Movchan i ego zapisnaia kniga." *Kievskaia starina* 11 (1885).

Anushkin, A. *Na zare knigopechataniia v Litve.* Vilnius, 1970.

Badecki, K. *Zaginione księgi średniowiecznego Lwowa.* Lviv, 1928.

Bainbridge, V. *Gilds in the Medieval Countryside: Social and Religious Change in Cambridgeshire, c. 1350–1558.* Woodbridge, 1996.

Baletskii, É. "Égerskii rukopisnyi irmologii." *Studia slavica* (Budapest) 4, fasc. 3–4 (1958).

[Balyk, B.] "Rukopysy Peremys'koï hreko-katolyts'koï kapituly v Narodovii Bibliotetsi u Varshavi." *Bohosloviia* 37 (1973): 193–213; 38 (1974): 237–43.

Bardach, J. "Bractwa cerkiewne na ziemiach ruskich Rzeczypospolitej w XV–XVIII w." *Kwartalnik Historyczny,* 1967, no. 1.

Barron, C. M. "The Parish Fraternities of Medieval London." In *The Church in Pre-Reformation Society: Essays in Honour of F. R. H. Du Boulay.* Woodbridge, 1985.

Barvins'kyi, O. "Stavropihiis'ka tserkva Uspeniia Pr. Bohorodytsi u L'vovi i zakhody kolo ïï obnovy i prykrasy." In *Zbirnyk L'vivs'koï Stavropihiï. Mynule i suchasne. Studiï, zamitky, materiialy.* Ed. Kyrylo Studyns'kyi. Lviv, 1921.

Bassi, I. B. *Tractatus de sodalitiis seu de confraternitatibus ecclesiasticis et laicalibus.* Rome, 1725.

Bednarski, S. "Dzieje kulturalne jezuickiego kolegium we Lwowie w XVIII wieku." *Pamiętnik Literacki* 23 (1936).

Bednov [Bidnov], V. *Pravoslavnaia tserkov' v Pol'she i Litve po "Volumina Legum."* Ekaterinoslav, 1908.

Belorusskii prosvetitel' Frantsisk Skorina i nachalo knigopechataniia v Belorusii i Litve. Moscow, 1979.

Bieńkowski, L. "Organizacja Kościoła Wschodniego w Polsce." In *Kościół w Polsce.* Vol. 2. Cracow, 1969.

Bilets'kyi, O. "Zarodzhennia dramatychnoï literatury na Ukraïni." In his *Pratsi v 5-ty tomakh.* Vol. 1. Kyiv, 1965.

Biriulina, O. "Dzherela do istoriï Luts'koho bratstva." In *Istoriia relihiï v Ukraïni.* Kyiv, 1997.

_____. "Reiestr dukhovnykh osib Luts'koho brats'koho pom'ianyka." In *Pam'iatky sakral'noho mystetstva Volyni na mezhi tysiacholit'.* Lutsk, 2000.

Black, C. F. *Italian Confraternities in the Sixteenth Century.* Cambridge, 1989.

Blasting, R. "The German Bruderschaften as Producers of Late Medieval Vernacular Religious Drama." *Renaissance and*

Reformation 13, no. 1 (1989).

Boner, A. G. "So znakom vladel'tsa." *Voprosy bibliotechnogo dela, bibliografii i istorii knigi v Sibiri i na Dal'nem Vostoke.* Novosibirsk, 1975.

Bošnjak, M. *A Study of Slavic Incunabula.* Zagreb and Munich, 1968.

Budilovich, A. *Russkaia pravoslavnaia starina v Zamost'e.* Warsaw, 1885.

Burke, P. *Popular Culture in Early Modern Europe.* New York, 1978.

Celestino, O., and A. Meyers. *Las cofradías en el Perú, región central.* Frankfurt am Main, 1981.

400 let russkogo knigopechataniia. Vol. 1. Moscow, 1964.

Chiffoleau, J. "Les confréries, la mort et la religion en comtat venaissin à la fin du Moyen Age." *Mélanges de l'École française de Rome: Moyen Age, Temps Modernes* 91 (1979).

Chodynicki, K. *Kościół prawosławny a Rzeczpospolita Polska. Zarys historyczny 1370–1632.* Warsaw, 1934.

Chubatyi, M. *Istoriia khrystyianstva na Rusy-Ukraïni.* 2 vols. Rome and New York, 1965–76.

Chynczewska-Hennel, T. *Świadomość narodowa szlachty ukraińskiej i kozaczyzny od schyłku XVI do połowy XVII wieku.* Warsaw, 1985.

Cleminson, R. "First Slavonic Primers to 1700." *Australian Slavonic and East European Studies* 2 (1988).

Confraternitas: Bulletin of the Society for Confraternity Studies. Ed. K. Eisenbichler. Vols. 1–11 (1990–2000). Serial is being continued.

Corpi, "fraternità," mestieri nella storia della società europea. Ed. D. Zardin. Rome, 1998.

Čyževs'kyj, D. *A History of Ukrainian Literature (From the 11th to the End of the 19th Century).* Littleton, Colo., 1975.

Czacharowski, A. "Die Bruderschaften der mittelalterlichen Städte in der gegenwärtigen polnischen Forschung." In *Bürgerschaft und Kirche.* Stadt in Geschichte, vol. 7. Ed. J. Sydow. Sigmaringen, 1980.

Czerniatowicz, J. *Książka grecka średniowieczna i renesansowa.* Wrocław, 1976.

Dąbkowski, P. *Miscellanea archiwalne.* Lviv, 1930.

Dashkevich [Dashkevych], Ia. "Pervyi armianskii knigopechatnik na Ukraine Ovanes Karmateniants." *Patma-Banasirakan Handes (Istoriko-filologicheskii zhurnal)*, 1976, no. 1.

De La Roncière, C. M. "La place des confréries dans l'encadrement religieux du contado florentin: l'exemple de la Val d'Elsa." *Mélanges de l'École française de Rome* 85 (1973).

De Rosa, G. "Le confraternite in Italia tra Medioevo e Rinascimento." *Ricerche di storia sociale e religiosa* (Rome), n.s. 17–18 (1980).

De Sandre Gasparini, G. "Appunti per uno studio sulle confraternite medievali: problemi e prospettive." *Studia patavina* 15, no. 1 (1968).

Delaruelle, É. *La piété populaire au Moyen Age*. Turin, 1975.

Dēmētrakopoulos, Ph. *Arsenios Elassonos (1550–1626). Bios kai ergo. Symbolē stē meletē tōn metabyzantinōn logiōn tēs Anatolēs*. Athens, 1984.

———. "On Arsenios, Archbishop of Elasson." *Byzantinoslavica* 42 (1981).

Deschamps, J. *Les confréries au Moyen Age*. Bordeaux, 1958.

Dietrich, D. H. "Confraternities and Lay Leadership in Sixteenth-Century Liège." *Renaissance and Reformation* 13, no. 1 (1989).

Dmitriev, M. *Pravoslavie i Reformatsiia: Reformatsionnye dvizheniia v vostochnoslavianskikh zemliakh Rechi Pospolitoi vo vtoroi polovine XVI v*. Moscow, 1990.

Dmitrievskii, A. "Arsenii arkhiepiskop Ėlassonskii (Suzdal'skii tozh) i ego vnov' otkrytyia istoricheskiia memuary." *TKDA* 17 (1898).

Dobrianskii [Dobrians'kyi], A. *Istoriia episkopov trekh soedinennykh eparkhii*. Lviv, 1893.

Dolyns'ka, M. "'Khronika' Stavropihiis'koho bratstva Denysa Zubryts'koho iak dzherelo dlia vyvchennia nerukhomoï vlasnosti Stavropihiï." In *Rukopysna ukraïnika u fondakh L'vivs'koï naukovoï biblioteky im. Stefanyka NAN Ukraïny ta problemy stvorennia informatsiinoho banku danykh*. Lviv, 1999.

Doroshenko, D. *A Survey of Ukrainian History*. Ed. O. W. Gerus. Winnipeg, 1975.

Dragomiretskii, F. "Mestechko Lantskorun'." *Trudy komiteta dlia istoriko-statisticheskago opisaniia Podol'skoi eparkhii.* No. 2. Kamianets-Podilskyi, 1878–79.

Drukarze dawnej Polski od 15 do 18 wieku. Fascicles 5 and 6. Ed. A. Kawecka-Gryczowa. Wrocław and Cracow, 1959–60.

Druziuk-Skop, H., and L. Skop. "Myttsi z drohobyts'koho bratstva: novi znakhidky." In *Provisnyk* (Drohobych), 2 (1991).

Duhr, J. "La confrérie dans la vie de l'Église." *Revue d'histoire ecclésiastique* 35 (1939).

Durand, H. "Confrérie." *Dictionnaire de droit canonique.* Vol. 4. Paris, 1949.

Efimenko [Iefymenko], A. *Iuzhnaia Rus'.* Vol. 1. St. Petersburg, 1905.

Efimenko [Iefymenko], P. "Shpitali v Malorossii." *Kievskaia starina* 5 (1883).

Eisenbichler, K. "Italian Scholarship on Pre-Modern Confraternities in Italy." *Renaissance Quarterly* 50, no. 2 (1997).

Eisenstein, E. L. *The Printing Press as an Agent of Change.* Vol. 1. Cambridge, 1979.

Fedalto, G. *Ricerche storiche sulla posizione giuridica ed ecclesiastica dei Greci a Venezia nei secoli XV e XVI.* Florence, 1967.

Fefelova, O. *Pravoslavnye bratstva na vostochnoslavianskikh territoriiakh Rechi Pospolitoi vo vtoroi polovine XVI–pervoi polovine XVII vekov* [dissertation abstract]. Tomsk, 2001.

Felmy, K. C. "Der Aufbruch der orthodoxen Laien in Polen-Litauen im 16. und 17. Jahrhundert." *Zeitschrift für Kirchengeschichte* 98 (1987).

Fiamingo, R. *Le confraternite nel diritto canonico e civile.* Naples, 1917.

Figol', V. "Tserkovni bratstva Halyts'koï hreko-katolyts'koï provintsiï XVIII st." *Bohosloviia* 15–16 (1938).

Fiorani, L. "Discussioni e ricerche sulle confraternite romane negli ultimi cento anni." *Storiografia e archivi delle confraternite romane.* Ricerche per la storia religiosa di Roma, 6. Ed. L. Fiorani. Rome, 1985.

Flerov, I. *O pravoslavnykh tserkovnykh bratstvakh, protivoborstvovavshikh unii v Iugo-Zapadnoi Rossii v XVI, XVII, XVIII stoletiiakh.* St. Petersburg, 1857.

Floria, B. "Kommentarii." In Makarii (Bulgakov), *Istoriia russkoi tserkvi*. Vol. 5. Moscow, 1996.

_____. "Polozhenie pravoslavnoi i katolicheskoi tserkvei v Rechi Pospolitoi. Razvitie natsional'no-konfessional'nogo soznaniia zapadnorusskogo pravoslavnogo obshchestva vo vtoroi polovine XVI v." In *Brestskaia uniia 1596 g. i obshchestvenno-politicheskaia bor'ba na Ukraine i v Belorusii v kontse XVI–nachale XVII v.* Pt. 1. *Brestskaia uniia 1596 g. Istoricheskie prichiny*. Moscow, 1996.

Flynn, M. "Rituals of Solidarity in Castilian Confraternities." *Renaissance and Reformation* 13, no. 1 (1989).

_____. *Sacred Charity: Confraternities and Social Welfare in Spain, 1400–1700*. Ithaca, N.Y., 1989.

Fonkich, B. L. "Grecheskie teksty Ostrozhskoi Biblii." *Fedorovskie chteniia 1981*. Moscow, 1985.

_____. *Grechesko-russkie kul'turnye sviazi v XV–XVII vv.* Moscow, 1977.

Franko, I. "Do istoriï tserkovnykh bratstv v Halyts'kii Rusi." *ZNTSh* 21 (1898).

_____. *Narys istoriï ukraïns'ko-rus'koï literatury*. Lviv, 1910.

_____. *P'ianyts'ke chudo v Korsuni*. Lviv, 1913.

_____. "Z polia nashoï kul'tury." *Narod* 4 (1893).

_____. "Zapysky proty knyhokradiv u starykh knyhakh i rukopysakh." *ZNTSh* 77 (1907).

_____. *Zibrannia tvoriv*. Vol. 41. Kyiv, 1984.

Frantsysk Skaryna i iaho chas: Èntsyklapedychny davednik. Minsk, 1988. Russian edition: Minsk, 1990.

Frick, D. *Meletij Smotryc'kyj*. Cambridge, Mass., 1995.

Gajecky, G. "Church Brotherhoods and Ukrainian Cultural Renewal in the 16th and 17th Centuries." In *Millennium of Christianity in Ukraine: A Symposium*. Ottawa, 1987.

_____. "The Stauropegian Assumption Brotherhood of Lviv." In *Millennium of Christianity in Ukraine: 988–1988*. Winnipeg, 1989.

Garin, E. *L'educazione in Europa, 1400–1600*. Bari, 1957.

Goldblatt, H. "On the Language Beliefs of Ivan Vyšens'kyj and the Counter-Reformation." *HUS* 15, nos. 1–2 (1991).

_____. *Orthography and Orthodoxy: Constantine Kostenecki's Treatise on the Letters*. Florence, 1987.

Golenishchev-Kutuzov, I. N. *Gumanizm u vostochnykh slavian (Ukraina i Belorussiia)*. Moscow, 1963. Repr. in his *Slavianskie literatury*. Moscow, 1970.

Golovatskii [Holovats'kyi], Ia. "Sprava Vilenskago tserkovnago bratstva s Grekovichem pered Vilenskim tribunalom." *Chteniia v Obshchestve istorii i drevnostei rossiiskikh*, 1859, no. 3.

Golubev, S. "Drevniya i novyia skazaniia o nachale Kievskoi Akademii." *Kievskaia starina*, 1885, no. 2.

_____. "Drevnii pomenik Kievo-Pecherskoi lavry." *Chteniia v Istoricheskom obshchestve Nestora letopistsa* (Kyiv) 6 (1892).

_____. *Kievskii mitropolit Petr Mogila i ego spodvizhniki*. 2 vols. Kyiv, 1883-98.

Grendler, P. F. *Schooling in Renaissance Italy: Literacy and Learning, 1300–1600*. Baltimore and London, 1989.

Gudziak, B. *Crisis and Reform: The Kyivan Metropolitanate, the Patriarchate of Constantinople, and the Genesis of the Union of Brest*. Cambridge, Mass., 1998.

Guzman, A. *Tratado del origen de la Confraternidad*. Madrid, 1730.

Hajda, L. Review article about Ia. Isaievych, *Bratstva ta ïkh rol' v rozvytku ukraïns'koï kul'tury XVI–XVIII st. Recenzija: A Review of Soviet Ukrainian Scholarly Publications* 1, no. 1 (Fall 1970).

Halenchenka, H. "Bratskae knihadrukavanne." In *Frantsysk Skaryna i iaho chas: Entsyklapedychny davednik*. Minsk, 1988.

Hall, B. "The Trilingual College of San Ildefonso and the Complutensian Polyglot." *Studies in Church History*, 1969, no. 5.

Hallam, H. *Introduction to the Literature of Europe in the Fifteenth, Sixteenth, and Seventeenth Centuries*. Vol. 2. London, 1838.

Hardtwig, W. *Genossenschaft, Sekte, Verein in Deutschland*. Vol. 1. *Vom Spätmittelalter bis zur Französischen Revolution*. Munich, 1997.

Heller, W. "Orthodoxe Bruderschaften und ihre Schulen in Polen-Litauen im 16. und 17. Jahrhundert." In *Der Ökumenische Patriarch Jeremias II. von Konstantinopel und die Anfänge des Moskauer Patriarchates*. Oikonomia. Quellen und Studien zur orthodoxen Theologie, vol. 27. Erlangen, 1991.

Henderson, J. "Confraternities and the Church in Late

Medieval Florence." In *Voluntary Religion*. Worcester, 1986.

Hering, G. *Ökumenisches Patriarchat und europäische Politik 1620–1638*. Wiesbaden, 1968.

Hochenegg, H. *Bruderschaften und ähnliche religiöse Vereinigungen in Deutschtirol bis zum Beginn des zwanzigsten Jahrhunderts*. Innsbruck, 1984.

Holovats'kyi, Ia. F. "L'vovskoe Stavropihiiskoe bratstvo i kniaz' Ostrozhskii," *Vremennik Instituta Stavropihiiskoho* (Lviv, 1867), 79–81.

_____. "Poriadok shkol'nyi ili ustav stavropihiiskoi shkoly v L'vovi 1586 hoda." *Halychanyn: Literaturnyi Sbornyk* 2 (1863): 69–79.

Horden, P. "The Confraternities of Byzantium." *Studies in Church History* 23 (1986).

Hradiuk, P. "Do istoriï Mariis'kykh Druzhyn v Ukraïni." *Analecta OSBM*, ser. 2, vol. 1 (7) (1953).

Hrinchenko, B. *Bratstva i prosvitnia sprava*. Kyiv, 1907.

Hrushevs'kyi, M. *History of Ukraine-Rus'*. Vol. 7. Edmonton and Toronto, 1999.

_____. *Istoriia ukraïns'koï literatury*. Vol. 6. Kyiv, 1995.

_____. *Istoriia Ukraïny-Rusy*. Vol. 6. Kyiv, 1907. Repr. New York, 1955; Kyiv, 1995.

_____. *Kul'turno-natsional'nyi rukh na Ukraïni v XVI–XVII vitsi*. Kyiv, 1912.

Hrytsak, E. "Kapitul'na biblioteka v Peremyshli." *S'ohochasne i mynule* (Lviv), 1939.

Hurs'ka, L. *Pravoslavni bratstva v Ukraïni iak chynnyk formuvannia natsional'noï samosvidomosti (kinets' XVI–persha polovyna XVII st.)*. Dissertation abstract. Kyiv, 2000.

Iakovenko, N. *Narys istoriï Ukraïny z naidavnishykh chasiv do kintsia XVIII st*. Kyiv, 1997.

_____. *Ukraïns'ka shliakhta z kintsia XIV do seredyny XVII st. (Volyn' i Tsentral'na Ukraïna)*. Kyiv, 1993.

Iakovenko, S. "Pravoslavnaia ierarkhiia Rechi Pospolitoi i plany tserkovnoi unii v 1590–1594 gg." In *Slaviane i ikh sosedi*. Vol. 3. *Katolitsizm i pravoslavie v srednie veka*. Ed. B. N. Floria et al. Moscow, 1991.

Iasynovs'kyi, Iu. *Ukraïns'ki ta bilorus'ki notoliniini Irmoloï XVI–XVIII st.: Kataloh i kodykolohichno-paleohrafichne doslidzhennia.* Lviv, 1996.

Isaievych, Ia. "Biblioteka L'vivs'koho bratstva." *Bibliotekoznavstvo i bibliohrafiia* (Kharkiv) 3 (1966).

_____. *Bratstva ta ïkh rol' v rozvytku ukraïns'koï kul'tury XVI–XVIII st.* Kyiv, 1966.

_____. "D. I. Zubryts'kyi i ioho diial'nist' v haluzi spetsial'nykh istorychnykh dystsyplin." *Naukovo-informatsiinyi Biuleten' Arkhivnoho upravlinnia URSR,* 1963, no. 1.

_____. "Der Buchdruck und die Entwicklung der Literatursprachen in der Ukraine (16.–1. Hälfte des 17. Jh.)." *Zeitschrift für Slawistik* 36, no. 1 (1991).

_____. *Dzherela z istoriï ukraïns'koï kul'tury doby feodalizmu XVI–XVIII st.* Kyiv, 1972.

_____. "Dzherel'ni materialy z istoriï ukraïns'koho mystetstva XVI–XVIII st. v arkhivi L'vivs'koho bratstva." *Tretia respublikans'ka naukova konferentsiia z arkhivoznavstva ta inshykh spetsial'nykh istorychnykh dystsyplin: Druha sektsiia.* Kyiv, 1968.

_____. "Greek Culture in the Ukraine: 1550–1650." *Modern Greek Studies Yearbook* 6 (1990).

_____. "Ian Amos Komens'kyi i Ukraïna." *UIZh,* 1967, no. 3.

_____. *Literaturna spadshchyna Ivana Fedorova.* Lviv, 1989.

_____. "Naidavnishi dokumenty pro diial'nist' bratstv na Ukraïni." *Istorychni dzherela ta ïkh vykorystannia* (Kyiv), issue 2 (1966): 13–18.

_____. "'Navity'—nevidoma pam'iatka ukraïns'koï publitsystyky XVII st." *Naukovo-informatsiinyi Biuleten' Arkhivnoho upravlinnia URSR,* 1964, no. 6.

_____. "Nevidoma pam'iatka ukraïns'koï istoriohrafiï druhoï polovyny XVII st." *UIZh,* 1970, no. 2.

_____. "Novye materialy ob ukrainskikh i belorusskikh knigopechatnikakh pervoi poloviny XVII veka." *Kniga: Issledovaniia i materialy* 34. Moscow, 1977.

_____. *Pershodrukar Ivan Fedorov i vynyknennia drukarstva na Ukraïni* [= *Pershodrukar*]. Lviv, 1975. 2d ed. Lviv, 1983.

_____. "Pervye graviury na medi v knigakh tipografii Ukrainy." *Pamiatniki kul'tury: Novye otkrytiia, ezhegodnik 1978*. Leningrad, 1979.

_____. "Pochatky derzhavnosti i ranni etapy formuvannia skhidnoslovians'kykh narodiv." In *Etnichna svidomist': natsional'na kul'tura*. Ed. H. A. Skrypnyk. Kyiv, 1991.

_____. *Preemniki pervopechatnika*. Moscow, 1981.

_____. "Rol' bratstv v izdanii i rasprostranenii knig na Ukraine i v Belorussii (konets XVI–XVIII vv.)." In *Kniga i grafika*. Moscow, 1972.

_____. *Ukraïna davnia i nova: Ukraine Old and New*. Lviv, 1996.

_____. *Ukraïns'ke knyhovydannia: vytoky, rozvytok, problemy*. Lviv, 2002.

_____. "Zv'iazky bratstv z Zaporoz'kym kozatstvom." *Seredni viky na Ukraïni* (Kyiv), issue 2 (1973). 2d ed.: *Kyïvs'ka starovyna*, 1992, no. 1.

_____., and I. Z. Myts'ko. "Zhyttia i vydavnycha diial'nist' Kyryla-Trankviliona Stavrovets'koho." In *Bibliotekoznavstvo ta bibliohrafiia*. Kyiv, 1982.

Istoriia kul'tury drevnei Rusi. Ed. B. D. Grekov. 2 vols. Moscow and Leningrad, 1948–51.

Iubileinoie izdanie v pamiat' 300-lětiia osnovaniia L'vovskoho Stavropigiona. Lviv, 1886.

Iubileinyi sbornik v pamiat' 350-lětiiu L'vovskoho Stavropigiona. Lviv, 1936.

Jaworski, F. *Uniwersytet Lwowski*. Lviv, 1912.

Jobert, A. *De Luther à Mohila. La Pologne dans la crise de la chrétienté, 1517–1648*. Paris, 1974.

Kamanin, I. "Eshche o drevnosti bratstva i shkoly v Kieve." *Chteniia v Imperatorskom obshchestve istorii i drevnostei rossiiskikh* 9 (1895).

Kapral', M. "Aktovi materialy do biohrafiï Ivana Krasovs'koho za 1574–1619 rr." In *Ukraïna v mynulomu*, 4 (1993).

_____. "Braty Rohatyntsi—stariishyny L'vivs'koho Uspens'koho bratstva." In *Ukraïna v mynulomu*, 2 (1992).

_____. "Chy isnuvalo L'vivs'ke Uspens'ke bratstvo pered 1586 rokom?" In *Uspens'ke bratstvo i ioho rol' v ukraïns'komu natsional'no-kul'turnomu vidrodzhenni*. Lviv, 1996.

_____. "Istoriohrafiia L'vivs'koho Uspens'koho bratstva." In *Ukraïna v mynulomu*, 2 (1992).

Katzinger, W. *Die Bruderschaften in den Städten Oberösterreichs als Hilfsmittel der Gegenreformation und Ausdruck barocker Frömmigkeit in Bürgerschaft und Kirche.* Stadt in der Geschichte, vol. 5. Ed. J. Sydow. Sigmaringen, 1980.

Kashuba, M. "Reformatsiini ideï v diial'nosti bratstv na Ukraïni: XVI–XVII st." In *Sekuliaryzatsiia dukhovnoho zhyttia na Ukraïni v epokhu humanizmu ta Reformatsiï.* Kyiv, 1991.

Keenan, E. *The Kurbskii-Groznyi Apocrypha: The Seventeenth-Century Genesis of the "Correspondence" Attributed to Prince A. M. Kurbskii and Tsar Ivan IV.* Cambridge, Mass., 1971.

_____. "On Some Historical Aspects of Early Book Printing in the Ukraine." *Recenzija: A Review of Soviet Ukrainian Scholarly Publications* 5, no. 1 (Fall-Winter 1974).

Kempa, T. *Konstanty Wasyl Ostrogski (ok. 1524/1525–1608). Wojewoda kijowski i marszałek ziemi wołyńskiej.* Toruń, 1997.

Kharlampovich, K. *Malorossiiskoe vliianie na velikorusskuiu tserkovnuiu zhizn'.* Vol. 1. Kazan, 1914.

_____. *Zapadnorusskiya pravoslavnyia shkoly XVI i nachala XVII veka.* Kazan, 1898.

Khudash, M. *Leksyka ukraïns'kykh dilovykh dokumentiv kintsia XVI–pochatku XVII st.* Kyiv, 1961.

Khyzhniak, Z. I. *Rektory Kyievo-Mohylians'koï Akademiï, 1615–1817.* Kyiv, 2002.

Kiriiak, V. *Cartea şi tiparul în Moldova în secolele XVII–XVIII.* Chişinău, 1977.

Kiselev, N. P. "Grecheskaia pechat' na Ukraine v XVI veke." *Kniga: Issledovaniia i materialy* 7 (1962).

_____. "Knigi grecheskoi pechati v sobranii Gosudarstvennoi biblioteki SSSR im. V. I. Lenina." *Kniga: Issledovaniia i materialy* 26 (1973).

_____. "O moskovskom knigopechatanii XVII veka." *Kniga: Issledovaniia i materialy* 2 (1960).

Kisilevich [Kysylevych], L. "Vymiraiushchiia tipy ukrainskoi derevni." *Kievskaia starina*, 1884, no. 8.

Klymenko, P. *Tsekhy na Ukraïni.* Vol. 1. Zbirnyk Istorychno-filolohichnoho viddilu Vseukraïns'koï Akademiï nauk, no. 81. Kyiv, 1929.

Kmet', V. "Inventari Uspens'koï ta Sviatoonufriïvs'koï monastyrs'koï tserkvy u L'vovi 1919 r." *Visnyk L'vivs'koho universytetu.* Historical series, 35–36 (2001).

_____. "Monastyr sv. Onufriia Velykoho u L'vovi." In *Nad Buhom i Narvoiu* (Bielsk Podlaski), 1998, nos. 3–4 (37–38).

_____. "'Zhyttiepysy l'vivs'kykh iepyskopiv hrets'koho obriadu'—pam'iatka ukraïns'koï istoriohrafiï druhoï polovyny XVII st." In *Lwów: miasto, społeczenstwo, kultura,* vol. 4. Cracow, 2002.

Knyha i drukarstvo na Ukraïni. Kyiv, 1965.

Kohut, Z. *Russian Centralism and Ukrainian Autonomy: Imperial Absorption of the Hetmanate, 1760s–1830s.* Cambridge, Mass., 1988.

Koialovich, M. O. "Chteniia o tserkovnykh zapadno-russkikh bratstvakh." *Den',* 1862, no. 36.

Koliada, H. "Knigoizdatel'stvo L'vovskogo bratstva v XVI veke." *Uchenye zapiski Stalinabadskogo ob"edinennogo pedagogicheskogo i uchitel'skogo instituta im. T. G. Shevchenko,* Filologicheskaia seriia, issue 1 (1952).

Koperzhyns'kyi, K. "Ostroz'ka drukarnia v Ostrozi ta v Dermani pislia Beresteis'koï uniï (1596), ïï vydannia ta diiachi." *Bibliolohichni visti,* 1924, nos. 1–3.

Kopiec, J. "Bruderschaften als Ausdruck barocker Frömmigkeit." *Archiv für schlesische Kirchengeschichte* 44. Sigmaringen, 1987.

Kostomarov, N. *Istoricheskie proizvedeniia. Avtobiografiia.* Kyiv, 1990.

Koval's'kyi, M. P. "Politychni zv'iazky zakhidnoukraïns'kykh zemel' z Rosiis'koiu derzhavoiu v druhii polovyni XVII st." *Pytannia istoriï SRSR* (Lviv) 6 (1957).

Krachkovskii, I. *Izbrannye sochineniia.* Vol. 6. Moscow and Leningrad, 1960.

Krajcar, J. "Konstantin Bazil Ostrozskij and Rome in 1582–1584." *Orientalia Christiana Periodica* 34 (1968).

Kraliuk, P. *Dukhovni poshuky Meletiia Smotryts'koho.* Kyiv, 1997.

_____. *Luts'ke Khrestovozdvyzhens'ke bratstvo.* Lutsk, 1996.

Krekoten', V. "Z istoriï ukraïns'ko-bilorus'koho literaturnoho spivrobitnytstva: Poema Khomy Ievlevycha 'Labirynt.'"

In *Ukraïns'ka literatura XVI–XVIII st. ta inshi slov'ians'ki literatury.* Kyiv, 1989.

Krylovskii, A. *L'vovskoe Stavropigial'noe bratstvo: Opyt tserkovno-istoricheskago issledovaniia.* Kyiv, 1904.

Kryp'iakevych, I. "Borot'ba netsekhovykh remisnykiv proty tsekhiv u L'vovi." *Z istoriï zakhidnoukraïns'kykh zemel'.* No. 1. Kyiv, 1957.

_____. "Deshcho zi zvychaïv u l'vivs'kii shkoli ta bursi." *Zhyttia i znannia*, 1934, no. 6.

_____. "L'vivs'ka Rus' v pershii polovyni XVI st." *ZNTSh* 77–78 (1907). 2d ed. Lviv, 1993.

_____. "350-littia seredn'oï shkoly u L'vovi." *Zhyttia i znannia*, 1936, no. 1.

_____. "Ukraïns'ki shpytali u L'vovi v XVI–XVII st." *Likars'kyi visnyk* (Lviv), 1930, no. 1.

_____. "Z istoriï halyts'koho shkil'nytstva XVI–XVIII st." *Ridna shkola* 1933, no. 2.

_____. *Zv'iazky Zakhidnoï Ukraïny z Rosiieiu do seredyny XVII st.* Kyiv, 1953.

Kryvonosiuk, P. "Stavropihiis'ka bursa v 1751 r." *Istorychnyi visnyk* (mimeographed publication of students of the Lviv Ukrainian Underground University), 1923, nos. 2–3.

Kudriavtsev, P. "Osvitni mandrivky vykhovantsiv Kyïvs'koï akademiï za kordon u XVIII st." *Kyïvs'ki zbirnyky* (Kyiv) 1 (1930–31).

Kudryk, B. *Ohliad istoriï ukraïns'koï tserkovnoï muzyky.* Lviv, 1937. 2d ed. Lviv, 1997.

Kulish, P. A. *Istoriia vossoedineniia Rusi.* Vol. 1. St. Petersburg, 1874.

Kumor, B. "Kościelne stowarzyszenia świeckie na ziemiach polskich w okresie przedrozbiorowym." *Prawo Kanoniczne* 10 (1967).

Kurganovich, S. *Dionisii Zhabokritskii, episkop Lutskii i Ostrozhskii.* Kyiv, 1914.

Kuźmak, K. *Bractwa Matki Boskiej Wspomożycielki Chrześćijan na ziemiach polskich w XVIII st.* Rome, 1973.

Kyievo-Mohylians'ka akademiia v imenakh, XVII–XVIII st.: Entsyklopedychne vydannia. Comp. Z. I. Khyzhniak. Kyiv, 2001.

Kyrychuk, O. "Perekhid L'vivs'koho Stavropihiis'koho bratstva pid iurysdyktsiiu sv. Apostol's'koho Prestolu (za materiialamy TsDIA Ukraïny u L'vovi)." In *Uspens'ke bratstvo i ioho rol' v ukraïns'komu natsional'no-kul'turnomu vidrodzhenni*. Lviv, 1996.

Labyntsev, Iu. "Pervoe izdanie Ivana Fedorova i Petra Timofeeva Mstislavtsa v sobranii GBL." *Kniga: Issledovaniia i materialy* (Moscow) 47 (1984).

Lauwers, L. Review of A. Vauchez, *Les laics au Moyen Age*. *Revue d'histoire ecclésiastique* (Louvain) 83, nos. 3–4 (1988).

Lazarevskii, A. [Lazarevs'kyi, O.]. *Opisanie staroi Malorossii*. Vol. 2. Kyiv, 1893.

_____. "Statisticheskie svedeniia ob ukrainskikh narodnykh shkolakh i gospitaliakh v XVIII veke." *Osnova*, 1862, no. 5.

Le Bras, G. "Les confréries chrétiennes: problèmes et propositions." *Revue historique de droit français et étranger* (1940–41). Repr. in *Etudes de sociologie religieuse*, vol. 2 (Paris, 1956).

_____. *Études de sociologie religieuse*. Vol. 2. Paris, 1956.

Lebedintsev, T. *Bratstva, ikh prezhniaia i nyneshniaia sud'ba i znachenie*. Kyiv, 1862.

Levyts'kyi, O. "Vnutrishnii stan zakhidnorus'koï tserkvy v Pol's'ko-lytovs'kii derzhavi v kintsi XVI st. ta Uniia." In *Rozvidky pro tserkovni vidnosyny na Ukraïni-Rusy XVI–XVIII vv.* Rus'ka istorychna biblioteka, 8. Lviv, 1900.

Lewin, P. "The Ukrainian School Theater in the Seventeenth and Eighteenth Centuries: An Expression of the Baroque." *HUS* 5, no. 1 (1981).

Little, L. K. *Libertà carità fraternità: Confraternite laiche a Bergamo nell'età del comune*. Bergamo, 1988.

Litwin, H. "Catholization among the Ruthenian Nobility and Assimilation Processes in the Ukraine during the Years 1569–1648." *Acta Poloniae Historica* 55 (1987).

Löffler, P. *Studien zum Totenbrauchtum in den Gilden, Bruderschaften und Nachbarschaften Westfalens vom Ende des 15. bis zum Ende des 19. Jahrhunderts*. Münster, 1975.

Longinov, A. *Pamiatnik drevnego pravoslaviia v Liubline: Pravoslavnyi khram i sushchestvovavshee pri nem bratstvo*. Warsaw, 1883.

Lotots'kyi, O. *Ukraïns'ki dzherela tserkovnoho prava*. Warsaw, 1931.

Łoziński, W. *Patrycjat i mieszczaństwo lwowskie w XVI i XVII wieku*. Lviv, 1892.

———. *Złotnictwo lwowskie*. Lviv, 1889.

Lutsiv, V. O. "Tserkovni bratstva v Ukraïni." *Bohosloviia* 37 (1973).

Mackenney, R. *Tradesmen and Traders: The World of the Guilds in Venice and Europe, c. 1250- c. 1650*. London and Sydney, 1987.

Makarii, Metropolitan of Moscow. *Istoriia russkoi tserkvi*. 12 vols. St. Petersburg, 1883–1903, repr. Moscow, 1994–97.

Maksymovych, M. *"Kiev iavilsia gradom velikim": Vybrani ukraïnoznavchi tvory*. Kyiv, 1994.

Malyshevskii, I. *Aleksandriiskii Patriarkh Meletii Pegas i ego uchastie v delakh Russkoi tserkvi*. 2 vols. Kyiv, 1872.

Marker, G. "Russia and the 'Printing Revolution': Notes and Observations." *Slavic Review* 41 (1982).

Maslov, S. I. *Kirill Trankvillion-Stavrovetskii i ego literaturnaia deiatel'nost'*. Kyiv, 1984.

Mathiesen, R. "The Making of the Ostrih Bible." *Harvard Library Bulletin*, 1981, no. 1.

———. Review article on the first edition of Ia. D. Isaievych, *Pershodrukar Ivan Fedorov i vynyknennia drukarstva na Ukraïni* (Lviv, 1975). *Recenzija: A Review of Soviet Ukrainian Scholarly Publications* 8 (1977–1978).

Matkovs'ka, O. *L'vivs'ke bratstvo: kul'tura i tradytsiï (kinets' XVI–persha polovyna XVII st.)*. Lviv, 1996.

Mazurkiewicz, J. *Jurydyki lubelskie*. Wrocław, 1956.

Medlin, W., and C. G. Patrinelis. *Renaissance Influences and Religious Reforms in Russia: Western and Post-Byzantine Impacts on Culture and Education (16th–17th Centuries)*. Geneva, 1971.

Medynskii, E. *Bratskie shkoly Ukrainy i Belorussii v XVI–XVII vv. i ikh rol' v vossoedinenii Ukrainy s Rossiei*. Moscow, 1954. Ukr. translation: *Brats'ki shkoly Ukraïny i Bilorusiï v XVI–XVII st*. Kyiv, 1958.

Meersseman, G. G. *Ordo fraternitatis: Confraternite e pietà dei laici nel Medioevo*. Italia sacra, vols. 24–26. 3 vols. Rome, 1977.

Meyers, A., and D. E. Hopkins, ed. *Manipulating the Saints: Religious Brotherhoods and Social Integration in Postconquest Latin America*. Hamburg, 1988.

Michelin, G., and M. Segalen. *La Confrérie des Pénitents blancs du Puy*. Paris, 1978.

Mikulec, J. *Barokní náboženská bratrstva v Čechách*. Prague, 2000.

Mironowicz, A. "Orthodox Centers and Organizations in Podlachia from the Mid-Sixteenth through the Seventeenth Century." *Journal of Ukrainian Studies* 17, nos. 1–2 (1992).

_____. *Podlaskie ośrodki i organizacje prawosławne w XVI i XVII wieku*. Białystok, 1991.

Modest (Strel'bitskii), Bishop of Lublin. "Svedeniia o sostave tserkovno-arkheologicheskago muzeia pri Kholmskom Sviatobogorodichnom bratstve po oktiabr' 1882 goda." *Kholmsko-Varshavskiia eparkhial'nyia vedomosti*, 1882, no. 2.

Mombelli Castracane, M. "Ricerche sulla natura giuridica delle confraternite nell'età della controriforma." *Rivista di storia del diritto italiano* 55 (1982).

Monticone, A., G. De Rosa, G. Alberigo, G. De Sandre Gasparini, C. de la Roncière, G. Vitolo. "La storiografia confraternale e le confraternite romane." *Le Confraternite romane: esperienza religiosa, società, commitenza artistica*. Colloquio della Fondazione Caetani, Rome, 14–15 May 1982. Ricerche per la storia religiosa di Roma, 5. Ed. L. Fiorani. Rome, 1984.

Moreno Navarro, I. *Cofradías y hermandades Andaluzas: estructura, simbolismo e identidad*. Seville, 1985.

Moroziuk, R. "The Role of Patriarch Jeremiah II Tranos in the Reformation of the Kievan Metropolia." *Patristic and Byzantine Review* 5 (2) (1986).

Mosxona, N. G. "Threskeutikes adelphothetes laikon sta Ionia nesia." *Ethnikon idryma epeunon Kentron Byzantinon epeunon symmeikta* 7 (1987).

Le mouvement confraternel en Moyen Age: France, Italie, Suisse. Actes de la table ronde organisée par l'Université de Lausanne avec le concours de l'École française de Rome et de l'Unité associée 11011 du CNRS, Lausanne 9–11 mai 1985. Geneva, 1987.

Mukhin, V. *Kievo-bratskii uchilishchnyi monastyr'*. Kyiv, 1900.

Muratori, L. A. "De piis laicorum confraternitatibus, earumque origine, flagellantibus et sacris missionibus: Dissertatio septuagesimaquinta." In his *Antiquitates Italiae Medii Aevi.* Milan, 1747.

Myhul, I. M. "Politics and History in the Soviet Ukraine: A Study of Soviet Ukrainian Historiography." Ph.D. diss. Columbia University, 1971.

Myts'ko, I. "L'vivs'ki sviashchenyky ta vchyteli XVI–pershoï tretyny XVII st." In *Uspens'ke bratstvo.* Lviv, 1996.

_____., comp. *Materialy do istoriï Ostroz'koï akademiï, 1576–1636: Bio-bibliohrafichnyi dovidnyk.* Kyiv, 1990.

_____. "Ostrozhskii kul'turno-prosvetitel'nyi tsentr." *Fedorovskie chteniia 1981.* Moscow, 1985.

_____. *Ostroz'ka slov'iano-hreko-latyns'ka akademiia.* Kyiv, 1990.

Naumenko, F. I. *Pedahoh-humanist i prosvitytel' I. M. Borets'kyi.* Lviv, 1963.

Naumow, A. "Zmiana modelu kultury a kwestia ciągłości rozwojowej." *Zeszyty Naukowe KUL* 27, no. 4 (108) (1984).

Nazarko, I. "Bratstva i ïkh rolia v istoriï ukraïns'koï tserkvy." In *Ukraïns'kyi myrianyn v zhytti Tserkvy, spil'noty i liudstva.* Paris and Rome, 1966.

Nemirovskii, E. L. *Frantsisk Skorina.* Minsk, 1990.

_____. *Ivan Fedorov, okolo 1510–1583.* Moscow, 1985.

_____. *Ivan Fedorov v Belorussii.* Minsk, 1979.

_____. *Nachalo slavianskogo knigopechataniia.* Moscow, 1971.

_____. *Vozniknovenie knigopechataniia v Moskve: Ivan Fedorov.* Moscow, 1964.

Nichyk, V. M. *Petro Mohyla v dukhovnii istoriï Ukraïny.* Kyiv, 1997.

Ohienko [Ohiienko], I. (Metropolitan Ilarion). *The Ukrainian Church.* Trans. Orysia Ferbey. Vol. 1. Winnipeg, 1986.

_____. "Zahublenyi kremianets'kyi starodruk 'Synod Luts'kyi 1638 r.'" *Elpis*, 1931, no. 5.

Orioli, L. "Per una rassegna bibliografica sulle confratenite medievali." *Ricerche di storia sociale e religiosa* (Rome), n.s. 17–18 (1980).

Orlevych, I. *Stavropihiis'kyi instytut u L'vovi (kinets' XVIII–60-i rr. XIX st.).* Lviv, 2000.

Orlovskii, P. "Uchastie zaporozhskikh kazakov v vosstanovlenii ierusalimskim patriarkhom Feofanom pravoslavnoi zapadnorusskoi tserkovnoi ierarkhii v 1620 godu." *TKDA*, 1905, no. 8.

Ovsiichuk, V. *Ukraïns'ke mystetstvo druhoï polovyny XVI–pershoï polovyny XVII st.: humanistychni ta vyzvol'ni ideï.* Kyiv, 1985.

Padokh, Ia. *Sudy i sudovyi protses staroï Ukraïny: Narys istoriï.* Vol. 209 of *ZNTSh* (1990).

Pamiatniki russkoi stariny v zapadnykh guberniiakh Imperii izdavaemyia P. N. Batiushkovym. Vol. 7. St. Petersburg, 1885.

Pan'kevych, I. "Pidkarpatorus'ka zapyska students'koï virshi z 1751 r." *Podkarpatska Rus'*, 1928, no. 3.

_____. "Pokraini zapysy na pidkarpats'kykh tserkovnykh knyhakh." *Zbirnyk Naukovoho tovarystva "Prosvita"* (Uzhhorod) 6 (1929).

Papkov, A. *Bratstva: Ocherk istorii zapadno-russkikh pravoslavnykh bratstv.* Sergiev Posad, 1900.

Pappenheim, M. *Die altdänischen Schutzgilden.* Breslau, 1885.

Pátková, H. *Bratrstvie ke cti Božie: poznámky ke kultovní činnosti bratrstev a cechů ve středověkých Čechách.* Prague, 2000.

Paulsen, F. *Geschichte des gelehrten Unterrichts auf den deutschen Schulen und Universitäten vom Ausgang des Mittelalters bis zur Gegenwart.* Vol. 1. Leipzig, 1919.

Pavlovskii, I. "Ostatki bratstv v prikhodakh Pereiaslavskago uezda." *Poltavskiia eparkhialnyia vedomosti*, 1880, no. 5.

_____. *Prikhodskiia shkoly v staroi Malorossii i prichiny ikh unichtozheniia.* Kyiv, 1904.

Peretts, V. "Novi dani dlia istoriï shkoliars'kykh bratstv na Ukraïni." *Zapysky Istorychno-filolohichnoho viddilu VUAN*, 1923, nos. 2–3.

Petrov, N. I. "Kremenetskoe pravoslavnoe Bogoiavlenskoe bratstvo." *TKDA* 3, no. 9 (1887).

Picchio, R. *Letteratura della Slavia ortodossa (IX–XVIII sec.).* Bari, 1991.

Plokhii, S. *Papstvo i Ukraina: Politika rimskoi kurii na ukrainskikh zemliakh v XVI–XVII vv.* Kyiv, 1989.

Polska-Ukraina. 1000 lat sąsiedztwa (Przemyśl), ed. S. Stępień, 3 (1996).

Presniakov, A. E. *The Formation of the Great Russian State.* Chicago, 1970.

Price, B. B. "Master by Any Other Means." *Renaissance and Reformation* 13, no. 1 (1989).

Prochaska, A. *Historia miasta Stryja.* Lviv, 1926.

Ptaśnik, J. *Cracovia impressorum XV et XVI saeculorum.* Lviv, 1922.

_____. "Walki o demokratyzację Lwowa od XVI do XVIII w." In *Księga pamiątkowa ku czci prof. Oswalda Balzera.* Vol. 2. Lviv, 1925.

Pylypiuk, N. "Eucharisterion. Albo, Vdjačnost': The First Panegyric of the Kiev Mohyla School. Its Content and Historical Context." *HUS* 8, nos. 1–2 (1984). Special issue. *The Kiev Mohyla Academy: Commemorating the 350th Anniversary of Its Founding (1632).*

Remling, L. *Bruderschaften in Franken: Kirchen- und sozialgeschichtliche Untersuchungen zum spätmittelalterlichen und frühneuzeitlichen Bruderschaftswesen.* Würzburg, 1986.

Robinson, A. *Bor'ba idei v russkoi literature XVII veka.* Moscow, 1974.

Rybakov, B. A. *Remeslo drevnei Rusi.* Moscow, 1948.

Savych, A. *Narysy z istoriï kul'turnykh rukhiv na Ukraïni ta Bilorusiï v XVII–XVIII st.* Kyiv, 1929.

Sawicki, J. "'Rebaptisatio Ruthenorum' in the Light of 15th and 16th Century Polish Synodal Legislation." In *The Christian Community of Medieval Poland.* Ed. J. Kłoczowski. Wrocław and Warsaw, 1981.

Schindling, S. "Schulen und Universitäte im 16. und 17. Jh." In *Ecclesia Militans.* Paderborn, 1988.

Schnyder, A. *Die Ursulabruderschaften des Spätmittelalters: ein Beitrag zur Erforschung der deutschsprächigen religiösen Literatur des 15. Jahrhunderts.* Stuttgart, 1986.

Schreiber, G. "Der Barock und das Tridentinum: Geistesgeschichtliche und kultische Zusammenhänge." In *Das Weltkonzil von Trient.* Vol. 1. Freiburg, 1951.

Segalen, M. *Les confréries dans la France contemporaine; les charités.* Paris, 1975.

Senyk, S. "Marian Cult in the Kievan Metropolitanate: XVII–XVIII Centuries." In *Intrepido pastori.* Rome, 1984.

Sharanevych, I. *Nykolai Krasovs'kyi (Krasuvs'kyi)*. Lviv, 1885.

Shustova, Iu. "Arkhiv L'vovskogo Uspenskogo Stavropigiiskogo bratstva kak fenomen kul'tury." In *Tekst v gumanitarnom znanii: Materialy mezhvuzovskoi konferentsii.* Moscow, 1997.

_____. "Biblioteka L'vovskogo Uspenskogo Staropigiiskogo bratstva v kontekste ukrainskogo natsional'no-kul'turnogo vozrozhdeniia v kontse XVI–nachale XVII vv." In *Biblioteka v kontekste istorii: Tezisy dokladov i soobshchenii vtoroi nauchnoi konferentsii.* Moscow, 1997.

_____. "Blagotvoritel'naia deiatel'nost' L'vovskogo Uspenskogo Stavropigiiskogo bratstva." In *Mezhslavianskie vzaimootnosheniia i sviazi: Srednie veka–rannee Novoe vremia. Sbornik tezisov.* Moscow, 1999.

_____. "Dokumenty L'vovskogo Stavropigiiskogo bratstva kak istoriko-antropologicheskie istochniki po istorii Ukrainy XVI–XVIII vv." In *Istoricheskaia antropologiia: Mesto v sisteme sotsial'nykh nauk, istochniki i metody interpretatsii. Tezisy dokladov i soobshchenii nauchnoi konferentsii.* Moscow, 1998.

_____. *Dokumenty L'vovskogo Uspenskogo Stavropigiiskogo bratstva kak istoricheskii istochnik (1586–1788).* Dissertation abstract. Moscow, 1998.

_____. "Sovokupnost' pis'mennykh, veshchestvennykh i izobrazitel'nykh istochnikov kak osushchestvlenie istoricheskogo dialoga kul'tur (na primere pamiatnika renessansnoi arkhitektury—l'vovskoi Uspenskoi tserkvi)." In *Istoricheskii istochnik: Chelovek i prostranstvo. Tezisy dokladov i soobshchenii nauchnoi konferentsii.* Moscow, 1997.

_____. "Ukraïns'ki bratstva iak providnyky diial'noï relihiinosti v kintsi XVI–na pochatku XVII st." In *Istoriia relihiï v Ukraïni: Materialy VIII mizhnarodnoho kruhloho stolu.* Lviv, 1998.

Skabalanovich, N. A. "Zapadnoevropeiskiia gil'dii i zapadnorusskiia bratstva." *Khristianskoe chtenie,* 1875, nos. 9–10.

Skochylias, I. "Protokoly iepyskops'kykh i dekans'kykh vizytatsii tserkov Kyïvs'koï uniats'koï mytropoliï XVIII st." In *Rukopysna ukraïnika u fondakh L'vivs'koï naukovoï biblioteky im. V. Stefanyka NAN Ukraïny ta problemy stvorennia informatsiinoho banku danykh: Materialy mizhnarodnoï naukovo-praktychnoï konferentsiï 20–21 veresnia 1996 r.* Lviv, 1999.

Skoczek, J. *Lwowskie inwentarze biblioteczne.* Lviv, 1939.

Smotryts'kyi, M. (Smotrzyski). *Paraenesis.* Cracow, 1629. Repr. HLEUL, Texts. Vol. 1. Cambridge, Mass., 1987.

Solov'ev, S. "Bratchiny." *Russkaia beseda,* 1856, no. 4.

Srebnitskii, I. "Sledy tserkovnykh bratstv v Vostochnoi Malorossii." *Trudy IV Arkheologicheskago s''ezda v Kazani.* Vol. 2. Kazan, 1891.

Sribnyi, F. Review article about A. Krylovskii, *L'vovskoe stavropigial'noe bratstvo. ZNTSh* 75 (1907).

_____. "Studiï nad organizatsiieu l'vivs'koï Stavropigiï vid kintsia XVI do polovyny XVII st." *ZNTSh* 106, 108, 111–12, 114–15 (1911–13).

Stakhiv, M. *Khrystova tserkva v Ukraïni, 988–1596.* Stamford, Conn., 1985.

Stepovyk, D. *Ukraïns'ka hrafika XVI–XVIII stolit': Evoliutsiia obraznoï systemy.* Kyiv, 1982.

Stetsiuk, K. I. *Narodni rukhy na Livoberezhnii i Slobids'kii Ukraïni v 50–70-kh rokakh XVII st.* Kyiv, 1960.

Strakhova, O. "K voprosu ob otnoshenii k grecheskomu iazyku v slavianskoi pis'mennosti (XI–XVII vv.)." In *Ėtnogenez, ranniaia ėtnicheskaia istoriia i kul'tura slavian.* Ed. N. I. Tolstoi et al. Moscow, 1985.

Studyns'kyi, K. "'Adel'fotes'— hramatyka vydana u L'vovi v r. 1591." *ZNTSh* 7 (1890).

_____. "Try panehiryky XVII st." *ZNTSh* 12 (1896).

Stupperrich, R. "Bruderschaften/Schwesterschaften/Kommunitäten." *Theologische Realenzyklopädie.* Vol. 7. Berlin and New York, 1981.

Stus, I. "The Early Years of the Kievan-Mohylian Academy." In *Millennium of Christianity in Ukraine, 988–1988.* Ed. O. W. Gerus and A. Baran. Winnipeg, 1989.

Sumtsov, N. "Shpital' v m. Boromle." *Kievskaia starina* 7 (1883).

Svientsits'kyi, I. *Pochatky knyhopechatannia na zemliakh Ukraïny.* Zhovkva and Lviv, 1924.

Sydorenko, A. *The Kievan Academy in the Seventeenth Century.* Ottawa, 1977.

Sysyn, F. *Between Poland and the Ukraine: The Dilemma of Adam Kysil, 1600–1653.* Cambridge, Mass., 1985.

_____. "The Cultural, Social and Political Context of Ukrainian History-Writing: 1620–1690." *Europa Orientalis* 5 (1986).

_____. "Peter Mohyla and the Kiev Academy in Recent Western Works: Divergent Views on Seventeenth-Century Ukrainian Culture." *HUS* 8, nos. 1–2 (1984).

_____. Review of Ja. D. Isajevyč, *Džerela z istoriji ukrajins'koji kul'tury doby feodalizmu. Recenzija: A Review of Soviet Ukrainian Scholarly Publications* 4, no. 2 (Spring-Summer 1974).

Syvokin', H. *Davni kyïvs'ki poetyky.* Kharkiv, 1960.

Ševčenko, I. "The Many Worlds of Peter Mohyla." *HUS* 8, nos. 1–2 (1984). Reprinted in his *Byzantium and the Slavs in Letters and Culture.* Cambridge, Mass., 1991 and *Ukraine between East and West: Essays on Cultural History to the Early Eighteenth Century.* Edmonton and Toronto, 1996.

_____. "Religious Polemical Literature in the Ukrainian and Belarusian Lands in the Sixteenth and Seventeenth Centuries." *Journal of Ukrainian Studies* 17, nos. 1–2 (1992).

Šmurlo, E. *Kurie a pravoslavný východ v letekh 1609–1654.* Prague, 1928.

Terlets'kyi, O. *Vasyl' Konstantyn kniaz' Ostroz'kyi: Istoriia fundatsii kniazia Ostroz'koho v Ternopoli.* Ternopil, 1909.

Terpstra, N., ed. *The Politics of Ritual Kinship: Confraternities and Social Order in Early Modern Italy.* Cambridge, 2000.

Thomas, C. "Two East Slavonic Primers: Lvov, 1574 and Moscow, 1637." *British Library Journal* 10, no. 1 (1984).

Thomson, F. "Peter Mogila's Ecclesiastical Reforms and the Ukrainian Contribution to Russian Culture. A Critique of Georges Florovsky's Theory of the 'Pseudomorphosis of Orthodoxy.'" *Slavica Gandensia* 20 (1993).

Topolska, M. B. *Czytelnik i książka w Wielkim Księstwie Litewskim w dobie Renesansu i Baroku.* Wrocław, 1984.

Trunte, H. "Die zweisprächigen Teile des 'PROSPHONEMA.' Zu Autorschaft und Entstehung des lemberger Panegyrikos vom 1. Februar 1591." In *Studien zu Literatur und Kultur in Osteuropa: Bonner Beiträge zum 9. Internationalen Slawistenkongreß in Kiew.* Ed. H.-B. Harder and H. Rothe. Cologne and Vienna, 1983.

Tryjarski, E. "Studia nad rękopisami i dialektem kipczackim Ormian polskich, 3." *Rocznik Orientalistyczny* 24, no. 1 (1960).

Tsehel's'kyi, I. *Deshcho pro tserkvy ta chudotvornu ikonu Materi Bozhoï v Kamiantsi Strumylovii.* Lviv, 1932.

Turilov, A. A., and B. N. Floria. "K voprosu ob istoricheskoi al'ternative Brestskoi unii." In *Brestskaia uniia 1596 g. i obshchestvenno-politicheskaia bor'ba v Ukraine i Belorussii v kontse XVI–pervoi polovine XVII v.* Pt. 2. Moscow, 1999.

Tysiachenko, H. [pseud. of H. Salyvon]. "Kazkovyi i real'nyi obraz pershodrukaria." *Bibliolohichni visti,* 1924, nos. 1–3.

Ul'ianovs'kyi, V. *Istoriia tserkvy ta relihiinoï dumky v Ukraïni.* 3 vols. Vols. 1–2. *Seredyna XV–kinets' XVI stolittia.* Kyiv, 1994.

Uspens'ke bratstvo i ioho rol' v ukraïns'komu natsional'no-kul'turnomu vidrodzhenni. Dopovidi i povidomlennia naukovoï konferentsiï 4–5 kvitnia 1996 roku. Lviv, 1996.

Uspenskii, B. *Arkhaicheskaia sistema tserkovnoslavianskogo proiznosheniia.* Moscow, 1968.

V. A. "K istorii iuzhnorusskikh bratstv: Osnovanie tserkvi i bratstva pri nei v m. Sribnom Poltavskoi gubernii, Prilukskago uezda." *Kievskaia starina* 16 (1886): 186–90.

Vasilenko [Vasylenko], K. "Ostatki bratstv i tsekhov na Poltavshchine." *Kievskaia starina,* 1885, no. 13.

Vauchez, A. "Les confréries au Moyen Age: esquisse d'un bilan historiographique." *Revue historique* 275 (1986).

_____. *Les laics au Moyen Age.* Paris, 1987.

Velyhors'kyi, I. "Iavorivs'ke molodets'ke bratstvo XVIII st." *Nasha kul'tura,* 1936, no. 4.

_____. "Svidky nashoï kul'tury." *Nasha kul'tura,* 1936, no. 4.

Vientskovskii, D. *Tserkovni bratstva na Rusi.* Lviv, 1878.

Vlasovs'kyi, I. *Narys istoriï Ukraïns'koï pravoslavnoï tserkvy.* Vol. 1. New York, 1955.

Voluntary Religion: Papers Read at the 1985 and 1986 Meetings of the Ecclesiastical History Society. Studies in Church History (Worcester) 23 (1986). Ed. W. J. Sheils and D. Wood.

Vozniak, M. *Istoriia ukraïns'koï literatury.* Vol. 2. Lviv, 1921.

_____. *Pys'mennyts'ka diial'nist' Ivana Borets'koho na Volyni i u L'vovi.* Lviv, 1954.

Vuitsyk, V. "Novi dokumental'ni vidomosti pro ukraïns'koho hravera i drukaria XVIII st. Ivana Fylypovycha." *ZNTSh* 236 (1998).

Wilda, W. E. *Das Gildenwesen im Mittelalter*. Berlin, 1831. Repr. Aalen, 1964.

Williams, G. H. *Protestants in the Ukrainian Lands of the Polish-Lithuanian Commonwealth*. Cambridge, Mass., 1988.

Wipszycka, E. "Les confréries dans la vie religieuse de l'Egypte chrétienne." *Proceedings of the XII International Congress of Papyrology* (1970).

_____. Świeckie bractwa w życiu religijnym chrześcijańskiego Egiptu." *Przegląd Historyczny* 59 (1968).

Wiśniowski, E. "Bractwa religijne na ziemiach polskich w średniowieczu." *Roczniki Humanistyczne* 17, no. 2 (1969).

Wlasowsky (Vlasovs'kyi), I. *Outline History of the Ukrainian Orthodox Church*. New York, 1956.

Wynar, L. *History of Early Ukrainian Printing, 1491–1600*. Denver, 1962.

Zaikin, V. *Episkop Iosif Shumlianskii i Stavropigiia*. Lviv, 1935.

_____. *Uchastie svetskogo elementa v tserkovnom upravlenii, vybornoe nachalo i "sobornost'" v Kievskoi mitropolii v XVI i XVII vv*. Warsaw, 1930.

Zalozetskii [Zalozets'kyi], V. "Neskol'ko svedenii o gorode Strye." *Chervonaia Rus'* (Lviv) (1890).

Zapasko, Ia. P. *Mystets'ka spadshchyna Ivana Fedorova*. Lviv, 1974.

_____. *Mystets'ki rukopysni pam'iatky Ukraïny*. Lviv, 1997.

_____. *Mystetstvo knyhy na Ukraïni v XVI–XVIII st*. Lviv, 1971.

_____. *Ornamental'ne oformlennia ukraïns'koï rukopysnoï knyhy*. Kyiv, 1960.

_____., and Ia. Isaievych, comp. *Pam'iatky knyzhkovoho mystetstva na Ukraïni: Kataloh starodrukiv, vydanykh na Ukraïni* [= *PKM*]. Vols. 1–2, pts. 1–2. *1574–1700, 1701–1764*, and *1765–1800*. Lviv, 1981–84.

_____. *Pam'iatky knyzhkovoho mystetstva. Ukraïns'ka rukopysna knyha*. Lviv, 1995.

Zhukovich, P. *Seimovaia bor'ba pravoslavnago zapadnorusskago dvorianstva s tserkovnoi uniei*. Vol. 5. St. Petersburg, 1910.

Zimorowicz, J. B. *Opera*. Lviv, 1899.

Zoltan, A. "K predystorii russkogo *gosudar'*." *Studia slavica* (Budapest) 29 (1985).

Zoric, K. *Le confraternite in Dalmazia studiate nei lor manoscritti ed il loro influsso sulla vita religiosa.* Rome, 1949.

Zubritskii [Zubryts'kyi], D. "Lĕtopis' L'vovskago Stavropigial'nago bratstva." *Zhurnal Ministerstva narodnago prosveshcheniia*, 1849, nos. 4–6; 1850, nos. 5–7. 2d ed. Lviv, 1926.

Zubrzycki [Zubryts'kyi], D. *Kronika miasta Lwowa.* Lviv, 1844. Ukrainian translation: *Khronika mista L'vova.* Trans. I. Svarnyk. Commentary M. Kapral'. Lviv, 2002.

Zwoliński, P. "Psalmów kilka słowieńskich Łukasza Górnickiego i ich pierwowzór." *Slavia Orientalis*, 1963, no. 2.

Index